Strategic Human Resource Management

People and Performance Management in the Public Sector

Dennis M. Daley

North Carolina State University

Upper Saddle River, New Jersey 07458

Library of Congress Cataloging-in-Publication Data

Daley, Dennis M.
Strategic human resource management : people and performance management in the public sector / Dennis M. Daley.
p. cm.
Includes bibliographical references.
ISBN 0-13-028260-X
1. Civil service--United States--Personnel management. 2. Personnel management. 3. Strategic planning. I. Title.

JK765 .D36 2001
352.6′234′0973--dc21

00-069170

For my brother
Alan T. Daley
And my uncle
Alex N. Taleff

VP, Editorial Director: Laura Pearson
Senior Acquisitions Editor: Heather Shelstad
Assistant Editor: Brian Prybella
Editorial Assistant: Jessica Drew
Project Manager: Merrill Peterson
Cover Director: Jayne Conte
Cover Design: Bruce Kenselaar
Director of Marketing: Beth Gillett Mejia
Prepress and Manufacturing Buyer: Ben Smith

This book was set in 10/12 Times New Roman by TSI Graphics
and was printed and bound by Courier Companies, Inc.
The cover was printed by Phoenix Color Corp.

Printed in the United States of America

10 9 8 7 6 5 4 3 2 1

ISBN 0-13-028260-X

PRENTICE-HALL INTERNATIONAL (UK) LIMITED, *London*
PRENTICE-HALL OF AUSTRALIA PTY. LIMITED, *Sydney*
PRENTICE-HALL CANADA INC., *Toronto*
PRENTICE-HALL HISPANOAMERICANA, S.A., *Mexico*
PRENTICE-HALL OF INDIA PRIVATE LIMITED, *New Delhi*
PRENTICE-HALL OF JAPAN, INC., *Tokyo*
PEARSON EDUCATION ASIA PTE. LTD., *Singapore*
EDITORA PRENTICE-HALL DO BRASIL, LTDA., *Rio de Janeiro*

Contents

Preface

The movement to reinvent and reengineer government services is transforming public administration. The hierarchal, command-and-control structure is giving way to a new organization whose remaining workforce is concentrated on service delivery. Staff functions previously administered by central offices are now carried out by the first-line supervisor and field manager. No place is this change more evident than in the realm of personnel administration/human resource management.

Strategic Human Resource Management gives the student and first-line supervisor a practical overview of human resources/public personnel practices as tools for management in today's knowledge-based organization. Emphasis is placed on using individual-oriented functions for achieving organizational missions and purposes. Personnel techniques and central personnel functions are addressed from the perspective of their ability to provide value-added assistance to the first-line supervisor and field manager.

Strategic Human Resource Management encompasses three distinct foci. First, the text is focused on a strategic perspective. All personnel or human resource functions are examined in terms of their ability to enhance the organization's ability to accomplish its mission. Second, a practical focus describes how to actually implement and use the personnel techniques examined. Third, research and illustrative examples are drawn not only from the federal government but from state and local organizations and nonprofits as well.

This text serves the basic graduate or undergraduate public personnel/human resource management course. The text focuses on management techniques rather than on political policy issues and has a first-line supervisor or field manager perspective rather than that of a central personnel office.

Strategic Human Resource Management provides a more thorough treatment of the techniques used for managing people than is found in most personnel texts. Students are first introduced to the general personnel function and then provided with an overview of the specific applications or options they have at their disposal. Finally, emphasis is placed on more fully describing in a how-to-do-it fashion those techniques that are most appropriate and recommended.

The book is directed at the decentralized, knowledge-based organization. This organization accomplished its work more through coordination by ideas than by organization. The command and control of the central personnel office serving executive-level officials is replaced by a coach-and-consult philosophy of assisting line officials. The performance of personnel functions, including the choice of their appropriateness, is the responsibility of the first-line supervisor and field manager.

Strategic Human Resource Management is written from the perspective of a professional, knowledge-based organization. The organization's needs link the accomplishment of its strategic mission to human resources activities. The student or first-line supervisor is taught to approach organizational problems in terms of adding value through the application of the personnel techniques. Hence, tying the personnel process into the planning and reward systems is highlighted.

The inclusion of historical material is limited to brief explanatory segments. Similarly, political policy issues are treated as means for illustrating the framework or environment within which personnel/human resources techniques is practiced. The text includes extensive and recent references to the research in public personnel administration. This enables students to quickly follow up on topics of interest.

ACKNOWLEDGMENT

I would like to acknowledge my students and colleagues whose questions and interests helped shape this work. I would also like to recognize Beth Murtha and Jessica Drew of Prentice Hall and Merrill Peterson of Matrix Productions for their professional assistance. Finally, I would like to thank Kathryn G. Denhardt (University of Delaware), Nancy Geist Giacomini (University of Delaware), and LaVonna Blair Lewis (University of Southern California) for their helpful reviews, comments, insights, and suggestions.

Dennis M. Daley

About the Author

Dennis M. Daley is a professor of political science and public administration at North Carolina State University. He has taught classes in Human Resources/ Personnel Management since 1978. He has also taught graduate classes in Organization Theory and Organizational Behavior as well as specialized courses in both Performance Appraisal and Labor Relations.

He earned a Ph.D. in political science at Washington State University (Pullman). He also received an M.A. in political science from the University of Montana and B.A.s in history and government from Montana State University. He has previously been on the faculty at Minnesota State University (Mankato), Iowa State University, and the University of Mississippi.

He is the author of *Performance Appraisal in the Public Sector: Techniques and Applications* (1992). He has also published extensively on human resources topics in the leading public administration journals. He is a senior editor for the *Review of Public Personnel Administration* and serves on the executive board of the American Society for Public Administration Section on Personnel and Labor Relations.

chapter 1

Organization of the Personnel Function

This chapter introduces the topics of personnel administration/human resource management within a strategic human resource management framework. The objectives in this opening chapter are fourfold:

1. It provides an overview of the strategic human resource management concept. It briefly introduces and examines a number of the personnel processes and techniques used in implementing strategic human resource management.
2. The chapter examines the civil service movement with its goal of protecting the public service from partisan politics.
3. It also details the continuing executive reform movement and its concern for the efficient provision of governmental services. The ebb and flow of the "centralization" engendered by protection and efficiency is discussed.
4. Finally, it examines the differing organizational perspectives for viewing personnel management.

How things are done determines what can be done. Although our interest in personnel administration is more likely to be focused on specific practices or administrative functions, the importance of structural aspects should not be neglected. How one goes about organizing (or reorganizing) the delivery of personnel functions can have significant consequences for what is actually accomplished.

This strategic interest in what organizations accomplish is transforming the field of personnel administration into one of human resource management. The focus is shifting away from an emphasis solely on the practices and techniques to a more inclusive view that looks at their relationship to and impact on the human workforce and the organization. While the traditional techniques remain the foundation of the personnel function, the purpose is now paramount in judging their usefulness and success.

The shift to human resource management is only accelerated in organizations that are knowledge-based. As the competitive advantage or value of an organization is more and more attributable to the talents of its human assets rather than to its physical equipment, attention to the maintenance and development of these human investments becomes ever so more crucial (Coff, 1997; Klingner and Lynn, 1997).

Who is responsible and what they perceive as their goals are important issues for the management of personnel. Job analysis, job evaluation, compensation, selection, training and development, planning, performance appraisal, and labor–management relations are techniques. The organizational structure and its goals breathe purpose into these techniques by providing them with direction.

Structurally, personnel management is characterized by two, somewhat competing trends: a decentralization of functions and, concomitantly, a centralization of authority. Surprisingly, both of these have responsiveness to the public as their objective. Reconciliation of these trends is an important problem.

STRATEGIC HUMAN RESOURCE MANAGEMENT

The modern public service is a professional service. For the modern organization, success is ultimately dependent upon how effectively this professionalism functions. Professions are built on knowledge and expertise. This is not a matter that readily lends itself to a temporary or part-time workforce. Knowledge is not gained overnight; it's earned the old fashion way—by hard work. Professional workers must be sought out and guaranteed an environment in which their careers can be nurtured and prosper. Only in this way can an organization itself hope to succeed. This is the task set for strategic human resource management.

Strategic Planning

For motivation and incentives to work, they first must be tied to a goal. An organization must employ needs assessment and human resources development strategies in pursuit of its vision or mission. Needs assessment (of where an organization wants to go) and human resources development (of those who are to get it there) focus on the specific organizational and individual needs whose satisfaction will lead to enhanced productivity.

The combination of the vision and the path for fulfilling it form the concept of *strategic human resource management.* The goals derived from strategic planning are put into practical perspective through the use of tools such as group-level total quality management (TQM) and individual-level management by objectives (MBO). Personnel processes and techniques are then used in achieving these operationalized objectives.

Strategic planning is rational analysis (Nutt and Backoff, 1992; Klingner, 1993; Perry, 1993; Berry, 1994; Mintzberg, 1994; Ledvinka, 1995; Bryson, 1996). It takes "what is" and develops ideas of "what should be" along with plans for "how to get there." With a realistic organizational strategy focused on what the future should look like, strategic planning provides the "road map" for fulfilling that future.

Through environmental scanning, strategic planning helps size up what the existing organization's capabilities are and what the real world it exists in is. The planning process explores alternatives—in terms of both the vision involved and the courses of action necessary to accomplish them. Finally, strategic planning helps an organization settle on one choice of direction and mesh it with the appropriate objectives and action plans. Strategic planning should also incorporate the human resources necessary for accomplishing its goals (Mesch, Perry, and Wise, 1995; Perry and Mesch, 1997).

The foremost advantage derived from strategic planning is that it helps improve organizational performance. Strategic planning focuses on the future—what should be. As such, it serves as a guiding star by which to steer the organization's development. Individual and team effort can be devoted to accomplishing the organization's goals (Keen, 1994).

Strategic planning also helps to concentrate individual efforts into a team effort. It can assist in developing total quality management and objective-based performance appraisal systems. Accountability for results can be assigned. The strategic planning process itself can serve as a team-building exercise. Finally, the process itself transforms perceptions away from separate and distinct projects and toward systemic viewpoints (Keen, 1994).

It is perhaps the primary task of an organization's leadership to provide vision. Organizations are often large, cumbersome entities with only vague, general notions of what it is they are supposed to do (i.e., the individuals assembled under its rubric have only vague, general notions about what they hope to do and accomplish). It is the job of those individuals occupying top management positions to provide detail and substantive direction to those notions. Here is where Osborne and Gaebler's (1992) analogy of "steering rather than rowing" is called for. It is the vision that serves to bring together and reinforce people's sense of belonging to an organization. It makes them stakeholders and active, contributing participants.

In addition to leadership support, those engaged in strategic planning need to be aware of other potential problems. As occurs with all management techniques, individuals will need extensive training and refresher training (to answer unforeseen questions that arise in response to implementation). Conflict, confusion, and chaos will prevail initially and for some time thereafter. Only as individuals learn how to do it and see its value will the benefits of strategic planning be realized (Merjanian, 1997).

The value of strategic planning is highly dependent upon those in the agencies who assemble and provide the data seeing that it also helps them do their jobs better. Excessive requests for information and data unconnected to an organization's mission undermine the strategic planning process. Although such information is useful in a command-and-control environment, strategic planning is essential for the more complex, knowledge-based organization's coaching and coordination. However, in such complex organizations the nonlinear nature of management is recognized. Strategic planning serves to define boundaries (Kiel, 1994). Planning is successful because it is useful (Merjanian, 1997).

In the modern, knowledge-based organization strategic planning is quite clearly strategic human resource planning. In noting the impact of strategic human resource management on organizational performance, John E. Delery and D. Jarold Doty (1996) identify seven general employment practices:

1. Internal career ladders
2. Formal training systems
3. Results-oriented performance appraisal
4. Performance-based compensation
5. Employment security
6. Employee voice
7. Broadly defined jobs

Career Ladders

For government, career ladders mean that a balance between inside and outside selection must be struck. Career services such as those associated with rank-in-person (pay and status adhere to the individual and not the specific work assignment) approaches virtually limit their recruitment to internal selection. The ideal of the rank-in-position approach (pay and status adhere to the job the individual is assigned to), on the other hand, invokes images of external selection. Reality lies somewhere in between. Even rank-in-position career systems have discovered the benefit of importing talented outsiders (or providing their members with significant outside, sabbatical experiences).

A career system is necessary to focus individual attention on the strategic issues facing an organization over the long term. Objectives and reward systems tied to the short term lead to dysfunctional behavior and goal displacement. Government with its two-year, four-year, and six-year electoral cycles has always suffered from this myopia.

A long-term perspective induces organizational commitment and loyalty. It enables individuals and organizations to invest in training and productivity improvements knowing that they will reap the benefits from that enhanced knowledge and technique.

Internal selection is also easier. The employee has already been attracted. The questions on whether an individual will fit in and adapt to an organization's culture are now moot. The problems of orientation and socialization (which are fraught with disappointment and turnover) have been overcome. The not inconsequential costs of recruitment (which are often an unfortunate, limiting factor among governments) are dramatically reduced.

However, internal selection exposes an organization to the dangers of "inbreeding." While it promotes a more harmonious, homogeneous workforce, it also can blind the organization to what is going on in the world at large. Outside selection stirs up an organization. All the problems mentioned above that are avoided by internal selection are also lost opportunities.

Training Systems

Training and development is the philosopher's stone. The modern organization is indeed its people and the knowledge they possess. We must recognize that this knowledge is, at best, only the beginning of the mystery. It can no longer be taken for granted that employees will arrive at work with all the requisite skills. Too much of what goes on in today's organization requires specific adaptation. The most knowledgeable and skilled worker still requires training in order to fit into the organization and become a valuable contributor to the team (Quinn, Anderson, and Finkelstein, 1996).

The chief function of the supervisors is the development of the people in their unit. Managers who have often been promoted from a technical position must remember that they are now the coaches; others have the responsibility of carrying out the plays on the field. The manager/coach can have the greatest effect only by assuring that the employee/player is truly prepared for action.

Unfortunately, training and development is one of the most neglected aspects of government. Well into the 1950s and 1960s, governments denied the value of training and development. Individuals were hired for specific jobs and were assumed to already possess all the skills that would be needed. While the importance of training and development is now recognized, it remains a neglected area. Employees, like the buildings and equipment of government, are allowed to depreciate through an underinvestment in maintenance (Elmore, 1991; Gray, Hall, Miller, and Shasky, 1997).

Performance Appraisal

Performance appraisal is used as an aid in making judgment decisions pertaining to promotion, demotion, retention, transfer, and pay. It is also employed as a developmental guide for training needs assessment and employee feedback. Performance appraisal also aids with a number of more general organizational functions as a means for validating selection and hiring procedures, promoting employee–supervisor understanding, and supporting an organization's culture. Modern performance appraisal systems combine an objective appraisal instrument with supervisory and employee training in its proper use.

Two formats dominate the arena of objective appraisal techniques: behaviorally anchored rating scales (BARS) and management by objectives (MBO). Behaviorally anchored rating scales and management-by-objectives approaches essentially involve the same components; however, the objective components that are common in both approaches are introduced into the appraisal process in a somewhat different order. BARS appraisals work best with large groups and subgroups of individuals whose job descriptions can be standardized; MBO, on the other hand, is more suited to cases that can be tailored to each individual job. MBO is best when it is focused on the results to be expected from job performance; BARS appraisals handle behavioral processes where outputs are more identifiable and assurable than outcomes. Both employ variations on participative management in order to guarantee their effectiveness. A somewhat more passive approach to participation guides BARS, whereas a more proactive style is found in MBO.

Although the use of objective appraisal instruments is recommended, many jurisdictions still employ subjective graphic rating scales. Although invalid, for the most part, they are relatively inexpensive and prove adequate "paper systems" for jurisdictions wherein performance appraisal is not realistically relied upon as an aid in decision making. Often effective and trusted supervisors can compensate for the shortcomings of inadequate systems. Unfortunately, supervisory (and employee) training in the proper use of the appraisal process tends to lag significantly. This often results in systems failures in that the advantages of an objective appraisal are dissipated through assorted managerial mistakes and rater errors.

Pay-for-Performance

Strategic pay requires that all decisions relative to compensation and benefits be designed to attract, retain, or motivate employees. As such, the entire organization's reward structure is designed to fully serve its mission or purpose. In reality, most organizations limit incentive pay to only a portion of the compensation package. All employees who perform satisfactorily are guaranteed a set base pay and benefits package. Even so, this guarantee serves to calm fears with regard to financial security and, hence, helps attract and retain individuals.

Extrinsic incentives primarily use monetary rewards as their motivating factor. Career development and training opportunities that can lead to promotion or interesting, fulfilling assignments (which also provide intrinsic motivation through their recognition of merit) are another source of extrinsic motivation in the sense that, in addition to higher compensation levels, they pay individuals in terms of power and responsibility.

Pay-for-performance is an application of expectancy theory. Expectancy theory posits that employees will be motivated to the extent to which their calculation of the desirability of rewards, the effort required to perform a task, and the probability of successful performance (and of the organization's paying off) are viewed favorably. Pay-for-performance schemes concentrate on providing or determining the right balance between extrinsic reward (pay) and required effort (performance).

A wide array of extrinsic pay-for-performance schemes exist. The modern pay-for-performance scheme builds upon a base-pay system. The salary or wage put "at risk" is such to encourage or motivate the worker without jeopardizing his or her basic financial security. One can address overall individual performance or specific instances; focus can be on group performance at the organizational or team level. Individual systems based on merit pay step increases, annuities, bonuses, and suggestion awards as well as skill or competency-based approaches abound. In addition, group or organization rewards are the focus of gain- or goal-sharing programs.

Performance appraisal systems are the trigger instrument for operationalizing pay-for-performance. The individual performance rating is used to determine which employees are eligible for individual and group awards as well as the amount of reward an individual is entitled to. Management-by-objectives systems may also serve as the measurement instrument for a pay-for-performance system (appraisal-by-objectives formally incorporates MBO into the performance appraisal process).

Merit pay annuities reward individuals' overall performance by an addition to their base salary (hence, the term *annuity*). What is essential is that the amount be substantial enough from the employee's perspective to serve as a motivating factor. This is likely to depend on both the economic situation and the individual's relevant equity comparisons. Merit pay annuities may be applied as a set percentage (or dollar) increase added to the base salary of all who achieve a specified performance rating. On the other hand, different performance rating levels may trigger different percentage (or dollar) increases.

The bonus (like the single-event suggestion award) is a lump-sum payment. Its advantage is that it recognizes exceptional performance occurring during the year without entailing a commitment to continuous future payments. Because they are one-time rewards, bonuses need to be more substantial than merit pay annuities. Bonuses, like merit pay annuities, can also be prorated to correspond with differing performance rating levels.

Skill- and competency-based pay rewards employees more for organizational potential than for actual performance. In a way, it is an expanded variation of "on-call" pay. Employees are paid extra for possessing the ability to step in and use their acquired skill or competency. The organizational advantage is that needed talent is on call in case of emergency or special circumstances. It allows the organization the ability to temporarily (or permanently) transfer individuals to more needed tasks. In addition to the extra pay, individuals benefit in the intrinsic motivation and revitalization inherent in the learning process and job rotation. They also are able to explore career options without having to abandon their current jobs.

One serious problem faced by most pay-for-performance schemes in the public sector is the tendency to cap awards. Locked into older notions of classification pay grades, individuals who have obtained the maximum pay allowed within their official pay grade may be deemed ineligible for merit annuities or bonuses. Because these awards are touted as being earned through meritorious performance, their denial greatly undermines perceptions not only of the program's efficacy but of organizational fairness as well.

Gain sharing or goal sharing is the primary group or team incentive system employed to measure and reward organizational performance. It is an outgrowth or refinement of the profit-sharing plans (such as Scanlon, Rucker, or Improshare). Profit sharing focuses on the entire organization and rewards individuals on the basis of its overall performance. Because individual employees materially share in the organization's success, profit sharing serves to motivate their performance.

Gain sharing is quite appealing to public sector organizations. It capitalizes on both the public sector's lack of a profit system and its greater reliance on group processes. As such, gain sharing complements TQM efforts by providing a mechanism for extrinsic rewards.

A recent refinement to gain sharing has been the notion of goal sharing. Instead of rewards being based on documented budget savings, they are tied to the achievement of specified group or team goals. Goals derived from TQM (or strategic planning or MBO) programs are thereby linked to extrinsic rewards for the individual. This serves to assure the individual's attention and motivation.

For gain sharing or goal sharing to be effective, the goals or savings gains must be based on measurable factors under the control of employees in the unit. Individual employees must understand what the goals are and feel that they are indeed obtainable through their group's combined teamwork. Employee participation in the selection of the goals is an added means for ensuring that understanding and sense of stakeholder status.

Employment Security

The knowledge-based environment also heightens the importance attached to employee rights along with the instrumental grievance and discipline system. Employees are human beings and work better when their humanity is recognized and respected. The employer–employee relationship is not that of master and servant (although much of the legal system is based on that design). Foreshadowed by the work of Mary Parker Follett and commencing with the Hawthorne studies in the late 1920s, motivational research has clearly pointed this out. With the transformation of the organization into an entity based on the skills of its employees rather than the efficiency of its machinery, this lesson becomes even more important.

Employee rights and the mechanism for enforcing them (i.e., the grievance process) serve as a safeguard for assuring that employees are accorded the basic dignity that every human being is entitled to. Like similar safety devices, we hope that we never will really need to use them. Although most organizations would prefer to do without such legal and formal systems, reality requires them. If there were no past abuses, there would be no need for laws prohibiting such practices.

Although all employees possess legal rights vis-à-vis the employment relationship or "contract," those in the public sector are afforded even greater protections. Public employees are both employees and citizens. As citizens, they are extended the basic protections that the federal and state constitutions provide citizens against the abuse of government power. In essence, the Bill of Rights becomes part of the employment contract.

Employee Voice

Employee motivation and, consequently, organizational productivity do not flow from the application of cut-and-dry, mathematical incentive models. To a great extent, success depends upon psychological factors. In general, it is not enough for individuals to simply receive a payment or reward for their efforts. They must also perceive their involvement as equitable and, perhaps more importantly, as an expression of their free will.

J. Stacy Adam's (1963) equity theory posits that each individual decides the extent to which the reward-effort balance is fair. Imbalances can be adjusted through increasing (or decreasing) the work effort into accord with a perceived higher (or lower) reward. Alternatively, a psychological adjustment can reassess the balance as indeed fair (or, in cases previously seen as fair, unfair).

Besides reconciling the reward-effort nexus, employees are interested in asserting "ownership" of their actions. Instead of merely being "cogs in the machine," they desire to be partners in decision making. This raises the issue of locus of control or participation.

In *Exit, Voice, and Loyalty,* Albert O. Hirschman (1970) proposes a typology of responses to dissatisfaction. It is this effort to change the situation which gives rise to voice. Voice is seen to represent a political dimension which can encompass a gamut of behaviors ranging from grumbling through participative management to full scale democracy.

Voice enhances the motivational level employees exhibit. Voice gives the employee a greater sense of ownership in and, hence, commitment to their work effort. The unfeeling, unthinking "cog" is transformed into an "expert system;" the "job" becomes a "profession."

According employees voice recognizes their human importance. When employees are consulted or involved in decisions for which they possess appropriate knowledge and skill, the benefits to an organization are three-fold. The organization benefits from accurate and often insightful information upon which to base its decisions. Having participated in the problem definition and solving process, the employee better understands what he or she is being asked to implement. Having participated in the decision making, and employee is also more likely to accept its legitimacy.

Broadly Defined Jobs

The "triumph of technique over purpose" is also evident here. The rigidity invested in the use of pay scales (and the concommitant job analyses upon which they are based) denies organizations the flexibility to adjust to and meet change. Individuals cannot readily be reassigned duties. This is especially a problem if those duties are from jobs officially designated as having lower grades. Even if pay remains constant, a lower grade assignment might be seen psychologically as a career setback. Reward for exceptional performance is thwarted by the formal attachment of pay ceilings or maximum salaries to specific job grades.

Broadbanding has been introduced as a means to cut through the Gordian knot of classification. Whether "broad grades" or "career bands" are used, management obtains greater flexibility. The employee is seen to benefit from both more challenging and meaningful work assignments and the possibility of pay increases (Risher and Schay, 1994).

Broad grades are simply a recalibration of the existing pay scales. Under broad grades, a system of, say, fifty pay grades is collapsed into one of ten or twelve grades. The range for each broad grade is from 50 to 100 percent of the minimum, starting salary. These new grades are subsequently divided into steps. The advantage of this simple, incremental approach is twofold. First, within each broad grade individuals can take on any of the previously lower-grade duties without loss of pay or prestige. Second, for all but the formerly top-rung employees in each of the broad grades, there is now more "headroom" between them and the pay ceilings. However, this flexibility introduces a higher degree of uncertainty or fussiness in the calculation of appropriate pay.

Career bands are more innovative and dynamic. While career bands also reduce the number of pay grades from, for example, fifty to ten or twelve, they do not impose any internal step structure onto this new system. Managers are given the flexibility to freely assign (and reassign) duties and salaries (limited only by overall budget figures). Individuals need not begin at the minimum, starting salary nor serve their time prior to receiving increases. Managers are often permitted to hire at any salary between the minimum and range midpoint; offers above the midpoint would be permitted but require approval. Ideally, salary determination within broadbanding is calculated from a midpoint base. The base is set by the market or competitive salary, which should be the median or average salary.

PUBLIC VERSUS PRIVATE SECTOR DIFFERENCES

Personnel management in the public sector is indeed different. However, the important question here is whether these differences really matter. Public and private organizations are different, but so are large and small, manufacturing and service, or staff and line organizations. As Wallace Sayre noted in his statement that "public and private organizations are fundamentally alike in all unimportant respects," it is the nature of the differences that is significant. The very study of public administration is predicated on the assumption that these differences do indeed matter.

The public sector arena introduces legal, economic, and political distinctions into personnel management (Gortner, Mahler, and Nicholson, 1987: 18–42). Each of these three dimensions affects the manner in which personnel practices are used by federal, state, and local governments.

Legal Differences

Even though private organizations must also operate within the rule of law, legal distinctions distance public organizations from those in the private sector. A public organization is specifically charged with administering the law. The public organization has a positive responsibility, whereas most private organizations are only charged with the somewhat more negative duty of merely avoiding proscribed conduct and activities. Public sector organizations have their responsibilities mandated to them; private sector organizations are free to choose the business they're in. The public organization is imbued with a degree of authority, including the legitimate use of force, that dwarfs anything even remotely similar to be found in the private sector (Gortner, Mahler, and Nicholson, 1987: 18–42). With respect to personnel practices and techniques, they are often externally prescribed by law.

Legal authority is the hallmark of the public sector, especially in the administrative realm. The basic legitimacy of the American administrative state is open to question. Nowhere is the governmental bureaucracy explicitly provided for. Because European administrations served absolutist monarchs, the bureaucracy has always been cognitively suspect as a potential threat to individual freedom. The American administration, therefore, obtains its legitimacy by endeavoring to cloak itself in the Constitution and by rigorously adhering to the strictures of the rule of law.

In order to assure that this power is not abused, the requirements for accountability in the public sector are also quite extensive. In particular, power is fragmented among a myriad of competing and overlapping jurisdictions. Hence, public employees are more likely to not fully control the tasks on which they work (Gortner, Mahler, and Nicholson, 1987: 18–42).

Democratic government is designed not for efficiency, but for protecting individuals. Rational efficiency is consciously sacrificed for the sake of political security. Administration is subject to the red tape of rules and regulations more so than is the case in the private sector. The introduction of these political safeguards does not occur without corresponding costs. Generally, the public sector binds managerial flexibility.

Economic Differences

Economic distinctions address the role of government in a free-market system. America, more than almost any other nation, attempts to relegate government to a narrowly defined role of providing for what the market economy fails to deliver. The provision of public goods and regulations designed to correct for other market imperfections due to extraordinary transaction costs, spillover or spinoff externalities, and oligopoly or monopoly are viewed as the economic tasks of government. Efforts for any more expansive governmental role or even for somewhat more liberal interpretations of those accepted tasks are often subject to acrimonious political controversy (Gortner, Mahler, and Nicholson, 1987: 18–42).

Because government resources are allocated through a political market rather than an economic one, productivity often proves difficult to measure, if not elusive altogether. In addition to the economic bottom line, there are many alternative measures of success in the public sector. Since the choice faced by the public sector official is not necessarily that of choosing one measure from among the alternatives but rather of simultaneously satisfying many of them, this adds to the difficulties inherent in measuring performance (Gortner, Mahler, and Nicholson, 1987: 18–42).

Finally, government participation in the economic market itself can be political. Purchases and whole projects can be undertaken for political, pork-barrel as well as for economic, business reasons. Is there a government anywhere that is not allowed legally and, in fact, encouraged to reject the lowest competitive bid for that of a slightly higher but local, nearby, or made-in-the-USA offer? Public works and economic revitalization are, to a great extent, seen as synonymous (Gortner, Mahler, and Nicholson, 1987: 18–42).

Political Differences

Political distinctions focus on the conflict resolution function that is at the essence of the public sector. For government organizations, politics means that agency missions and goals are set by external, elected, and citizen actors rather than by internal, organizational experts. This is in startling contrast to the manner in which private sector business firms are run.

In addition, the political setting is prone to ambiguity. In fact, politics can be best termed as the "art of the ambiguous" rather than the oft-cited "art of the possible." With goals that are unclear, public organizations face great difficulties in assessing performance.

Finally, the political world conducts its business in the open. "Life in the fishbowl," "before the camera," "in the sunshine," or "on stage" are all apt descriptions of public decision making. Furthermore, in addition to organizational members, external actors, including individual citizens, are integrally involved as participants in those decisions (Gortner, Mahler, and Nicholson, 1987: 18–42). Few private sector organizations allow even their stockholders, let alone their clientele, such extensive involvement in their decision making and operations. And who has ever heard of opening the door to one's competitors and opponents? Yet, this is the regular practice among public organizations.

Although many of these legal, economic, and political distinctions have begun to blur as society has extended its notions of what is "public," they still account for marked differences separating public and private organizations. Furthermore, the growth in the governmental public and nonprofit public sectors adds to the overall importance of the public sector itself.

Hence, the distinctions between public and private organizations are the focus of sustained interest (Rainey, Backoff, and Levine, 1976; Perry and Rainey, 1988; Rainey, 1989, 1991). In contrast to either the generic or the uniqueness perspective, others see a public–private organizational continuum (Allison, 1974) in which the role of "publicness" can be quite extensive. In fact, Barry Bozeman (1987) tends to see all organizations as public to some extent—due to the growing concerns for equity and responsiveness and the interdependence of organizations.

Woodrow Wilson (1887) could admire "a murderous fellow sharpening a knife cleverly . . . without borrowing his probable intention to commit murder with it." Yet, the circumstances in which and purpose for which we intend to employ our tools is also important. They affect whether the knife is used to cut bread or a throat.

For organizations, the public arena makes an important difference. Federal, state, and local governments are far larger today than they were at the turn of the century or even a generation ago. Expenditures have increased from under $2 billion and around 10 percent of the gross national product (GNP) early in the twentieth century to under $100 billion and about 25 percent of the GNP in the 1950s and 1960s to nearly $2 trillion and over 33 percent of the GNP in the 1990s. This growth has entailed an expansion both in the amount of services delivered and in the scope of the services provided by government (Denhardt, 1991: 32–44; Fesler and Kettl, 1991: 23–38).

Management practices in the public sector are more important as areas of study today because government and nonprofit organizations employ a substantial part of the workforce. Over 15 million people work in the public sector; this is approximately one out of every six jobs in the United States. Another 5 to 10 million (5 to 10 percent) are employed in nonprofit organizations. In total, from a fifth to a quarter of the American workforce earns its living from serving the public.

PROTECTION VERSUS EFFICIENCY

The primary organizational problem personnel management faces is that of balancing the goals of protection and efficiency. Should public administration be organized to protect employees from the "adverse" consequences of political patronage and the abuse of power, or to maximize the efficiency of service delivery? The answer to this question pivots on the role played by the political executive.

In American history, executive power has with rare exceptions been distrusted. Weak executives have tended to be the norm. Even in the era beginning with the New Deal (which has witnessed strong executives at both the national and state levels), periods of "imperial" leadership have been few and brief.

Even so, the modern era has been one of heightened power for elected executives like mayors, governors, and the president. The nineteenth-century view that the role of the state should be limited to that of a "night watchman" gradually gave way before the development of the administrative state. As the United States changed from an agrarian to an industrial society, government was called upon both to coordinate these changes (the development of regulatory agencies) and to directly provide services (social welfare, transportation, health care, and education). The administrative state is even seen as an extension of the Constitution and Bill of Rights—necessary if each individual is to receive the benefit of modern society (Rohr, 1986).

Chief executives are just as interested in the next election as any other politicians. This factor, however, poses the dilemma that confronts the public service. For the chief executive, the question is what approach will win more votes—jobs as rewards and incentives for campaign workers or the electoral benefits derived from good government.

The public service is a tool of executive power. However, the question remains as to what kind of tool. First, the patronage issue raises the spectre of the spoils system. For much of our history, this has been the prevailing view with regard to the public service. It can be argued that patronage was a major factor contributing to the development of political parties and of democratic government.

A different perspective, which emerged in the late nineteenth century to dominate the thinking behind the twentieth century's executive reform movement, views the political executive as the chief beneficiary and benefactor of an efficient public service. The reputation derived from efficiently providing governmental services can often be translated into electoral support. To a great extent, the administrative state has replaced political parties as the provider of public services. Whereas previously political parties secured voter loyalty from the various and sundry activities they performed, these activities (as well as many more) are today conducted by various public agencies.

Public service jobs were viewed as rewards for loyal party work under the spoils system. However, the second perspective of an efficient public service required that these jobs be protected. An efficient public service enables its employees to perform their jobs without fear that they will suffer arbitrary dismissal by hostile politicians, or that their duties will be influenced by political considerations.

Protection from Patronage

Although the abuse of patronage is among the charges laid against King George III in his indictment in the Declaration of Independence, the practical tasks of nation building rapidly introduced patronage into the new American regime (White, 1948, 1951; Mosher, 1982). From George Washington onward, government posts were used to win support for the new nation and its government.

The Jacksonian era marked an open break with the past (White, 1954). While devoted to restoring Jeffersonian Republican principles, the Jacksonian era was also a time of expanding political participation. The development of mass politics required permanent party organizations. Political parties could no longer be run by a handful of notables simply speaking to their friends and neighbors. The new party cadres needed jobs in order to support themselves while engaged in political activities. The only jobs at the disposal of the political leaders, however, were those they controlled through their positions in government. Although Andrew Jackson did not envision patronage as a damaging force, it soon became so. The spoils system that dominated the public service from the 1840s to the 1880s undermined the government's ability to function (White, 1958; Van Riper, 1958).

Following the Civil War, a "good government movement" began to advocate serious civil service reform. An early start occurred with the Grant Civil Service Commission (1871–1875), which pioneered many of the practices that guided future reform efforts. The civil service reform movement began a concerted attack on the growing abuses of the spoils system and emerged as an important moral factor in the political arena.

Sparked by the assassination of President Garfield, the Pendleton Act of 1883 established a merit-based civil service system in the United States. The public service was formally organized into a civil service system with selection and promotion based on individual skills and abilities. Merit principles slowly developed over the years to guide the administration of the public service. Figure 1.1 displays the rules and regulations outlining these merit principles as ultimately codified into law under the Civil Service Reform Act of 1972.

Although strongly advocated for decades by the Old Progressives of the good government movement, the inauguration of the civil service system was itself the result of political expediency. Republicans, tainted by corruption scandals stemming from the spoils system and fearful of losing control of the executive branch (which they did in the 1886 election), wrapped themselves in the "flag" of civil service reform. Democrats were even less fond of the notion (as they looked forward to their chance for the spoils of electoral victory). Neither Woodrow Wilson nor Franklin

Figure 1.1
Merit Principles

(1) Recruitment should be from qualified individuals from appropriate sources in an endeavor to achieve a work force from all segments of society, and selection and advancement should be determined solely on the basis of relative ability, knowledge, and skills, after fair and open competition which assures that all receive equal opportunity.
(2) All employees and applicants for employment should receive fair and equitable treatment in all aspects of personnel management without regard to political affiliation, race, color, religion, national origin, sex, marital status, age, or handicapping condition, and with proper regard for their privacy and constitutional rights.
(3) Equal pay should be provided for work of equal value, with appropriate consideration of both national and local rates paid by employers in the private sector, and appropriate incentives and recognition should be provided for excellence in performance.
(4) All employees should maintain high standards of integrity, conduct, and concern for the public interest.
(5) The Federal work force should be used efficiently and effectively.
(6) Employees should be retained on the basis of adequacy of their performance, inadequate performance should be corrected, and employees should be separated who cannot or will not improve their performance to meet required standards.
(7) Employees should be provided effective education and training in cases in which such education and training would result in better organizational and individual performance.
(8) Employees should be—
    (A) protected against arbitrary action, personal favoritism, or coercion for partisan political purposes, and
    (B) prohibited from using their official authority or influence for purposes of interfering with or affecting the result of an election or a nomination for election.
(9) Employees should be protected against reprisal for the lawful disclosure of information which the employees reasonably believe evidences—
    (A) a violation of any law, rule, or regulation, or
    (B) mismanagement, a gross waste of funds, an absence of authority, or a substantial and specific danger to public health or safety.

Source: Section 2301, Title 5, United States Code.

Roosevelt were active proponents of the civil service; in fact, the proportion of federal employees under the civil service declined during their administrations.

Initially 10 percent of the public service was covered or included in the new civil service; however, presidents often found it in their interests to expand coverage. Partisan appointees could be "blanketed in," thereby receiving a permanent job for their loyalty. Upon their retirement, the vacant position would be subject to replacement under full merit system rules.

Although the Civil Service Commission (CSC) created by the Pendleton Act was designed primarily to protect the public service from the pressures of the patronage system, efforts were also devoted to introducing efficient personnel practices. Drawing upon the earlier efforts by the Grant Civil Service Commission, for example, practical tests were developed for selecting employees.

The CSC sought to dampen political, specifically partisan, influence over personnel in two ways. First, the CSC was an independent agency. Within its nineteenth-century context, this clearly implied that the agency was not subject to the control and direction of the chief executive. Independent meant precisely that—it was outside the executive's zone of control. Presidents might not have liked the creation of independent agencies, but they had more pressing concerns. In fact, most executives had difficulty exercising control over their own executive agencies.

The second means for protecting civil servants from political pressures was in the composition of the commission itself. The CSC was not only an independent agency but was headed by a plural executive. Of the three commissioners (each appointed to a seven-year term), only two could be from the same party. This "ensured" that each party had an in-house watchdog who could bark an alarm if anyone attempted to manipulate the public service for partisan purposes. Furthermore, as commissioners were appointed to staggered terms, no one president was expected to appoint all three commissioners (since few commissioners served out their full terms, most presidents ultimately did appoint all members).

Although the CSC was independent, it was also charged with the duty of advising the president on personnel matters. In turn, the president was also responsible for officially promulgating civil service rules and regulations. This duality forced presidents to steer a course between a political Scylla and Charybdis.

The New Patronage

The CSC always faced a difficult task in balancing its mandated roles as protector of the public service and as executive advisor on personnel management. However, it was relatively successful in achieving that protection. Over the decades, fears about patronage gradually gave way to concerns for efficiency. Ultimately, the Civil Service Reform Act of 1978 (which reorganized the old Civil Service Commission into the Office of Personnel Management) granted paramountcy to efficiency (protection was relegated to the back burner under a separate Merit Systems Protection Board). Efficiency is even more the focus under the various reinvention proposals that emerged in the 1990s (Osborne and Gaebler, 1992).

However, beginning with the Nixon administration the CSC's protective role had already begun to dissipate. Partisan influences in personnel matters had begun to grow. Toward the end of his first term, President Nixon rediscovered Franklin Roosevelt's "Administrative Presidency" (Nathan, 1975, 1983). The administrative presidency recognizes that public policies are dependent upon the implementation process. In turn, implementation requires the support and cooperation of administrators. Hence, the ability to exercise control over administrators is transformed from a technical to a public policy issue.

Presidents since then have used the tactics of the administrative presidency. The Civil Service Reform Act of 1978, in part, institutionalized them. Because the public service tends to mirror the population in its political composition, the activities of the administrative presidency are more noticeable under Republican administrations (Aberbach and Rockman, 1976).

This is the foundation of the new patronage. Whereas the spoils system found jobs for party workers, the new patronage focuses primarily on policy issues. The executive seeks to find places where those who share his views on policies (which are quite often highly ideological and partisan) can exercise influence over their implementation. Career administrators can then be prevented from diverting or thwarting the politically elected leaders and their mandate (Meier, 1981).

The new patronage represents a logical extension of the executive reform movement. Basically, public enterprise is viewed as nearly identical to private enterprise. The contractual-based principal–agent relationships of the private sector (e.g., stockholder–manager, client–lawyer, patient–doctor, or investor–broker) are seen as appropriate models for the administrative hierarchy in government (Moe, 1984). Administrators are viewed as accountable to executives who are themselves responsible to the electorate.

However, the new patronage carries with it at least three major assumptions that need to be more fully examined (Aberbach and Rockman, 1988). First, the principal–agent relationships of the private sector are not wholly transferable to the public hierarchy. The legitimate role afforded to other political actors is virtually ignored. The Constitution and the role it grants to Congress and the judiciary are quite often neglected. Within the political system of the United States, power is shared. The electorate does not confer a political mandate on any *one* institution—be it executive, legislative, or judicial. In the United States, pyramids end in broad, flat tops and not pinnacles.

Second, the new patronage has a quite negative view of the role played by administrators (Aberbach and Rockman, 1988; Mitchell and Scott, 1987). Public policy implementation is fraught with complications. Unfortunately, things do go wrong. Because administrators are basically the "messengers" of public policy, they are ready targets for the venting of frustrations. Third, although the new patronage does not propose a return to the spoils system, it may not preclude it (Newland, 1987; Pfiffner, 1987). Likewise, few could have envisioned Andrew Jackson's commitment to the Jeffersonian principle of rotation-in-office as leading to such. The temptations posed by the new patronage may be hard to resist.

A major task facing personnel systems in the near future will be to strike a balance between providing direction for personnel policies and protecting public employees from partisan pressures. This cannot be an either/or situation; hence, the task will not be easy. Counterpoised to the new patronage are the protectionist concerns of our heritage; that these are still valid is evident from U.S. Supreme Court rulings such as *Elrod v. Burns* (1976), *Branti v. Finkel* (1980), and *Rutan v. Republican Party of Illinois* (1990). Nonpolicy positions are being afforded more and more protection as employees' "property interests" in government positions are legally recognized. A legal fiction in a renewed politics/administration dichotomy may well become an important factor in personnel management (Daniel, 1992; Roback and Vinzant, 1994).

Administrative Efficiency

The Civil Service Commission (as with the early Grant Commission) did not limit itself to the task of protecting the public service from the abuses of the spoils system. From its earliest days, efforts were made to enhance the efficiency of the service. Many of the founders of the civil service movement were sympathetic to the scientific management movement. The application of scientific management principles to administration quickly occurred.

Administrative management (initially identified with the New York Bureau of Municipal Research and the city manager movement) was a driving force behind the executive reform movement during the early twentieth century. The recruitment efforts during World War I as well as the Classification Act of 1923 are clear examples of administrative management's influence.

Organizationally, the CSC attempted to cope with the concerns for personnel management versus partisan protection on an ad hoc basis. Gradually, a hybrid structure was developed that designated the CSC's chair as the chief executive's advisor on personnel matters. The chair was also assigned responsibility for the day-to-day administration of the CSC.

By the 1940s, the civil service system was a pastiche of functions and purposes that had been assembled over the course of the century. The effect of this was to inhibit efficiency. As Wallace Sayre (1948) noted, personnel management had become a "triumph of technique over purpose." Individual techniques, themselves efficient, were in combination inefficient and often inadequate for the tasks set for them. This overall inefficiency led to strategies for circumventing the formal limitations imposed by specific personnel procedures. Unfortunately, this also contributed to undermining the civil service system's legitimacy (Shafritz, 1973, 1975).

Beginning with the Brownlow Committee on Administrative Management (1937) and running through the Hoover Commissions on Organization of the Executive Branch of the Government (1949, 1955), the reform movement strongly advocated that the personnel function be placed under the direction of a single head. This single personnel head was envisioned as part of the Executive Office of the President.

Underlying the demands for a single-headed personnel agency was efficiency. Efficiency finally prevailed with the Model Civil Service Law of 1970 and the Civil Service Reform Act of 1978. Both these "laws" incorporate the notion of personnel management as primarily an executive function. The efforts at reinventing government also have this theme (Osborne and Gaebler, 1992; Kettl, 1994; Kamensky, 1996).

Inasmuch as executives are motivated by the need for efficient management, these reforms provided them with enhanced capabilities. Efforts can more easily be directed at rationalizing the personnel system for productivity. One of the disadvantages of the CSC's role of protecting employees was the myriad rules constraining and inhibiting executive action. Although due process affords individual protections, it does not necessarily concern itself with the overall conditions of service. However, the pursuit of efficiency does not negate the need that gives rise to such protections (Kettl, 1994; Kettl and DiIulio, 1995; Thompson and Ingraham, 1996).

An executive personnel agency charged with providing the government with efficient personnel services has much to offer. It is at the heart of our notions of what modern staff services should be. After a couple of generations of civil service reform and public administration education, the spoils system was hardly seen to be a credible threat to the public service. The dangers that the spoils system had engendered were, for the most part, forgotten. Without the perceived threat of a spoils system, the need for the protection provided by the centralization of the personnel function was seen as less essential.

The Decentralization of Personnel

Under the Civil Service Reform Act of 1978, efficiency was to be achieved through the decentralization of the personnel function. The Reagan revolution's ideological emphasis on deregulation helped strengthen this trend. The permanence of these changes is demonstrated by the continued interest in such concepts as the hollow state and reinventing government. The reassertion of the pre–New Deal state, in which government directed and monitored public activity but contracted out for the actual provision of services, calls upon the line official to engage in a myriad of personnel decision making.

However, deregulation and decentralization are not synonymous. Decentralization moves the locus of personnel decision making from the central personnel office to the line supervisors and agency personnel managers. Yet, decentralization may be accompanied by detailed rules and regulations that structure and check personnel decisions (Davis, 1969). Deregulation, on the other hand, gives more discretion to new decision makers. Deregulation is the focus of the movement for reinventing government or the new public management. Deregulation is seen clearing the way for the practice of strategic human resource management (Kellough, 1999). Although deregulation is often accompanied by decentralization, this need not be the case. In the Reagan administration, the new patronage introduced a strong element of centralization.

Both Gulick (1937) and Simon (1957) noted that there are great advantages in allowing the first-line supervisor or street-level bureaucrat "independence." These individuals are indeed the only ones who truly see the nature of the specific problem to be solved. It is only when the "costs" inherent in centralized organization can be offset by the "benefits" of coordination, expertise, and responsibility that centralization is deemed warranted.

Advancements in personnel administration (e.g., the acceptance of training and development as a government function) make it feasible for decentralization to occur. Personnel functions can be delegated with confidence that agencies possess the ability to actually perform those tasks. Organizational "economies of scale or scope" (e.g., recruitment and test administration, payroll and benefits) become the criteria for determining which functions are to be delegated or outsourced under reinventing privatization schemes.

Although outsourcing or contracting out (i.e., hiring nonorganizational employees to perform a task or service) is often undertaken to reduce administrative headcount or to reap cost savings, these can produce futile, short-term benefits. Outsourcing personnel functions must always be based and evaluated on quality and service performance. In general, it is highly recommended that any performance management function (e.g., performance appraisal or employee relations) that contributes to an organization's competitive advantage not be outsourced. On the other hand, many of the other personnel functions (job analysis, recruitment, testing, payroll, benefits administration, and training) can be contracted out (Greer, Youngblood, and Gray, 1999).

When outsourcing any personnel service, the organization must treat this as it would any other product or service purchase. Outsourcing must use periodic and competitive bidding, adequate contract monitoring must be provided for, and services must be evaluated for performance (Greer, Youngblood, and Gray, 1999).

Although appealing because of its image of reducing unnecessary government, privatization (i.e., outsourcing to or contracting with a nongovernmental organization) is fraught with peril. Because the privatized activities are still fulfilling a public purpose, privatization serves only to create an unofficial, hidden, or shadow government. When in the guise of nonprofits, privatization may also contribute to understaffing and underfunding of needed services (Kettl, 1993; Milward and Provan, 1993).

Virtually all personnel functions can benefit from decentralization. If first-line officials possess the requisite personnel skills, they may be able to perform many tasks more effectively than a central personnel office. The problem traditionally has been that organizations have simply not provided these officials with the necessary skills. In such circumstances, the central personnel office's performance of these functions was indeed the only logical solution.

At the federal and state levels, the failure to provide personnel training for first-line supervisors has receded before a growing tide of public administration professionalism. The personnel office is no longer needed to perform the command-and-control tasks of personnel management. It is free to engage in the staff role for which it was originally intended. The central personnel office can serve as consultant and trainer. In human resource management, command and control is replaced by coaching and coordinating.

Recruitment should remain a preserve of the central personnel office. However, this is primarily due to the convenience and efficiency it affords both to individuals seeking government jobs and to agencies seeking employees. Basically, the central personnel office acts as a hiring hall. Even so, individual agency officials are responsible for "listing" jobs as well as defining them. Job analysis and the selection process already entail a great deal of work on the part of the line-agency official who must determine what the job is and who among the eligible applicants best meets its requirements. The personnel office should limit its role to providing common formats and broad guidelines. In administering selection exams, the central personnel office again serves as a meeting place; it also introduces economies of scale into the process.

The performance appraisal process should be left to individual supervisors with the personnel office serving as a staff resource and coordinator. Symbolically, in this case, the central personnel office also serves as an objective, "honest broker." It thereby designs, underwrites, and guarantees the fairness of the entire performance appraisal system (Daley, 1992b).

The will of the central personnel office remains paramount in the areas of pay and benefits, due primarily to the overarching character of these tasks. Furthermore, the central personnel office, freed from having to perform many of its former personnel functions, should have more time to devote to the job evaluation and compensation tasks.

Labor–Management relations remains an area that will involve the central personnel office. While first-line supervisors are responsible for the day-to-day administration of the labor contract, the central personnel office is responsible for teaching them how to do this. The central personnel office's direct involvement is limited primarily to the collective negotiations. This function is centralized because contracts apply to entire organizations (those negotiated for small subunits often serve as models). Hence, they must be negotiated by those with an organizational point of view.

The New Patronage Versus Decentralization

The new patronage and decentralization represent two important trends in personnel administration. Both advertise continuing problems for the future (Peters and Savoie, 1996). However, whether these two trends will come into conflict remains a concern. The task personnelists face is how to assure the reconciliation of the two.

The new patronage focuses on political responsiveness to elected officials. Centralization is viewed as a means for achieving that responsiveness. Yet, responsiveness is also the focus of decentralization. Whereas the new patronage is primarily concerned with providing political appointees the necessary power to oversee the functioning of government, decentralization involves delegating that authority to career civil servants in order to assure the same.

Inasmuch as the problems regarding governmental responsiveness may, in fact, partially stem from the centralization of staff functions like those in personnel administration, the decentralization of personnel functions may actually contribute to enhancing responsiveness.

The civil service system created under the Pendleton Act of 1883 was designed to protect public employees from the abuses of the spoils system. It was also a merit system designed to promote efficiency. A growing emphasis on efficiency coupled with a lessening fear of partisan abuse supported the centralization of authority. Yet, in order to maintain efficiency the very growth of modern government also demands the decentralization of governmental functions. For modern government, the reconciliation of centralized authority with decentralized functions poses the problem and prospect.

THE ORGANIZATION AND PERSONNEL MANAGEMENT

Personnel management occurs in and is part of an organization. Organizations are themselves subsystems within society that mediate and translate society's demands into the purposeful actions performed by individuals. In order to accomplish these desired tasks, organizations through the application of various mechanisms such as specialization and hierarchy create the techniques and processes that enable individuals to engage in coordinated, productive behavior.

The role of the personnel management process as a component in such organizational systems is often overlooked. The process of personnel management is both influenced by and itself influences the organization. In understanding and judging the effectiveness or success of a personnel management system, the role played by the organization is crucial (Becker and Gerhart, 1996; Delery and Doty, 1996; Youndt, Snell, Dean, and Lepak, 1996; Pfeffer, 1998; Pfeffer and Veiga, 1999).

Organizations are methods for the coordination of work. They perform a quite extensive array of activities—technical, commercial, financial, security, accounting, and managerial—only one of which involves management (Fayol, [1916] 1949: 3–6). In turn, this managerial activity is itself subdivided into numerous and various categories (Yukl, 1989: 92–95). Employing a statistical factor analysis, Gary Yukl (1989) derives fourteen empirical categories. Herbert Mintzberg (1973) designates ten managerial categories, while Robert House and Terence Mitchell (1974) deduce but four. Into these categories, the task-oriented techniques and processes of personnel management are grouped and arranged. However categorized, personnel management is an important tool in the manager's leadership role.

Organizations are also important because they can help foster and contribute to organizational commitment among public employees. Extensive examinations detail the positive role of employee involvement or commitment in developing and maintaining job satisfaction and organizational effectiveness (Buchanan, 1974a, 1974b, 1975a, 1975b; Romzek, 1985a, 1985b, 1989, 1990).

Organizational Culture and Climate

Organizational culture is the combination of assumptions, values, and artifacts that invest the organization with a sense of identity and mission (Schein, 1985). Organizational culture combines assumptions about human nature and the causal relationships of how things work with a set of philosophical, societal, and ideological values as to what should be done. These assumptions and values are further supported and clarified by an internal collection of myths, symbols, and rituals (Heffron, 1989: 211–238; Tosi, Rizzo, and Carroll, 1986: 65–72).

Organizational culture is the first and most general statement of what an organization strives to be. It represents its vision of what it is and what it wants to be. As such, it is meant to serve all as a guide to their actions. This is an especially important task in today's world where management is constantly faced with an ever-changing environment and beset by a veritable quandary of techniques and processes. A well-defined organizational culture can help individual managers and employees cut through the management jungle.

The concept of an organizational climate focuses more narrowly on the topic of how well the organization achieves its cultural goals. Specifically, organizational climate addresses what behaviors the organization actually supports and rewards. Are the organization's actions consistent with its pronouncements? Are individuals who act in behalf of the organization's culture rewarded or punished for their efforts? The consistent translation and interpretation of the guiding principles envisioned in an organization's culture into the specific work behaviors necessary for carrying out its tasks is a complex phenomenon.

The distinction between culture and climate is witness to the problems faced in this process. Public profession of a specific organization's culture may not accord with that organization's internal allocation of rewards and punishments. The climate perceived by employees is an accurate gauge of an organization's effective culture. Aligning the desired culture with an appropriate climate is among the central tasks faced by top management.

Organizational culture in the public sector is shaped by the basic regime values of American democracy (Fried, 1976: 43–81; Rohr, 1978). A distinctive public ethos pervades public administration counterbalancing the demands for efficiency, equity, and responsiveness. Notions of the public interest are important and real considerations for public employees. The oath public employees take in support of the Constitution is viewed as a serious and meaningful commitment (Rohr, 1991).

The nineteenth century civil service reformers launched a moral crusade against the laxity and corruption that had transformed political patronage into the spoils system. They endeavored to substitute a more efficient administration based on the concept of a professional civil service system (Van Riper, 1958; White, 1958). The success of their efforts culminated in the enactment of the Civil Service Act of 1883 and the creation of the merit system. Its successor, the Civil Service Reform Act of 1978, actually enshrines these merit principles in statute.

Whereas the reformers' early efforts were concentrated on combatting the evils of the spoils system, the work of younger scholars and reformers such as Frank Goodnow (1900) and Woodrow Wilson (1887) was directed somewhat more toward developing the positive aspects of the civil service system. In particular, they focused on establishing an administration separate from the political realm that would be guided by an imperative for efficiency. Good works would drive out the immorality of the spoils system.

Whether reality or myth, politically separate or not, public administration during most of the twentieth century clearly viewed itself as an arena dominated by neutral-competent officials (Appleby, 1952; Bailey, 1966; Redford, 1969). Even today, the notion of the neutral-competent official is seen as means for melding efficiency into democracy (Caiden, 1981; Daley, 1984a; Heclo, 1977; Meier, 1987; Mosher, 1982; Yates, 1982). On a somewhat more practical level, this attitude is also seen in the series of private sector commissions devoted to importing business efficiency into government.

The value placed upon equity as a component in the public sector organizational culture raises dual concerns for individual freedom and social justice. Allowing individuals the freedom to live their lives as they wish yet protecting these selfsame individuals as members of society from the deprecations of other individuals is a delicate task. This is made all the more difficult in that it requires the skills of a juggler to adjust for the constantly changing balances that are made necessary in order to keep everything in place. Administratively, freedom and justice both have distinctive external and internal applications.

Basically, freedom consists of the general natural rights possessed by individuals; many of these rights are further, specifically guaranteed under the federal Constitution as well as in many state constitutions. Their support and protection is, in fact, one of the reasons for the establishment of the United States (Rohr, 1989: 157–224).

Constitutional law articulates and protects these general rights. In organizational terms, administrative law also addresses issues involving citizens' rights. Case law regarding liability and constitutional torts is meant to assist in protecting citizens from the abuse of governmental authority (Lee, 1987, 1992; Wise, 1985, 1989; Rosenbloom, 1991). The cases themselves provide both for the redress and compensation of individuals whose rights have been violated as well as guidance designed to discourage and avoid future violations.

As public employment theory replaced the doctrine of privilege with a doctrine of substantial interest, civil liberties were also accorded to public employees (Rosenbloom, 1971, 1975, 1981, 1988, 1990). Public employee rights extend the notion of freedom into the organization itself. This assists in reinforcing the value placed on freedom by the organizational culture in the public sector.

Justice is a closely related aspect of the concern for equity (Rohr, 1989: 97–158). The focus here is on citizens in similar circumstances being accorded equal treatment before the law. The question of *caeteris paribus*—all things being equal—is, of course, the crux of the matter. Perhaps the bulk of administrative law is precisely devoted to the issues of administrative due process designed to guarantee citizens this equality.

Justice is also a concern of the civil rights movement. Equal employment opportunity and its implementation strategies such as affirmative action and cultural diversity focus on obtaining justice in the workplace. Organizationally, the Civil Rights Act of 1964 and the subsequent case law flowing from it form the basis for many of the legal requirements that drive modern personnel management practices. In fact, most of the court rulings vis-à-vis personnel management were handed down under the jurisdiction of the civil rights statutes.

Responsiveness is the third value shaping organizational culture in the public sector (Caiden, 1981; Daley, 1984a; Meier, 1987). The American Revolution originated in reaction to an unresponsive government. A continued uneasiness exists in American society with regard to the role and nature of government. The Whig tradition that imbues American democracy is especially distrustful of government, in general, and of administration, in particular. With the growth of the administrative state in the twentieth century, the fears of an elitist and hegemonic administrative class have once again burst forth. These fears are only heightened by the often complex, technical and professional nature of the tasks government is called upon to perform. However, academic research has consistently indicated how little reality there is to these fears. Administrators in the United States are among the most fervent supporters of democracy (Aberbach, Putnam, and Rockman, 1981; Aberbach and Rockman, 1976, 1988; Wynia, 1974; Daley, 1982, 1984b).

Managerial and employee roles along with the tools they use are influenced by the culture and climate of an organization. In creating a sense of identity for itself, an organization is also creating a work environment in which its managers and employees function. Organizational culture and climate affects individuals in three distinct ways. These three planes or levels of generalization—institutional, managerial, and operational—each provide a different perspective for analyzing the impact of organizational culture and climate (Thompson, 1967: 10–12).

The overall, long-term organizational environment sets the institutional tone and enunciates the basic principles that are used to guide individual behavior. Organizationally, this institutional tone tells individuals what is important. At the managerial level, these general principles are translated into and applied to the specific tasks required by the organization. Here, the linkage between theory and practice is central. Finally, the operational process of actually getting the specific job or task done reflects on how the organizational culture is actually implemented. At this level, the manner in which specific tools and interpersonal relationships are employed comes to the forefront.

American Democratic Values

American democracy is founded on ideals of liberty, effectiveness, and responsiveness (Fried, 1976: 43–81). The institutions of government and the electoral processes associated with them are means for safeguarding and pursuing those ideals. Furthermore, these ideals are not limited to the political arena but rather permeate society as a whole. In essence, these values guide our behaviors in politics, in economics, and in a host of other social activities.

Perhaps more than any other nation, the United States' social fabric is interwoven with a sense of individualism. Although much may occur in a private setting, it is still refereed by government. In American political theory, government is constituted to afford each individual the benefits of life, liberty, and the pursuit of happiness.

Yet, we recognize that with freedom there is also responsibility. Free individuals are also held accountable for their actions. Within the sphere of an individual's work-life, this accountability is the goal of performance appraisal.

A career open to talent and the rewarding of individual merit require individual judgments. Whether they are formal or informal, these assessments are made. Given the chances for mistake, formal methods are often to be preferred where tasks are either complex or particularly important.

American democratic values for liberty, effectiveness, and responsiveness set the stage upon which the performance management drama is played out. Although these values apply to both public and private sector organizations, the public sector setting only heightens the importance attached to them.

The Institutional Organization and Personnel Management

At the institutional level, the organization must decide the extent to which it will employ formal personnel management systems. Can the introduction of a personnel management system accomplish the goals envisioned for it? Furthermore, can it do so without creating an employee backwash so counterproductive as to negate all the benefits obtained?

The organization must choose personnel practices that suit its organizational culture. These must also be compatible with the other personnel and management techniques employed in that organization. Finally, it needs to fit in with the patterns of interpersonal relationships that the organization desires to foster (Zammuto, London, and Rowland, 1982).

As a manifestation of that culture, the organizational climate in which a personnel management system operates is crucial. Whether their results are real or imagined, individuals strive to bring order to their surrounding environment, especially their work environment. They also often adjust their behavior to accord with that perceived environment (Schneider, 1975, 1985). Although this is to some extent an interactive relationship, effectiveness is more likely to be associated with organizations that are categorized as emphasizing high involvement—management based on employee commitment, participative management in the decision-making process, and the ability to change in order to meet environmental demands (Lawler, Mohrman, Resnick, 1984; Lawler, 1986, 1990).

The Managerial Organization and Personnel Management

As a special aspect of organizational culture, management style performs the task of mediating that overall culture to the employees. Rensis Likert (1961, 1967) contrasted four different management styles—exploitative authoritarian, benevolent authoritarian, consultative, and participative. Each style characterizes a distinct approach to managing an organization. While paralleling the concepts discussed in organizational culture, management style differs from organizational culture in that it specifically focuses on the manager's role in the transmission of that culture.

Management style is a key factor in the creation and maintenance of employees' perception of the organization's climate. Subordinate employees take their cues from the behavior of those in managerial positions (Lawler and Rhode, 1976). How their immediate supervisors and hierarchal superiors behave is read by employees as how the organization itself behaves. Managerial actions can either reinforce or negate the formal statements of organizational culture and mission. Furthermore, managerial behavior is also interpreted as how the organization wants employees to behave.

Hence, management style is an important factor for encouraging the relationship between top-management support and personnel management needs to be carefully nurtured and handled. Performance management is, basically, a long-term process that seems to work best under conditions of openness and participation. Rensis Likert (1967) suggests that participative management approaches require from five to six years in order to fully gain employee confidence and trust.

Ever since the abuses of the scientific management movement were perpetuated at the turn of the century, employees have expressed reservations with regard to the introduction of new techniques and processes. They must be convinced that it is not some passing fad that will be replaced by next season's management fashion; they also need to be convinced that it is not some gimmick for exploiting them. Only after these systems have obtained the confidence and trust of employees will they commence showing productivity results.

Unfortunately, managers often feel themselves pressed for time and consequently unwilling to wait for real and lasting results. Geared as it is to two-, four-, and six-year electoral cycles, the public sector is especially vulnerable to such pressures. Authoritarian "get the job done now" attitudes willingly sacrifice the long-term advantages of participative approaches for smaller, short-term benefits. This is what underlies much of the employee distrust for management that has built up over the past half century. To win employee support for any new system, this distrust must first be overcome. This process of building trust now takes from two to three years in most organizations (hence, the five- to six-year lag for results discussed by Rensis Likert).

In nonparticipative systems, further problems may arise simply because the employees do not understand what is actually expected of them. Nonparticipative systems tend to suffer from serious communication problems. One of the advantages of participative management is that employees, having been in on the decision making itself, are better able to implement those decisions. Even the mild, informed consent aspect of participative management entails a vigorous feedback process. Employees and supervisors talk with one another. In essence, a true process of democratic centralism can be said to exist. Although managers may still retain full decision-making authority and expect employees to carry them out, decisions themselves are fully discussed.

In a nonparticipative environment, many more implementation questions are likely to arise. If this environment is accompanied, as it often is, by an authoritarian culture as well, employees may be reluctant to ask questions. Inquiries are often perceived as challenges to authority in such systems or, at the minimum, indicators of individual incompetence. In these systems, the performance management process is, indeed, a part of the command-and-control structure. Hence, employees learn to avoid seeking feedback or asking for assistance.

Top managers may also suffer from unrealistic expectations of what can be accomplished. Their desire for substantial results often leads them to minimize or trivialize potential problems (Janis, 1972; Whyte, 1989). When unrealistic expectations are set for employees, they simply give up. Although difficult but realistic expectations may not be fully meet, employees seem to be willing to put in the efforts such circumstances call for. Without something in the nature of a participative decision-making process, problems of this sort are quite likely to occur.

The Operational Organization and Personnel Management

The rewards determined or allocated with the assistance of performance management processes, whether extrinsic or intrinsic, are, most certainly, meaningful and important to individual employees. Inasmuch as individuals, especially Americans, derive more and more of their personal identity and sense of self-worth from the nature of their work, things that can affect that work environment take on greater salience. Hence, a personnel management can indirectly have effects on an individual that go well beyond the work setting.

However, this employee–supervisor relationship is not all one-sided. A formal personnel process establishes the "rules of the game." As with all sets of rules, employees can make use of these to structure and check supervisory and managerial behavior. In the more participatory processes, there is an even greater scope for influencing the outcome.

In this process of transformation and adaptation, managers are guided by an organization's culture. Economic circumstances, top-management support, the perceived efficacy and worthwhileness of personnel processes, the extent to which supervisors and employees received adequate training, and the degree to which the processes are participative all combine and interact to influence whether and to what extent the process is politicized.

Trust is the catalyst in organizational performance. Although the presence of a sense of organizational commitment does not itself directly lead to enhanced productivity, it establishes the framework in which that productivity can occur. More specifically, the expression of trust in an organization's supervisory and managerial leadership is associated with job performance (Becker, Billings, Eveleth, and Gilbert, 1996). Trust creates a positive or favorable environment in which employees are free to perform. More precisely, it establishes an organizational climate that encourages cooperation and allows them to devote their undivided attention to the task at hand (Barnard, 1938; Carnevale and Wechsler, 1992; Carnevale, 1995; Mayer, Davis, and Schoorman, 1995).

As Henri Fayol (1916) and Luther Gulick (1937) outlined at the beginning of the twentieth century, organizations are mechanisms for the coordination of work, that is, the coordination of human behaviors. This is even more the case with respect to today's knowledge-based or learning organization (Senge, 1990; Quinn, 1992a, 1992b; Quinn, Anderson, and Finkelstein, 1996). The primary assets of the knowledge-based organization in the information society are their networks of people. In the information society, the coordination of work is being transferred from traditional organizations to those based on ideas.

The centralized command-and-control organization is replaced by one emphasizing decentralized creativity of coaching and coordinating. Individuals no longer respond to command from hierarchal superiors but are allowed to exercise their creativity in solving problems. Hence, the purpose of the central authority ceases to be one of controlling its subordinates and becomes that of coordinating their efforts. To a great extent, this is a recognition of the nonlinear aspects of management (Kiel, 1994; Klingner and Lynn, 1997).

As such, it is important to understand the nature of human beings and the role that human behavior plays in organizational performance (Simon, 1985). To realize the benefits that these human assets provide requires an organizational climate in which trust predominates. One of the "general laws of management" must indeed be the importance and necessity of support from top management for specific programs and projects. There is not an administrative system or technique that does not specify this as a sine qua non for success. The generalized, overall sense of this support forms the perception of organizational trust.

The advent of renewed public sector reform movements in the 1970s (relying on organizational development) focused on the importance of a climate of organizational trust (Golembiewski and McConkie 1975; Golembiewski 1985). Organizational culture combines the assumptions, values, and artifacts that invest the organization that a sense of identity and mission (Schein, 1985). The related concept of an organizational climate narrows the focus to the topic of how well the organization achieves its cultural goals.

Organizational climate is a reality check. Conceptually, an organizational climate represents what actually has been implemented in an organization's culture. Hence, it serves to compare or contrast what an organization says it is with what it indeed is. How well does and an organization take the guiding principles espoused in its cultural vision and translate them into day-to-day reality? It is the difference between culture and climate that measures the extent to which the objectives of benefits of the cultural concept are achieved. The greater this difference is less likely it is that an organization can achieve its stated goals.

Aligning culture and climate, that is "walking the talk," involves building organizational trust among employees. Top management must transmit a clear and consistent message. What one wants the organization to be and the tools, including personnel practices, to be used for achieving this need to be rationally linked to one another.

The overall, long-term organizational environment sets the institutional tone and enunciates the basic principles that are used to guide individual behavior. Organizationally, this institutional tone tells individuals what is important. At the managerial level, these general principles are translated into and applied to the specific tasks required by the organization. Here, the linkage between theory and practice is central. Finally, the operational process of actually getting the specific job or task done reflects on how the organizational culture is actually implemented. At this level, the manner in which specific tools and interpersonal relationships are employed comes to the forefront (Becker and Gerhart, 1996; Delery and Doty, 1996; Youndt, Snell, Dean, and Lepak, 1996; Pfeffer, 1998; Pfeffer and Veiga, 1999).

SUMMARY

Strategic human resource management focuses on coordinating work to best achieve an organization's mission. Each and every process employed in the performance of work is assessed in terms of its ability to fulfill the purpose of the organization. While strategic planning is used to define that purpose, the techniques of personnel administration are employed to accomplish it.

Used separately and, more important, in tandem, techniques such as an internal career ladder, formal training systems, results-oriented performance appraisal, performance-based compensation, employment security, employee voice, and broadly defined jobs all serve to focus and achieve the mission, goals, and objectives of an organization.

Since the public sector differs in respect to legal, political, and economic dimensions, generic or business personnel practices must be adapted to fit. The private sector focus solely on maximizing efficiency and effectiveness needs to be modified. While the historical emphasis upon protecting the civil service from the dangers of patronage and the corrupting influences of the spoils system include a very important concern for efficiency and effectiveness, it also represents a strong force in support of democratic values and fairness. Current emphases on a new patronage (to enable elected political leaders to achieve their program objectives) and decentralization (to enable agencies to achieve their program objectives) enhance the strategic application of the personnel function. However, they may do so at the expense of employee protections and safeguards. The exercise of such managerial flexibility carries with it a pressing need for honoring and preserving the trust it also entails.

Every organization possesses a culture that governs how it is run. Management can occur successfully only when it is in accord with that culture. In America, that culture also includes the deeply held societal values underpinning democratic government—efficiency, equity, and responsiveness. Institutional, organizational, and operational systems must be aligned to support the organizational values and to obtain the organization's goals. This alignment is the aim of strategic management.

chapter 2

Planning

For motivation and incentives to work, they first must be tied to a goal. An organization must employ needs assessment and human resources development strategies in pursuit of its vision or mission. This chapter provides the reader with:

1. An understanding of the strategic planning process
2. The practical means for translating goals and objectives into results

Needs assessment (of where an organization wants to go) and human resources development (of those who are to get it there) focus on the specific organizational and individual needs whose satisfaction will lead to enhanced productivity. The vision and the path for fulfilling it, derived from strategic planning, are put into practical perspective through the use of macrotools such as total quality management (at the group level) and management by objectives (at the individual level).

STRATEGIC PLANNING

Strategic planning is rational analysis (Nutt and Backoff, 1992; Klingner, 1993; Perry, 1993; Berry, 1994; Mintzberg, 1994; Ledvinka, 1995; Bryson, 1996). It takes "what is" and develops ideas of "what should be" along with plans for "how to get there." With a realistic organizational strategy focused on what the future should look like, strategic planning provides the road map for fulfilling that future.

Although installing the strategic planning process appears relatively simple, in reality it requires that a learning organization exist. An organizational culture supportive of change must already be in place if strategic planning is to be anything other than a paper exercise. An organization must perceive that change may be desirable (i.e., recognize that the status quo is not the best of all possible worlds), be able to reflect and analyze that change (instead of following whatever is the current fad), have individuals who will champion the change, and, ultimately, have the ability to institutionalize that change throughout the entire organization. Without this learning environment, strategic planning is for naught (Mahler, 1997).

Through environmental scanning, strategic planning helps size up what the existing organization's capabilities are and what the real world it exists in is. The planning process explores alternatives—in terms of both the vision involved and the courses of action necessary to accomplish them. Finally, strategic planning helps an organization settle on one choice of direction and mesh it with the appropriate objectives and action plans. Strategic planning should also incorporate the human resources necessary for accomplishing its goals (Mesch, Perry, and Wise, 1995; Perry and Mesch, 1997).

The foremost advantage derived from strategic planning is that it helps improve organizational performance. Strategic planning focuses on the future—what should be. As such, it serves as a guiding star by which to steer the organization's development. Individual and team effort can be devoted to accomplishing the organization's goals (Keen, 1994).

By focusing on the truly important, strategic planning takes attention away from the day-to-day fire fighting and crisis management that so fruitlessly dissipates individual efforts. Its future-oriented techniques can warn an organization of dangers when there is yet time to prepare for them. Hence, it can be the basis for instilling habits fostering continuous improvement (Keen, 1994).

Strategic planning also helps to concentrate individual efforts into a team effort. It can assist in developing total quality management and objective-based performance appraisal systems. Accountability for results can be assigned. The strategic planning process itself can serve as a team-building exercise. Finally, the process itself transforms perceptions away from separate and distinct projects and toward systemic viewpoints (Keen, 1994).

Like electronic toys sold with the ubiquitous "batteries not included" attached in small print, strategic planning should be labeled with the warning "strategy not included." Planning is what strategic planning is about; the techniques are designed to assist in implementing strategy. The all-important vision of what is to be done, however, must be provided individually by those who choose to employ the planning process. Strategic planning is an aid to thinking; it is not a substitute.

It is perhaps the primary task of an organization's leadership to provide vision. Organizations are often large, cumbersome entities with only vague, general notions of what it is they are supposed to do (i.e., the individuals assembled under its rubric have only vague, general notions about what they hope to do and accomplish). It is the job of those individuals occupying top management positions to provide detail and substantive direction to those notions. Here is where Osborne and Gaebler's (1992) analogy of "steering rather than rowing" is called for. It is the vision that serves to bring together and reinforce people's sense of belonging to an organization. It makes them stakeholders and, more important, active, contributing participants.

Although vision is the chief responsibility of management, it is important that the vision be the organization's. A vision must be communicated and shared if it is to be an effective guide for performance. The participative development of formal mission statements serves both to communicate to and induce commitment among employees. Figure 2.1 displays three examples wherein a mission statement succinctly embodies an organization's purpose.

Leaders or management teams that "hammer out" a mission statement at some organizational retreat and then "broadcast" it to the organization are not providing a vision. Such catchy slogans are only a commercial message. A vision is also more than a "cult of personality" where the leader's personal vision, or merely his or her ego, is trumpeted loudly.

Figure 2.1
Mission Statements

United States

We the people of the United States, in Order to form a more perfect Union, establish Justice, insure domestic Tranquility, provide for the common defence, promote the general welfare, and secure the Blessings of Liberty to ourselves and our Posterity, do ordain and establish this constitution for the United States of America.

NASA/Johnson Space Center's Human Resources Office

We are in the people business.

We provide responsive, adaptable human resources programs and services which help the Center achieve its mission.

We partner with our customers to bring talented people into the Center, deliver services and product which provide for their development and well-being, and offer innovative solutions for human resources challenges.

State of Missouri Division of Personnel

To contribute expertise and leadership to human resources programs and strategies which support and enhance the efficient and effective operation of state agencies and which encourage and develop a high-performance state workforce. To administer the state's personnel systems with respect for the standards of professionalism and equity embodied in the State Personnel Law and for the public interest inherent in the missions of state agencies.

Visions are shared and voluntarily become guiding principles for each individual. Although they will originate in some individual's personal vision, they are transformed as they are subscribed to or adopted by others. Often they are modified and transformed by this process of conversion. A vision statement displayed on the wall is only a physical reminder. Only when the vision is within an individual is there a real vision (Senge, 1990).

Although the actual quality of a given vision remains elusive (a concept intricately associated with the interplay of personal characteristics and environmental circumstances), there are techniques that can assist in its development. The development of vision is aided by two sets of techniques: the focusing techniques that enable us to see clearly and the forecasting techniques that allow us to see early (Starling 1988: 87–217).

In addition to leadership support, those engaged in strategic planning need to be aware of other potential problems. As occurs with all management techniques, individuals will need extensive training and refresher training (to answer unforeseen questions that arise in response to implementation). Conflict, confusion, and chaos will prevail initially and for some time thereafter. Only as individuals learn how to do it and see its value will the benefits of strategic planning be realized (Merjanian, 1997).

The value of strategic planning is highly dependent upon those in the agencies who assemble and provide the data seeing that it also helps them do their jobs better. Excessive requests for information and data unconnected to an organization's mission undermine the strategic planning process. Although such information is useful in a command-and-control environment, strategic planning is essential for the more complex, knowledge-based organization's coaching and coordination. However, in such complex organizations the nonlinear nature of management is recognized. Strategic planning serves to define boundaries (Kiel, 1994). Planning is successful because it is useful (Merjanian, 1997).

Environmental Scanning

First attention, however, must be given to determining the initial conditions from which we will proceed. Strategic planning begins with an organizational assessment of existing external and internal conditions: the strengths, weaknesses, opportunities, and threats (SWOT). This stage is primarily devoted to data gathering (with some preliminary interpretations). Although it lacks the glamour associated with later stages and techniques, it is the all-important foundation upon which the rest of the planning process rests. If the information gathered here is faulty, the interpretations flowing from it will be fantasy.

No organization is independent of the environment in which it exists (or it ceases to exist). In fact, the formal organization exists precisely to assess and coordinate with this environment. An external environmental scan monitors opportunities for and threats to the organization. It assesses economic and social conditions (and their implications). What does society need in the future? What methods will it allow for achieving those aims? The environmental scan tallies stakeholder interests and desires. Who does the organization serve? What are their interests? Also, who is opposed to the organization and why? Forecasting techniques often play a crucial role in assessing the implications of these findings.

The internal environmental scan focuses on the strengths and weaknesses of the organization. Of course, at this stage these are somewhat conjectural. Strengths and weaknesses are only such in light of the objectives that the organization sets for itself. Under differing conditions or goals a strength can become a weakness, and a weakness a strength. Past successes and failures are recorded. What does the organization do well, and what does it do poorly? Most important, the state or readiness of the workforce is noted. Its people and the knowledge they possess or can acquire are the chief assets of an organization.

Strategic planning begins with needs assessment. An organization must search out what its environment is and where it wants to go. Needs assessment techniques (suggestion systems, attitudinal surveys, turnover analysis, and exit interviews) help gather such information (McGregor 1988; Ospina 1992).

Suggestion systems and more systematic employee attitude surveys call upon the organization's workforce for ideas and information (Carnevale, 1993). Suggestion systems can directly focus on new ideas for improving productivity. Whether as individuals or in groups such as occur under a quality circle format, suggestions draw upon the workers' expertise with the specific tasks they regularly perform. In addition to asking for specific productivity suggestions, attitudinal surveys can test organizational commitment and measure motivation. These assessments, albeit indirect, are strongly related to organizational effectiveness. They can also serve as instruments for spotting potential trouble.

Turnover analysis and exit interviews are more specifically tuned as troubleshooting devices. By focusing on how many and why employees are leaving an organization, important, negative changes can be highlighted and, hopefully, addressed.

Turnover rates are indicators. In fact, some turnover is quite desirable. The removal of unproductive workers and the renewal of the organization through the replacement of older workers with younger employees can be positive factors. While public organizations may average a 10 percent turnover rate, this would include retirements (2 percent), dismissals (1 percent), deaths (under half a percent), and layoffs (under half a percent). Retirements and deaths are unavoidable, and dismissals and layoffs may be deemed desirable. Hence, only 6 percent reflect voluntary resignations. It is in these voluntary quits that we must look for potential problems (Elling, 1997).

While perhaps beneficial, high dismissal or discharge rates do indicate an organizational problem. The proportion of poor performers in an organization should be strongly influenced or mitigated by the selection process and training opportunities whose investment in human capital enhances productivity both objectively and psychologically. Proper selection and training can make performance problems manageable (Shaw, Delery, Jenkins, and Gupta, 1998).

It is turnover among star performers that is most watched for. In this case, selection and training have worked. However, the productivity "payoff" is lost. Stars not only do proportionately more work; they serve as role models for other workers, helping them to do more. Hence, the loss of a star performer can have a tremendous impact.

Turnover is likely among younger workers who decide that they do not enjoy the job or fit in with the organizational culture. These voluntary quits are often mutually beneficial. Turnover rates can focus attention on misalignment in the work effort–incentive contract. Average turnover rates may mask problems in parts of an organization (the high stress and low pay in corrections and health care) or in high-demand job areas (accountants, engineers, and computer specialists are often subject to intense turnover). Pay inequity is most often the factor triggering voluntary quits. High turnover rates can be highly costly both in terms of lost productivity and because resources must be devoted to the recruitment and training of new workers (Cotton and Tuttle, 1986; Cascio, 1991; Kellough and Osuna, 1995; Elling, 1997; Shaw, Delery, Jenkins, and Gupta, 1998). Hence, stemming such problems can result in major contributions to an organization's retained resources.

Exit interviews glean information from those leaving the organization. Because employees may fear "negative" references if they complain, six- or twelve-month follow-up surveys are often a better source of critical information. They are especially designed to detect negative reasons for the exit. Such follow-up surveys (conducted by a more "neutral" personnel or human resources specialist) often highlight reasons not mentioned in the original exit interviews, especially if they were related to employee–supervisor conflicts. While not all these complaints are valid or completely accurate, they can serve to alert the organization to interpersonal skill problems or abusive supervisors. Also important is to ask when the employee began to think about leaving. By identifying "warning signs" at this stage, an organization can intervene to retain employees before the decision to leave (and underlying job dissatisfaction) has become irrevocable. In general, the exit interview can spotlight turnover problems. If early corrective action is appropriate, major mistakes and their costs can be avoided.

A specific aspect of turnover analysis relates to succession planning. Succession planning for managerial positions and, more generally, for all the key positions within an organization is especially important in periods of turmoil and change. The loss of key people is a serious impediment at any time; it is especially fraught with peril during the uncertainty of change (Gilmore, 1988; Schall, 1997).

An organization needs to identify who its key people are (talent, not management status, is what is important here). First, these people need to be motivated or induced to stay with the organization. Being informed of their key status may provide them with an extra sense of job security, thereby precluding efforts to find a more "secure" job elsewhere. Investing in their training (developing the skills that will be needed in the future role) can also give them a sense of job security. A financial "staying bonus" may hold them. Promotions or additional authority can also motivate people to stay.

Second, succession planning needs to occur. Individuals leave, retire, and die. They need to be replaced. Having identified the key people, it is also important to identify potential replacements. It is usually best to identify more than one in order to avoid "crown prince" problems. If sufficient internal candidates are lacking, then outside recruitment for such backup people should be undertaken. These internal and external individuals will not be ready to step into these jobs at once; the organization must plan for their training and development. The rank-in-person career systems tend to be much better at this than rank-in-position systems.

Although the vagaries of the electoral process make the planning of transitions in the public sector difficult, this problem is no greater than the competitive environment that private sector businesses face. Succession occurs in a turbulent environment whether the organization is public or private. The task is to manage within that turbulence (Schall, 1997).

Finally, succession planning needs to be linked and guided by overall organizational strategy. The choice of successors must fulfill the organization's goals for its future. Merely replacing or duplicating existing "officeholders" may not be sufficient (Gratton and Syrett, 1990).

The employment of needs assessment instruments for strategic planning and incentive systems for rewarding the successful implementation of plans are the alpha and omega of productivity. Correlations between these items is most certainly not to be taken as evidence of any direct causal relationship but rather as indications of a more sophisticated, underlying management strategy. Although these relationships are not expected to be as strong as those associated with the more directly related TQM and MBO/performance appraisal systems, they should, nevertheless, be quite evident if well-developed productivity systems are present.

Needs assessment brings into focus the general problems along with the directions the organization needs to go in seeking their solutions. Yet, it is up to individuals to actually accomplish these tasks. Inasmuch as these tasks require group efforts and cooperation, total quality management provides the team-based environment and monitoring techniques necessary for success.

Goal Setting

Focusing techniques concentrate on improving our understanding of an organization's goals and the means for achieving them. Goal setting, brainstorming–scenario planning, and Ishikawa or cause-and-effect charts are but three methods used in focusing on problems and solutions.

Participatory goal setting is quite simple; surprisingly, it works extraordinarily well. Individuals work better with a goal in mind. Even when the reward for achievement is only intrinsic, goal setting can be used to increase productivity. Goal setting even in the looser form of work agendas helps focus efforts (Kotter, 1982; Barry, Cramton, and Caroll, 1997).

Goal setting works because human beings inherently seem to abhor wasting their time and effort. Providing them a goal focuses their efforts; teamwork is innate. Adding participation to the goal-setting process refines and improves its effect. Participation allows the employees to clear up misconceptions and obtain a far better understanding of what is desired. It can also foster the sense of goal ownership that transforms motivation into commitment (Locke, Shaw, Saari, and Latham 1981; Locke and Latham 1984).

Brainstorming and related techniques such as cognitive mapping and scenario planning begin the goalsetting process. The human mind is designed to act quickly. It can readily draw conclusions based on little information. While an advantage to our ancestors and to us in emergencies, this facility can preclude the consideration of more complex, worthwhile options. Brainstorming exists to overcome this limitation. Since its purpose is to generate ideas, judgment is suspended at this stage in the process.

A brainstorming session begins with each individual being asked to write down five to ten possible "answers" to the question being considered. This ensures that everyone participates, with the further advantage that the act of writing itself gives the individual an investment in the process. These answers are then shared with the group as a whole. Commonly, these answers are written on large Post-it notes that are stuck on the wall for all to see (they can be jotted down on large sheets of paper that are then taped to the wall or a bulletin board).

The ideas generated by the brainstorming process can be structured or grouped using techniques such as cognitive mapping or cause-and-effect charts. Cognitive mapping is a simple device wherein the various ideas are rearranged and grouped (easily done with the use of Post-it notes) into similar topics. Complementary topic groups can be physically positioned near one another.

More complex than cognitive mapping for structuring the ideas is the use of cause-and-effect charts. Devised by Kaoru Ishikawa (1976) as a TQM technique, the cause-and-effect chart (also referred to as a fishbone diagram) provides the skeleton around which individuals can structure their brainstorming. In an Ishikawa chart, the problem or effect forms the foundation stem (or backbone) from which the contributing causes branch out (see Figure 2.2). Main branches often are used to group problems for staff and line agencies around issues related to (1) procedures or methods, (2) plant or machinery, (3) policies or materials, and (4) people. Individuals will then identify subsidiary cause-and-effect relationships that branch from these main issues. Like cognitive mapping, the diagram helps to organize the discussion and assure that attention remains focused on the problem (and ultimately its solution). It also serves to group related issues together so that potential interdependencies and interactions may better be noticed.

These techniques all involve substantial efforts at discussion and deliberation. The importance of discussion in fostering stakeholder understanding is not to be underestimated. Although the main goal of focusing techniques is to bring clarity to what is to be done, the eager willingness to do it is also paramount. Participation, inasmuch as it creates this sense of shared ownership in decisions, enhances the commitment to succeed (Miller and Monge 1986; Wagner and Gooding 1987a, 1987b).

It is at this final stage in goal setting that judgment is introduced into the process. Because no formal analysis has yet been undertaken, it is still important to be cautious in rejecting ideas. To preclude premature foreclosure, the spectrum

Figure 2.2
Ishikawa Cause-and-Effect Chart

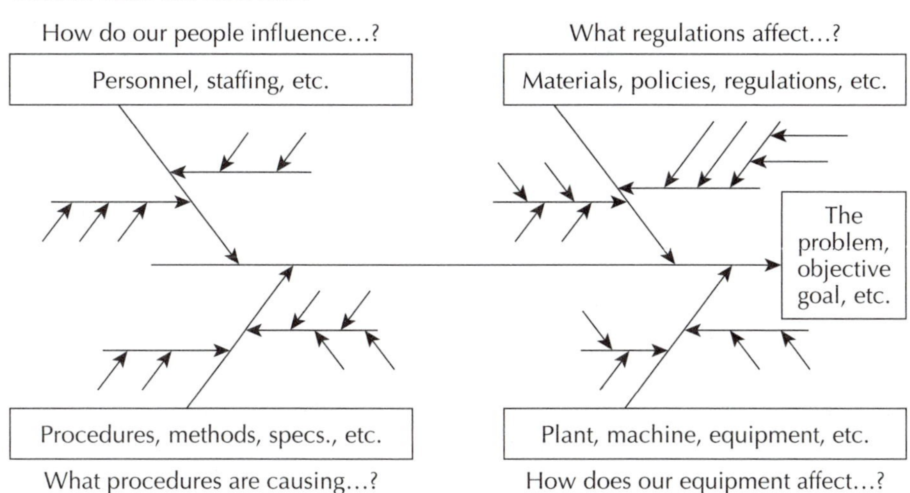

policy-planning technique is introduced (Prince, 1970; Shea, 1992). Under spectrum policy planning, each idea is assessed following a set protocol. First, the group as a whole attempts to list all of its advantages. They do this, in turn, for each of the ideas. Only after this has been done does the group turn to negative assessments. However, spectrum policy planning tempers negative judgments. When a disadvantage is noted, it then becomes the duty of the individual who pointed it out (and the others in the group) to think of ways to overcome that disadvantage. Only in this fashion will an idea be rejected from further consideration.

These techniques are designed to produce a marketplace of ideas from which to choose, and they do. Hence, it often is necessary to set priorities or reduce the set to a manageable size. This should only occur after the group has been exposed to each idea. Some form of quick or light voting can be used to accomplish this. Each individual ranks the top four or five ideas (five to the highest priority, four to the second most important, and so forth), and the scores are then tabulated. The items with the highest total scores continue to be focused on in further discussions and analysis.

Goals are a device for focusing attention and effort. In a knowledge-based organization this, in itself, helps to coordinate the actions of the entire workforce. In essence, coordination by organization has been supplemented (or replaced) by the equally powerful coordination by idea (Fayol, 1916; Gulick, 1937). Goals should, in general, share a number of attributes: specificity, difficulty, feedback, participation, and competition (Sims and Lorenzi, 1992: 118–129).

If they are to direct effort, goals must be specific about "what is to be done." This, first and foremost, requires that they be clearly measurable. Individuals must be able to "keep score." They must be able to judge for themselves that the goal is doable, and how well they are doing. Measurable goals reduce vagueness in assessing success.

By attaching a degree of difficulty to a goal, it is invested with value. Goals that are simple and easy to accomplish do not succeed in bringing out the extra effort in an individual. Only if there is a challenge in its accomplishment, do humans invest a goal with the psychological attention that motivation calls for. This also means that goals should avoid being too difficult, that is deemed impossible to achieve. Organizations in creating goals (and individual objectives) have all too often "stretched" them beyond reality. The plans look nice, but they fail.

Goals require performance feedback. Employees need to know how well they are doing in order to continue or take corrective actions. This is especially important when goals are long-term and big picture in nature. Intermediate and component assessments provide the small victories that encourage continuation.

Participation is, of course, designed to make the employee an actual stakeholder in the goal's achievement. By participating in the goal-setting process the individual assumes an ownership role in achieving that goal and, in addition, a far better understanding of what that goal is and what is necessary for its fulfillment.

Finally, some degree of competition (even if against one's self) can help. Although one must be careful in fostering competition to avoid damaging teamwork, humans are striving creatures. Like goal difficulty, the contest quality of goal setting adds to its intrinsic worth.

Forecasting

Forecasting techniques attempt to predict the future so that we can prepare for it (a realistic option) or, better yet, change it (our dream). Human beings hate uncertainty; the unknown frightens us fiercely. Forecasting becomes a means of assuaging these fears and, thereby, allowing us to work free from the paralysis of fright.

Forecasting techniques can use statistical methods (for projecting continuing trends) or human judgment (for assessing complex interactions). In either case, the more complex the question and the further into the future one looks, the more uncertain the answer. The confidence intervals or margin of error for predictions should always be included to visibly remind us of the imprecision of these measures. At some point, forecasting becomes little different from astrology or psychic readings.

Statistical methods take advantage of underlying mathematical relationships between events or variables to predict their future relationships (or actually the specific composition that the relationship will take at that future date). They work inasmuch as these relationships remain stable and relatively routine. Statistical methods run the gamut from bivariant correlations to Auto Regressive Integrated Moving Average (ARIMA) and regression models.

All statistical techniques are variations on the simple trend line (or bivariant correlation) that predicts future events by drawing a straight line through the past events. Because there are an infinite number of lines that can be drawn through any set of points, some rule of thumb is necessary to decide how to do so. Ours is to use the least squares approach (the mathematics being simpler than the alternative absolute value method). Under this method, we choose that line which minimizes the cumulative distance (squared to correct for the pluses and minuses of being above or below the line) between each separate point and the line. The result is a line that represents the "average" effect and enables us to predict that effect at future time periods.

Of course, not all lines are straight. Hence, we introduce various curve-fitting approaches (by mathematically introducing exponential and logarithmic functions).

Furthermore, these lines give equal weight to all points. Because these actually represent the same event at different time points, we would prefer to give preference or importance to those most recent (this assumes that they will have a greater impact on future events). To accommodate this adjustment, many formulas can also include a moving average or exponential smoothing component (in reality, fudge factors). A moving average simply takes the last three to five events and uses the average of their sum as the next prediction. Exponential smoothing bases its future prediction on the addition to the previous prediction of some proportion of the difference between the previous prediction and the actual result. These techniques are all brought together in the statistically sophisticated autoregressive integrated moving average (ARIMA) technique.

Finally, multiple regression techniques are also available for forecasting purposes. These extend the simple trend line by allowing us to deal with more complex relationships. In multiple regression, we can include more than one variable or item in the group used for making our predictions. The econometric forecasts of the economy (gross domestic product and revenue forecasts) are the most well known example of this technique. It is also the basis for market analyses.

More important, multiple regression enables us to theoretically study a complex relationship. The other approaches, no matter how sophisticated, only allow us to predict the future based on the past. They tell us nothing of how that past came to be or why these relationships exist. With multiple regression, this changes. We can examine these relationships for causal effects. By taking the mystery away, we can understand (and accept) the events that are transpiring. If successful, this would also allow us to manipulate present variables, not to predict but to produce the future.

Statistical techniques are, of course, not without their limitations—limitations that, in fact, can be quite serious. First, we live in an extraordinarily complex world. Statistical techniques often provide us with little more than the illusion of precision. The mathematics lull us into a sense of control that is unfounded. Our social science studies, as good as they are, are still only rudimentary. We know broad, general truths in many cases and in some instances specific applications. However, our knowledge map remains one where most territory is uncharted. Our statistical models are partial or conditional; they are pieces in a puzzle.

Second, statistical forecasts are all based on the world remaining unchanged. They are based on underlying structural relationships that are projected to continue into the future. If these relationships change (because we mapped out only a portion of the relationship upon which to base our predictions), then we are wrong. Our experience is that much of the world operates in this manner. Human civilization represents a mere 10,000 years of even our short existence; the "modern" era is a scant few hundred years old.

The human judgment methods for forecasting are primarily based on group decision-making techniques. The deliberation entailed in the group process is used to sort out the important and unimportant aspects of a problem. Unlike in statistical techniques, equal weight need not be given to all aspects or more importance attached to the most recent (which could prove to be aberrations). The groups can be composed of nonexperts or experts.

Nonexpert groups (surveys, public forums, and citizen panels) highlight the importance of citizen participation in the ultimate acceptability and success of public policy initiatives. Groups draw upon the added strength that differing experiences and perspectives bring to the decision-making process.

However, they do suffer from the social consequences inherent in group decision making. Groups exert pressure for social conformity and agreement. In fact, agreement may displace a valid forecast as the goal of the group. Merit may take second place to persistence. The number and intensity of the comments on an issue may be substituted for the validity underlying their argument. Individuals (and their reputations and egos) may take an interest in specific positions; subsequently, winning displaces arriving at a valid forecast as their goal (Janis, 1972; Martino, 1975: 19–20).

The survey is a well-developed technique for gathering information and assessing preferences (Rea and Parker, 1992; Fowler, 1993; Babbie, 1995). Though surveys lack true group deliberation, neither do they suffer from the adverse social consequences.

The public forum assembles citizens together and can indeed be a quite lively arena. Like the old-fashioned New England town meeting, it can focus deliberation on the problem and thoroughly explore the options and consequences from which a choice is to be made. As such, it can also suffer the social disadvantages of groups and follows the call of those who attend. In today's world, it is quite unlikely that any public forum will be as representative and democratic as the New England town meeting. Although a survey can be used to scientifically represent public opinion, it fails to capture the salience of issues and intensity of belief inherent in a public forum. The mere act of attendance in itself indicates a degree of concern well beyond the simple response to a survey's queries. A public forum can help serve to identify (or verify) the stakeholders on any specific issue.

The citizen panel attempts to synthesize the representativeness of the survey with the deliberation of the group. Citizen panels may follow the format of the jury system, the focus group, or a kiva technique. The legal system's jury of peers is the classic example of a group of citizens deliberating. Focus groups (which can be deliberately constructed to ensure various stratified representations) are another aspect of this method. Because the focus group employs a facilitator to moderate it, those monitoring or conducting it can interject additional comments or questions in order to clarify or follow up on information presented in the focus group's discussion (Krueger, 1994; Templeton, 1994). A modification on this is the kiva technique, developed by the Hopi Indians, in which the deliberating group is observed by other groups. After the initial group makes its decision, the next group discusses that decision; this is followed by another group that continues the discussion. Finally, the original group again deliberates (Nutt and Backoff, 1992: 232–233). Of course, others might prefer the Germanic double deliberation—first drunk, then sober.

Groups can also be composed of experts (citizen panels can actually be viewed as groups involving experts in popular opinion). A number of techniques (key informant, expert panel, nominal group, delphi, scenario, and expert system) have been devised. Because most technical and social issues are complicated by interactions, their ramifications can be cut through, to some extent, by having the various experts deliberate among themselves.

The key informant technique is simply the employment of a single expert. The chief advantage of the key informant lies in its ability to quickly and knowledgeably focus on the technical issues that must be dealt with. Of course, a key informant is not really a group.

An expert panel brings together a true group of key informants. Hence, the deliberation that occurs is tempered by a shared (or complementary) knowledge of the problem. An expert panel differs from a nonexpert, citizen panel in that its members possess the professional knowledge with which to weigh and judge complex, technical issues.

However, an expert panel is also a social group and suffers just as much, if not more, from the disadvantages inherent in the group decision-making process. The nominal group and delphi techniques were developed to overcome these social problems. These techniques can be used with nonexpert groups; however, the added expense often limits their practicality to cases involving serious technical issues.

The nominal group technique avoids the social disadvantages of group decision making through the simple device of never physically assembling the group together. If brought together in order that all members receive the same information, the group members do not interact with one another. In reality, it is a set of separate key informants. Hence, the adverse social consequences of the group are avoided at the cost of losing the advantages of expert deliberation.

The delphi technique attempts to correct for this. Although the delphi group is also left unassembled (which dampens the negative effects present in groups), it creates a framework in which expert interaction and deliberation can occur. Under the delphi process, a central facilitator or coordinator transcribes each expert's response(s). These are then summarized and the results distributed to the members. Those who have taken "extreme" positions are encouraged to add supporting information explaining how or why they reached their conclusions. This enables the group to reassess the original question(s) in light of the collective evaluation. Because all the individuals who participate in the delphi are "unknown" to one another, discussion centers on the merits of each argument rather than on subsidiary group issues. The delphi is rerun through three or four interrelations in order to benefit from a thorough debate.

Experts may also be asked to deal with contingencies through the employment of scenarios. In such cases, the experts are asked to forecast for each of a set of conditions (e.g., declining economy, status quo, and improving economy). This is analogous to conditional cost-benefit and risk assessment techniques (payoff matrixes and decision trees).

Finally, an organization may make use of programmed experts in the form of expert systems such as are found in interpretative structural modeling (Warfield, 1977) or the community options model (Talhelm, 1993). Branching routines lead the individual decision maker(s) through a series of computer menus. Responses direct the individual to further questions or are subject to complex calculations. The end result is a forecast or prediction.

IMPLEMENTATION

Goals are not self-executing. They require the coordinated effort of people to transform the ideas into realities. Implementation is at the heart of the administrative process. It is the magical or mystical act of calling things into being. It is this act of creation that attracts and enthralls us.

Coordination involves linking organizational goals with individual interests. Total quality management, human resources development, and management by objectives are techniques that each address aspects of this need for coordination.

Strategic plans must be translated into actions. Total quality management (TQM) is an umbrella concept that includes in its subcomponents an array of scheduling and implementation techniques for monitoring and tracking the accomplishment of organizational goals. Equally important are the notions of human resources development and management by objectives. These focus on the people themselves.

Human resources development highlights the importance attached to training individuals. If goals are to be accomplished, then the individuals who are meant to accomplish them must be provided the capability of doing so. The modern organization is no longer a "simple" gathering of clerks or laborers. Productivity is derived from the value added by the knowledge that its workers apply to the tasks they are charged with carrying out. To assure that this is done successfully, it is necessary for the organization itself to take an active role in providing its members with the knowledge requisite for accomplishing its mission.

Finally, this knowledge must be applied to the task. That is the function of such individual scheduling techniques as management by objectives (and the performance appraisal process). Management by objectives (MBO) translates the organizational goals found within TQM into individual assignments. Teams are composed of individual players, each of whom executes specific tasks. It is the completion of these individual jobs that brings success to the team and organization.

Total Quality Management

Total quality management is a loose amalgamation of the productivity theories drawn from such scholars as Philip B. Crosby (1979, 1984, 1986), W. Edwards Deming (1982, 1986; also see Scherkenbach 1986 and Walton 1986), and Joseph M. Juran (1964, 1988). TQM is, in many ways, an extension or renewal of Frederick W. Taylor's (1911) initial call for a scientific management movement. Like Taylor and scientific management, TQM calls for a "revolution of the mind." It is meant to be far more than the mere application of a series of productivity techniques (Schacter 1989).

TQM focuses primarily on the development of an array of statistical process controls (SPCs) as a means for monitoring and improving organizational productivity. Productivity gains are viewed as being locked in the organization's management and technical processes. The application of SPCs can ferret out these hidden productivity potentials. Although to some extent TQM has taken on the aspects of another management fad, there is real public sector interest in the concept. Public sector application has been encouraged and, in some instances, attempted (Hunter, O'Neill, and Walter 1987; Berwick 1989; Carr and Littman 1990; Cohen and Brand 1990; Milakovich 1990; Berman and West, 1995). However, serious questions have been raised about the applicability of TQM to the public sector—for example, the service orientation of the public sector and the difficulty in identifying the public customer (Swiss, 1992; Durant and Wilson, 1993; Wilson and Durant, 1994). However, empirical studies are beginning to demonstrate that sustained TQM efforts are capable of producing substantive results (Mani, 1995; Poister and Harris, 1996, 1997).

Although TQM involves a number of different but related systems, it is possible to summarize its purpose or direction in terms of seven basic tenets (Swiss 1992). First, TQM was founded on the notion that the customer is the arbiter of quality. Hence, efforts are focused on ascertaining what it is the customer desires. Second, emphasis is placed on building quality into the product or service rather than weeding out failures through some form of postproduction inspection. Third, quality calls for consistency. Efforts are devoted to continuously reducing the variability or variance involved in a product or service.

Fourth, with especial respect to performance appraisal systems, TQM places emphasis on group or team performance rather than that of individuals. TQM envisions organizational effectiveness as the result of systemic factors rather than something that is substantially the product of individual efforts. For modern organizations, collective or group tasks are the reality; individuals accomplish things only by working with others. Cooperation and teamwork predominate.

Fifth, TQM advocates note that it is a continuous process. TQM does not inoculate or vaccinate an organization against the lack of quality. TQM requires perseverance.

Sixth, these efforts are substantially dependent for their success on the participation of the workers. The ideas that lead to enhanced productivity and the benefits of teamwork are both dependent upon employees. Employees must perceive themselves as being stakeholders in the organization's future. This entails top management commitment.

Seventh, TQM is demanding and, hence, requires the commitment of the organization. It cannot exist merely as one of a myriad of management methods.

Total quality management views productivity as an organizational or managerial rather than as an individual problem. Various SPCs—for example, cause-and-effect models, flow charts, control charts, scatter diagrams, correlations, trend lines, pareto charts, or histograms—are used to establish the parameters of the productivity system.

Systemic effects rather than unique occurrences are the focus of the TQM efforts. The construction of confidence intervals based on formulas using the standard deviations among observed data enable managers to focus on the systemic aspects of a problem. Hence, normal variation in output is separated from long-term inefficiencies in the productivity process. By continuously attacking these systemic factors and correcting them, the process itself is improved.

The confidence intervals that separate systemic from variable aspects are themselves affected by the elimination or correction of systemic outliers. Hence, previously classified variable conditions can themselves become systemic problems through the continuous application of SPCs. However, it is important to note that in doing so they do not become individual or performance problems. They are always treated as systemic; individuals are never deemed at fault or as the source of error. In TQM, the individual is always viewed as an asset in problem solving. Even when inadequate training or skills may be indicated, these are not deemed to be attributable to or the fault of the individual. By these means, each problem area receives attention only when it is the most pressing, remaining problem. The organization, thereby, is devoting its attention to finding the solution that will do it the most good.

In TQM, performance appraisal is viewed, at best, as a minor tool. At worst, it becomes one of W. Edwards Deming's seven deadly sins. For Deming, far more is gained from dealing with problems from a systemic perspective than from attempting to personalize them.

First, personalizing a problem draws attention away from the group and cooperative nature of the work environment. Because performance appraisal focuses on the individual and the rewarding or punishing of that individual, it undermines the work group and, concomitantly, its productivity. With a performance appraisal system, competition is emphasized rather than cooperation. The interdependent nature of the modern work process is also ignored. Since the nonprofit and public sectors are characterized by an even more interdependent, group-oriented work process, these concerns are doubly important.

Second, introducing this divisiveness between individuals gains little. Individual performance differences are relatively small when compared with the overall levels of productivity involved. Most performance appraisal systems somewhat arbitrarily magnify these small differences in order to create a psychological distance. Differences in productivity that occur at the margins are thereby distorted and blown all out of proportion. The productivity gains from improved performance are, therefore, also relatively small, especially when compared to those that can be reaped elsewhere.

Finally, according to TQM, most of the appraisal systems actually in use are also at fault. They are not objective measures, but rather highly subjective instruments such as the graphic rating scales. When coupled with work measures that are more influenced by interdependencies and organizational factors, these appraisal systems produce a climate of fear.

The subjective appraisal processes do not allow employees to perceive that a causal relationship between their actions and organizational rewards is in operation. Uncertainty breeds caution. Coupled with this behavioral response is the added negative feature entailed in what TQM proponents view as the widespread and inherent abuse of the appraisal process. Performance appraisal is a management systems command-and-control instrument used more to punish than to reward. It is primarily an instrument for reminding individuals of the extant power relationships and of their subordinate place in those relationships.

Although TQM is not without faults of its own (Hyde, 1990–1991; Swiss, 1992), its indictment of performance appraisal raises serious concerns. These concerns have also long been the focus of public personnelists; they have also long been the focus of efforts to develop solutions. The performance appraisal innovations, including objectives-based appraisal, introduced over the past few decades are a result of these research efforts. Over the years, many individuals have looked upon the appraisal process uneasily (McGregor, 1957). That unease remains with us today.

A number of public administrationists (Fox, 1991; Gabris, 1986; Halachmi and Holzer, 1987; Thayer, 1987) raise the same questions found in the TQM literature. It should be noted that many of these problems are designed to be addressed by objective appraisal systems (Daley, 1992a, 1992b).

Human Resources Development

A second component in a fully developed system of productivity and incentives is the training support provided to the employees who are asked to carry it out. Human resources development does for the individual what needs assessment does for the organization. It audits skills and abilities in light of goals or directions to be sought. In combination, human resources development matches the individual to the organization (Fitz-enz, 1990; Sims and Sims, 1991).

This is even more true for organizations that are called upon under the various TQM conditions to be more adaptable. A commitment and investment in the people who are the heart and mind of the organization is required. Educational leave, tuition incentives, and flexible work hours (flextime) are some measures of these activities. More general notions of organizational development (Golembiewski, 1985) are also appropriate (albeit a lot of these are now being subsumed under the TQM label).

Again the relationship between these items and productivity incentives is indirect, but it is indeed there. Training and organizational development programs provide employees with the wherewithall and skills to achieve those productivity improvements and win the incentive rewards attached to them.

Since efforts represented by such terms as *TQM* are only now coming into vogue in the public sector, it is too early to expect anything other than marginal relationships to be evident in all but the most highly involved organizations. Results here are perhaps more likely to be useful as a baseline for measuring future developments.

Human resources development parallels the group-level needs assessment–TQM relationship. Like needs assessment, it outlines the plans and goals; it is then left to the individual performance appraisal process or a management-by-objectives system to guide their implementation and monitor individual efforts. The human resources development–MBO relationship parallels and complements the needs assessment–TQM relationship. Each relationship is vested with strengths and weaknesses; together they combine to support and compensate for the other.

Management by Objectives

Ultimately, management by objectives (MBO) stems from the planning imperatives or requirements of Frederick W. Taylor's scientific management. Formally associated with the writings of Peter Drucker (1954, 1964, 1974), management by objectives has developed into a sophisticated managerial tool (Morrisey, 1976; Odiorne, 1965, 1987; Rodgers and Hunter, 1992). Public sector applications of MBO quickly followed its introduction in the generic business/management literature. As with many managerial techniques and practices, promotional pieces and qualitative assessments abound. However, empirical research has indicated that MBO, in addition to its participative advantages, is viewed as positively contributing to organizational productivity (Rodgers and Hunter, 1992).

At the heart of the MBO process is the psychological one-on-one contract between superior and subordinate. Even though an MBO system translates overall organizational goals into component parts (thereby providing direction) and assigns the responsibility for their obtainment to subunits and finally to specific individuals, its success stems from the personal responsibility that those specific individuals willingly assume. Hence, the participatory or negotiated aspect of the MBO process plays a crucial role.

James Swiss (1991) outlines five parts in the basic MBO agreement. First, all MBO agreements answer the basic question of "what is to be done?" by indicating a specific goal (along with a timetable for its completion) that is to be accomplished. Second, the resources necessary for the achievement of this task should be indicated and allocated. This is often lacking in public sector applications and, hence, is a significant factor in their failure or limited success. Third, the intervening or intermediate steps for arriving at the goal should also be detailed. Usually referred to as "milestones" from the important role that these indicators actually serve in the map analogy for measuring travel distances, this MBO aspect helps map out the route by which the objective will be reached and thereby makes the journey more readily understood and accomplished. Fourth, periodic monitoring or superior–subordinate discussion is necessary in order to ascertain that one is on-track to obtaining the specified objectives. This also allows for the introduction of readjustments and corrective action. Fifth, upon the completion of the MBO cycle an evaluation should occur. This not only deals with the issue of whether the objective was obtained (on time and on budget) but also whether it succeeded in accomplishing the desired goal or introduced any side effects or unanticipated consequences. Such assessments also are used to begin the process anew.

As a formal management system, MBO brings direction and benefits to an organization. Management by objectives focuses on results rather than processes (Swiss, 1991). It is directed on what is accomplished rather than the effort put into it. Of course, this is more of an advantage for private sector, product organizations than it is for the more typical public sector service provider (where TQM approaches with their focus on process are becoming more popular). However, it is important even for government organizations to remember that results are indeed the "bottom line." A public sector service organization is not a symbolic agency; it exists to provide a desired, if not necessary, service. While that service may be qualitatively difficult to define and measure (hence, the resort to processes), it is nonetheless real.

Management by objectives is an aspect of participatory management. As such, it improves organizational communications (Swiss, 1991). By "forcing" superiors and subordinates to negotiate an MBO contract face-to-face, an opportunity for them to talk together is created. Subordinates are in a position to obtain a clear understanding of precisely what is being asked of them and to receive immediate clarification on any areas not fully understood. Similarly, superiors are provided with a clear picture of their subordinates' concerns and capabilities. MBO is a reality check.

Management by objectives breaks the distortion of scientific management's planning. The notion that "managers plan; workers work" is discarded under MBO. MBO's reality check prevents the futility of strategic planning. Lofty visions and grandiose plans are forced to address the real concerns of those expected to carry them out (Swiss, 1991).

Finally, management by objectives allows for an objective assessment of individual performance. As such, it is the foundation for one of the basic methods of objective performance appraisal (Daley, 1992b). Inasmuch as the individual objectives included in the MBO process are indeed individual and within the realm of reality, an MBO-based performance appraisal is a highly accurate and valuable instrument. Even where group processes are involved, it may be possible to readjust objective statements to reflect the coordinated or process nature of the task.

Although generally viewed as effective, public sector use of MBO is not enthusiastically endorsed. As Poister and Streib (1995) note with respect to municipal governments, this may be due to the extent to which MBO systems are actually employed. Systemwide MBO (more often found in larger cities and in those with a professional focus or city manager) does receive rave reviews. However, it is the piecemeal and, indeed, often pilot programs that garner less support. MBO "systems" limited to top management or to one segment of an organization produce frustrations because they are indeed incomplete. In such instances, managers must not only learn how to effectively use the MBO approach (with all of its inherent learning difficulties) but must also retain and maintain the non-MBO techniques for coping with the rest of the organization.

EVALUATION

Planning is a continuous activity. Formal evaluation becomes an important step in the transition from one plan to another (Rossi and Freeman, 1982; Fischer, 1995). Without evaluation, that transition could easily turn into a misstep. Formal evaluation serves to reinforce the goal-setting requirements for specificity and measurability. Knowing that there will later be a "test" helps to concentrate the mind at these earlier stages.

Evaluations are immensely difficult. Not only are there the technical and methodological problems associated with measurement to contend with, but political and dynamic issues as well. There is a vast evaluation literature stemming from and following up on Donald T. Campbell and Julian C. Stanley's *Experimental and Quasi-Experimental Designs for Research* (1963) outlining the methodological requirements for successful evaluation.

Planning is a dynamic process; it is meant to be. In planning, forecasting and feedback are continuous. This information is gathered not merely to know where you are going. It is accumulated so that the direction the future takes can be influenced and, if need be, changed. The purpose of forecasting a future disaster is not so we can put our affairs in order but so that we might endeavor to avoid that fate. Hence, the plans that we begin to implement may be subject to necessary change and readjustment. Evaluations must of necessity also be altered to take these into account.

Perhaps more frustrating are the political aspects attached to evaluations. All programs have enemies or, at the very least, individuals who favor alternative uses for their resources. This is a condition inherent in pluralist societies. Also inherent in pluralism is the fact that these enemies can succeed in ending your program or transferring resources from it totally separate from any evaluation based on the merits of the program itself. A formal evaluation, then, can actually be used against your program. For an unsuccessful program, further resources need not be wasted. For a successful program, victory can be declared and further resources transferred elsewhere.

Program evaluation itself is a twofold process: efficiency and effectiveness. First, the organization must evaluate how well it achieved its goals. Second, it must assess whether in achieving those goals it has accomplished what it hoped for or intended to. Has purposeful action produced beneficial results?

SUMMARY

Just as no man is an island, no organization exists in a vacuum (or black box). Organizations must be aware and atuned to the environment that surrounds and nourishes them. Organizations exist because they provide value to that environment. When that ceases to be true, they cease to exist. Scanning the environment prepares an organization. It establishes what its limitations and opportunities are.

Within this setting, it is paramount for an organization to maximize its potential through a process of goal setting. Goal setting points the way for those in the organization; it enables them to coordinate their work efforts in pursuit of common purposes.

Using appropriate statistical and/or group forecasting techniques allows an organization to envision possible futures. These alternative scenarios can serve to provide a choice of future goals or forewarn of impending problems. Preparations made in light of such forecasts enhance an organization's flexibility. This ability to adapt is useful even if an unforeseen future develops.

Plans are thoughts; results require action. It is the combination of strategic planning with implementation techniques that assures successful results. Techniques such as total quality management (setting group priorities) and management by objectives (setting individual priorities) coupled with human resources development (providing individuals with the skills and capabilities to carry out those priorities) transform thought into reality.

chapter 3

Motivation and Productivity

Public administration is plagued by partial systems trumpeting the triumph of technique over purpose. Our efforts—whether PPB, MBO, ZBB, or TQM—quickly become failed fads rather than successful solutions. The problem is not that we lack vision but rather the narrowness of partial systems. Each of our proposals fails because it only addresses a piece of the problem. Hence, we are often left to perfect the technique (a doable task) while ignoring the problem it was meant to solve (undoable with the tools at hand).

Strategic human resource management is meant to address this problem. A central concern linking techniques to purposes lies in motivation. This chapter provides knowledge of the:

1. Various motivational needs theories
2. Processes wherein those needs are fulfilled
3. Psychological or cognitive calculations that frame motivation
4. Communications and feedback techniques for implementing motivational strategies

The ultimate goal of all management systems is effective organizations. To achieve this, techniques or practices must be considered as part of a total system. We have been plagued by failure in the past because we have ignored the complementary, supportive aspects of our various management practices. Just as James Madison in espousing the notion of the Compound Republic in *The Federalist,* No. 10, argued that past republics failed because they were too small rather than too large, we must turn our current thinking on its head. A truly effective management integrates both work group and individual. In essence, we must combine a group-oriented TQM with an individually focused MBO into a unified total quality management by objectives.

Theoretically, explanations of organizational effectiveness focus either on the individual as an agent responsible for change or on the organization itself as a structure that controls and shapes the transformation of the environment. However, cognitive theory integrates these two perspectives. The individual's cognitive sense-making process (scanning, interpretation, and action) deletes steps in response to prior successful outcomes (Mintzberg, Raisinghani, and Theoret, 1976; Walsh and Ungson, 1991; Thomas, Clark, and Gioia, 1993). In essence, individuals form structural algorithms of the successful outcomes and apply them to problems perceived as similar. The agent–structure problem is not only a theoretical concern but also a practical issue.

Although overall productivity programs, including TQM, focus on the organization, their success is totally dependent upon their ability to elicit individual responses. Individual motivation, as such, is linked to the availability of a system of extrinsic and intrinsic incentive rewards. This chapter outlines the conditions under which productivity programs, both those focused on more general needs assessment and human resources development practices as well as those involving TQM and MBO, are likely to succeed (or, at least, have the possibility of succeeding).

Organizational effectiveness is the product of parallel group and individual productivity systems. At a general level, needs assessment practices focus on the strategic planning for the group-related aspects of an organization whereas a parallel human resources development outlines individual requirements. The specific application of these planning systems is the focus of TQM and MBO/performance appraisal systems. Total quality management translates the general goals established from the needs assessment process into doable group efforts. Similarly, MBO/performance appraisal systems mediate the individual objectives derived from the human resources development process. In addition, needs assessment and human resources development and TQM and MBO must be cross-linked to function as parallel, tandem processes.

Organizational effectiveness is the end product from the efforts of individual people working together. To improve or enhance the efficiency and effectiveness of an organization, we have an array of productivity programs. However, these productivity programs, whether directed at the activities of separate individuals or at work groups, must capture the attention and engage the interest of the employees themselves if they are to be successful.

That means that productivity must inherently include individual incentives. Our human resources/personnel textbooks regularly note this relationship between productivity and incentives (Lee, 1987: 275-330; Shafritz, Riccucci, Rosenbloom, and Hyde, 1992: 407–456). In general, the key role played by and the growing importance of human resource management in successfully implementing productivity programs receives detailed attention (Cascio, 1991; Snell, and Dean, 1992). The growing focus on TQM and similar participatory or group programs only serves to accentuate this.

Productively is achieved through employee motivation. The motivational literature presents the material for a rich and complex conceptual framework. It provides an array of content theories on what it is that motivates people and process theories on how one goes about doing that. It also explores the cognitive or psychological processes that occur as individuals "make up their minds" about the motivational-reward nexus. As important as these theories are, they are not theories in the social science sense. Most have been assumed true; very little empirical work has been done testing any of the theories. In fact, many are indeed untestable; the failure of one condition is often conjecturally offset or compensated for by another. Yet, these conceptual frameworks are invaluable heuristics.

CONTENT THEORIES

Motivation entails tapping into the preexisting needs that each individual has. By fulfilling these individual needs, the organization obtains the coordinated work that enables it to accomplish its goals. Maslow's (1943) hierarchy of needs, Alderfer's (1972) existence-relatedness-growth (ERG), and Herzberg's (1966) motivator-hygiene two-factor models all posit similar and related notions for use in motivating individuals.

All these theories assume that the individual possesses preexisting needs. These needs are not artificial or whimsical but represent real conditions. Therefore, the organization is not guilty of creating an unnecessary demand or dependency that it then fulfills by manipulating the individual. Virtually all motivational literature recognizes that human needs are complex. This is not questioned; what is subject to debate is whether the organization's response need be simple or complex.

Scientific Management

Frederick Taylor (1911) advocated a simple solution to motivation—you paid the worker! Money motivates, and that's all one needs to know. For Taylor, the complexities of individual needs were worked out by the individual himself. The great permeability of money to buy other things took care of the multitude of human needs rather well. In addition, it also assured workers a modicum of privacy and respect for their individuality. Of course, Taylor's calculations were modified in order to assure a continued supply of labor and demonstrated a paternalistic concern for moral considerations.

Modern concerns with privacy rights according every individual a sense of human dignity and a reluctance for imposing moral standards make such simple, classical approaches to motivation again appealing. However, even though money is a quite flexible medium of exchange, the market approach itself may symbolically serve to undermine individual motivation. The acknowledgment of the existence of the various human needs is also an important aspect of motivation. One of the strengths of the complex or multiple-need solutions to motivation is that they do so.

The Needs Hierarchy

Called upon to transfer the success of clinical psychology in dealing with mental illnesses to motivating workers, industrial and organizational psychology was developed in the early part of the twentieth century. Recognizing that workers were healthy rather than sick or abnormal required that new frameworks be developed. Abraham Maslow (1943) developed the premier needs theory in his five-stage "hierarchy of needs."

Maslow outlined five distinct needs levels—physiological, safety, social, esteem, and self-actualization—that somewhat progressively rose from the basic to the sublime. Satiation or marginal utility rather than fulfillment guided Maslow's mix of needs. Hence, individuals were always beset with multiple motivations. Satisfaction or satiation of a lower-ordered need set the stage or redirected the individual's attention to the unmet higher-level needs. Healthy individuals would continue to climb the needs hierarchy in their desire to develop and fulfill their human potential.

However, Maslow also allowed for psychological displacement to occur wherein the blockage of one needs level could be "satisfied," "fulfilled," or compensated for from higher- or lower-level needs. Unfortunately, this makes Maslow's theory methodologically untestable; that is, it cannot be "proven" to really work. Because its tenets are not subject to falsification, it cannot be verified. Yet, Maslow provides an archetypical framework from which to view human motivation.

Maslow's hierarchy of needs begins with the physiological. These are the basic essentials of animal existence. Individuals need food, clothing, shelter, and sex. The satisfaction of these needs was the primary focus of Taylor's notion of money as a motivator. Their importance even today is paramount. Much of the intensity and emotion in the health care debate arises from the physiological fears that illness engenders.

As these needs were more or less provided for, a concern for safety would arise. Human beings have a distinct dislike for uncertainty. In a world fraught with danger, things that were not recognized were most safely assumed to be things to avoid. Much of our effort is spent in spinning visions of normalcy, of weaving a world of routine and familiarity. This need is not limited to questions of physical safety. Questions ranging from that of job security to the rules and regulations governing organizational practices to procedural safeguards protecting workers from managerial abuses all tap into our concern for safety.

With social needs, Maslow began to address higher-level human concerns. Friendship and love, a sense of belonging are essential to the well-being of each and every person. As Aristotle well noted, "Man is a Social Animal." People do not really exist as separate individuals; they require the presence and interactions of fellow human beings. The modern, industrial world has wrecked havoc on many of the traditional underpinnings of social needs. Almost alone the work organization remains a major source of an individual's sense of community. "What do you do?" or "What is your job?" is one of the typical questions asked of a new acquaintance; it indeed really means "who are you?" Work is the defining experience.

Work as a social arena is also evident in the transformation of the dating/romantic setting. After college (and its spate of graduation marriages), it is the workplace that becomes the principle environment in which individuals search for that significant other. Friends and family are seen as a lesser network for finding someone with whom you share interests. The social atmosphere of the organization is more supportive of personal relationships. Those with whom you work already share career interests; the daily proximity allows for the exploration of other mutual interests.

Of course, any organization that serves as a matchmaker in order to motivate workers needs also to be aware of the negative aspects of such arrangements. A climate that fosters romantic relationships is not far removed from one that tolerates sexual harassment. The differences, while real and distinct, are neither remote nor innocuous. Similar advantages and disadvantages are associated with the organization acting as a friendship factory. The introduction of personal and social relationships into the workplace adds volatility that can both motivate and dissipate organizational energies.

Maslow's fourth level is esteem. Individuals are motivated by the esteem that they hold for themselves and in which they are held by others. Confidence in our own abilities and achievements is an important source of self-motivation. Although real achievements are rewards in themselves, we still very much enjoy the recognition and respect of others. An accomplishment is all that more appreciated when friends or an organization favorably comments on it.

The use of public honors and displays has long been an important element in human society. From the laurel wreath awarded to the Greek athlete and the triumph received by the Roman general to today's honorary award presentations and the organizational use of incentive trophies, recognition and adoration have been vigorously sought after. Sought-after symbols are potent motivators.

Self-actualization is the final and, perhaps, most complex stage in Maslow's hierarchy of needs. Self-actualization not only encompasses individuals' need for growth and development but also their craving for human fulfillment. Organizations are adept at providing assistance in the former, but at a loss when it comes to the latter.

Career development and training opportunities are readily available to feed the individual's appetite for personal and professional growth. Training and development are clearly recognized as benefiting the organization and enhancing productivity. As a motivation tool, this aspect of self-actualization is immensely cost-effective.

Human fulfillment, the achievement of one's full potential as a human being, opens onto an entirely new vista. Maslow's other stages and the growth aspect of self-actualization all can be accomplished within and with the help of the organization. This complimentary relationship benefits both individuals (who obtain the fulfillment of their needs) and the organization (which obtains productivity). The ultimate transformation of the individual need not include, and perhaps cannot include, a partnership with the organization.

As Abraham Maslow discusses in his *Eupsychian Management* (1965), self-actualization transcends the boundaries of ordinary, everyday relations. Self-actualization requires in individuals a religious fervor to fulfill their full human potential. Human existence extends beyond the organizational or economic realm. It encompasses all that life is—it is work, it is play; it is the ordinary, it is the sublime. Although the fulfillment of this potential may be accomplished with the assistance of the work organization, it is not necessary. In fact, because self-actualized individuals are *called* and act on an inner direction, they are much more independent and self-confident.

Many organizations, locked into command-and-control cultures, are unable to tolerate or understand such independence, let alone value it. For Maslow, when the interests of organization and individual diverge in the search for self-actualization, it is the individual and not the organization that must take precedence. For most organizations, such a notion is totally anathema. Hence, self-actualization beyond its early training and development phrase is downplayed by organizations. The lower stages of motivation prove safer.

As popular as it is, Maslow's hierarchy of needs lacks the precision of a social science theory. Since the blockage of one need can be addressed through displacement (i.e., substitution satisfaction from a higher- or lower-level need), the needs hierarchy is untestable. This problem is further compounded in that need satisfaction need not be complete before individuals turn their attention to higher-level needs. Marginal satiation, which varies from individual to individual, is all that Maslow specifies; any given individual may be operating under a set of multiple motivations.

Clayton Alderfer (1972) in his existence-relatedness-growth (ERG) theory has modified Abraham Maslow's needs hierarchy. Maslow's five stages have been turned on their side and regrouped into three concepts. No longer are we dealing with a vertical hierarchy of "lower" and "higher" level needs, but with a horizontal arrangement of equal needs. Existence combines Maslow's physiological and safety needs. Relatedness encompasses the social and esteem needs. Growth represents the self-actualization stage (with the emphasis perhaps placed a bit more upon its training and development components). In Alderfer's motivation model, relatedness assumes a pivotal role in balancing and adjusting the mix between existence and growth needs. In addition, Alderfer recognizes growth as an asymmetric component whose satisfaction doesn't lead to satiation.

Two-Factor Theory

Frederick Herzberg's two-factor or motivator-hygiene theory was developed independently of the work of Maslow (and Alderfer). However, its empirical results are often offered as evidence supporting Maslow's hierarchy of needs. Herzberg focused on the two factors of job satisfaction and dissatisfaction. Workers were asked to record what they enjoyed about the best job they ever had and what upset them about the worst job they had experienced.

The resulting list of job experiences forms the foundation of the two-factor theory. Although all items were listed by individuals as reasons for both the best job and the worst job, a pattern emerged in which certain practices tended to be associated with the best jobs (achievement, recognition, the work itself, responsibility, advancement, and growth), while others lined up with the worst (company policy and administration, supervision, relationship with the supervisor, work conditions, salary, relationship with peers, personal life, relationship with subordinates, status, and security). Herzberg labeled these two dimensions satisfiers and dissatisfiers (and later motivator and hygiene factors).

Interestingly, Herzberg's dissatisfier/hygiene items closely matched in ascending order Maslow's physiological, safety, and esteem needs while the satisfier/motivator category encompassed the esteem and self-actualization levels. This rough equivalency was quickly touted as an empirical verification or validation of Maslow's hierarchy-of-needs theory. This is, of course, not the case. Herzberg's model, while certainly related (after all he was studying the same phenomenon), is an independent explanation of motivation.

Although only one of Herzberg's factors is labeled motivation, it would be a mistake to confuse the label with the concept and to ignore the motivational role played by dissatisfiers. If we think in terms of productivity instead of motivation (the motivation of workers adjusted for effort, skills, and luck is what creates productivity), we can see the importance of both factors.

Under Herzberg's model, the employee comes to the job prepared to give a "fair day's work for a fair day's pay." This set level of productivity can be reduced if the organization fails to eliminate or alleviate the dissatisfier or hygiene items. Although hygiene items do not serve to motivate extra work, their impact on productivity levels is quite significant. Most of the success of Frederick Taylor's scientific management was owed to the enhancement of productivity obtained by correcting dissatisfier or hygiene problems. Organizations often throw away substantial amounts of productivity through such mismanagement (or, as Taylor would claim, the failure to plan the work).

Beyond the medieval social value of a "fair day's work for a fair day's pay," employees are willing to do more if they are motivated. Motivation entails an additional psychological contract between employer and employee. The extra productivity that the employer or organization obtains from the worker is "paid for" by providing the employee with substantial intrinsic rewards—opportunities for esteem and self-actualization.

Need Theory

If we think that all motivation theories fit together so easily, David McCelland (1961, 1975) offers another and different view of a human needs theory of motivation. McCelland also bases his theory on meeting or providing for inherent human needs. However, his classification of needs differs markedly from those offered by Maslow, Alderfer, or Herzberg. McCelland's research has focused on three inherent needs—the need for achievement (nAch), the need for power (nPwr), and the need for affiliation (nAff).

Motivation is inculcated in children through the stories and role models presented to them as things admired in their society. As adults, they seek to emulate the heroes and values of their childhood lessons. The entrepreneurial spirit, necessary for the creation of productive enterprises, emerges from stories focused on achievement and individual accomplishments. Leadership, necessary for managing or coordinating large organizations, is honed on stories of individual competition and intellectual legerdemain. Social harmony and teamwork flow from the affiliation needs fostered by an emphasis on "getting along" and the "good of the whole."

PROCESS THEORIES

How one taps these motivational needs is the focus of the process theories. The psychological/learning theories represented by B. F. Skinner's operant conditioning with its emphasis on rewarding desired behavior is the conceptual framework that predominates. Expectancy theory (that undergirds pay-for-performance schemes) is a more specific application of this.

Operant Conditioning

Earlier work in psychology developed conditioning theories (S-R) such as that of Ivan Pavlov. The experimental subjects were presented a stimulus to which they were conditioned to respond. Pavlov's experiments with hungry dogs linked a call to dinner with the provision of the food. The dogs were conditioned to associated the two events together. The dogs' salivation at the sight of the food was transferred to the artificial stimulus of ringing the bell. Ultimately, the bell alone was enough to trigger the salivation response in the dogs.

Operant conditioning (S-O-R) extends this work to require that the experimental subject upon hearing the stimulus produce a positive operation in order to receive the response or reward. In essence, the animal is trained to perform some trick—the dog must now sing for its supper!

Although the logic is clearly evident (and may have appealed to managerial prejudices), the leap from training experimental animals to do tricks to motivating human workers is not that easily accomplished. The parsimonious language of experimental psychology leaves little room for the niceties of polite and civilized human discourse. Yet, it is these very differences that help define the human condition.

For operant conditioning to work as a motivational tool, it must fully include the worker as a thinking participant in the system. Even the dogs had to be hungry for Pavlov's experiments to work, and humans are much more complex than dogs. People respond to rewards and punishments. Desirable behavior can be reinforced and encouraged by providing a positive reward (a motivator or satisfier) or by eliminating a negative feature (a hygiene factor or dissatisfier). Undesirable behavior may be curtailed by punishing its occurrence or by denying a valued reward. The extinction of reward or punishment for an event—it no longer counts in the scheme of things—may also lead to its elimination (inasmuch as it does not serve other functions).

As with Maslow and other motivational scholars, Skinner does not advocate the use of punishment. From a utilitarian perspective, punishment just does not guarantee the desired outcomes. The fear of punishment itself may reduce the overall effort and curtail the frequency of success. Relationships between supervisor and subordinate are also likely to suffer, especially if the reasons underlying the punishment are vague or open to question. Finally, punishment is an aggressive act and may elicit an aggressive response.

Success in the reinforcement of desired behavior (or in the elimination of undesired behavior) is also dependent upon the scheduling or timing of that reinforcement.

Continuous reinforcement rewards and punishes every event; modern technology makes such close monitoring possible for many organizations. Learning is quick, but so is extinction. Compliance occurs only as long as a police-state environment is maintained.

The scheduling of reinforcement is a mix of fixed versus variable effects in interaction with interval (time) or ratio responses. Fixed interval effects follow a set time schedule. Many organizational functions are linked to annual schedules. Hence, learning is somewhat slow, yet resistant to extinction. Variable interval effects trigger rewards at random time periods. Like pop quizzes, this approach encourages employees to review and think about their activities constantly. Although learning remains slow, what is learned is highly resistant to extinction.

Ratio responses are divorced from temporal considerations. Fixed ratios reward on a piece-rate schedule. Following a set number of responses, the employee is rewarded. Quantifiable productivity is what triggers the reward mechanism. In this method, learning is slow with moderate resistance to extinction. A variable ratio is also based on the number of responses, but differs in that the number necessary to trigger the reward mechanism is itself random (rewards are proportionally adjusted to match quantity). In this instance learning is also slow, but it is highly resistant to extinction.

Operant conditioning is predicated on the efficacy of extrinsic rewards. This can have serious drawbacks. When rewards are withdrawn, extinction of the desired behavior often results. Even more important, extrinsic rewards can replace the desired behavior as an individual's primary focus. This both lessens the intrinsic "value" of the desired behavior and refocuses productive effort/attention on the extrinsic reward at the behavior's expense (Kohn, 1993).

Expectancy Theory

Expectancy theory lays out the interrelated requirements that link productivity and incentives. In deciding whether to engage in a specific activity (which enhances or contributes to organizational productivity), an individual calculates the likelihood for successfully completing the task, the value of the promised reward for doing so, and the probability of actual payment once the task is completed. The cost-benefit calculations of the efforts and incentives entailed in this process are the key to initiation.

Combining the rational choice theories of classical economics with the cognitive theories of psychology, expectancy theory posits employee motivation as the outcome of rational decision making on the part of the employee. Associated with the work of Victor Vroom and of Edward Lawler, expectancy theory is composed of a series of calculations in which the worker judges the degree to which a task is realistic, the effort needed to accomplish it, and the desirability of doing so.

Sizing up the job is a two-step process. First, an individual must deem the requested task or job as something that can indeed be done. This initial reality check determines whether a fuller analysis is warranted. Only when tasks are seen as being firmly grounded in reality are they worth considering further. Second, the employee assesses the amount of effort required to assure success or a probability of success. How much "work" does the job entail? The answer to this question forms the foundation for the work–reward calculus that is at the heart of expectancy theory.

The desirability of performing the requested task is based on the degree to which the individual judges that the rewards being offered match the effort that would be required. This is crucial. Although most organizations have little difficulty in developing jobs that are realistic and doable, they often fail in tying commensurate rewards to these requests. They expect far more from their employees than they are willing to give in return. The work–reward calculation is very much a cognitive process involving all of J. Stacy Adam's notions of equity theory.

The employee's calculation of the desirability of doing a task includes not only the balancing of the effort–reward bargain but also the probability of the reward actually being paid on delivery of the effort. Most discussions of expectancy theory tend to overlook this problem. However, just as organizations must write off some of their accounts receivable as lost, the possibility of the organization reneging on its promised payouts must also be factored into the equation.

COGNITIVE REALITIES AND PRODUCTIVITY

Although computer analogies have replaced the machine model in discussions of how the mind works, neither model accurately reflects the actual cognitive process. Computers and machines alike invoke images of precision, rationality, and logic. The human mind, however, is also a vast realm given over to nonanalytical, nonrational thinking.

As highly interested participant-observers, we humans prefer to view our mind as the culminating result of a rational, evolutionary process. However, the brain may be nothing more than an appendix with an education. Evolution is accident. Bearing in mind the uncertainties of chance, the useful accidents are encouraged by evolution and may survive long after they have outlived that initial, expedient usefulness.

Developments are not undertaken with a definitive purpose in mind. The nose may be ideal for holding one's glasses; yet, it was not intended for that Panglossian purpose. In the human brain's triune makeup—reptilian complex, limbic system, and neocortex—rationality and reason are associated with the last stage in this evolutionary development (MacLean, 1973; Sagan, 1977; Restak, 1979). This thought that human intelligence may be nothing more than an artifact is as troublesome as it is humbling.

Efforts in the development of artificial intelligence grope with this nonrational problem in their attempts at constructing algorithms mimicking the fuzzy logic that guides human decision making. It appears that human beings are quite capable of making great inferential leaps on the basis of quite little information. The combination of an innate ability for pattern recognition and a memory for the past underlie human intelligence. This is a talent that also leads one to "jump to conclusions." Yet, these jumps often do prove highly successful.

Cognitive research focuses on discerning how the mind functions (DeCotiis and Petit, 1978; Landy and Farr, 1980; Feldman, 1981; Ilgen and Feldman, 1983; DeNisi, Cafferty, and Meglino, 1984; Gardner, 1985). How do individuals go about making decisions? How do they perceive that a problem is a problem? How do they know that a proposed solution is feasible? Once the cognitive processes are understood, can this information or understanding aid us in making better decisions? The question further devolves into the more specific concern—what is the role of cognitive behavior in the performance appraisal process?

A number of ideas vis-à-vis cognitive behavior stem from the decision-making work of Herbert Simon (1947). The development of Herbert Simon's notion of *satisficing* along the lines later outlined by Robert Axlerod's (1976) search concept leads to the empirical schema theory. Human beings recognize patterns; new events are compared against the set of existing patterns stored in an individual's memory.

New problems are quickly classified according to their essential characteristics and then compared with the set of previous problem–solution schema. When the mind registers a sufficient similarity between present and memory patterns, the memory match solution is applied to the present problem. This search process moves from the simple and more recent patterns to the more complex and older memories.

Schemas enable humans to make quick decisions on the basis of incomplete information. As such, they are also easily prone to error. A match need not be perfect in terms of schema theory for it to occur; it only need be one of sufficient similarity. The schema profile then would be the basis on which any further analysis would proceed. Hence, schema notions would impart the nonmatching characteristics as well as those that matched when interpreting the cognitive process.

There is a strong hint of traits in the working of the schema concept. Individuals profile basic traits or behavioral characteristics that affect performance rather than compiling lists of results. There also is a tendency to concentrate on defining boundary conditions that separate one schema from another. Outlines rather than details are important in schemas. Further, these profiles appear to focus on defining what is not to be done or doesn't fit into the schema rather than on more positively defining what it is.

Individuals operate with a set number of schemas or scripts (Abelson, 1976; Ilgen and Feldman, 1983; Gioia and Poole, 1984; Schott, 1991). Scripts are prototypes for behavior. In many ways, they are like the plays available to a sports team. Although innovation can occur, preference is given to the application or slight adaptation of those plays already proven successful. The standard operating procedures that undergird organizational behavior witness the widespread employment of this approach.

For the most part, routine suffices. Only when it fails to meet the challenge does an organization wake up. Innovation requires the expenditure of extraordinary effort. Although individual tailoring results in clothes that fit better, it also entails greater costs than purchasing clothes off-the-rack. Is the better fit worth the additional cost? As devices for reducing the costs of administrative transactions, organizational economics posits that organizations endeavor to avoid innovation or individual tailoring wherever possible (Barney, 1990; Donaldson, 1990; Hesterly, Liebeskind, and Zenger, 1990).

Prospect and Attribution Theories

Cognitive research also introduces us to two other substantive aspects—prospect and attribution theories—that affect the performance appraisal process. Both of these cognitive theories deal with how individuals receive and recall information. Basically, they focus on the mind's limitations as a central processing unit.

Prospect theory directs its attention to the various limitations humans face in processing large amounts of information (Tversky and Kahneman, 1974; Kahneman and Tversky, 1979; Nisbett and Ross, 1980; Kahneman, Slovic, and Tversky, 1982; Quattrone and Tversky, 1988; Houston, 1988). Prospect theory posits an asymmetric relationship between risk and information. Potential losses loom larger than prospective gains; however, this risk aversion is temporarily reversed into a speculative frenzy when faced with a chance for restoring recent losses.

From prospect theory research, a number of decision-making heuristics or rules of thumb are also apparent. The presence of too few schema or categories in an individual's repertoire can lead to a representativeness problem. In the search process, comparisons are made against an overly narrow model of success. While the chosen schema indeed is an example of success, it need not be the only possibility. In addition, it is also likely to include extraneous items that are subsequently and incorrectly perceived as essential ingredients.

In another heuristic, initial impressions anchor our overall perceptions, especially with regard to numeric or statistical manipulations. New information is introduced only as adjustments to the initial perception and tends to be heavily discounted. In addition, the total amount and type of material that we can recall influences our decision making. Finally, besides the question of how much information is available to us, the vividness or dramatic value of individual items has its own significance. The more noteworthy an item, the more likely it is to actually register with us and also to be considered as "typical."

Attribution theory addresses the influence that causal perceptions impart to the appraisal process (Green and Mitchell, 1979; Feldman, 1981; Knowlton and Mitchell, 1980; Lord and Smith, 1983; DeVader, Bateson, and Lord, 1986). The extent to which supervisors perceive or credit external factors with influencing the outcomes of individual initiatives is important. Similarly, the extent to which these causes are viewed as temporary or as permanent conditions are also taken into consideration.

If external or systemic conditions are deemed culpable in cases where objectives were not met, an employee's efforts are more likely to be rewarded. On the other hand, if the ball was deemed playable, failing to catch it or dropping it is an error to be counted against an individual. Similarly, problems attributable to a lack of sufficient motivation or effort are viewed more severely than those perceived as a failure of ability. Doing the best you can is always expected.

Attributional factors influence the evaluation processes both for employee performance and for training needs assessment. Supervisors, who often enjoy a greater locus of control over their own jobs than they are willing to grant to their employees, are more likely to make individual attributions. On the other hand, employees are more aware of the role played by external, environmental conditions.

Within the parameters of an organization's culture the supervisor's overall and initial causal attribution can influence the subsequent strategy. An external attribution can lead to leniency and the concomitant recommendation of developmental remedies. An internal attribution; that is, a question of innate ability, can put the employee on the skids to dismissal.

Equity and Exit-Voice-Loyalty-Neglect Theories

Prospect and attribution notions of motivation are only made somewhat more complicated when Adams's (1963) equity concerns or Hirschman's (1970) exit, voice, and loyalty options are included in the calculus. Both theories focus on the worker as an active participant in the motivational process. Individuals evaluate their situation and react accordingly. Complications arise, from a managerial point of view, in that these employee assessments incorporate both objective and subjective perspectives. Hence, anticipating employee reactions proves a difficult task fraught with cognitive complexity.

J. Stacy Adams (1963) suggests in his equity theory that employee assessments are comparative. In evaluating the balance in the reward–effort nexus, an individual employee while cognizant of the work performed and the reward received for it assesses their worth cognitively. The objective situation is analyzed through subjective, comparative lenses.

Each individual decides the extent to which the reward–effort balance is fair. Although situations in which an imbalance is deemed to exist can be adjusted for through increasing (or decreasing) the work effort to accord with a perceived higher (or lower) reward, they can also be psychologically adjusted by reassessing the balance as indeed fair (or, in cases previously seen as fair, unfair). The crucial fulcrum on which this balance rests is the comparative referent employed by the individual. Fairness is perceived as a result of general principles or of specific instances guiding how others are treated. An employee most likely will compare his or her wage–effort arrangement with that of fellow workers. The amount of reward received is thrown into the scales with the perceived effort expended by each colleague. An external referent can also be employed where some social or industrial standard exists. Because referents as well as workload can be adjusted, the cognitive responses guarantee no simple bottom-line equation for balancing the reward–effort bargain.

As such, it is imperative that the organization make a concerted effort to demonstrate the fairness of its motivation and reward structure. This is an underlying precept in the use of both internal job evaluation and external market wage determination techniques. Job evaluation constructs an elaborate and integrated system of what each job contributes or is worth to the organization and rewards it accordingly. The market technique focuses on external factors and anchors pay and benefits in the global supply and demand.

Consistent standards are essential for success. Pay-for-performance schemes often fail this test. While performance or productivity demands make extensive reference to the market and real-world practices, salary and wage practices rely on internal measures or political whim. The rewards and risks of the external market system are not included along with the demands for businesslike efficiencies.

In *Exit, Voice, and Loyalty,* Albert O. Hirschman (1970) proposes a typology of responses to dissatisfaction. A theory of individual self-interest that not only operates in terms of the economic market but with respect to sociopolitical values is primarily an attempt to explain an organization's survival. Although Hirschman's theory focuses on decisions regarding the acceptance/rejection of an organization's products or services, it can also be interpreted with regard to similar decisions by an organization's own personnel vis-à-vis the organization itself.

Exit is a conceptual representation of the market or economic system. The individual consumer chooses to buy or not buy, that is, to stay or exit. By exiting a product line or service, individuals register their market judgment. Similarly, an employee can express dissatisfaction with the organization by leaving it.

For such a market system to work, basic economic assumptions must be met. The consumer or employee must have viable alternatives from which to choose (as well as knowledge of the situation). Even so, Hirschman notes that the exit option, as such, is not made lightly. Hence, he suggests that prior to such a step being taken, a consumer or employee is likely to make other attempts to rectify the perceived problems or dissatisfactions.

It is this effort to change the situation that gives rise to voice. Voice is seen to represent a political dimension that can encompass a gamut of behaviors ranging from grumbling through participative management to full-scale democracy. It represents a viable, nonmarket means for assuring organizational survival.

Whereas voice focuses internally on the advocacy of reform, loyalty represents the employee's willingness to "stand up" for the organization. In this instance, advocacy is in response to outside criticism and is an expression of confidence in the organization.

In a series of articles, Farrell and Rusbult (Rusbult, 1980; Farrell and Rusbult, 1981; Rusbult, 1983; Rusbult and Farrell, 1983; Farrell, 1983; Rusbult, Farrell, Rogers, and Mainous, 1988) explicitly extend Hirshman's concept to personnel matters. As a result of a multidimensional scaling of job dissatisfaction, Farrell (1983) was able to demonstrate support for a modified version of Hirschman's typology. To the categories of exit, voice, and loyalty, Farrell added one for neglect. Neglect indicates a condition in which employees give up but stay to draw a paycheck. Neglect may involve absenteeism and obstructionism or merely a passive "I don't care" attitude.

Farrell arranges these four categories into a two-dimensional structure: (1) constructive versus destructive, and (2) active versus passive. Voice and loyalty are constructive while exit and neglect are destructive of the organization. Crosscutting this, we find that voice and exit are active.

Rusbult and Farrell identify motivation as being affected by previous job satisfaction, investment in the job, and job alternatives. These lead to different dissatisfaction responses. Specifically, high levels of job satisfaction are linked to constructive voice and loyalty responses (and retard exit and neglect). A high degree of job investment also encourages constructive voice and loyalty responses while retarding destructive exit and neglect tendencies. Finally, the presence of job alternatives is linked to active exit and voice options (while inhibiting loyalty but not neglect).

COMMUNICATIONS

Henri Fayol (1916) defined management as a dual structure requiring the integration of task accomplishment with a concern for people if it is to be successful. This is true for personnel management no less than for any other aspect of management. The vast array of techniques at our disposal are for naught if the human link is lacking. Interpersonal skills are an intricate part of management.

Employee relations focus on the nexus of interpersonal structures that pose serious challenges to supervisors and managers. Clearly, communication—focusing on performance feedback—is the most essential. As goal-setting research indicates, employees are extremely more productive when they know what it is that they are expected to do (Roberts and Reed, 1996). This is the underlying reason for the great success that Frederick Taylor's scientific management experienced at the beginning of the twentieth century.

The knowledge organization makes communication even more imperative. Today's professional employee is both a worker carrying out tasks and a "manager" planning for them. The communication of knowledge is essential for success.

Feedback is integral to the performance management process. Whether judgmental or developmental purposes are the focus of the management process, feedback is an essential mechanism for their working. Without an adequate means for informing employees of their performance, desired changes in motivation and productivity cannot occur.

Performance management feedback can take place in a number of ways. However, the primary means in which feedback occurs is through the performance appraisal interview. The appraisal interview is a formal meeting between employee and supervisor that is explicitly devoted to the discussion of the employee's job performance. Preparations necessary for properly conducting an appraisal interview along with the requisite interviewing skills for carrying it out are, therefore, important elements in the supervisor's job domain.

Feedback

Feedback is an essential component of the learning cycle. It also plays a pivotal role in the performance management process. The feedback from the performance management process serves as a productivity tool for managers; it provides employees with an indication of how they are doing.

From an organizational perspective, feedback serves as a means for enhancing productivity. It helps to convey to the worker the message of what is to be done. Feedback on job performance is a vital mechanism for the organization in other ways as well. It can be a means for clearing up misunderstandings and for providing supervisors with a better picture or sense of what is going on. Under a "worst case scenario," feedback represents the organization's good-faith effort at assisting poor performers in their improvement.

From an employee perspective, feedback is itself a means of intrinsic motivation. The feeling of accomplishment from doing a job and doing it well can be quite stimulating. It helps foster a sense of craftsmanship that can rather mystically transform an ordinary job into a professional calling.

Research studies, conducted in a number of settings and under widely differing circumstances, link feedback to increased productivity and enhanced worker motivation (Ilgen, Fisher, and Taylor, 1979; Greiner, Hatry, Koss, Millar, and Woodward, 1981: 158–160; Yeager, Rabin, and Vocino, 1985; Alexander, Helms, and Wilkins, 1984; Murphy and Cleveland, 1995: 274). In addition, feedback is also found to be an important element in the theory of goal setting (Locke, Shaw, Saari, and Latham, 1981; Earley, Northcraft, Lee, and Lituchy, 1990; Roberts and Reed, 1996).

There is relatively clear evidence that employees seek out feedback on their performance (Longenecker and Gioia, 1988; Ashford and Tsui, 1991). However, the seeking of feedback on one's performance is tempered by considerations of what impression it may make on those being asked. The act of seeking feedback itself marks and makes more vivid the substantive nature of feedback being requested than would otherwise be the case. The request for feedback serves to uniquely spotlight the performance itself (Ashford and Tsui, 1991; Morrison and Bies, 1991).

Psychologically, there is a heuristic tendency to take a specific piece of good or bad performance as an example of an individual employee's normal or typical work. While an employee may see such vividness as desirable when performance has been good, employees whose work has been marginal or even bad are less likely to want that brought to the attention and into the long-term memories of their supervisors.

There are a number of ways other than interviews with which to provide employee feedback vis-à-vis job performance. One of the various notions entailed by the term *critical incidents* suggests the immediate feedback of examples of good and bad behaviors to the employee. This is also advocated in all the basic "management by walking around" schemes (Ouchi, 1981; Pascale and Athos, 1981; Peters and Waterman, 1982). Of course, this is not a new concept but can be traced back, at least, to Frederick Taylor's (1911) recommending that his functional teachers (foremen) step in immediately whenever they saw an employee performing a task incorrectly and demonstrate how to do it right.

For feedback purposes, the performance appraisal interview is the next most advocated method to the critical-incident approach. Although it lacks the immediacy of the critical-incident technique, it compensates for this with a more measured or well-rounded evaluation of employee job performance. By examining an individual's efforts over an entire management cycle, a more balanced picture of his or her entire performance can be drawn. It can also be drawn under less hasty circumstances.

The performance appraisal interview is a formal meeting between employee and supervisor that is devoted entirely to a discussion of the employee's job performance. This can be an exciting or traumatic experience—both for the employee and the supervisor.

Objective appraisals, especially those employing an MBO approach, are explicitly built around a participative management concept. While such participative approaches are designed to encourage positive employee–supervisor interactions, even in these systems the appraisal interview often proves difficult. For the most part, performance appraisal systems involve judgmental rather than developmental purposes. As a result, feedback is often focused on what can only be deemed as questions of the individual's personal worth and identity rather than on topics addressing means for assisting the employee in improving the performance effort.

Properly used, a 360-degree appraisal (a combination of supervisory appraisal, self-appraisal, peer appraisal, and subordinate appraisal) can provide insightful feedback. As long as the 360-degree instrument is used for development and not employed in judgmental decisions, the various nonsupervisory inputs can provide objective lessons (DeNisi and Kluger, 2000; Ghorpade, 2000).

The feedback process can involve important consequences for the entire organization. Systems in which feedback is seen to be positively linked to goals are also likely to be viewed as being more concerned with the attainment of those goals. Hence, organizational support, supervisory effectiveness, and even the usefulness of the MBO technique itself are all accorded a greater degree of efficacy when used in conjunction with an adequate means of employee feedback. In addition, individual job satisfaction is enhanced when feedback is provided (Aplin and Schoderbek, 1976; Roberts and Reed, 1996).

Supervisory training in the art of providing feedback is an essential requirement, especially as few individuals exhibit a natural talent in this area. In fact, it is the lack of training in this area that substantially contributes to supervisors' sense of ill ease when faced with the need to conduct a management interview. Simulations, role-playing exercises, and behavioral modeling can all be used for training supervisors in conducting a management interview (Martin and Bartol, 1986).

Ideally, training should include both supervisors and employees. They should be apprised of their individual roles and how they interact with one another. This also provides them with an understanding of or an expectation as to what the appraisal interview entails. Training should include not only the mechanics of the appraisal system (i.e., job analysis, setting performance standards, how to use the forms, etc.) but the behavioral skills for motivation as well (Pajer, 1979).

Interview Preparation

The performance interview should not just happen. It is an important management tool requiring careful preparation and planning. The tendency, in part because it often is an unpleasant experience for both supervisors and employees, is to treat the management interview as an ad hoc event. This only contributes to and perpetuates its undesirable features and reputation for failure.

The physical and psychological situation under which the interview is to occur must also receive serious consideration. Attribution theory indicates that situational circumstances have important interpretational affects on the performance management process (Knowlton and Mitchell, 1980; Feldman, 1981; Lord and Smith, 1983; DeVader, Bateson, and Lord, 1986). The purposes for which a performance management process is intended as well as the conditions or environment in which that performance occurs are an intricate part of the assessment process. A number of other employee, supervisory, job, and organizational factors can also be seen to affect the interview (Clement and Stevens, 1986).

The purpose underlying the use of the performance appraisal influences how employees as well as supervisors approach the process. The distinction between a judgmental and a developmental process is not trivial. Different purposes lead to different assessments. Even when an objective appraisal instrument is employed, the supervisor approaches its terms and behavioral anchors in light of the specific purpose for which the appraisal is viewed as serving.

The characteristics of individual employees can be significant factors in determining performance ratings. The extent to which employees are actually experienced in doing a job may matter as much as or more than their actual level of job performance. Newer employees may be allowed greater latitude than those "who should know better." In addition, the personal needs of an employee can play a role in the assignment of ratings. A higher rating may be needed to build up an employee's confidence; a lower rating than objectively warranted may serve to instill caution or humility.

Similarly, the experience an individual has as a supervisor can also be an important factor. More experienced supervisors are often more comfortable with the employee–supervisor relationship. When it comes to performance appraisals, they are often more at ease in exercising their authority and in fulfilling their responsibilities. In addition, they possess a greater experiential base vis-à-vis employee performance with which to guide their assessment of job behavior. The development of specific skills in conducting the performance management process, including interviews, are also a factor. Finally, the personal and organizational needs the supervisor brings to the table may also play a substantial role.

In addition to an employee's performance in a job, the nature of the job itself can influence the appraisal and interview process. Numerous job- or position-related factors can influence how an individual's performance is assessed. How routine are the tasks performed? Do individual employees have clear perceptions of their job role? How new is the position? The answers to questions such as these help frame the environment for the appraisal process and set the tone in which the interview is conducted.

Organizational culture and climate help shape the entire process from beginning to end. The time available in which to actually conduct the interview (which is influenced by the number of interviews to be conducted) sets the boundaries on what topics can be adequately covered. Last, organizational or personal politics may be involved.

Preparation for an employee interview should be continuous. Keeping a critical-incident log on individual employee performances can greatly aid in this task. This also enables the supervisor to respond with feedback immediately—correcting errors and acclaiming successes. Although critical-incident logs entail additional paperwork and suffer from many of the problems commonly associated with essay appraisals, they can also help in avoiding the introduction of rater errors into the management process (Pajer, 1979).

Preparation for the interview should also actively include the employee. Advance notice as well as the scheduling of a mutually convenient time are important considerations. Both the supervisor and employee need sufficient time prior to the actual interview so that both can conscientiously analyze and evaluate the employee's performance (Pajer, 1979).

For the feedback interview itself, Robert Pajer (1979) recommends that supervisors prepare a script of what it is they want to accomplish in the interview. Although it is unnecessary and perhaps even counterproductive to rigidly follow such a script, it provides a structured outline with which to assure that the interview covers all the important points.

In terms of developmental opportunities, supervisors should have an assessment not only of the employee's needs but of the organization's capability in meeting and resolving them. Specific plans for employee development set a positive tone in an interview. This is an especially important consideration when indicating to employees "areas in need of improvement." In such circumstances it is absolutely essential, as well as legally required, to provide accompanying corrective actions.

Finally, the physical location where the interview is conducted must be taken into consideration. The physical conditions pertaining to the interview should be chosen so that they help reduce the stress inherent in the performance appraisal process.

Employees do not want to experience an appraisal interview, even one with a developmental focus, amid a crowd. An enclosed office space that assures privacy is what's called for under these circumstances. Even within this setting, it is important to put the employee at ease—if that is the desired message the supervisor wishes to convey. Instead of confronting an employee from across a desk, a more conversational arrangement can work better. In addition, the interview should be free from interruptions, either by a phone or from others dropping in (Pajer, 1979).

Interview Techniques

Having set the tone for the interview, the supervisor begins by providing a general assessment of the employee's performance evaluation. Each distinct dimension is then examined with the employee being afforded opportunities to participate in the discussion. It is important that the interview remain an open process. The interview is a means for managers to obtain additional information on organizational and individual performance. Maintaining an open process in which the "conclusions" are still subject to change can assist in enhancing organizational effectiveness. Even what are initially deemed as "self-serving excuses" may, in fact, turn out to be valid arguments that fairness and justice demand be taken into consideration.

Hence, conducting a performance interview calls upon the supervisor to avidly employ a number of interpersonal communication skills. First, the style in which a supervisor chooses to conduct an interview is an important determinant of what follows (Clement and Stevens, 1986). Norman R. F. Maier (1958, 1976) distinguishes three interview styles—tell and sell, tell and listen, and problem solving—with a preference for the last. These approaches run the gamut from judgmental to developmental.

The tell-and-sell approach sees the supervisor as a judge handing down a sentence. Communication is centered on convincing the employee to accept the verdict. This is an authoritarian style. It assumes that employees appreciate such frank and honest appraisals. However, unless employees respect their supervisors (and trust in the organization), hostility and the development of evasive behaviors can result.

The tell-and-listen style attempts to integrate the judgmental pronouncement of the management evaluation with a hearing of grievances on the part of the supervisor. Unfortunately, in a tell-and-listen format the listening is viewed more as a means for allowing the employee to "let off steam" than as a legitimate means for redressing grievances. However, even this limited listening can help to successfully reduce employee stress.

The listen component of the interview is used to symbolically express the organization's acceptance of the employee as a member. In essence, even when the specific message is negative, the tell-and-listen style is designed to convey a sense of belonging and job security. This long-term commitment implied by a tell-and-listen approach can reduce resistance to change.

Because the supervisor is free to change the evaluation as well as to convey information to others in the hierarchy, the process still remains somewhat open. This ability to change the evaluation can also help enhance the supervisor's standing with employees.

The problem-solving approach is an example of a developmental, participative application. It is the interview style preferred by Norman Maier as well as most other management scholars; it is also the style that is most favored by employees. The problem-solving approach is designed to be a true discussion of job performance focusing primarily on stimulating employee development.

Active Listening

The problem-solving style involves the employment of active listening skills on the part of the supervisor. Although this approach can contribute to employee growth, organizational problems may not necessarily be solved or solved in the manner anticipated by the supervisor.

Active listening is a technique that encompasses a wide range of verbal and nonverbal communication skills (Kikoski and Litterer, 1983; Bolton, 1986; Clement, 1987; Murphy, 1987; Kikoski, 1998). They are all aimed at creating an environment that both is conducive to an employee–supervisor dialogue and assists in the effective interpretation of that dialogue.

As Robert Bolton (1986: 15–26) notes, active listening is designed to suspend the behavioral barriers that inhibit communications. Dialogues are hindered by an array of premature judging, solution sending, and avoidance habits. Individuals reply before they have received the complete message. Unfortunately, the complexities of modern American society have instilled these behaviors. Although they are basically defensive mechanisms for coping with a modern world, their indiscriminate application proves harmful.

Instead of listening to what is being said, individuals are engaged in evaluating the incoming messages before they have even been completely transmitted. English grammar, unlike that of such languages as German, does not force the listener to await the verb at the sentence's end in order to evaluate the meaning of the sentence's message. Individuals are also likely to respond during this process in such a manner as to affect the remainder of the message transmission, that is, to cause the sender to change or abruptly end the message. In addition, individuals may choose to avoid the content of the message either because they prefer not to deal with it or because they deem it unimportant in comparison to what they want to say.

Nonverbal skills focus on demonstrating the listener's participation in the conversation qua listener. Physically, individuals position themselves to catch the speaker's message. The listener must treat the message very much as if it were a ball being tossed or pitched to them; they must keep their attention focused on it. Such attending skills entail both posture and natural body motions. Avoiding physical distractions is also an important consideration (Bolton, 1986: 34–38).

Specific verbal skills are designed to aid the listener in receiving the message and in interpreting it. These skills include those that fall into the more traditional area entailed by deliberative communications. The translation or interpretation of the main or substantive message is the focus of attention and analysis (Bolton, 1986: 30–34).

Other verbal skills—following and reflective—focus on the medium in which the message is transmitted. Although not focusing on the message's substantive content, they can be just as important. These skills are used to interpret the additional messages that emphasize, reinforce, or negate the substantive message being sent.

Following skills begin with sizing up the senders' state and then providing the appropriate climate for receiving their message. This consists of providing the attentive silence—physical and psychological—in which to actually listen to the message. Questions should be infrequent and open-ended. Questions are designed to clarify and encourage the conversation; they are not meant to serve as analytical vehicles (Bolton, 1986: 38–48).

Reflective skills aid in the interpretation of the message. The speaker's message is paraphrased in the listener's own words in order to aid understanding and to verify its content from the speaker. The speaker's emotions and other feelings need to be interwoven with the spoken message. Reflective skills serve as a reality check; they also convey the important notion of "message received" back to the sender (Bolton, 1986: 50–113).

SUMMARY

The foundation of motivation lies in an individual's desires. Only if individuals are aware that a need exists (or is created) will they respond. Motivational theories focus on eliciting that response in a coordinated manner that both fulfills the need and contributes to the organization. There are various theories (e.g., Taylor, Maslow, Herzberg, and McCelland) outlining how needs are generated and their relationships to one another. In addition, there are theories (e.g., Skinner and Vroom) that focus solely on the process by which these needs are activated and used.

At the center of both content and process motivational theories is individual choice. The cognitive psychological aspect of motivation is recognized as significant in this respect. Whether this is framed through a "manipulative" operant conditioning or a more "free" expectancy theory, how the individual sees and interprets events defines the motivational needs and extrinsic and intrinsic incentives for fulfilling them.

Although content and process theories can outline what and how to motivate individuals, communication is necessary. Feedback techniques are essential for guiding motivation. They both remind or reinforce the motivation and allow for adjustments in its pursuit. Drawing upon active listening techniques enables the development of a positive employee-supervisor relationship. This trust forms the foundation for motivation.

chapter 4

Position Management

Position management identifies the specific jobs or tasks that individuals perform (in order for the organization to plan for and coordinate their efforts) that form the basis for the strategic pay decisions to attract, retain, and motivate. The work to be done and the incentives for doing it must be linked. This is a problem that daunts the public sector with its separation of powers between the executive (doing) and legislative (paying) branches.

This chapter focuses on job analysis and job evaluation techniques. The chapter provides:

1. An overview of the differences between rank-in-person and rank-in-position approaches to organizing jobs
2. Knowledge of the job analysis process and specific techniques used in defining job content
3. An examination of the use of competencies or skills, knowledges, and abilities in defining jobs
4. Knowledge of the job evaluation process and techniques for relating one job to another within an organization for purposes of career development and pay competitiveness and equity

Position management directly arose in response to Frederick Winslow Taylor's *Principles of Scientific Management* (1911). Yet, it was just as much a political solution as a technical breakthrough. Although the Old Progressives had setback the spoils system in the late nineteenth century, they did not succeed in vanquishing political bossism and its public corruption. Civil service systems, once installed, were readily subverted and patronage restored. The Young Progressives such as Woodrow Wilson and Frank Goodnow saw in Taylor's principles a technical solution for sustaining the moral crusade against bosses and political patronage (White, 1958; Van Riper, 1958). Moreover, scientific management was a solution that would also positively enhance the capabilities and products of government.

Job analysis and evaluation define and describe the essential work and tasks entailed in individual jobs or positions and how they relate to one another. Staffing, especially in the testing aspect, identifies individuals capable of performing those jobs. The arbitrariness and corruption that previously characterized government work is thereby replaced with clearly delineated, objective job requirements and an open, public recruitment of prospective candidates.

Even so, there are serious issues with regard to position classification itself. Position classification was the focal point for Wallace Sayre's (1948) famous book review on the "triumph of techniques over purpose." The problems he outlined fifty years ago have hardly gone away. Job analysis and evaluation systems are even more complex. Emphasis is placed on positions rather than on individual judgment and performance. A one-size-fits-all mentality limits flexibility. Hierarchical empire-building and budget-maximization are rewarded (Ban, 1995; Wamsley, 1997).

CAREER SYSTEMS

Although often overlooked, the job analysis and evaluation processes are designed to facilitate and serve a career system. In contrast to the patronage or spoils era approach to public employment, government jobs under the civil service concept are intended to be part of a permanent, lifelong career. Whether this career is built on the basis of employment that offers the individual rank-in-person or rank-in-position becomes the central question.

Under the Jacksonian justification for patronage, public employment was viewed as a temporary feature in an individual's career. Public service provided the basic, practical skills necessary for an individual to succeed in a burgeoning America. In a sense, government provided advance training for people assuming roles in business (something it still does today). Whatever disadvantages might be experienced due to inexperience were offset by the democratic turnover among personnel.

Industrialization changed this equation. A modern society requires the expertise of a permanent public service. Government must be well versed in the problems and solutions affecting society. The corruption of the patronage system into a spoils system demonstrated that the Jacksonian model could not be adapted to these new demands. A permanent public service must be a professionalized public service if it is to properly carry out the governmental functions associated with industrial (and postindustrial or postmodern) society.

Rank-in-Person

The European system of administrative classes represents the classic rank-in-person approach (Heady, 1995: 202–289). While the basis for quite effective public administrations, they are unfortunately associated—in American minds—with authoritarian, elitist regimes. The administrative class served as the means for an aristocratic oligarchy to perpetuate its subjugation of a people. Members of the administration were themselves often drawn from this elitist, aristocratic group. Indeed, efficiency was gained, but at the cost of democracy.

Yet, the United States has extensively relied upon rank-in-person systems in conducting the business of government. The military along with the Foreign, Public Health, and National Park Services are all rank-in-person systems found at the federal level; state and local governments employ police, firefighters, and teachers under rank-in-person arrangements. Although the image is one of an exception to the "normal" rank-in-position approach, a rough tabulation of the number of employees under rank-in-person career systems reveals that they compose a substantial proportion of public employment. This is hardly an exception.

While rank-in-person and rank-in-position systems overlap a great deal (both are aimed at the efficient performance of the same jobs), there are some significant contrasts. The long-term, career perspective inherent in the rank-in-person approach better focuses attention on strategic, organizational goals and human resource planning.

Recruitment centers on young, entry-level employees who are then subjected to extensive training and development. This enables the organization to foster a highly motivating esprit d'corps among its employees. The long-term relationship among a cadre of public servants also facilitates an in-depth understanding of each's strengths and weaknesses. This understanding is enhanced by a performance appraisal process focused on promotability. Whereas a rank-in-position appraisal asks "how well was the job done?" a rank-in-person appraisal asks "what does the performance of the job tell about the individual's future abilities?" The focus is more on characteristics and competencies (knowledge, skills, and abilities) than on behaviors and results (Hays and Kearney, 1995).

Rank-in-person systems can become somewhat myopic. They allow for little lateral entry of individuals with divergent talents and experiences. The focus on promotability can also lead to less attention being paid to the efficient performance of the actual job. Promotability may introduce an "up-or-out" rule where otherwise competent individuals are removed from service because they are not deemed promotable (thereby making room for others who are).

Rank-in-person systems possess greater flexibility in the placement and assignment of individuals. With the career distinct from the specific job, individuals can be more readily moved. This not only facilitates employee development but can assure the assignment of the individual with appropriate skills for the job. This flexibility underlies, in part, the broadbanding technique. Pay flexibility is also possible with rank-in-person systems (Hyde, 1995).

From the perspective of a knowledge organization, the rank-in-person system is quite ideal. This should not come as a surprise. Rank-in-person systems are indeed built for knowledge-based organizations. Rank-in-person systems are found wherever government has a need for the service of professionals. Hence, as society's professional needs increase we are going to see more personnel systems that mimic rank-in-person approaches.

Rank-in-Position

The rank-in-position system was an American innovation. While a rank-in-person approach has great strengths, it is also subject to some significant weaknesses. Ignoring the democratic versus elitist contentions, rank-in-position systems better focus on actually doing the job at hand. While certainly important, this is a somewhat secondary concern under rank-in-person systems. With the retching experience of the spoils era as a stark lesson, American reformers were well aware what consequences awaited those who neglected job performance.

The ad hoc focus on the job itself under the rank-in-position approach neglects the need for overall planning and goal setting. This was not accidental, but part of the system's design. The American reforms undertaken by the Young Progressives such as Frank Goodnow and Woodrow Wilson were based on Frederick Taylor's scientific management. Planning was not neglected, but rather a function assigned to others elsewhere. For those in public administration, this fit ideally into their notion of a politics/administration dichotomy. An efficient rank-in-position civil service could be created without the antidemocratic authoritarianism common to the European states.

The rank-in-position approach concentrates its attention on the job itself. The job is subject to analysis to determine its exact tasks and responsibilities. The skills, knowledge, and abilities (SKAs) required to perform each task are also determined. These are used to design tests for use in the selection of employees. Every individual is selected solely on the basis of his or her capability to perform the job. No uncertainty due to some magical measure of potential is allowed. Individuals are selected neither because they can be better trained to perform the job nor because they hold greater potential for advancement.

This steadfast focus on the job and its performance is the hallmark of the rank-in-position system. It is an important factor in the historical acceptance of the civil service system in the United States. A practical rank-in-position system based on the objective job analysis and selection principles of scientific management inoculated the American administrative state from the authoritarian, elitist diseases of European versions. Without this guarantee, there might well have been no civil service system.

Theoretically, every job in a rank-in-position system is open. Unlike rank-in-person approaches, the rank-in-position system takes advantage of experience gleamed from outside the organization. With every position subject to open competition, lateral entry is encouraged. This also enhances the chances for hiring the most appropriate individual for a specific job.

In reality, most rank-in-position systems are hybrids. Not all positions are open to competition. Some recruitment efforts are limited to agency, department, or government-wide searches. More important, the qualifications attached to many positions may narrowly focus on government-only skills. Yet, these systems do include a substantial proportion of positions open to competition at the middle and upper levels.

Job analysis is the application of scientific management to organizational positions. It is a technique that clearly enhances the focus and potential for productivity of individual jobs. Politically, its emphasis on practical, merit-based criteria served as a foundation for the construction of a permanent, professional civil service.

JOB ANALYSIS

Job analysis is the basic building block in professional personnel/human resource management. It is the foundation upon which the other personnel activities are built. The job analysis results in a *job description* (encompassing the duties and responsibilities to be performed) and/or a shorter *job specification* (which describes the most important aspects or duties performed in that specific job). The job description is used for recruiting candidates. It is the document upon which selection and testing is based and a guide for orientating new employees. It also serves as the benchmark for determining training needs and for establishing performance appraisal standards.

The job analysis contains three parts: job content, job context, and job requirements. Job content focuses on the internal role, the specific responsibilities and duties to be performed. Job context scans the external role, the environment—working conditions, budget and resources, supervision, and so on—in which the work is performed. Job requirements assess what skills, knowledges, and abilities are needed to successfully perform the work.

The individual job tasks or responsibilities that are identified in the job analysis process may be either narrowly or broadly defined. Narrowly defined job analyses focus on specific tasks that usually occur in a stable, routine environment (and allow for centralized administration). Broadly defined job analyses such as are involved in broadbanding emphasize the requirement for situational adjustments and flexibility in the performance of tasks. Because these usually entail decentralization, the results may be referred to as functional profiles rather than as job analyses or position descriptions.

The job context documents the situation or conditions under which the work occurs. It becomes a measure of the difficulties faced in performing the job content. It also addresses how a position functions in relationship to the other positions it interacts with. Hence, it recognizes the interdependence and team nature inherent in most positions. As such, the external role contributes to job performance (Van Dyne and LePine, 1998).

Job requirements focus on the individual. They delineate the skills, knowledges, and abilities that an individual would need to perform the job. These may also include personal characteristics that have been validated for specific jobs.

Individual jobs are grouped together with similar jobs in job classes. If jobs are narrowly defined, this results in many distinct classes. Narrowly defined jobs create career paths (often with limited labor pools) and a psychological feeling of progress as promotion and advancement is rapid. The trend toward more broadly defined job classes, while introducing greater flexibility, has also created psychological uncertainty. Employees see more job competition (while ignoring the greater opportunities afforded them) and fewer promotions (even though wage and salary increases may, in fact, exceed those under the older system).

Uses and Misuses of Job Analysis

Job analysis is the foundation upon which the other personnel activities are built. The resulting job description is used for attracting candidates in recruitment. It is the document upon which selection and testing is based. It is a guide for orientating new employees. It helps determine training needs for job performance and promotional opportunities. It serves as the benchmark for establishing performance appraisal standards. Finally, it can provide the basis for employee–supervisor understandings (Clifford, 1994).

The job specification serves as a quick guide for recruiting prospective candidates. Its one or two pages provide an overview of the job behind the title. By highlighting the essential tasks entailed in a job, individuals can judge whether this is a position that interests them and for which they are qualified. Because of their use in recruitment, job specifications also often include more generic information about the organization and geographic location.

Selection and testing is explicitly tied to the notion of job-relatedness. Although this is clearly entailed in our notions of the merit system, its modern incarnation arises from Frederick W. Taylor's *Principles of Scientific Management.* The scientific management movement engenders the early development of industrial and organizational psychology, including personnel psychology. The federal Position Classification Act of 1923 is a recognition of this. In the latter half of the twentieth century, job-relatedness has been reemphasized through the Civil Rights movement. The Civil Rights Act of 1964 and subsequent court interpretations such as *Griggs v. Duke Powe*r (1971), the Age Discrimination in Employment Act of 1967, the Equal Employment Opportunity Act of 1972, and the Americans with Disabilities Act of 1990 all refocus attention on the requirements for specific jobs. Individuals are judged and hired on the basis of their ability or potential for performing the tasks and responsibilities of a specific job. For this to work, job analysis is essential.

Once hired, the job description can aid in orienting the individual to the job. The job description outlines the specific job tasks that are expected. Properly done, the job description can serve as an instrument for goal setting. It can also be used in the design of more general, organizational orientation material.

A job analysis also is important with regard to the development of training programs. For some jobs, the job description also entails or lists tasks for which the development of additional proficiencies—skills, knowledge, and abilities (SKAs)—is required. This serves to trigger the training needs assessment process by focusing on these precise areas. It alerts those in charge of training and development of the need to provide such programs. More generally, the basic job description serves to set the job's performance boundaries. When performance discrepancies arise, a job description focuses attention on the areas in which training would be a meaningful solution. This, thereby, avoids the misapplication of training resources to performance problems attributable to non-SKA origins.

Similarly, the job description and its training parameters would assist individuals seeking promotional opportunities. By outlining job duties and the requisite knowledge, skills, and abilities needed to perform them, employees are provided with a career map. They can scan an organization's set of job descriptions for positions that interest them and make use of their talents. They can also seek out training and development opportunities that will enable them to qualify for these positions. The organization can, of course, encourage this by providing these promotional or career training and development opportunities. Internal promotional or career paths are a means for enhancing motivation and organizational commitment.

The job responsibilities identified in the job analysis also form the basis for evaluating an individual's performance. In conjunction with measurable performance standards, they compose the objective performance appraisal instrument. They can serve to set employee goals, monitor progress, and plan for the future—of the employee and the organization.

Running throughout these uses is the omnipresent notion that the employee–supervisor relationship is enhanced by job analysis. A job analysis clarifies and improves the job understanding of both the employee and the supervisor. It focuses attention on job responsibilities, duties, tasks, elements, and so on; the SKAs required and the conditions under which they are performed; and the performance standards, objectives, results, outcomes, and so on.

A discussion of the uses of job analysis would not be complete without detailing what drives many to fear the process. Like all tools, job analysis can be used for purposes it was not intended for. These misuses can turn out to be, surprisingly, beneficial or, as is perhaps more likely, harmful.

The application of the job analysis technique stresses the separation of the position from the person. It is the job and not the individual who is the position's incumbent that is the subject of analysis. However, most abuses center on the application of the analysis to the individual. Although it is indeed the individual and not the position that is the key to productivity, this is not the stated focus of the job analysis technique. To make it so is to sow distrust among employees.

Job analyses can become subtle, or not so subtle, performance audits designed to downsize the organization. By disguising performance audits as job analyses and evaluations, it is hoped that employees will more honestly and openly provide the necessary information (for eliminating their own jobs!). After all, one can't simply ask if one's job is unnecessary. Given the extent to which Americans see their personal identity and well-being in their jobs, this poses a truly vital threat. Eliminating unnecessary jobs also eliminates "necessary" people.

Similarly, job analysis instead of focusing on the position may be misused as a productivity measure of the individual incumbent. Redefining the job can lead to the inclusion of additional responsibilities (without compensating adjustments in wages and salary). Again this raises concerns with regard to openness and trust.

The misapplication of job analysis can result in the incumbent's performance rating or length of service being used in assessing the job's contribution rather than the position itself.

The Americans with Disabilities Act has provided legal reinforcement to the application of job analysis. In determining the essential responsibilities of a job, Equal

Employment Opportunity Commission regulation 1630.2(n) (3) emphasizes (1) the organization's judgment as to what is essential, (2) written job descriptions, (3) the amount of time spent on a task, (4) the consequences of not performing the task, and (5) past and current work experiences (along with collective bargaining agreements). All are factors included in a proper job analysis. A function is "essential" if (1) the job exists solely to perform that task, (2) there are limited number of employees who can perform the task, or (3) the task is so specialized that the incumbent is hired for his or her skills in performing it (Smith, 1998b).

The Job Analysis Process

Job analysis and evaluation is a two-stage process. First, the job analysis identifies the essential job tasks or responsibilities. Second, the job evaluation compares and contrasts the resultant positions and sorts them into categories. This enables the organization to identify similar and different positions and the value or worth they add or contribute.

For most organizations, job analysis and evaluation is a perennial back-burner issue (with the burner turned off). Its physical cumbersomeness and psychological stressfulness make it difficult and expensive. However, the Americans with Disabilities Act of 1991 has refocused attention on this issue. More important, this spotlight has brought with it the power of a legal mandate. While doing the right thing is nice, doing the legal thing is a must.

Following an initial job analysis process, each position should, ideally, be reanalyzed within a five-year framework. Many organizations have allowed this to slip to a ten-year cycle, and some have neglected things for up to thirty years. Old job analyses, like old maps, may have certain historic value, but their current usefulness is rather suspect. Even the attempt at reanalyzing the positions involving the most individuals is an unsatisfactory option. Although it leads to accurate descriptions for the lower-level positions, it furthers the neglect accorded to the technical and professional positions.

Job analysis and evaluation is one of the more centralized techniques. Although the employee and supervisor play the pivotal role in developing the raw data upon which the analysis and evaluation process is based, the central personnel office and, most likely, outside consultants play the crucial role of transforming and standardizing this information into usable material.

Consultants bring their specialized knowledge and experience to this task. Smaller consulting firms or individuals have the advantage of relatively lower costs and a truly tailored product. The larger, major firms (such as the Hay Group or Ernest & Young), on the other hand, provide a more costly and, at-best, made-to-measure product. However, these are offset by their vast knowledge and experiential base.

In planning a job analysis survey, previous job analyses as well as appropriate legal strictures need to be examined. The practices followed in comparable organizations or jurisdictions are also quite useful. Given the psychological aspects and fears likely to be engendered, it is essential that plans include provisions for keeping employees fully informed of and involved in the process. Although active employee participation is not as essential for the completion of the job analysis and evaluation process as it is in other personnel techniques, it is essential for controlling all the negative, secondary effects that might arise from it. What good is a successful operation if the patient dies from related complications?

Following the formal announcement that a job analysis and evaluation is be conducted and the introduction of the professional staff (this may entail a number of meetings before employee groups), every employee, often referred to as a subject matter expert (SME) in the literature, should be sent a job analysis questionnaire. For vacant positions or vacationing employees, the supervisor should be provided with the questionnaire as the next best source of information. Although individual employees should be allowed sufficient time in which to complete their job analysis questionnaire (in which they provide the raw information describing what it is that they do), a week should suffice for this task.

There are a number of methods for obtaining job information. All, more or less, use the employee as the primary source. They differ in the degree to which the employee is allowed to actively participate in the process.

A number of methods rely directly upon information provided by the employee. Open-ended or close-ended survey approaches are often employed. They can run the gamut from asking employees to record their activities in a diary through structured questionnaires to activity matrixes and formal checklists of specific job tasks deemed likely or appropriate for the positions under analysis (these latter devices are based on prior work).

These survey methods are quite cost-effective. They are easy to administer to a large number of employees, cause little disruption of the work flow, and guarantee a degree of anonymity to the employee. Surveys, especially the more structured, may not allow for free expression or responses that "don't fit."

The job analysts can also engage in the direct observation of the employee at work. The employee's participation is limited; emphasis is placed on the interpretative expertise of the job analyst. Activities can be sampled at random intervals or critical incidents noted. Video monitoring can be employed in some situations.

Observation need not disrupt the employee's work (although it is hard to imagine how an employee would remain unaffected). Assuming the expertise of the job analyst, these approaches enable the positions to be quickly and clearly assessed. However, it is this "expertise" requirement that is also their chief limitation. It simply cannot be assumed to exist. Furthermore, observation may be viewed by employees as "spying."

An interactive job analysis integrates the above employee and job analyst formats. This can be in the form of either a one-on-one interview or a group discussion. In each case, the job analyst and employee or employees exchange information. Focus groups might also be used.

The interactive approaches combine the richness of employee surveys with the expertise of observation. Group discussions can greatly assist in clarifying what tasks indeed are common to a position and, in fact, what those tasks are. Of course, interactive approaches are time-consuming and labor-intensive, hence expensive.

Finally, job information may be obtained from external sources. The organization may have prior reports and records that detail the tasks performed by various positions. This can also include the use of key consultants or media sources.

Reports and records, including prior job analyses, can be highly valuable sources of information. Inasmuch as circumstances have not been subject to drastic changes, these documents can indeed be quite up-to-date. Unfortunately, there are often changes. Although sudden changes in the nature of a job—what activities are performed or the process followed—often catch our attention, incremental adjustments can also lead to substantial change. Governments are notorious in overlooking both these forms of change. Consultants and media information can be invaluable in addressing relevant external conditions.

The information gathered through job analysis traditionally has been task-specific to the particular job. However, the technique may be used with a systemic focus so that it can be used within a TQM framework (Siegel, 1996).

Having collected the raw job information, the personnel professionals and consultants, often with the assistance of employee or SME groups, examine and determine which represent different jobs and which are variations of the same job. For each job class so identified, they winnow the myriad of individual job statements into a set of standardized statements. The Department of Labor's Occupational Information Network (O*NET), which replaces the *Dictionary of Occupational Titles,* also serves as a data source for activity/behavior statements (http://www.doleta.gov/programs/onet/).

At this stage, a sampling of the employee position analysis questionnaires is taken, and the jobs are subject to an observational desk audit in which the professionals and consultants monitor or verify what occurs. This results in a set of preliminary position classes and accompanying job descriptions. Although these individuals are highly trained in the use of job analysis techniques, they remain subject to the limitations of the "state of the art" (Clifford, 1994).

The preliminary job evaluation is also performed at this point. Using the information included in the job descriptions, positions are evaluated against a set (or series of sets) of factors deemed relevant to the organization. These external or internal factors are viewed as the means through which the organization is made productive or effective. Hence, they help measure the value or worth that each job adds or contributes to the organization's mission.

These preliminary job descriptions (along with the job evaluation implications) are returned to the job incumbents for their review and comment. Job incumbents may appeal what they consider to be oversights or mistakes. These are especially likely to arise in regard to the job evaluation part of the process if rank or grade changes (with or without adjustments to pay) are being suggested. In cases where downgrading is being suggested, it is common to "red-circle" the position's pay. The job incumbent in this case is not subject to a pay cut (or, is exempt for, say, five years); however, neither is he or she eligible for pay increases until such time as that position's pay levels have been adjusted to encompass the incumbent's salary range.

Only after this process has been completed is the new job analysis implemented. This is usually accompanied by a formal announcement of its adoption. This serves to clearly indicate to all employees in the organization the completion of the job analysis and evaluation.

Job Analysis Systems

The job analysis technique itself is a dual approach that integrates various systems for describing job tasks with differing methods for obtaining this information. Job task systems focus on traits or activities; information-gathering methods rely on expert opinion or employee statements (Gael, 1988).

Figure 4.1 displays the "pure" options that may be used in job analysis. Job analysis systems may encompass either the (1) activities, behaviors, and results or the (2) traits and competencies entailed in a job. A "full" or complete approach will list all tasks entailed in a job whereas a "reduced" set focuses solely on the essential or major tasks.

The basic tasks that compose an individual job can be defined either in terms of the underlying traits or work behaviors that the worker possesses which enable him or her to perform the job or in terms of the specific work activities or results that are expected. "Task statements are used to describe work behaviors by incorporating (a) what the worker does, (b) to what or to whom a behavior is directed, (c) upon what instructions, (d) how the behavior is performed, and (e) why the action is taken (Feild and Gatewood, 1989: 156).

Because of concerns over fairness and discrimination, work activities are given legal preference due to their more straightforward face validity. Behaviors or traits, while perhaps more appealing in that they focus on what it takes to get things done, require a difficult, two-step validation. First, a valid instrument measuring the work behavior or trait must be constructed, and then that instrument must be demonstrated to be job-related. Work activity methods only require the latter.

Figure 4.1
Job Analysis Systems

	Full	Reduced
Activities, Behaviors, and Results	Functional Job Language, Performance Expectation, Results-Oriented,	Critical Incident
Traits and Competencies	Position Analysis Questionnaire	Job Element

Psychological traits focus on the inherent factors that motivate people to perform. Basically, traits are a question of character or personality. As such, traits are highly desirable as a method for defining job tasks. Personality studies have begun to group traits into the "big five" categories: neuroticism, extraversion, openness, agreeableness, and conscientiousness (Digman, 1989, 1990; Goldberg, 1993; John, 1990; McCrae and John, 1992; Wiggins and Pincus, 1992).

These five trait categories form separate personality dimensions. Neuroticism assesses emotional stability focusing on tension and stress. Extraversion examines sociability and friendliness. Openness touches upon the role of creativity and imagination. Agreeableness records levels of trust or skepticism. Conscientiousness registers the individual's sense of self-worth and competence along his or her degree of discipline.

Personality traits are certainly a major factor in determining individual performance. It is not known which specific traits or combination of traits are necessary (let alone the "amount" required of any trait), and, in fact, this may be unknowable. In addition, some traits may be inherent (or learned at a very early age) and, as such, not easily altered or remedied. This can pose questions of fairness.

Unfortunately, the question of legal validity poses a costly and difficult problem. The indirect relationship between traits and job performance raises questions of fairness and accuracy. In addition to linking the trait to the specific performance of a given job's duties, the instrument for measuring the trait itself must also be validated. This twofold validation makes the use of trait approaches prohibitively costly.

Because of these legal and cost considerations, trait systems have been left primarily to the realm of academic research. Job analyses may endeavor to comprehensively detail all the relevant job-related traits and work behaviors involved as with the original position analysis questionnaire (McCormick, 1979) or focus only on the most essential traits and work behaviors as in a job element inventory (Primoff, 1975). The Americans with Disabilities Act of 1990, focusing on a job's essential functions, adds support to the use of such systems (Bishop and Jones, 1993).

Work activities possess the advantage of being quite visibly linked to job tasks. Even so, they should be subject to psychometric validation to ensure that the activities are indeed keyed to job performance. Like trait systems, activity approaches may detail all of a job's tasks and the defining activities performed in each, as in the original functional job language (Fine and Wiley, 1971; Fine, 1974; Fine and Cronshaw, 1999), or limit itself only to those deemed essential, as in the critical-incident technique (Flanagan, 1954).

Expanding upon Felix Lopez's (1988) threshold traits analysis (TTA), Donald Klingner advocates the use of a results-oriented description (ROD) or performance expectations. Drawing upon changes in the performance appraisal process designed to enhance its objectivity, the specification of results or performance standards clarifies and refines the job tasks. Klingner sees RODs as a means for obtaining the benefits of trait approaches without the costly and difficult validity problems. By adapting the work activities systems to include the measurable outcomes that each job task is expected to accomplish, the trait approach's motivational advantage is duplicated in an activities-based job analysis (Klingner and Nalbandian, 1985: 77–79).

Klingner also includes as part of his results-oriented descriptions the specification of the conditions or processes under which the job duties are performed. The inclusion of such circumstantial characteristics is an essential ingredient in developing realistic position descriptions that reflect what a job actually does. Especially in the public sector, the process by which something is done can be just as important as the substantive results themselves.

Among private sector organizations one can also find a few experimenting with "no descriptions." Adapting to an environment grown more uncertain and interdependent, these ad hoc organizations hire people (on the basis of a holistic assessment of organizational peers) and then require them to figure out how to be useful. This provides for a quite flexible organization in which individuals move to where they're most needed.

Although referred to as "jobless" or "open," these organizations do have a job description. However, it focuses on the skills, knowledge, and abilities (SKAs) that an individual possesses rather than on-the-job tasks he or she will perform. Specific tasks and processes are subject to rapid change in today's world; in fact, they are expected to change if the organization is to be successful. Hence, the basic competencies that enable an individual to successfully perform specific tasks are the focus of the job analysis. By rewarding these competencies, an organization can reinforce desired behavior (Luthans and Stajkovic, 1999). In an open organization, internal divisions and jurisdictional claims aren't allowed to hamper the task of getting the job done and concomitantly the organization's survival (Bowen, Ledford, and Nathan, 1991; Quinn, 1992a, 1992b; Pickett, 1998).

Competencies have much in common with personality traits or attitudes. The important difference that transforms a trait or attitude into a competency is job-relatedness. Unfortunately, many organizations do not make the effort to carry out the validation studies that establish the competency link to performance.

The individual job tasks or responsibilities that are identified in the job analysis process may be either narrowly or broadly defined. Narrowly defined job analyses focus on specific tasks that usually occur in a stable, routine environment (and allow for centralized administration). Broadly defined job analyses such as are involved in broadbanding emphasize the requirement for situational adjustments and flexibility in the performance of tasks (which are usually decentralized). Reinventing government and new public management efforts emphasize the flexibility advantages of broadbanding (Kellough, 1999).

The skills- and competencies-based "position expectation description" or "functional profile" really focuses on what the individual can do. Misleading organization charts with their evenly regimented boxes of job descriptions are replaced by individual profiles. These greatly enhance supervisory understanding of what an organization's real capabilities are.

By highlighting skills and competencies instead of tasks and behaviors, the organization is targeting the very things it needs to do to succeed. Competencies encompass results; specifically, they indicate the effort necessary for a task or activity to be performed successfully. Individuals think of achieving goals and results rather than narrowly focusing on one specific means of accomplishing an often vaguely defined task. By assuring that the skills and competencies necessary for fulfilling the strategic plan are possessed or provided for through employee training and development, the organization's managers and supervisors concentrate their efforts on the factors essential for success (Sullivan, 1996; Pickett, 1998).

Skills, Knowledge, and Ability

Included almost as an afterthought in the job description (and often treated as such) is the specification of the skills, knowledge, and abilities (SKAs or KSAs) necessary if one is to perform the job.

Skills, knowledge, and ability measure three levels of job performance. Skills indicate that one can and does perform the job. It is the highest level representing actual experience. Knowledge registers the possession of information for successful job performance. Finally, ability argues that, in general, there is nothing that would prevent one from performing the job. The individual is physically, psychologically, and intellectually capable and could perform the tasks once trained (Feild and Gatewood, 1989: 151; Clifford, 1994: 326).

As a way of illustrating the relationships involved in the concepts of skills, knowledge, and ability, take bread making. Skill indicates that one can and has successfully baked loaves of bread. Knowledge implies that one is familiar with the process and has read a cookbook. Ability suggests that there is nothing that would prevent one from carrying out the task—enjoys eating bread, willing to make it, capable of mixing the ingredients, could learn how to use the equipment, and so on.

For each separate, distinct work behavior or activity there should be designated, corresponding SKAs. The SKAs map out what human capital inputs are necessary to successfully complete the task. They serve as a reminder and guide as to what should be done in performing a task. When difficulties arise, they direct immediate attention to possible solutions. While somewhat difficult (as is job analysis itself), the added effort required to chart out SKAs is merited. Skills, knowledge, and ability can be analyzed in just the same fashion as job tasks are (Clifford, 1994: 331–333).

Unfortunately, too many position descriptions are conducted in a slipshod fashion. The part devoted to the SKAs is often shortchanged. Instead of individual task assessments, general requirements such as academic degrees and other credentials along with years of prior experience in similar or related jobs are focused on. These are, at most, rudimentary efforts. As far as any meaningful use goes, these are virtually worthless.

Properly done, the documentation of the skills, knowledge, and ability necessary to perform a job successfully is a key element in planning for training and for individual career advancement (Wooten, 1993). The identification of similar SKAs also enables organizations to recognize jobs with comparable work and aids in the job evaluation process. Inasmuch as SKAs focus on characteristics and traits (including efforts to validate their use), they are homing in on the very core requirements in the knowledge organization.

Skills, knowledge, and ability designate the minimum competencies required for a job. However, they can also include advanced SKAs that can lead to greater proficiency (and, ultimately, to advancement). Although these would not be required for an individual to assume a position, they would indicate that the minimum expected standards were not also the maximum effort expected.

The inclusion of such proficiency SKAs would assist in justifying pay-for-performance schemes. Currently, public acceptance suffers from the perception that individuals are paid more for doing the "same" job. Position descriptions that only detail the minimum standards perpetuate the notions that government jobs are simple (especially inasmuch as the generic qualifications that are often listed imply such). Such job descriptions discourage the growth potential that exists within jobs. This has lead dynamic individuals to focus on promotion as the sole means of development.

Of course, placing an emphasis on SKAs is not without danger. The difficulty in constructing instruments that can measure the various competencies and characteristics and link them to job-related functions is not trivial. However, extensive research has already been conducted on the big-five model of personality traits.

The big-five model groups personality traits into five major dimensions—neuroticism/emotional stability, extraversion/introversion, openness, agreeableness/antagonism, and conscientiousness/undirectedness—and has now gained wide acceptance among researchers (Digman, 1989, 1990; John, 1990; Barrick and Mount, 1991; McCrae and John, 1992; Wiggins and Pincus, 1992; Goldberg, 1993)

However, as many of the critics of the big-five model of personality traits research have noted, it is important to devote our attention to those competencies and characteristics over which individuals exert some degree of control. If personality traits are inherent, then regardless of how well they predict job performance they are likely to be perceived as unfair. Personality traits that individuals can develop and modify are more likely to gain acceptance.

As a practical matter beyond the academic construction and validation of instruments, the costs associated with such double validations is a barrier. Organizations, especially those in the public sector, do not favor "diverting" resources away from their primary mission to pay the expenses of administrative overhead.

Perhaps even more important, the perception of fairness and, hence, employee acceptance is questionable. The advantage of job tasks based on worker activities is quite straightforward; it is the visible part of the job. The competencies and characteristics that are needed in order to perform those tasks are inherently invisible or latent.

The knowledge organization exists in a changing world where job tasks do not remain fixed. Work behaviors and activities, in fact, the very jobs themselves, are undergoing constant and rapid evolution. To remain constant to the organization's purpose, attention must be focused on the workers themselves. It is their knowledge and their ability to change and learn that is essential.

Although the SKAs identified in a job analysis are linked to the performance of specific tasks, they tend to be adaptable to or inherent in evolving needs. The open or jobless organization reflects this notion. Individuals are hired on the basis of their SKAs and then turned loose to use them. Such knowledge workers must be self-directed. Guided by the organization's strategic plan, workers align their capabilities with its goals. Knowledge workers are also able to learn and adapt. In the pursuit and fulfillment of their organization's goals, they can see the rise of new technical needs and engage in their own development to address them (Quinn, 1992a, 1992b; Arthur, Claman, DeFillippi, 1995; Quinn, Anderson, and Finkelstein, 1996).

JOB EVALUATION

Job evaluation compares and contrasts the individual job analyses and sorts these separate positions into similar and different job categories. This sorting or ranking provides the basis for determining each individual job's (and not that of the individuals themselves) contribution to the organization. Job evaluation allows an organization to compare individual jobs to one another, thereby enabling it to develop an overall picture of how various positions are related to and support one another. It also enables the organization to assess the direct and indirect contribution each position makes to the organization's mission. In addition, job evaluation can also be the basis for compensation and benefit systems.

Typically, an organization (often with directional assistance from a management consulting firm) determines which factors are essential to carrying out its mission. Although anywhere from a dozen to twenty overall factors may be developed, specific jobs may only relate to three to six factors. Compensable factors can delineate such things as data, people, and things found in the functional job language; job requirements, difficulty of work, responsibility, personal relationships, and other factors from the federal Factor Evaluation System; or mental activity (problem solving), know-how, and accountability according to the Hay method. Individual jobs are ranked or rated on the extent and degree to which they are involved in each factor.

The composite score from these separate evaluations (with the factors treated equally or weighted, however the organization feels best reflects its structure) indicates the overall worth or contribution of the job to the organization. Each method provides for detailed instruction and training in its use along with guide charts for assigning appropriate point levels under the point-factor systems.

Job evaluation is a matter of equity. It is an attempt to identify the relationships that link various jobs or positions to the organization's mission. Each position is assessed on a factor or set of factors that have been chosen because they encompass the major, compensable components or dimensions that lead to successful performance. By identifying what each position contributes to achieving the organizational success, the internal value or worth of that job vis-à-vis all the other jobs within the organization can be determined.

The focus on compensable factors reflects the primary use of job evaluation as a method of establishing pay equity. Although the job evaluation process can indeed produce a uniform pay structure, the subjectivity inherent in the process itself means that different systems (along with the choice and weighting of different factors) will lead to divergent pay systems. The application of job evaluation techniques does not imply that there is one, underlying correct answer to the question of pay equity (Madigan and Hoover, 1986; Madigan and Hills, 1988; Lewis, 1989; Clifford, 1996).

Job evaluation is traditionally linked with an organization's compensation system. The Equal Pay Act of 1963 gave impetus to the employment of job evaluation systems in determining compensation (Greenlaw and Lee, 1993). Although legal requirements have not been extended to matters of comparable worth, the Equal Pay Act has been interpreted to require, in addition to equal pay for equal work, equal pay for comparable work (Moore and Abraham, 1992, 1994; Abraham and Moore, 1995). Benchmark jobs are used in establishing pay relationships. Even so, job evaluation has been effectively used to target gender-related pay differentials (Thompkins, 1987, 1988; Lewis and Stevens, 1990; England and Kilbourne, 1991; Scholl and Cooper, 1991). Ethnic differences are also subject to examination through job evaluation (Green, Veres, and Boyles, 1991).

Although this focus is important, it is not the only use of job evaluation. Inasmuch as job evaluation provides a picture of how the individuals in the organization work together to achieve its mission, it serves as a road map for planning activities. The organizational analysis aspect of job evaluation is just as valuable as its role in compensation. In fact, without a sense of how each job assists in accomplishing the organization's mission, an adequate compensation system cannot be constructed.

The disadvantages of job evaluation cannot be ignored. This can be an overly rigid and inflexible system that stifles creativity. It focuses attention on the managing of positions rather than on accomplishing the organization's mission. People, not positions, perform the work.

When "job responsibility" is included among the factors, "bureaucratic" empire-building and budget-maximization are encouraged. Job responsibility, including the number of individuals one supervises (a measure of greater responsibility), reinforces hierarchy and the development of "ranks." By focusing individual attention on the tasks that compose their jobs, boundaries are established. These boundaries are rigorously guarded and defended. In addition, those tasks, no matter how important or necessary, that are "beyond the pale" readily fall prey to the not-my-job claim.

This concern with "turf protection" also tends to direct attention internally. Great effort is spent on monitoring what goes on within the organization rather than scanning the environment for potential opportunities and threats. Management may buy internal peace by imposing uniform policies and procedures on all. While a "one size fits all" approach appears egalitarian, it can readily discourage necessary adaptation and change.

When associated with pay systems (as it usually is), job evaluation can lead to various "point grabbing" and job design games. In organizations that eschew pay adjustments for inflation or rewarding meritorious individuals (common, if not universal, among public sector organizations), grade inflation becomes the only means by which a supervisor can make things "right." These games serve only to undermine the system's and the organization's credibility.

Finally, under job evaluation schemes rewards are attached more to promotion than to job performance. This can contribute to goal displacement. Because job evaluations are often "adjusted" to "correctly" reflect exiting reality (which enhances their acceptability), they perpetuate the biases and social discrimination included in current pay scales. This places undue emphasis on the importance of promotion and formal tasks over that of doing a job well (Lawler, 1990: 139–150).

The Job Evaluation Process

Job evaluation is conducted in conjunction with job analysis. The completed, individual job analyses are assessed using a job evaluation technique (market-pricing, ranking, grading, factor, or point-factor). These techniques employ holistic approaches or ones based on objective factors. These are further subdivided into analyses based on global, comprehensive factors or analyses measured against "job-specific" performance standards operationalizing these comprehensive measures. These assessment criteria are used to evaluate each position's worth or contribution in fulfilling the organization's vision.

Classification specialists and subject matter experts drawn from the organization's workforce (trained in whichever job evaluation techniques are being used) examine the position classes or job descriptions derived from the job analyses. These are compared with the job evaluation standards guide charts and "classified." Classification may be a simple sorting (ranking and grading techniques) or a complex calculation (factor and point-factor techniques).

This process enables the organization to set a value on each job (just as a market can set a price on different commodities). This is a "value" based on the organization's own goals as determined by its members. It enables the identification of jobs that may be totally different in nature but that make similar contributions to the organization. Equity considerations call for these jobs to receive similar treatment.

If the wrong factors are selected (or important factors left out), the job evaluation will be distorted. It will fail to account for tasks that make valuable contributions to the organization's well-being. This is one of the invaluable safeguards that participation affords. By involving employees in the process, they can identify potential mistakes or oversights. "Suspect" comparisons—jobs thought similar that receive different values, jobs felt to be more or less important grouped together—will also raise questions. These may indicate a faulty job evaluation process or serve to correct original, but biased, misperceptions.

Job Evaluation Systems

There are numerous job evaluation systems on the market. For convenience, they can be grouped into five categories: (1) market-pricing, (2) ranking, (3) grading, (4) factor, and (5) point-factor. The choice of system depends on a number of features. Organizational size, scope, and technology all influence the type of job evaluation system used. Larger, more diverse organizations employing complex technologies (and the professional staff necessary for their use) are going to require more complex job evaluation systems.

Administrative criteria are also important considerations. Organizations seek job evaluation systems that are inexpensive and easy to administer. They shouldn't require complex specialization or eat up prodigious amounts of staff time. They should not be readily subject to manipulation and gaming (or make supervisors and employees want to engage in such activities). Yet, these systems must also meet the legal tests for validity and employee perceptions of objectivity and fairness. In addition, supervisors want a system they can easily explain and defend. Different job evaluators should produce consistent results for the same or similar cases. Documentation should be straightforward.

For employees, the emphasis is on an objective and fair system. The link to the reward structure should be explicit and encompass all the tasks or contributions expected of the job. The application of job evaluation needs to be seen as evenhanded and fair. Motivation is in the "eye of the beholder." The best systems are therefore worthless if they are not perceived as such.

Market-pricing is wholly focused on external compensation as the arbiter of a job's worth. As such, it is relatively simple to use. All one basically needs is a copy of the appropriate newspaper classified section's job ads. Even a knowledge-based organization needs little more than a subscription to the professional society newsletters (professional associations, being quite practical, are concerned with the placement of their members). With some trial and error a wage–effort bargain can soon be struck.

However, market-pricing ignores internal concerns not only for equity but for teamwork. It focuses effort onto "billable hours" (the needs of special interest groups is the public sector equivalent) at the expense of long-term maintenance activities.

When reward is tied to market perceptions, efforts are concentrated on influencing those perceptions. Activities that highlight the individual roles are preferred to those where one is part of a "cast of thousands." Public relations and self-promotion become part of the job (if indeed personal "spin doctors" are not employed to take care of these tasks).

Market-pricing ignores the fact that market is not necessarily a rational arena. It is strongly influenced by short-term considerations. Supply and demand, expectations and speculations, and information availability and transaction costs all work to distort the operation of the market.

More important, market-pricing overlooks the fact that not all public sector jobs have a "market." Two of the reasons government is called upon to perform tasks is that they are deemed too important to be left to the market or the market has difficulty in transforming consumers into customers. The professional services provided by government are either things we don't want private individuals "owning" (e.g., the military and police) or things requiring start-up costs, risks, and economies of scale beyond corporate abilities (e.g., public education and firefighters). When permitted, private involvement in these functions is limited to supplemental roles.

Market-pricing job evaluation is basically a salary survey. First, it is necessary to identify the appropriate labor market. Managers and professional staff will require national searches, especially for the more specialized positions. Administrative and technical jobs may necessitate a regional hunt while it should be sufficient to only look at local wage levels for the clerical and support staff. The labor market also needs to encompass the entire set of appropriate jobs. In the fast-food industry, McDonald's does not just compete with Burger King and Wendy's but must also be aware of Kentucky Fried Chicken and Subway. Ideally, these labor markets should also reflect similar conditions to that in which the organization operates.

Second, the wages and salaries (and benefits) associated with these jobs needs to be discovered. Since the expense of costing out all jobs is prohibitive, only selected benchmark jobs are costed out. The full job analyses for each need to be compared with those of their market compatriots. These are then used to assign appropriate salary figures to the other positions. However, this requires some other job evaluation technique for establishing these job-to-job links.

The remaining four systems—ranking, grading, factor, and point-factor—strive to create internal equity. As displayed in Figure 4.2, these systems combine approaches that place emphasis on looking at the whole job or objectively analyzing its components while measuring or evaluating each job comparatively against other jobs withing the organization or against a set (or sets) of performance standards.

Ranking and grading are holistic (nonquantitative or qualitative) approaches to job evaluation. They examine the job *in toto.* Using their expertise or informed opinion, the classification specialists (and SMEs) form a gestalt impression of the value or contribution of the job. The limitations of the "state of the art" are most noticeable in these instances. Holistic approaches take into account the dynamic functioning of the overall job. Hence, they are able to recognize interactive effects or added value when a series of separate, simple tasks are combined into a complex job greater than the sum of its parts.

As a job evaluation technique, ranking is extraordinarily simple. One sorts out jobs based on their perceived overall importance to the organization. This is a comprehensive evaluation using a single, global criterion (very important, moderately important, somewhat important, less important, etc.) or by comparing one job to

Figure 4.2
Job Evaluation Systems

	Comparative	Standards
Holistic	Ranking	Grading
Objective	Factor	Point-Factor

another. Ranking is most effective in smaller organizations where an individual or set of individuals has in-depth knowledge of all the jobs in the organization.

Jobs can be compared by "peeling the onion" (i.e., identifying the most important and least important jobs, then the next most important and least important, and so forth) or through a series of paired comparisons (i.e., each job is matched cheek-by-jowl with every other job, and the jobs are ranked in order of the total number of "more important" scores each job has). These techniques result in a list of jobs ranked from the most important to the least important.

Grading (or classification) is another holistic approach to job evaluation. This is the formal origin of the whole notion of job classification and pay grades and is often (somewhat confusingly) used as a generic description for the whole job analysis and evaluation process. Instead of a comprehensive comparison, however, grading employs a series of performance standards. Rather than compare job to job, each job is assessed against a predetermined template.

Used in larger organizations, the holistic global, comprehensive criterion is refined under a grading job evaluation. Under a grading approach to job evaluation, appropriate "job-specific" examples or applications of the comprehensive criterion serve to guide the classification specialists' and SMEs' decisions. Individual jobs are examined against these standards and classified into various grade levels. The government grades jobs as it does eggs and meat. Although the result is not a list of rank-ordered jobs, it does provide a list of grouped jobs. Each group contains jobs that add a similar value or make a similar contribution to the organization.

The development of the decisionband job evaluation technique introduces an advanced, "factor" approach to grading. The decisionband method argues that one factor, the extent of decision making involved in the performance of a job, is all that is needed to adequately capture its overall worth. This technique claims to offer the sophistication and validity of the objective methods while retaining the simplicity and ease of use of the qualitative, holistic approaches.

With the development of more complex, diversified organizations in the second half of the twentieth century, the qualitative, holistic job evaluation techniques gave way to quantitative, objective factor and point-factor approaches. The quantitative approaches were designed not only for use in even larger organizations but for organizations that encompassed a wider range of activities and functions.

The factor and point-factor methods objectively break the evaluation of jobs into separate dimensions or factors. This allows for a fuller, more correct assessment of what it is each job does and how that contributes to the organization. In essence, multiple indicators are used in calculating a job's worth. The factors chosen for use in the job evaluation can be either accorded equal status or weighted. This results in an overall, more balanced view. However, different weighting formulas can produce different results that may not be all that benign (Davis and Sauser, 1993). Factor and point-factor job evaluations are personnel applications of the more general trade-off analysis decision-making tool (Fisher, 1980: 319–335).

The use of factor and point-factor job evaluation systems usually requires the employment of a management consulting firm (or job evaluation specialists). This is often done in conjunction with a thorough job analysis. Although costs can be somewhat reduced by contracting for the training of an organization's own employees in the use of both the job analysis and the evaluation techniques, the consulting firm must also be contracted for the system's maintenance and updating.

Hybrid systems, as they are called in organizations that forgo the "service contract," tend to rapidly deteriorate. The job evaluation expertise decays as those employees originally trained in it leave, are promoted, or just get tied up with other matters. Without practice, these skills atrophy.

To provide an image of uniformity, formal factor systems may contain up to a dozen factors (albeit only five or six are expected to apply to any one job). Alternatively, many factor evaluation systems employ only three factors; however, these contain subdimensions that are applied differently to jobs at various levels in the organizational hierarchy.

Factor evaluation occurs as classification specialists and trained SMEs examine jobs against each factor using a comprehensive or comparative approach. This is analogous to the ranking method except instead of a single dimension, jobs are ranked on three to six distinct factors. These individual, ordinal scores are combined for the overall evaluation. Statistical analysis can be conducted with trade-off analyses to determine if the differences among scores are indeed statistically significant.

The point-factor (or point-rating) method expands upon the factor method by introducing interval metrics instead of the ordinal ratings used in the factor approach. On a particular factor, the factor method will designate that job A is first, job B second, and job C third. These are ordinal measures; the "distance" from first to second and from second to third is uncertain. The planetary system illustrates this. The fourth planet, Mars, is farther from the Sun than the third planet, Earth, and the fifth planet, Jupiter, is farther out than Mars. However, the distance from Earth to Mars (48 million miles) is not the same as that from Mars to Jupiter (341 million miles).

The point-factor method is a specialized application of the trade-off technique of cost-benefit analysis. As such, many of the computer software packages, such as Expert Choice, can be used to perform the mechanical aspects of this process.

Just as "miles" provide an interval metric for the more finely honed measurement of planetary distances, point-factor job evaluation claims to be able to make the same sort of distinctions. Of course, the social science realm within which job evaluation occurs does not usually have such distinct metrics as miles, kilometers, or light-years. The assessment from a point-factor system is not simply that one job contributes more to an organization's mission than another (as is the case with factor scores) but precisely how much more that contribution is.

To some extent, this is another case of the "illusion of precision." Under the influx of comparable-worth lawsuits, most organizations have backed away from such definitive claims. However, point-factor systems remain useful when organizations feel that some sense of "distance" can be ascertained. Minimally, point-factor systems can be viewed as factor systems with a whole lot of categories.

Classification Wars

Classification systems restrain public managers. Introduced to bring order and fairness to the hodgepodge of positions, titles, and salaries that plagued government at the beginning of the century, classification schemes have seriously suffered a lack of flexibility in dealing with the requirements imposed by the end of the century's changing environment.

Classification systems give rise to problems as they attempt to maintain rigid command-and-control systems and preserve an internal-equity vision of fiscal uniformity. Attuned to a simpler and more stable era of government, such classification systems now impose inequities and inefficiencies on the public service. These problems are often compounded in jurisdictions that fail to maintain and modify their classification systems and provide inadequate or no training to their classification specialists.

Carolyn Ban (1995: 205–215) details these problems and the strategies for overcoming them in her study of federal managers. First, managers must decide if they want to become actively involved in the classification process (or to passively try something else).

Once involved, classification becomes a question of conflict resolution or negotiation. A choice must be made between cooperation and confrontation. These strategies reflect the need to sustain long-term relationships and take short-term advantages. Political appointees and fast-track careerists (who expect to move on quickly) are often more willing to sacrifice an organization's long-term relationship. The resultant atmosphere of mistrust and suspicion makes it more difficult for future classification changes.

Cooperation or confrontation is also determined by the stakeholder interests of managers and classification specialists. If the classification system is still seen as an accounting means for command and control, cooperation is unlikely to work. On the other hand, if a human resources perspective exists, a cooperative relationship can benefit both groups.

Ban (1995: 205–215) notes that a manager can approach reclassification in either a technical or a political manner. Technical modifications can be made through job redesign. A position can have an "accretion of duties" due to mission and technology changes. Simpler yet, is to have the position retitled (recognizing a change in classification) into a higher grade range.

These techniques have often been used to reward and retain "superstars" or even regular employees when replacement is doubtful. Although this is something that a pay-for-performance system should do, many governments simply fail to face that need. Fiscal austerity and antigovernment rhetoric combine to deny public employees adequate compensation.

Politically, a manager can search out precedents among existing position descriptions and argue for grade changes as a matter of equity. Alternatively, the supervisor can master the classification system itself and rewrite position descriptions to reflect the desired grade-level outcome. Finally, one can go to the "boss" and with his or her support "pressure" the classification office into the change.

SUMMARY

A civil service can be organized using either a rank-in-person or a rank-in-position format. A rank-in-person system focuses on specific jobs and the skills, knowledges, and abilities needed to perform it. It enhances both job-related efficiency and hiring equity. On the other hand, a rank-in-person system focuses on developing the individual to optimize performance over a career and many different specific jobs.

Job analysis is the basic building block of personnel administration. It is through job analysis that the content of specific positions is defined. Knowing the tasks that a job is to perform then allows recruitment and selection for those skills, training to develop them more fully, and appraisal of the efforts and results of incumbent jobholders.

While job analyses focus primarily on determining the internal-role, job-related tasks performed by a specific position, attention is now also focusing on the competencies or skills, knowledges, and abilities that enable one to perform those tasks. External-role, organizational relationships are also beginning to be given credence.

Job evaluation distinguishes the relationships between the different positions defined through job analysis. In essence, the job evaluation creates the "organization chart." This is important for both pay determination (in order to offer competitive salaries for recruiting and retaining individuals) and internal equity (recognizing and paying equal contributions equally).

chapter 5

Staffing

The staffing function or recruitment and selection arose directly in response to Frederick Winslow Taylor's *Principles of Scientific Management* (1911). Yet, it was just as much a political solution as a technical breakthrough. Although the Old Progressives had set back the spoils system in the late nineteenth century, they had not vanquished political bossism and its public corruption. Civil service systems once installed were readily subverted and patronage restored. The Young Progressives such as Woodrow Wilson and Frank Goodnow saw in Taylor's principles a technical solution for sustaining the moral crusade against bosses and political patronage (White, 1958; Van Riper, 1958).

Moreover, scientific management was a solution that would also positively enhance the capabilities of government. It promised politicians a government fully capable of delivering the programs and services that they saw as solutions to the problems facing American society. This politically sustained the public administration movement from the New Deal and through the Great Society.

This chapter examines the techniques used in the recruitment, testing, and selection of employees. This chapter provides:

1. An understanding of why positive and active recruitment is important
2. Knowledge of fundamental recruitment strategies and techniques
3. Knowledge of various test formats available for assisting in the hiring decision
4. An overview of the role played by the mechanics of administering examinations in influencing hiring decisions
5. A review of extra-merit or features added onto the selection process that serve other organizational purposes
6. An examination of the role played by orientation in completing the transition from selection to employment

Staffing is the most thoroughly studied and researched area within the human resources/personnel field. The importance of people to effective government was recognized very early. Unlike other academic aspects of human resources/personnel management, staffing also benefited from substantial resources in support of scholarly research activities. The almost immediate, practical benefits and payoff from such research was recognized. This proved a major contribution not only to research on staffing but to personnel research in general.

However, such abundance is not without problems. We have benefited from the discovery and development of many objective recruitment and selection techniques. Yet, this very abundance results in a complex array of techniques not so easily sorted out from one another. From phenology and personality profiles at the beginning of the century to graphology and psychics at its end, objective techniques have been forced to compete with the bizarre.

Staffing links a number of actions designed to bring together the people who make an organization work. It begins with efforts at recruitment (and retention), progresses through the testing of job candidates, and concludes with the selection of those deemed most appropriate and their orientation into the organizational culture and teamwork environment.

The modern staffing process (as is human resource management in general) is the product of equal employment opportunity/affirmative action (EEO/AA). Equal employment opportunity calls for a true, free market on jobs. Competition is based on talent and merit regardless of gender or ethnic status (Lee and Greenlaw, 1997; Greenlaw, Kohl, and Lee, 1998). Affirmative action is one method for achieving those goals.

Beginning with the Civil Rights Act of 1964 and its implementation in the personnel arena through *Griggs v. Duke Power* (1971), the Equal Employment Act of 1972, the "Uniform Guidelines on Employee Selection" (1978), and subsequent court cases, EEO/AA has helped shape a modern, objective approach to the management of human resources. In fact, it has sparked the transformation of personnel administration into human resource management (Straus and Stewart, 1995).

Equal employment opportunity requirements are not limited to ethnic minorities and women. The Age Discrimination in Employment Act (ADEA) of 1967 extends coverage to workers over forty years old (jury decisions are especially favorable to anyone over fifty). In *O'Connor v. Consolidated Coin Caters* (1996), the Supreme Court ruled that the basic criteria for bringing a case under the ADEA are that an individual (1) was in the protected age class, (2) was discharged or demoted, and (3) at the time of the discharge or demotion, was performing his or her job at a level that met the employer's legitimate expectations. The age of the individual replacing the employee is immaterial. The Americans with Disabilities Act (ADA) of 1990 provides extensive protection for those with physical or mental impairments who are capable of performing the essential responsibilities of a job. It has focused renewed attention on the importance of job analysis (Boller and Massengill, 1992; Cozzetto, 1994; Mello, 1995; Hollwitz, Goodman, and Bolte, 1995).

Although objective techniques existed for some decades, their use languished. It was not until the courts mandated that organizations adhere to equal employment requirements that the use of objective techniques for staffing were seriously undertaken. This is one of the great legacies of the Civil Rights movement—the effective operationalization of the merit principle.

As a method for implementing equal employment opportunity, affirmative action is politically controversial. Equal employment opportunity has given way to arguments over hiring preferences and quotas. When correctly carried out, affirmative action is quite effective.

The U.S. military is an exemplary example of how affirmative action can be correctly employed. First, the military maintains performance standards (if anything, they have actually been increased). No one holds on to a job if they cannot do it. It then concentrates its efforts at providing those who possess the ability to do the job with the necessary remedial knowledge and skills required. Remedial education to correct for the failures of the elementary and secondary school (and, growingly, college) systems is intensely frustrating (for those who thought they had received an education) and costly. Since most organizations are unwilling to go to such efforts and expense, affirmative action programs degenerated into preferences. This has, in turn, generated a political backlash (Daniel, 1986).

In establishing the requirements for affirmative action litigation, the burden of proof is an important factor. The presumption of innocence is a quite advantageous position as the burden of proof is a costly and laborious requirement. In order to protect organizations from frivolous lawsuits while enabling relatively poor individuals to address alleged wrongs, a series of threshold tests on adverse impact are employed: blatant discrimination, the 80 percent rule for selection rates or utilization, and validity.

Disparate treatment occurs in the case of intentional or blatant discrimination. Validation provides the strongest defense in these cases. Blatant discrimination (which is seldom admitted to) is tantamount to a "guilty" plea. Another means for an individual to establish a prima facie case (thereby shifting the burden of proof to the organization) is to establish only that he or she is a member of a protected class, qualified for the job, was not hired, and that the same job remained open or unfilled (*McDonnell Douglas v. Green,* 1973).

On the other hand, validation is offered as clear statistical evidence of "innocence." Validation claims that employment decisions are job-related on the basis of content, construct, or criterion-related tests. However, these tests are costly and result in evidence that accounts for only a portion of the variability (i.e., it only partially explains or predicts).

Adverse impact merely establishes that different groups are treated differently; it is not itself proof of discrimination. Under *Griggs v. Duke Power* (1971) the establishment of adverse impact shifted the burden of proof from the plaintiff to the organization. *Wards Cove Packing v. Atonio* (1989), modified by the Civil Rights Act of 1991, additionally requires that an intent to discriminate or an identifiable causality relationship be demonstrated before such a shift.

The 80 percent (or four-fifths) rule examines the outcomes of employment decisions. Because there is nothing inherently job-related in an individual's gender or ethnic status that should affect his or her job selection, the division or sorting of individuals into different groups (based on gender, ethnic status, right- or left-handedness, ice cream preferences, etc.) should exhibit no differences among applicant selection rates. The 80 percent rule actually allows for these groups to vary by as much as 20 percent.

For two applicant "groups," one can have a selection rate that is a fifth lower than another without adverse impact. If in one group of a thousand applicants one hundred are selected (10 percent), a second group of two hundred should see twenty individuals (10 percent) selected. The 80 percent rule creates a margin of error that would consider nothing amiss even if the second group selected only sixteen individuals. However, anything less than this opens the organization and its practices to question. *Wards Grove Packing v. Atonio* (1989) requires that a specific practice be established or identified as causing this disparity. Even so, the organization is allowed to demonstrate that the adverse impact is spurious and that its actions are indeed job-related.

The utilization rule shifts the focus from selection rates to the proportion of employees available in the appropriate labor market. The "defense" is based on a claim that either women or ethnic minorities are not hired because they simply don't exist (for this specific job). Educational efforts, especially apprenticeship programs, are pointed to as eventual remedies to this problem.

RECRUITMENT AND RETENTION

Before there can be an organization, there must be workers. Employees do not spring like Athena fully armed from the head of Zeus. As with the batteries for children's toys, workers are not included in the organizational package. Hence, the attraction and recruitment of employees is an important, crucial step in the development of the organization. With so much effort spent in obtaining workers, efforts designed at their retention is a highly related concern (Armacost and Jauernig, 1991; Carnevale and Housel, 1995).

Why Recruit?

Recruitment is a twofold process. Indeed its main purpose is to, ultimately, find the right person for the job. Naturally, this is where the primary focus of the recruitment process is directed. Job analysis sets the stage by clearly defining what tasks and responsibilities are to be performed and what characteristics and skills are necessary to successfully do so. Hence, recruitment becomes a search for the individual who matches these criteria.

However, a secondary function in recruitment is to instill in those making the hiring decision the psychological confidence and ease of mind that indeed they did make the right choice. Although the absolute right candidate may be the first person who walks in the door, how would one know that unless there were other candidates to compare with? This confidence is quite important. It influences how a new employee is treated. If there is confidence in the selection, then the new employee will be more readily provided a locus of control over his or her job. With the flexibility that this latitude and autonomy provide, new employees perform their jobs with more confidence and a resultant higher chance for success.

Labor Markets

Attracting individuals as job candidates is no different than seeking customers for the organization's product or service. It is a marketing operation. One is faced with the classical equation of supply and demand. It is a matter of determining what performance is desired—whether from a job candidate or a product or service—and what one is willing to or can pay for it.

Because jobs are not composed of simple tasks where people are merely interchangeable parts, labor markets are important to recruitment. This is even more the case with respect to the professional, knowledge organization. The number of individuals available for a specific job is limited. The entire population is immediately reduced by simple demographic factors. We are limited to the working-age population. Although what constitutes "too old" is, more and more, a matter of conjecture, there is definite agreement that there is an age at which people are too young.

Changing demographic patterns also are at work. Workforce diversity is merely a statement of the coming reality. The proportion of "minority" people in the population is increasing. This, in itself, is forcing organizations to transform themselves. Recruitment patterns (along with most of the other techniques employed in management) must be revalidated.

Similarly, the need for skilled workers militates against the exclusion of women and ethnic minorities. With this increase in demand will also come other adjustments (e.g., the introduction of family-friendly workplaces) necessary if jobs are to be filled.

Each technical requirement imposed more finely filters this labor pool. Education requirements (attesting to general competencies) may have a significant influence on shaping the job market. Furthermore, the call for specific degrees or skills can place substantial limits on the number of individuals available.

To individual candidates the type of industry or work may matter. To put it bluntly, they may not want to work for government. Similarly, some individuals may prefer to seek out public employment while shying away from business. In America, choice—whether in jobs or ice cream—is part of our sense of freedom. Personal preferences matter.

The "bash the bureaucrat" atmosphere that has dominated political discourse over the past two decades (and has been an undercurrent in American politics since the beginning) has painted a rather uninviting picture of public employment. More important, it has led to the neglect of and disrespect for the public service. The rhetoric has been used to justify actions that have indeed undermined the civil service system. The image of government built on the success of the New Deal and World War II has been replaced by one derived from the quagmire of Vietnam and the unraveling of the Great Society. A negative image of governmental service has been created in the minds of many individuals. Today's image of the public service requires that efforts be spent in attracting individuals to careers in the public sector (Kilpatrick, Cummings, and Jennings, 1964).

The organization itself may limit the number of available candidates through a series of added requirements (e.g., residency, citizenship, veterans preference). Governments especially feel the political pressure to reserve jobs for their citizens. Although a business may hear complaints when it fails to hire locally, it is accorded the right to hire whomever it wants. This same latitude is often not extended to governments. Furthermore, state and local governments often insist (or strongly encourage) public employees to reside within their political jurisdiction. They want to capture the economic effects of the public payroll. In the case of police and firefighters, they also capture the benefit of their "off-duty" expertise and availability.

Political conditions may also affect employment decisions. Civil service positions normally attempt to restrict and limit partisan involvement. These protect public employees from partisan pressures. In addition, the Hatch Acts of 1939 and 1940 were also designed to protect legislators from executive-dominated political machines. Even so, the public service in many states and cities still suffers from extensive and inappropriate partisan influences. Even in the best situations, there is widespread interaction with political officials and personnel experts (Stein, 1987).

Working for political appointees is a related factor that may deter an individual from seeking public organizations. Although all organizations suffer from unsuccessful managers, they and their failures are far more visible in the public arena. Having to work for or around such individuals can be discouraging. The private sector benefits from an image of efficient business practices quite opposite of that "bungling bureaucrat" picture of the public sector. Neither image is correct.

Internal selection or former employee preference (RIF or rehire lists) may be used. In many instances, job openings are limited to existing employees already in the agency, the department, or in government-wide employment. Sufficient qualified applicants are felt to exist while the limitation speeds up the entire process. In the public sector, a vacant position is more likely to become victim to an unrelated political wrangle, fiscal problem, or downsizing effort. Filling the position may be frozen even if it is direly needed.

Recruitment Strategies

The Jacksonian perspective of government as a provider of temporary jobs requiring little beyond the basic skills of reading and writing did not call for any major effort at recruitment. The night-watchman state of the nineteenth century served to start people on their careers—careers that would be pursued, for the most part, in agriculture or private business. The democratic fervor of the era also eliminated any need whatsoever to seek out candidates for governmental posts.

This passive approach to governmental recruitment still prevails along with the sleepy, night-watchman image. However, the industrial and postindustrial society of the twentieth and twenty-first centuries requires a more active government involvement. This also necessitates an active approach to attracting candidates for governmental posts. Government, like any other organization, must seek out and compete for the talent it needs. The public service, if it is to be successful, must market itself.

For high-demand jobs (where organizations almost always have vacant positions or are training internal candidates), a proactive approach is called for. In a proactive recruitment, the organization goes out to other organizations and raids their talent or to schools (intern relationships are ideal for establishing a "first refusal" or "first look" program). In both cases, the organization begins "recruiting" talent before it actually has a formal vacancy. It may even identify someone and then proceed to "create" the needed position for him or her. The use of name requests is considered part of the human resources netherworld as it raises questions of equal opportunity and fairness. When it is legitimately used, there is no problem. If the position (written to match the identified candidate) is actually advertised ("spinning the register" so the preferred candidate "surprisingly" comes out ahead), the high demand would lead to other qualified candidates also being hired.

The modern public service is a professional service. Professions are built on knowledge and expertise. This is not a matter that lends itself to a temporary workforce. Knowledge isn't gained overnight. It's earned the old-fashioned way—by hard work. Professional workers must be sought out and guaranteed an environment in which their careers can be nurtured and prosper.

For government, this means that a balance between inside and outside selection must be struck. Career services such as those associated with rank-in-person approaches virtually limit their recruitment to internal selection. The ideal of the rank-in-position approach, on the other hand, invokes images of external selection. Reality lies somewhere in between. Even rank-in-position career systems (e.g., the elite French *grands corps)* have discovered the benefit of importing talented outsiders (or providing their members with significant outside, sabbatical experiences).

A career system is necessary to focus individual attention on the strategic issues facing an organization over the long term. Objectives and reward systems tied to the short term lead to dysfunctional behavior and goal displacement. Government with its two-year, four-year, and six-year electoral cycles has always suffered from this myopia.

A long-term perspective induces organizational commitment and loyalty. It enables individuals and organizations to invest in training and productivity improvements knowing that they will reap the benefits from that enhanced knowledge and technique.

Internal selection is also easier. The employee has already been attracted. The questions on whether an individual will fit in and adapt to an organization's culture are now moot. The problems of orientation and socialization (which are fraught with disappointment and turnover) have been overcome. The not inconsequential costs of recruitment (which are often an unfortunate, limiting factor among governments) are dramatically reduced.

Internal selection exposes an organization to the dangers of "inbreeding." Although it promotes a more harmonious, homogeneous workforce, it also can blind the organization to what is going on in the world at large. Outside selection stirs up an organization. All the problems mentioned above that are avoided by internal selection are also lost opportunities.

Recruitment forces an organization to campaign. Like candidates for elected office, the organization must go out into the real world and find out what its concerns and issues are. Recruitment forces an organization to scan its environment. The turmoil involved in addressing the questions that revolve around organizational fit force an organization to reexamine its own organizational culture and climate. Does it best serve the purposes that the organization is set on accomplishing? The problems of orientation and socialization expose the organization to ideas and ways of doing things drawn from different organizations. New ideas, different ideas can foster creativity. Even the costs of recruitment can serve to remind the organization how valuable its human "investment" is.

Different jobs require different markets. The attraction of employees cannot be managed with a one-size-fits-all plan. An adequate number of candidates is the goal. This may be achieved through word of mouth among current employees or posters on a wall; it may require an international search with extensive, individual negotiations. Whichever is the case, it is predicated on the goal of confidently hiring the right person.

There are costs to recruitment. These are often ignored in the public sector with dire consequences. The public sector often approaches recruitment as an inconvenient nuisance, best gotten over with as quickly as possible. They overlook that recruitment is a natural part of organizational life. It is also an important part. Every hiring decision is a million dollar decision. The costs of the process itself, the lifetime salary and benefits involved, and the productivity derived from the employee all add up to a substantial figure. Hence, recruitment needs to be treated as the major investment it indeed is.

First, a vacant position entails costs in terms of temporary employees and lost productivity (no matter how competent, the temporaries lack a long-term perspective and organizational commitment). Governments often fail to fill these positions and assume that the salary saved is all "profit." Just because it is undocumented does not mean that the lost productivity or morale effects (when the work is dumped on others) did not occur. Second, there are the direct costs of recruitment itself. Individuals in the personnel office and the work group must take time from their schedules to plan, organize, and manage the recruitment process. Recruitment expenses (advertising, search fees, job fairs and college visits, and referral bonuses) are also included.

All in all, this is an important investment of organizational human resources (and quite worth it given the consequences involved). Although cost-per-hire will vary depending on the level of the position and nature of the organization, it can be calculated with models from the Employment Management Association (Cluff, 1999) or Saratoga Institute (http://www.sarins.com/). Cost-per-hire data can be used to evaluate whether the recruitment dollars are being used effectively. In doing so, however, it is also important to take into consideration the (1) quality of the hires, (2) its affect on service, and (3) the timeliness of hiring (Trice, 1999).

There are also the costs involved in assembling and interviewing candidates, including recruitment trips. While small compared with the other costs discussed here, they are crucial. The hiring process (and especially the interview) is dyadic. Not only is the organization seeking out the best candidate, but the candidates are "testing" the organization. These are the items that directly influence the impression a job candidate gets of the organization (Rynes, Bretz, and Gerhart, 1991; Smither, Reilly, Millsap, Pearlman, and Stuffey, 1993).

Although applicant tracking is a difficult task, this is one area where advances in information technology have produced major dividends. Much of the work can now be done by computer programs that scan resumes, allow for on-line application processes, and run preliminary tests and checks on the applicants' credentials. Organizations with a large volume of hiring, security or competitiveness needs, or specialized report requirements may prefer to control their own system (e.g., purchasing a Personic, Restrac, or Resumix system). Smaller organizations can still benefit by contracting out for these applicant-tracking services (e.g., using Hire Systems or I-Search) (Wheeler, 1999).

These costs all need to be put into perspective. Tabulated, they form the basis for calculating the cost-per-hire. This cost is compared against a number of organizational benefits. The productivity (or performance ratings) of employees can be used to gauge the value they add to the organization. Retention enters the equation when we look at the length of time the organization benefits from a recruited employee's work.

Although these are all post hoc determinations, they can be used to make projections about "similar" recruitment activities. The value of techniques used in recruitment, their application to specific job types, whether geographic markets or educational institutions are worth the effort can all be assessed.

The use of realistic job previews, especially for professional organizations, has gained widespread acceptance. The realistic preview that balances the fun and exciting parts of the job with some of the routine and boring is designed to maximize the retention of new hires. Although it discourages individuals from applying or continuing their employment interest, it pays off later in lower turnover among those hired. For those with prior experience of the job area, realistic previews are more likely to remind them of the negatives and discourage their application (Meglino, Ravlin, and DeNisi, 1997). Knowing more about what a job actually entails reduces the disappointment among new employees. Given the costs of a "failed" recruitment, realistic previews are highly cost-effective (Premack and Wanous, 1985; Meglino, DeNisi, and Ravlin, 1993; Phillips, 1998).

Recruitment Techniques

Traditionally, recruitment has relied upon word of mouth by employees among their friends and neighbors. These networks are often the means by which job applicants hear of an opening. Although extensive formal advertising is "broadcast" by organizations, the word from a friend or family member assures that the "message" was received. Employee referral is one of the strongest and most viable recruitment techniques. For prospective employees, the recommendation of current employees is a strong indicator that the organization is a desirable place to work.

In addition to attracting new workers, employee referrals also afford the organization a number of safeguards. Because the "recruiting" employees work there too, they are going to be cautious about recruiting anyone unqualified for the job. The supervisors can query the recommending employee about the job candidate. Because an unqualified placement not only would adversely affect the organization but would also personally reflect poorly on the recommending employee's judgment among his or her colleagues, the sponsor has an added incentive to see to it that the new employee succeeds.

Of course, this networking method can fail if it is based on too narrow a set of friends and family. The goal displacement of a buddy system focused on taking care of one another rather than on guaranteeing organizational success can easily arise. Similar-to-me hiring practices can also lead to the exclusion of talented but different individuals. It is especially likely to exclude women and ethnic minorities who are not currently part of the organization's demographic makeup.

Employee referrals can be encouraged. Rewarding successful referrals is an added means of assuring a flow of high-quality applicants. Often employees are awarded $50 to $100 for every recommended applicant that is hired. The referral bonus rate may vary with the level of the position. Entry level and internships may be worth $100, technical and support personnel referrals $200 to $400, and professional staff $800 to $1,000. In more knowledge-intensive organizations where skilled employees are essential, referral bonuses can be as high as $5,000. These referral bonuses are divided with half being paid on initial hiring and the remaining half after six months or a year. Additional rewards may be based on the longevity of the new hire (which can foster mentoring). Alternatively, referring employees could be rewarded with extra vacation days, free parking, or prizes (donated by vendors or public-spirited citizens). Intrinsic recognition can be provided through employee-of-the-month displays and newsletter mentions.

Referral bonuses can also be awarded to a team or group as well as to the supervisors of those making referrals. "Token" awards for referrals that were unsuccessful can be made in order to encourage the employee to make future referrals. Recruitment packages and "referral" training can be provided to employees as a means of enhancing these efforts (these may also provide a side benefit in heightened employee commitment).

The display of posters and job announcements in public places is the other traditional approach to recruitment. This was designed to assure open competition for governmental posts. Often requiring prospective candidates to seek them out, these announcements are a somewhat passive method.

However, the transformation of government calls for more active and energetic approaches to recruitment. Professional employees cannot be expected to respond to passive techniques when so many others are actively vying for their attention (Rynes, Bretz, and Gerhart, 1991; Smither, Reilly, Millsap, Pearlman, and Stuffey, 1993). Advertisements, organizations, and search firms all are part of professional recruitment approaches.

Advertisement now goes beyond the simple poster on the post office wall (ideally, separated from those advertising others who are wanted by the government). A wide variety of media outlets are available. General newspapers as well as radio and television can be effectively used at reasonable costs. Cable television can be used to target specific markets (in terms of virtually any demographic distinction desired). Promotional literature can be printed and distributed; it can also be placed on the Internet. Even the office voice mail can be programmed to play recruiting messages while people are "on hold."

The Internet with its Web pages is becoming a major recruitment instrument. Although created to inform current government employees of job openings, the Federal USAJOBS (www.usajobs.opm.gov) is readily available for use in "open searches." Although the Internet has rapidly become the primary recruitment tool, a survey of recent federal hires indicates that only about half had access to the Internet (U.S. Merit Systems Protection Board, 1999b). The Web allows the organization to place extensive information regarding itself on Web sites along with lists of job openings (e.g., although decentralizing much of the personnel function, South Carolina has developed a convenient, centralized Web page listing state jobs). It can broadcast/e-mail job announcements to appropriate listserves. In addition to directly applying to such job announcements, those seeking employment can have their resumes listed in college and university placement or professional association Web pages (or other similar services). Prospective employers can readily search these electronic placement files.

Professional associations and educational institutions are special sources for recruitment efforts. Every professional organization and school is interested in the placement of their members and alumni. Professional organizations publish job announcements in their newsletters; they often run their own recruitment services. Representing that first job linkage between childhood and adult status, schools are especially involved in placement efforts. They encourage the formation of networks to foster placement and assist in the development of internships and cooperative education experiences.

Schools (and larger organizations) can sponsor job fairs that attract many candidates. Government agencies (and job candidates) are often induced to attend these job fairs by being granted "direct hiring authority"—the ability to make a job offer right on the spot!

Executive search firms (also known somewhat affectionately/perversely as headhunters) focus on specialized recruitment problems. An executive recruitment firm possesses an expertise in a specific human resources market. By concentrating their efforts, they gain a specialized expertise on what is required and who is available. An executive search firm can also assure some degree of confidentiality in an area where egos may collide (Ammons and Glass, 1988).

Conceptually related to the executive search firm, placement and temporary agencies are increasingly being used. The temporary service agency is an outsourced human resources office. It handles the entire recruitment process (and perhaps other personnel functions as well). The organization then has the option of "testing" the temporary through on-the-job performance.

Recruitment, Reward, and Retention

Recruitment requires effort. In some instances, extra inducements are needed to "close the deal." Unfortunately, government is often limited in what it can legally do. Because recruitment inducements are individualized, they can be perceived as being inequitable. Why is one individual offered something extra while another is not? If this influences the decision to accept a job offer (as it is intended to do), what are the repercussions?

Governments can offer an individual a "signing bonus." Although this cannot generally be done as such, it can be accomplished with the creative use of honorarium or consultation contracts. Salary flexibility is also an important factor. Under pay scale systems, starting salaries can be set above the minimum as an inducement. Broadbanding approaches offer even more discretion in setting salaries. Managers are often permitted to offer salaries anywhere between the minimum and the range midpoint on their own authority. If a salary above the midpoint is deemed necessary in order to obtain a suitable candidate, permission from superiors would be required. The jobs themselves can be redesigned to make them more appealing.

The expense of relocating is a major, up-front cost that an individual faces in accepting a job. This can be especially burdensome on younger workers just starting out. Organizations can reimburse or advance relocation expenses. These need not be limited solely to the costs of moving. The expenses of selling and buying a house may be covered. The organization can even "pay the difference" if the employee-seller must take a loss on the sale. Subsistence expenses covering rent and meals while in a temporary residence awaiting closing can be included in the package. If there are concerns with regard to the employee "jumping ship" or leaving, reimbursement can take the form of a promissory note payable after the probationary period.

Assistance in finding employment for a trailing spouse is more and more a necessity. Dual-career couples are now the norm (especially with the "office" having become the primary social network for meeting people). Lifestyles are based on dual incomes; hence, job decisions must be calculated in terms of how they affect both partners. Creating second jobs or a strong network of local employers is a must.

Relocation incentives that focus on the whole family are important. Bringing the entire family on the interview or, at least, on a post-offer visit can make all the difference. More and more recruitment efforts fail not because the candidate is not convinced but because the family has reservations. By bringing the family to the job site and community they are given a real experience on which to base their judgments. Special relocation welcoming packages can be provided. A regular feature in the military is the availability of a person or family (who have recently gone through the same process) to help orientate the newcomers.

The effort spent in attracting employees is wasted if they cannot be retained. Workforce planning, employing turnover analysis and exit interviews, is necessary to alert the organization of recruitment problem areas. More generally, employee attitude surveys and suggestion systems provide an early warning device for potential problems (Carnevale, 1993).

Retention of desired workers focuses on managing turnover. Pay and job satisfaction are the key strategies involved. The pay package (salary/wages and benefits) must be deemed adequate for the employee's needs. Without a fair and equitable pay structure, employees and their knowledge will exit the organization (Coff, 1997).

Pay flexibility can allow managers the ability to retain valued employees. This enables them to make counteroffers when an employee is offered a job elsewhere (or better yet to preempt such job seeking by adjusting pay in advance). In a variation on longevity pay, the organization may provide retention bonuses to targeted employees. This is especially useful where downsizing is occurring. The uncertainty that often accompanies downsizing can lead to the more highly prized (and marketable) employees leaving. Unfortunately, most public organizations operate with a fixed pay scale system providing them with little flexibility in matters of wages and salary. Older workers possessed of critical skills can be retained through the use of phased retirement and deferred retirement option plans.

Retention can also be encouraged by making it part of the manager's duties. Where managerial bonuses are used, part of the bonus can be tied to retention rates (of good performers). These can be based on organizationally normed turnover rates with some adjustment to reflect the effect of employees the organization wants to keep compared to those it's happy to see leave.

Just as important as pay satisfaction in retaining employees is job satisfaction. Although pay is a component of overall job satisfaction, supervisory relations, coworker relations and working conditions, promotional and developmental opportunities, and the intrinsic value of the job itself are all factors. A mixture of these factors, especially those which are more difficult for other organizations to match (i.e., the nonfinancial) plays a key role in retention. By developing favorable perceptions of the job and organization, employee retention can be enhanced (Rusbult, Farrell, Rogers, and Mainous, 1988; Coff, 1997).

Organizational trust (which is the foundation for the motivating organizational citizenship behavior) is an important factor in retention. It focuses first and foremost on the first-line supervisor. Training managers (and eliminating those who fail to learn) is the primary step an organization can undertake in encouraging the retention of high-performing employees.

Similarly, the elimination of poor performers (who continue to fail after extensive developmental efforts) can also serve to enhance the retention of high performers. Resources freed from poor performers can be used to hire new people more likely to produce. The sense of belonging to a meaningful and productive organization is in itself a retention factor. The tolerance for poor performers dissipates that esprit de corps.

Reemployment

With the more fluid work environment that has begun to emerge, the question of rehiring former workers arises. In the recent past, most organizations shied away from or even prohibited reemployment. Workers who had left the organization were deemed to be disloyal. Because organizations can no longer assure their workers reciprocal loyalty (and job security), the decision to rehire or not needs to be examined on a case-by-case basis.

Reemploying a former worker has both advantages and disadvantages. On the plus side, the "new" employee really does know what the organization is about and is very likely to fit in with its organizational culture and climate. The rehired worker will need less time to learn the job and, hence, will be a full contributor to the organization's productivity sooner. It is, of course, important to verify this through an examination of previous performance appraisals as well as discussions with former supervisors and colleagues (Frazure, 1997).

A specific concern lies in assessing the reason the employee originally left. Have those conditions sufficiently changed so that a repeat episode is unlikely? Obviously, those unable or unwilling to meet the expectations of the job are not desired. A returned employee may also help spread the word that things are not all that better elsewhere; he or she may actually serve to discourage turnover by giving others a realistic view of "life on the other side."

Reemployment also raises some serious equity concerns. Will the rehired employee obtain pay and promotion considerations (due to enhanced training and development received in the other job) that put him or her ahead of those employees who were loyal and stayed. If professional advancement and development is better obtained by leaving, this will have a negative morale effect on employees. Ultimately, the decision to rehire must be based on the benefits it brings to the organization (Frazure, 1997).

Promotional Opportunities

Retention of valued employees may hinge on the availability of "promotional opportunities." These may be, as traditionally thought of, increases in rank and pay grade or enhanced responsibility and locus of control over the job. Equity considerations suggest that every position be open to all applicants with the "best" being selected. On the other hand, restricting some positions to qualified insiders (agency-only, department-wide, or government-wide candidate fields) creates an incentive for retention. Restricted recruiting can also be speedier than the full blown, open search.

Even in the case of an open search, current (or former) employees may be given some form of "preference." In essence, current employees receive treatment similar in nature to veteran's preference. Having established their passing qualifications, employees may be awarded bonus points on the examination (thereby placing higher on the list of eligibles) or even receive an absolute preference (with all current employees automatically ranked above any outsiders). The use of absolute preferences is not really recommended as it may prove far too restrictive and hurt the overall quality of the public workforce.

TESTING

The crux of the staffing endeavor is testing. Although recruitment may bring candidates into the organization, only testing can enable it to sort through those individuals. Testing matches individual skills to job requirements. It is the life spirit of the effective organization. Without this linkage, talent can waste away and jobs be boggled. Effective testing puts the right person in the right place at the right time.

Drawing on the same job analysis that defines "what is to be done," testing designs measurement instruments to assess those capabilities. Hence, all tests are endeavors in forecasting individual potential. As with any forecast, tests are subject to a wide array errors. In fact, testing compounds these. Because the job description itself is prone to error (an imperfect picture of the job), efforts at measuring the potential performance of someone derived from this job description passes those errors on and, in addition, contributes to them.

Objects of Measurement

In the haste to test candidates to fill vacant jobs, O. Glenn Stahl (1976) reminds us not to ignore the fact that different tests can measure different things. The myriad of tests that we have available for our use are neither interchangeable with one another nor a linear combination that can simply be added together. Each test has a specific object of measurement—a distinct dimension.

Although some tests are indeed designed as alternative measurement instruments, many are designed to measure independent factors. To do well on one test carries with it no implication for doing well on another. More important, the scores from these tests share in common only the fact that they are numbers.

Yet, organizations are wont to add these scores together. This makes as much sense as adding a person's height, waist size, and weight together and calling the result the person's volume. The result is a number, but it is meaningless.

We have tests designed to measure an individual's general potential (aptitude), specialized potential (abilities), actual performance (achievement), health, physique, and dexterity (physical), and emotional stability and psychological stress (personality). Each can provide valid, job-related information. They can help in the selection of a candidate to fill a position. However, they must be used with appropriate care.

Tests

Tests come in a wide variety of forms and serve many different purposes. Some purport to measure the same or similar qualities; others focus on completely different objects. Alongside those tests commonly used and accepted are a rash of neophyte and neolithic instruments. Separating the new technique from the fashionable dross is not an easy task.

Individual tests are judged in terms of their job-relatedness (validity-reliability), cost-effectiveness, and perceived fairness. However, organizations almost always use tests in conjunction with one another. Organizations use tests serially by employing them to winnow the applicant pool to a manageable size. Tests are also used side by side, especially those measuring different objects, to put together a multidimensional picture of the candidates. When a number of tests are used in conjunction, decisions must be made as to whether each test has a minimum score required or the extent to which good performance on one will compensate for poor performance on another (McKinney, 1987).

Test validity is the ability of a specific test to predict successful job performance. Reliability is an indicator of the consistency of that test score on "repeated" measures. Validity is measured in terms of correlational scores that are seldom larger than $r = .50$ (i.e., the variation explained by the test is only .25). Work samples (.54), general mental ability tests (.51), structured interviews (.51), and assessment center (.36) are among the better tests in use (U.S. Merit Systems Protection Board, 2000: 16). Hence, the use of multiple tests is encouraged.

The Americans with Disabilities Act has sharpened the focus in the selection process. Its emphasis on essential responsibilities has added legal authority to employing correct job analysis techniques that more precisely or clearly define job-relatedness issues. The ADA also introduces the notion of reasonable accommodation. Flexibility rather than rigidity has always been desired by managers in filling positions. As long as individuals can do the "job," how they ethically do it makes little difference.

Reasonable accommodation focuses on making facilities physically accessible, reassigning or redistributing marginal job functions, altering processes or modifying schedules, and providing special tools. Reasonable accommodation takes into account the size and resources of an organization; even so, most accommodations cost only a few hundred dollars. Organizations need not accede to the specific accommodation requested by an employee. However, they must demonstrate that an effort has been made to reach an accommodation (even when the employee has refused to accept it). Accommodations do not require redesigning jobs to eliminate essential responsibilities or shifting the performance of various duties to other employees. Organizations already do these things in other contexts (e.g., religious accommodations); now, the ADA extends a legal requirement that they be explored for the benefit of those with disabilities (Smith, 1998b).

From biodata, references, and peer assessments through written aptitude, ability, personality, and performance tests to interviews, assessment centers, and probationary appointments the organization has an extensive set of selection tools at its disposal. Figure 5.1 displays these various tests and assessments of their relative validity, fairness, and cost. As we work our way through this list, job-relatedness of the instruments tends to improve, but so do the costs. Fairness, on the other hand, is associated with the familiar; for the most part, it is the written tests that are presently most accepted (even though there are actually better tests available). As these other tests become more widely used, their perceived fairness should also improve (Rudner, 1992).

Biodata is the standard application form or resume. It is relatively inexpensive yet contains a wealth of basic information. It forms the basis for education and experience or training and experience tests. Credentials and degrees along with previous job experience are strong predictors of future job success (Warrenfeltz, 1989; Lavigna, 1992). Suitable candidates can be requested to submit supplemental applications in which they are asked to provide more details about what it is they actual did. These questions can, in fact, be structured around the skills, knowledge, and

Figure 5.1
Tests

Test	Validity	Fairness	Cost
1. Application			
Resume	moderate	moderate	low
Supplemental Application	high	moderate	low
2. References			
Letters of Recommendation	low	low	low
Background Check	moderate	low	moderate
3. Potential Intelligence			
Aptitude (General)	moderate	high	low
Abilities (Specific)	moderate	high	moderate
4. Personality			
Characteristics	moderate	low	low
Psychological	moderate	low	high
5. Performance			
Work Samples	high	high	moderate
Performance Appraisal	moderate	moderate	moderate
Peer Assessment	high	moderate	low
Assessment Center	high	moderate	high
6. Interviews			
Unstructured	low	moderate	high
Structured	high	moderate	high
7. Job Appointment			
Internship	high	low	moderate
Probationary Appointment	high	low	high

abilities that will be required in the new job. The biodata resume is the basis of federal "case examining."

Although standardized applications allow for the specification of desired job-related information, they may discourage candidates from applying. This is not desirable where tight job markets and star talent are involved. Hence, organizations should be willing to accept resumes (with formal "applications" requested only from those being called for interviews). In many cases, computer scanning programs such as the federal OPM Micro-computer Assisted Rating System (MARS) can process resumes almost as efficiently as application forms. They are extremely useful in verifying simple yes/no items. Advanced artificial intelligence programs (primarily word search techniques) still remain "experimental," requiring hands-on checking (U.S. Merit Systems Protection Board, 1999b).

Of course, this information must be verified or checked out. Depending on the depth of such checking, this can be a costly activity. However, formal reference or background checking can wait until the later stages of the selection process or until making a job offer (the job offer being conditional on "passing" the background check).

Job candidates should be requested to sign a waiver allowing for the conducting of a reference and/or background check. Information collected by third parties (e.g., private investigators or background-checking firms) for use in employment decisions is considered a "consumer report" and is subject to the provisions of the Fair Credit Reporting Act (FCRA) administered by the Fair Trade Commission. The FCRA requires informed consent, copies provided to an individual if they would result in an adverse action (giving the individual an opportunity to respond), the right to request a reinvestigation, and a second notice if the material is used in an adverse action.

Any check should focus solely on job-related areas and avoid anything of a personal nature. It is also advisable to obtain information only on the last five to seven years. Licenses and academic degrees should be verified. Besides education and employment history, reference checks can also examine identity (through social security and fingerprints), criminal convictions (including drug and driving offenses), civil records, and finances (credit reports may require a separate consent or waiver form). Background checks are a specialized service and can be economically (from $500 for basic professional checks to $2,000 for full comprehensive checks) contracted for from professional organizations (Herman, 1994: 145–160; Bradford, 1998; Smith 1998c).

Although still considered a somewhat "personal" matter, a background check should in conjunction with other preemployment tests screen for violence. Workplace and domestic violence equally affect employee well-being and an organization's productivity. Violence has no privileged "private life."

References or letters of recommendation are a hold over from the nineteenth century when they were a precondition for employment. Because they once exerted so much influence in the hiring process, job-related and privacy concerns abound (Aamodt, Bryan, and Whitcomb, 1993). Hence, today references are little used (except by academics who subject them to deconstruction) for any practical purpose.

They remain required almost solely as a legal safeguard against negligent hiring claims. As such, reference and background checks (as a post-offer condition of employment) are highly recommended, and an organization actually has a positive requirement (failure to do so is prima facia evidence of negligence) to conduct such a check with respect to safety-sensitive positions. References from a previous employer are usually expected to be included. The failure by that employer to mention any serious concerns (which most avoid doing out of fear of slander and liable charges) makes them responsible in the event of a later negligent-hiring lawsuit. Some thirty states are now granting employers "good faith" exemptions (unfortunately, not yet validated through court litigation) in order to provide preventive measures against such negligent actions (Ryan and Lasek, 1991; Kinard and Renas, 1991; Walter, 1992; Baskin, 1998a, 1998b; Smith 1998c; Terpstra, Kethley, Foley, and Limpaphayom, 2000).

Peer assessments (often as part of a 360-degree performance appraisal program) from among an employee's colleagues are used in a growing number of internal selections. Instead of just relying on the supervisory appraisals, the more complete knowledge of those with whom an individual works is queried. Since subordinate or employee relations is an important aspect of most jobs, especially those in the professional, knowledge organization, this information can provide invaluable insights into questions of organizational fit.

Written tests measuring aptitude, ability, personality, and performance abound. Aptitude tests focus on general measures of intelligence (e.g., the Intelligence Quotient [IQ] test, Scholastic Aptitude Test [SAT], and Graduate Record Examination [GRE]). Ability tests focus on specialized fields of knowledge (e.g., the Advanced GREs for various academic disciplines or foreign language tests). Ability tests are written for specific jobs (or sets of jobs). Because it costs virtually the same to develop a test, aptitude tests that can be administered to a greater number of people are more "cost-effective" than ability tests that are designed only for those applying for the specific jobs. Of course, inasmuch as the ability tests are better able to identify individuals who can perform the jobs well, they are usually more cost-effective in the long run.

Personality tests focus on emotional and psychological issues (e.g., the Edwards Personality Preference Scale [EPPS] or Minnesota Multiphasic Personality Inventory [MMPI]). Concern over workplace violence has given an added emphasis to the use of personality tests. Personality tests measure traits that need to be validated as job-related (Smith, 1998f). Integrity tests that are designed to assess the honesty of the applicant are also used. Integrity tests, however, only focus on protecting the organization from potentially dishonest employees; they do nothing to protect the public from dishonest employees who are working on behalf of the organization (Brumback, 1996).

Because personality tests focus on questions of mental health, American society finds their use somewhat suspect. Although governments may need to establish a condition of substantial interest as with the safety-sensitive positions in law enforcement, these tests can be important aids in the selection process. Where the lives of others are involved, an individual's emotional stability and ability to handle psychological stress are not solely matters of privacy.

Performance tests measure actual achievement. Basically, they are exercises in work sampling. Health, dexterity, or other tests of physical ability (which can be job-related for police and firefighters) fall into this category as well (Hughes, Ratliff, Purswell, and Hadwiger, 1989; Arvey, Nutting, and Landon, 1992; Hoover, 1992; Hogan and Quigley, 1994). These tests, of course, are subject to close job-relatedness supervision under the Americans with Disabilities Act. If used for the purpose of selection, it is important that the tests focus more on capabilities than on injury reduction behaviors (Landy, 1998; Smith, 1998e). They test individuals' overall ability to do a job by engaging them in the performance of some of the specific skills they will need to use. The ability to do a job is basically tested by doing the job—if only briefly.

Interviews are ubiquitous to the selection process. Everyone uses them, and most do so poorly. They are considered so common and ordinary that most organizations don't bother training individuals in how to conduct a selection interview (outside a list of the legal do's and don'ts). This has led many to reject their use. Yet, the selection interview can be a highly valid instrument when properly used (Eders and Ferris, 1989; Herman, 1994; Graves and Karren, 1996).

The interview is unique among tests in that it is actually a dual test. While the organization is testing the individual, the individual is also testing the organization. Hence, interviews should be conducted as part test and part recruitment. This recruitment aspect can put an unusual spin on the process. Although supervisors and managers may be used to asking candidates if they have any questions, they are not used to candidates actually questioning them. Many are unable to respond immediately or even to provide the requested information later. Others react as if they have either been insulted or had their authority challenged.

An interview tests for oral presentation skills. The modern knowledge organization requires this of every employee. If employees are to work together on teams, they must be able to communicate effectively with one another. When problems arise, the appropriate, professional employee rather than a designated spokesperson needs to address it. Only an employee involved in an issue can understand the importance and implications of technical questions. Only such an employee can provide assurances that the problem will be dealt with.

Interviews are often included as the final test in a selection process. Hence, at this stage all the candidates still under consideration are deemed capable of performing the job. With the advent of total quality management approaches, the organization is not looking for someone who can merely fill a role but for a person who gives a "performance." Many feel that only in an interview can they recognize that "star" quality. What is tested, then, is the organizational fit or teamwork (Bowen, Ledford, and Nathan, 1991).

Effective interviews are structured. Although they still serve as a recruitment instrument, they are designed to test an individual on questions related to the job performed. In fact, this focus on relevant job dimensions also aids in attracting the interest of desired candidates. A structured interview assures that candidates can be compared to one another. Not only is each candidate asked job-related questions, but they are all asked the same questions (Baker and Spier, 1990; Daniel and Valencia, 1991; Lowry, 1994; Herman, 1994; Rosse and Levin, 1997).

Interviews are structured around questions designed to elicit examples of how they have previously handled problems or how they would hypothetically deal with them. A patterned behavior description interview (PBDI) uses past performance to forecast future potential. The situational interview asks the candidate to respond to hypothetical cases. This transforms the biodata material on education and experience into information specifically related to the job and responsibilities being interviewed for (Stohr-Gillmore, Stohr-Gillmore, and Kistler, 1990; Gabris and Rock, 1991). The job analysis guides in the selection of appropriate questions (Goodale, 1989; Herman, 1994).

Structured interviews are based on thorough job analyses from which a series of structured questions are formulated. They are designed around both job-related tasks and personal characteristics. The STAR—situation, tasks, action, and results—method (used by Innovative Management Concepts) demonstrates the process. Individuals are asked to describe or give an example of a specific situation. They are then asked "what tasks needed to be performed?" followed by "what actions did you actually take?" The method finishes with an overview of the results. The answers to these questions are benchmarked against answers obtained from employees who have successfully completed similar tasks. Hence, personal characteristics can be validly judged in addition to task accomplishment.

In addition to answering specific job-related questions and assessing organizational fit, an interview can lead to judgments on a candidate's motivation or willingness to perform the job and his or her overall suitability. Although global impressions of a candidate's overall suitability may focus on important ethical dimensions, they are more likely to lead one to founder on personality characteristics and other biases (Goodale, 1989: 311–312).

The interview can also be influenced by extraneous factors as well. Ethnic and gender differences may be highlighted instead of or despite job-related qualifications. Similarly, the physical attractiveness of the applicant may exert an influence (McDaniel, Whetzel, Schmidt, and Mauer, 1994; Cesare, 1996).

Preliminary telephone interviews, in addition to aiding in sorting through a large field of candidates in a cost-effective manner, can mitigate the influence of these extraneous factors. One tends to pay more attention to what is said (and "hear" it better) in a telephone interview. Without the inhibition that note taking can create in a physical-presence interview, the interviewer or interview team (conference calls readily enable such an assemblage—although an added effort must be made to identify who is speaking at any given time) is free to take notes. Telephone interviews set the stage for later, more complex, physical interviews.

In conducting the interview, the first step is preparation. The interviewer or, better yet, interview panel should review the position's job responsibilities and familiarize themselves with or write the structured questions. They also need to examine the application forms or resumes of the candidates prior to the interview. This will enable the interviewers to avoid irrelevant questions or asking for information they already have. It will also allow them the opportunity to seek elaboration or clarification (Goodale, 1989: 316; Herman, 1994: 133–138).

A panel is preferable to a single interviewer. It provides differing professional perspectives while safeguarding the decision process from the affects of individual biases.

The interview itself starts with efforts to put the candidate at ease. A general overview of the position and the organization often serves this purpose. Next, the candidate is allowed to ask his or her questions. This more freely elicits the candidate's concerns, uncolored by attempts to fit or respond to the perceived panel agenda. The questioning itself should be designed to let the candidate speak as much as possible. Active listening skills along with adequate periods of silence (thinking does take time) should be employed.

When a structured interview format is used, it should not be in the form of a rigid checklist or straitjacket approach. Although all items are to be eventually covered, the conversation can be allowed to flow more naturally.

Even though evaluation occurs during the interview itself, the interviewer or panel must take care not to make written notes at this time. Writing will distract the candidate and make him or her more self-conscious. Time should be allotted immediately after the interview for a written assessment. The same assessment form should be used for all candidates. The evaluation of the candidate must also distinguish between what an individual is capable of doing and what he or she is willing to do. Motivation is just as important as capability (Kaufman, 1960; Goodale, 1989: 317–320; Herman, 1994: 138–143).

Nowhere in the recruitment process should the organization attempt to solicit information that is suspect. Such information tends to pertain to matters that are not job-related and have been prohibited by law. Interviews are particularly vulnerable due to the often untrained interviewers and the lack of a written record. Suspect information includes personal and physical characteristics (including ethnic identity); anything that can be used to determine age, marital status, or family responsibilities; general questions about an individual's health; or salary history (Vodanovich and Lowe, 1992; Herman, 1994: 83–86).

Although the consideration of internal candidates should be encouraged in the selection process, additional expenses are imposed. Internal candidates are "on the clock" (i.e., being paid) while they are interviewing. Because an excessive amount of internal interviewing can adversely affect productivity, some added steps are necessary. First, the interview process can be monitored to minimize wasted time. This benefits everyone—internal and external candidates as well as those conducting the interviews. Second, before setting up an internal interview, the candidate's supervisor should be consulted as to his or her job performance. This has the added advantage of reenforcing current job performance as an important criterion in advancement.

Although the assessment center has more value as a tool for employee development, it can also be used as a selection test. The assessment center assembles a group of candidates together. Each candidate's performance is evaluated on predetermined criteria or standards based on the position's job analysis. Although measured against a set of standards, the candidates are, to some extent, directly competing with one another as well. This sense of competition adds intensity and motivation to the exercises (Yeager, 1986; O'Hara and Love, 1987; Lowry, 1996).

An assessment requires that each candidate be observed by one or more assessors. Ideally, each assessor is assigned to observe two (or, at most, three) candidates during each exercise. Assessors are rotated among the candidates in the other exercises. Even though the assessors are professionals drawn from the organization, each assessor is provided training in exactly what it is he or she will be looking for in each exercise (Lowry, 1988, 1991, 1992, 1993, 1996; Pynes and Bernardin, 1992).

As it can clearly be seen, assessment centers consume substantial resources. Their cost-effectiveness becomes evident in their validity. Even so, the costs tend to limit their use to managerial and upper-level professional positions (Olshfski and Cunningham, 1986). To run an assessment center, facilitators and consultants must be contracted for. Although public sector assessors often serve without pay (their organizations do absorb the costs of their "lost" time), assessor fees can cost $100–$150 per day (with another $50 toward incidental, logistic expenses). Overall, an assessment center can cost around $350 per candidate (Lowry, 1996). However, there are cases where the employment of assessment centers in the selection of entry-level positions may be justified (Coulton and Feild, 1995).

The assessment center is actually a collection of tests or exercises that mimic or simulate job activities. In an assessment center, the candidates must demonstrate the same skills, knowledge, and abilities as are required for performing the job. Assessment centers usually include leaderless group, in-basket, employee coaching, and other "business" or practical "hands-on" exercises. Developmental assessment centers will also include a personality profile.

The leaderless group exercise provides the assembled candidates with a realistic task and requires them to reach joint agreement on a proposed course of action. It tests an individual's assertiveness and group-management skills. Assessors look at how individuals influence one another and exert leadership through listening and negotiation skills.

The in-basket exercise provides each candidate with a series of realistic memos and reports. They are then expected to sort through this stack of material and respond accordingly. Of course, there is always more material than can be dealt with in the allotted time. As such, an in-basket is a time-management exercise in planning and organizing. An in-basket exercise can assess decisiveness, willingness to delegate, and judgment. It can also examine the extent to which an individual voluntarily adheres to management control.

Employee coaching exercises are designed to measure the interpersonal skills of the candidates. They assess a candidate's skills in communications, leadership, motivation, delegation, and decision making.

Additional "business" games can be constructed to test other dimensions involved in a job. These reflect specific tasks or skills that are required. Role-playing exercises are commonly used (Kaman and Bentson, 1988). The in-basket may include memo writing as a method of examining written communication skills. The leaderless group or a separate, short oral presentation may be used to assess speaking ability.

In developmental assessment centers, personality profiles (e.g., Performax or Myers-Briggs) are administered. However, these are not designed for use in selection! The personality profile provides candidates with insights regarding their attention to detail, capacity for handing ambiguity, decisiveness, desire for precision, ease of interpersonal interactions, need for rules and structure, and risk taking.

Personality profiles are clinical instruments. It is important that they be used by trained counselors and in conjunction with suitable follow-up, developmental opportunities. Although various profiles categorize individuals into assorted personality types, the scores on which these categorizations are based usually don't demonstrate such clear-cut dichotomies. They serve to focus an individual's attention on strengths and weaknesses that can, in turn, be enhanced or compensated for.

The probationary appointment is the last form of exam reviewed here. It is the most expensive; it is also the most valid. Essentially, an individual is tested by doing the job. Unlike a performance test, this is not a sampling of work skills or a short-term experiment. Probationary periods usually run from six months to a year (the academic tenure cycle is seven years). At the end of that period, a decision is made whether to grant permanent status to the employee (Elliott and Peaton, 1994).

Because probationary appointments carry with them the implication of permanency, they have not proven as effective as they should. The probationary employee is still an employee and benefits from a sense of the group loyalty. There is also the dread of having to admit that a mistake was made and one needs to start the process anew. This has lead to the use of temporary appointments, special assignments, cooperative education, apprenticeships, and internships as selection tests (Taylor, Giannantonio, and Brown, 1989; Riccucci, 1991).

Most organizations have a legitimate need to fill certain positions on a temporary basis. In doing so, they also have the opportunity to more thoroughly observe an individual and assess his or her potential for other or future permanent slots.

An internship is perhaps an even better test. Internships are arranged so that the student already comes to the organization with some professional skills. The organization helps refine these skills and provide the student with practical insights. Finally, the intern returns to complete his or her education (and share insights with fellow classmates and professors). Although interns hope that their internship may lead to a job opportunity, each has a built-in termination date.

There are some additional benefits to internships. Because this is an educational experience, interns can be paid less than a full professional staff member. More important, internships help establish relationships with professional programs. These collegial networks can be useful not only for recruitment but for managerial advice in general.

Exam Administration

The business of testing requires attention to detail. The simple mechanics of conducting examinations can greatly influence their results. Ultimately, the entire recruitment and selection process can be affected.

Tests must be prepared. An organization has to decide what kinds of exams it wants to use and how many different positions it will need exams for. These must then be either designed or purchased. Designing exams requires expertise. Even in purchasing exams, the organization must know what to request and how to assess it.

Once the exams have been acquired, the organization must institute policies designed to assure their security. Given the "prize" that is to be won by these exams, they are assets on par with bearer bonds. Fairness (not to mention perceptions of organizational competence) require test security.

Test security begins with the development of the exams themselves. The material and information used in the preparation of exams must be protected. Just as voter fraud requires ballot security provisions, the exams also need protection prior, during, and after their use. In discarding old exams, consideration must be given to their potential "usefulness" in preparing individuals for future exams (would possession of an old exam give an individual an unfair advantage over those without such access?). Although developmental feedback on the results of an exam is important for the individual, the release of this information can also compromise or limit the useful life of the exam (Kovalski, 1997).

Failure at any point in this process can undermine an organization's appearance of fairness and competence. More important, it can pervert the selection process. Not only can the organization be led to hire a less qualified individual, but it is also hiring someone who is quite willing to engage in unethical conduct in obtaining his or her personal goals.

In administering exams, decisions must be made on when and where. How often should exams be offered? When during the week should they be administered? Where should the tests be held? Who should pay for the cost of exams?

Exams should be offered frequently enough to guarantee that an adequate supply of candidates is available to fill anticipated openings. On the other hand, if offered too frequently, the lists of applicants will swell beyond reasonableness. If offered infrequently, the lists will be inadequate and out-of-date.

If exams are only offered Monday through Friday between 9:00 A.M. and 5:00 P.M., are working individuals discouraged or penalized? Many individuals may not be able to take time off from work (or have employers who would look askance at such behavior). Evening or weekend exams can help in making the testing process more convenient and open to all citizens.

Where are exams held? What is their physical location and how accessible is it? Organizations can facilitate the testing process by scheduling exams in a wide variety of locations. This is true just as much for a city as it is for a state or national government. Accessibility is another important factor. Having tests offered at different locations is futile if it is difficult for many people or segments of the population to get there. It is also important that each testing center also have whatever specialized equipment may be needed.

Exams cost money to produce and administer. Should those costs be absorbed by the personnel budget or underwritten from other revenue sources? Specifically, should agencies be charged—in full or only for special requirements—for the internal services they use? Should job applicants be assessed a fee? The value of additional revenue, even if it is directly deposited into the general fund, is clear. Offsetting this is that the answers to these questions can all affect the number and quality of applicants (Coffee, 1996; 1998).

While applicant fees can provide much-needed revenue in the form of user fees retained by the agency or contributions to the general fund, they can also be employed to discourage individuals from not showing up for scheduled exams. No-shows are a substantial problem and expense in many jurisdictions. If the purpose is solely reducing the number of no-shows, these fees can be refunded to those who take the examinations. Provisions can also be established to waive fees for those who cannot afford them (Coffee, 1996; 1998).

Finally, tests must be scored. What "scores" will be used? Will the exam be graded with numeric ratings (1 to 100, 200 to 800, etc.) or categories (adjective descriptions, pass/fail, letter grades, letters with plus/minus, etc)? Is there a "minimum passing score"? Most tests use a minimum passing score; it represents a determination that certain basic skills or performance standards are necessary if the job is to be done right. This scoring not only affects perceptions of merit but involves equal employment opportunity concerns as well (McKinney and Collins, 1991).

How reliable is each exam? In other words, how much can we count on it to give us a good reading of an individual's abilities. If more than one exam is used (either measuring the same thing or different objects), how are they to be combined? Exams can be set up as a series of elimination contests. An individual must pass one exam before moving on to the next. For large numbers of applicants, more general and less expensive tests can be used to winnow the crowd down and, thereby, save on the costs associated with administering the more expensive but more valid exams. Alternatively, scores can be added together. If added together, will the exams be weighted (some given added importance, others less)? Does each separate exam require a minimum score? To what extent can an individual use the results from one test to compensate for a poor showing on another?

SELECTION

Recruitment and testing are the opening and middle game in the staffing process; the endgame comes when an individual is selected to fill a position. Until the deal is closed, the efforts at staffing remain incomplete. Successful methods for attracting candidates and exceptionally valid and fair exams for identifying the most suitable are wasted investments if the wrong choice is made.

Certification

A list of eligibles is certified by the central personnel authority. This is a carryover from the days when the civil service required heavy monitoring to protect the government from patronage appointments and assure the public of fair competition for jobs. It is used far less today than is often realized. Concerns about test validity and the decentralization of personnel functions has led many agencies to substitute individual case examining for a centralized list of eligibles.

The certification of a list of candidates from which an agency can hire is a traditional aspect of the staffing process. It enables a centralized recruiting process to serve numerous agencies. Individuals can take one set of exams and, if eligible, be referred for jobs in a wide variety of agencies and locations.

The famous "rule of three" wherein the top three names or individuals would be certified upon an agency's submission of a request to fill a position originated as a legal opinion for assuring the constitutionality of the civil service system. The president's power to appoint was assured by allowing him three candidates to choose from (U.S. Attorney General, 1871).

Over the years, various other schemes have been employed varying the number of individuals (from five to ten) included on the list of eligibles sent over to an agency. Certifying all individuals in the top three to ten scores or categories (since there are numerous ties) is also used. In some instances, the top 10 or 15 percent of those passing the exam are certified; where demand is particularly heavy and all individuals are likely to receive job offers, the entire list may be block-certified. Large, economical lists may also be culled in a selective certification in which additional requirements are used.

Somewhat overlooked in the certification process are the changes that are rapidly transforming it. Although designed to assure fairness, central certification has also been a major factor delaying hiring. The safeguards instituted as protections lengthen the process inordinately and often result in the loss of the top candidates to other organizations. The knowledge organization can afford neither such delays nor having to settle for second choices (U.S. Merit Systems Protection Board, 1995).

The percentage of federal employees hired through central certification by the Office of Personnel Management or by larger agencies allowed to operate their own personnel offices declined from over half in 1984 to just over a third in 1992. Today, all federal hiring-related tasks are decentralized; OPM involvement is often as a contract provider. In federal agencies, delegated examining units (DEU) now exercise the personnel-hiring tasks. Case-examining methods in which the specific agency with the job vacancy takes responsibility has been on the rise. Under case examining, the specific job is analyzed and a "test," most often an education and experience examination of the resume, is conducted. Direct hiring authority along with internal selection (including selection from among temporary employees) now account for over half the employees hired. Another eighth enter the civil service through the outstanding scholar (undergraduate minimum GPA of 3.5 or graduate in top 10 percent of the class) and cooperative education route (U.S. Merit Systems Protection Board, 1994a, 1994b, 2000; Ban, 1997).

These changes mark a trend toward decentralization and allowing agencies greater flexibility over hiring. They are driven by the professional needs facing those charged with staffing governmental organizations. In the federal government, decentralization is felt to have increased the quality of hires by speeding up what was seen as an overly slow and long process. The old centralized process was a major impediment in hiring qualified individuals (U.S. Merit Systems Protection Board, 1999b).

Decentralization is seen to have some disadvantages. The economy of scale and "fairness" inherent in the old "single-source" centralized system is missed by many. More important, sufficient training in personnel techniques has not always accompanied the delegation of hiring responsibility. Nor have budgets been adjusted to contract for these services. In the federal system, the "merit promotion procedures" that govern internal hiring free agencies from the restraints of the "rule of three," veteran's preference, and candidate-ranking requirements (U.S. Merit Systems Protection Board, 1999b, 2000; Kellough, 1999).

Even greater flexibility is found in other systems such as the Canadian Public Service. Concerns for fairness are addressed by requiring each candidate to be informed of the reasons for the selection decision and allowing the appeal of that decision (U.S. Merit Systems Protection Board, 1992).

Extra-Merit

The testing process upon which certification is based is not precise. Although the numeric scores associated with all forms of tests imply a scientific precision, there is much illusion in the process. Even here, there are numerous cases in which tie scores result. In dealing with this and other factors not addressed by testing itself, extra-merit considerations are resorted to. Affirmative action, geographic location, and veteran's preference (with additional consideration for disabled veterans and including widows and spouses of injured veterans) are the three most well known extra-merit applications.

All factor into the hiring equation the political need to assure all citizens access to public jobs or, as is the case with veteran's preference, serve as a compensation or reward for military service. Veteran's preference has also served as an indicator of loyalty ever since the administration of George Washington. President Washington also began the use of geographic preferences to assure that individuals from New England, the Mid-Atlantic, and the South were all included in the new government.

All extra-merit provisions require that the candidate first meet the basic eligibility requirements for a position. In no case can any extra-merit provisions be used if the individual is unqualified or fails to meet the minimum passing score. Geographic preferences are often ensured simply by limiting the area coverage of the list of eligibles. Federal and state public services separate themselves into employment regions. Veteran's preference adds points to the final score or, in some cases, still requires "absolute" preference wherein all eligible veterans must receive a job offer or decline one prior to hiring any nonveteran (Elliott, 1986; Tummala, 1987).

Gamesmanship

The staffing process from recruitment to selection is overly cumbersome. Techniques separately designed to improve objectivity or assure fairness when combined create a quagmire (Wamsley, 1997). Hence, officials intent on finding the best person to fill a vacant position and help them with the tasks of government have discovered numerous means for short-circuiting or gaming the system. Although this is done for the purpose of expediently providing effective public services, it can also be subject to the abuse of buddy systems and cronyism (U.S. Merit Systems Protection Board, 1989; Ban, 1995, 1997).

A series of practices often identified with the "Malek Manual" (U.S. Senate Select Committee on Presidential Campaign Activities, 1974), which gave them more open notoriety, outline how appointed or civil service officials can get around the rules governing personnel selection. Associated with the Watergate scandal and the Nixon administration's reintroduction of the administrative presidency strategy, the use of these techniques carries negative connotations.

Rather above board is the practice of "name request." This is an open call that a specifically named individual be certified as eligible for a particular job. More subtle is the practice of "job tailoring" or "spinning the register." In this case a position description is drafted from the resume of the individual one desires to hire. Although the process may be directed by a central personnel office (where certification registers are employed), it will still call upon the agency itself for the input of subject matter experts. When the formal testing and selection process is carried out, the desired individual should easily qualify for consideration. The use of education and experience exams (which are scored off of the resume) and agency direct-hiring authority facilitate the process.

A list of eligibles is also open to manipulation. Because all lists lapse (so as to eliminate individuals no longer seeking employment), hiring can be delayed (or speeded up as the case may be) in order to enhance a preferred individual's chances. For a preferred candidate ranked lower on the list of eligibles, a number of tricks are available. A "realistic" preview can be employed to "solicit declinations" from individuals ranked higher. The list can further be worked by arranging for a buddy or buddies to make similar requests. This will temporarily remove the top names from active consideration elsewhere (permitted for reasons of efficiency). Following the selection, the other requested names will be returned and again take their place at the top of the general list.

Finally, an organization may resort to the use of special hiring practices. Individuals may be externally employed as consultants or through the contracting out of services. Privatization puts one outside most of the civil service rules (hence, a patronage threat may exist). Internally, the agency can hire individuals under emergency provisions, as temporary employees (less than a year), or as part-time workers (up to thirty-six hours per week, plus overtime). The experience gained in the job helps qualify an individual to compete if the position is made permanent.

ORIENTATION

Many would consider the staffing process as completed at this point; it is not. The purpose of recruitment and selection is to put a person on to the job. It is not complete until an employee has successfully completed his or her orientation to the organization and the work (Allen and Meyer, 1990; Ostroff and Kozlowski, 1992).

Orientation begins immediately with an employee's acceptance of the job offer. Employees will wonder if they have made the right decision; a proactive effort at welcoming them even before their first day helps alleviate this anxiety. This time period is also useful for providing detailed information on benefits and other complicated (and often irreversible) start-up, enrollment decisions. Community and family needs should also be considered.

Orientation should be more than signing up for payroll and making the benefit decisions required. Orientation reduces employee anxiety associated with starting a new job. Organizationally, orientation enhances productivity in that it establishes performance expectations early and helps the employee rapidly develop the appropriate job skills. Ideally, it will involve some general introduction to the organization and its culture. Executive orientation often begins with a stint in the central office in order to provide the individual with a strategic perspective. This is followed by rotation through each of the core or cognate line and staff functional areas before beginning the assignment at the post for which he or she was specifically hired.

This orientation process is repeated, in miniature, within the agency unit itself. In some organizations, each new employee will be assigned an advisor (or, in a misuse of the term, a mentor) to assist in answering questions. Orientation should both welcome individuals to the team and provide them with Q&A sheets, form examples, and other aids to ease them into the workforce.

SUMMARY

Strategic human resource management advocates an active and positive approach to recruiting for government and nonprofit positions. Recognizing the importance individuals make in achieving success, an organization cannot passively wait for the right people to descend like some *deux ex machina.* Legal requirements related to equal employment opportunity and the practical reality of a growingly diverse workforce add to this pressure for action. An organization needs to focus on the appropriate labor markets that "contain" the talent it is seeking and then proceed aggressively in getting those individuals to apply for positions.

Testing is essential if individual and position are to be successfully matched, and ultimately the achievement of the agency's goals and objectives obtained. Because different tests are designed to measure different objects and no test exhibits extraordinary validity, multiple tests are preferred in order to enhance the odds of a successful hire. However, this testing must be balanced in terms of both its cost-effectiveness and the perception of fairness. In addition to the tests themselves, the mechanics of their administration can affect the selection process. How often and where tests are offered as well as the security necessary to assure fairness can all influence the candidate pool seeking employment.

Although selection is strategically focused on hiring the individual most capable of performing the specific job, many organizations piggyback other purposes onto this process. Extra-merit affirmative action, geographic, and veteran's preference requirements have been attached to the selection process. Given the added concerns that arise from the moderate predictive validity of many of the exams employed in the selection process, supervisors and managers are also likely to engage in acts of gamesmanship or the netherworld tactics in their attempt to secure the best hires possible. Finally, the selection process is not complete until the individual has successfully been oriented to the new job.

chapter 6

Compensation

The high-involvement, knowledge-based organization can only achieve effectiveness if its compensation (pay and benefits) policies are in alignment (Lawler, 1990). The goals to be achieved must be supported with individual incentives for those meant to achieve them. Motivation theories clearly indicate that productivity is a composite "wage and effort" bargain.

Pay and benefits must be systematically tied to achieving an organization's purpose. It can no longer be dealt with as a separate issue (as is too often the case in the public sector). Although the separation of executive and legislative powers makes this task difficult, it is not insurmountable. Legislatures, besides granting the appropriations that fund pay systems, also create the organic statutes that spell out each organization's mission (and often the processes to be used in achieving them).

This chapter examines:

1. The concept of strategic pay as a means for achieving organizational goals
2. The techniques for determining organizational pay structures
3. The various pay-for-performance options used in strategic pay

The chapter also provides:

4. An overview of benefits systems
5. Knowledge of health care issues
6. Knowledge of retirement planning

STRATEGIC PAY

Strategic pay in the public sector faces a number of challenges. First, political leaders and the general public itself must move beyond the nineteenth-century, Jacksonian notion that government jobs are inherently simple tasks that anyone can perform. The clerical, night-watchman state of the agrarian nineteenth-century has been long replaced by one that calls for a knowledge-dependent, proactive partner in the industrial society. Government is no longer "relegated" to the role of a referee adjusting and balancing the actions of the major sectors of society. It is now called upon to be one of those major players itself. This role will only increase in importance as the twenty-first century highlights our growing interdependence with globalization and technology.

Second, governments must establish goals. Most efforts at productivity improvement fail because there is no agreed-upon meaning as to what is productivity. Legislatures and executives must go beyond general goals to establish measurable, qualitative and quantitative goals. To aid in their achievement, performance standards must be set like mileposts along a road. Finally, political leaders must then "stay the course," monitoring the progress toward achieving these objectives (Swiss, 1991).

Only when programs can be measured is it then possible to ascertain the efficiency and effectiveness with which they are carried out. All too often, we "bash the bureaucrat" when the fault actually lies in a failure to communicate "what is to be done." The incentives that are entailed in the strategic-pay concept can only work if they are harnessed to achieving an organizational strategy.

Attract, Retain, Motivate

Strategic compensation links all pay and benefits to attracting, retaining, and motivating employees. Some pay and most benefit options will be inflexible (i.e., equally provided to all employees); yet, these should be designed to aid in recruiting desired employees and for encouraging their continued commitment. Other pay options (e.g., the various pay-for-performance schemes) are flexible devices for motivating or enticing added effort.

Every manager and employee knows how important individuals are to success. Despite our machinelike analogies, the positions described with their listed responsibilities and requisite qualifications are not interchangeable parts. Recruitment and selection are among the most intensely studied and watched activities in administration. People make a difference.

Attracting those individuals and keeping them is the foremost ingredient in creating a successful organization. Adequate compensation is one of the factors that can attract individuals. Adequate compensation also helps retain them once they have been hired. A vacant position (or one filled with the wrong individual) is not costless. Work is not being done (or done poorly), and a mission is going unfulfilled. More important, by focusing individuals' attention on a desire for continued employment, it also focuses their attention on the long-term health and well-being of the organization (so it will be able to offer them that much desired continued employment).

Although public sector pay has often lagged behind that in the private sector, its benefits (especially the pensions, due process, and job security) have compensated for that in its ability to attract and retain employees. Because governments discriminate less than private sector companies, even their pay policies have often been attractive. Beginning in the 1980s, cost-control strategies and market-driven theories have been used to justify the reduction of public sector benefit packages without any commensurate adjustment in pay (Cayer, 1997).

Central to the strategic-pay concept is the use of pay to motivate. Because American society places such emphasis upon pay, extra pay options can be used to help focus individual attention and effort. Although total quality management proponents downplay the importance of individual differences (albeit even Deming never denied there were differences), they call for group incentives plans (such as are found in gain-sharing proposals).

Competitiveness

Research has placed greater emphasis on intrinsic motivation than it has on extrinsic rewards. This view is based, in part, on the assumption that pay would be relatively equal and, hence, not a competitive advantage. However, this assumption may not be met in some cases, and then pay can indeed be an advantage. While an extrinsic reward, pay is also an intrinsic item. In pay-for-performance systems, pay is an indicator of accomplishment. The amount of the extrinsic reward is an intrinsic recognition of achievement (Markman, 1997).

In approaching the concept of strategic pay, an organization must decide whether it wants to lead, meet, or lag the prevailing pay rates. The pay strategy chosen will influence how other pay information is interpreted (Weber and Rynes, 1991; Klass and McClendon, 1996). Although most public sector pay policies are based on a principle of uniformity, one size need not fit all. Different strategies may be pursued for different jobs. Jobs with different levels of difficulty (e.g., added technical or professional requirements) or in different areas that theoretically involve similar levels of difficulty can be treated separately.

The decision to lead the market in pay will serve to attract and retain the top candidates. However, these "hired guns" may leave as soon as another tops your offer. Even some leading private sector companies are reluctant to let money be their drawing card. They want the excitement and fun of working with their organization to take precedence (something that has always been in the forefront of public sector efforts).

For a public sector organization to lead the market also raises the specter of its distorting the market by unfairly driving up labor prices. Public organizations are just as deserving of good workers (who are also deserving of good wages) and can be just as, if not more, efficient as businesses in their use. However, in the United States preference is afforded private sector pursuits.

This argument is bolstered in that many government jobs are government jobs precisely because there is no private market for them. The necessity for a monopoly of services or security concerns may preclude private competition.

A decision to lag the pay market assumes there is a substantial unmet or captive demand (willing to settle for goods and services of a lesser quality). These jobs also are often more routine and less knowledge-intensive. In the public sector, such positions are often an on-the-job "residency" or internship that further adds to an individual's education. These jobs serve to qualify them for future, higher-paid positions.

Retention

Retention of desired workers focuses on managing turnover. Pay and job satisfaction are the key strategies involved. The pay package (salary/wages and benefits) must be deemed adequate for the employee's needs. Without a fair and equitable pay structure employees and their knowledge will exit the organization (Coff, 1997).

Pay flexibility can allow managers the ability to retain valued employees. This enables them to make counteroffers when an employee is offered a job elsewhere (or better yet to preempt such job seeking by adjusting pay in advance). In a variation on longevity pay, the organization may provide retention bonuses to targeted employees. This is especially useful where downsizing is occurring. The uncertainty that often accompanies downsizing can lead to the more highly prized (and marketable) employees leaving. Unfortunately, most public organizations operate with a fixed pay scale system providing them with little flexibility in matters of wages and salary. Older workers possessed of critical skills can be retained through the use of phased retirement and deferred retirement option plans.

Retention can also be encouraged by making it part of the manager's duties. Where managerial bonuses are used, part of the bonus can be tied to retention rates (of good performers). These can be based on organizationally normed turnover rates with some adjustment to reflect the effect of employees the organization wants to keep compared to those it's happy to see leave.

Just as important as pay satisfaction in retaining employees is job satisfaction. While pay is a component of overall job satisfaction, supervisory relations, coworker relations and working conditions, promotional and developmental opportunities, and the intrinsic value of the job itself are all factors. A mixture of these factors, especially those that are more difficult for other organizations to match (i.e., the nonfinancial) plays a key role in retention. By developing favorable perceptions of the job and organization, employee retention can be enhanced (Rusbult, Farrell, Rogers, and Mainous, 1988; Coff, 1997).

Social and Ethical Concerns

Strategic pay is also tempered by the very values society has created government to protect and foster. The public service is designed, in part, to be separate from the everyday economic world. Civil service structures foster a distinct public identity of true professionalism. Laws such as those that entail collective bargaining limitations and no-strike provisions also exclude public employees from normal economic remedies found in the market economy.

It is the duty of government to perform its job not only efficiently and effectively but responsibly. Every action undertaken by a government is symbolic. It is indeed the beacon guiding others to safety. Government must be a model employer.

The model employer responsibility entails numerous requirements. Governments must pay their employees a living wage as this is something our society values. It is being called upon to be in the forefront of family-friendly policies because the continuation of our society is dependent upon the existence of healthy families. Similarly, it is called upon to provide employees with health care benefits (just as it was a leader in introducing pensions). Governments are expected to set the example for nondiscrimination in hiring and employee practices. As Adam Smith recognized, all of these practices can distort the amoral, invisible hand of the economic market.

PAY STRUCTURE

Although pay and benefits can be dealt with on an individual or case-by-case basis, it is usually far better to provide a system that guides the application of specific pay policies. Not only does this limit the decision-making requirements (in terms of both effort and time), it greatly helps in establishing an image of equity and fairness. Compensation decisions are not simply single employer–employee transactions; they are part of and interact with an entire employment system.

The pay structure is the framework in which specific pay policies operate. It is used to guide the decisions on specific pay policies to assure that they are fulfilling the reward objectives attached to the organization's goals. Because benefits are provided to all employees virtually across-the-board, the main focus of the pay structure is the creation of an overall pay scale system (usually in conjunction with a position management system created through job analysis and evaluation).

Design and Administration

In creating a pay structure, specifically a pay scale system, thought must be given to the ease with which it can be administered, its perceived equity among employees, and its flexibility in handling differing conditions or circumstances. Administration, equity, and flexibility are, in fact, interrelated factors. Although compensation systems are subject to scores of federal and state laws, there still remain vast areas open to organizational choices.

The design of a pay structure must fit in with that organization's culture and climate. Just as rewards must be linked with the goals the organization desires to achieve, rewards for individuals or teams can only work if they exist in environments that encourage the appropriate effort whether individual or team. Individuals will not shine if rewards are granted across-the-board. Teams will not succeed if incentives are awarded to individuals.

Participation and communication are two important aspects in the design and administration of a pay structure. As is the case in all organizational matters, participation in the design of a pay structure enhances understanding of how it works and in conferring a sense of ownership makes it more acceptable to employees. Although separate from participation, communication also improves employee understanding of the reward structure. As part of a goal-setting approach, communication aids in concentrating employee efforts on the desired outcomes.

The extent that earnings are placed at risk is also a matter of design. The notion of strategic pay need not require that pay-for-performance schemes be employed. If an organization chooses to introduce individual or group incentives, it must decide on the mix or ratio of base pay (provided to all across-the board) and at-risk pay (extra-effort rewards). The appropriateness of these for the individuals and teams must be measured. Earnings-at-risk implies that individuals or teams possess the ability to sufficiently affect outcomes.

Flexible reward systems imply added managerial discretion and the ability to focus employee attention on goals. However, they may also be viewed as failing to provide enough security from arbitrary events. Base pay is not money thrown away. If it does not directly aid in motivation, it does serve to attract and retain. Base pay is indeed that—the secure foundation or base from which the employee has the security to launch or undertake more risky or problematic efforts. A mixture of flexible and inflexible pay and benefits is required in a successful organization.

Wage and Salary Surveys

Whether an organization relies upon internal or external equity considerations in designing its pay structure, it will resort to the use of wage and salary surveys. This is obvious for the case of organizations that employ external, market-based approaches. However, wage and salary surveys are also essential in internal equity studies. The market, even if only as a factor determining the cost of living, must be dealt with. Public sector organizations, for the most part, rely on internal equity approaches. They especially note public–private differences that place less attention on materialistic factors among public sector employees. However, the employees in most public agencies see their jobs as being not that much different from those in the private sector (Gabris and Simo, 1995).

Wage and salary surveys are indeed that—plural. Surveys of benchmark jobs are conducted in the appropriate labor markets—from local to national (if not international). The surveys are dependent upon the geographic scope necessary for a job search to elicit a sufficient number of applicants to ensure both the hiring of a successful candidate and the psychological confidence that this has indeed been done. Because this will vary from job to job, an organization will, most likely, require that more than one wage and salary survey be conducted. However, regardless of how many are necessary, they are conducted similarly.

Because it is impossible to check out the wages and salaries for every job within an organization, benchmarking is used. A stratified selection of jobs is chosen from all hierarchal levels and segments of the organization. This selection should include the most important or typical jobs (since comparable jobs need to be found in other organizations).

These jobs are linked to one another and the other jobs in an organization through the application of job evaluation. The information obtained on them through the wage and salary survey are used as benchmarks in guiding wage and salary decisions for the other jobs.

It is crucial that the jobs being used as comparative benchmarks are indeed comparable. Each is subject to a thorough job analysis. Job titles alone are not enough; one must be assured that all the tasks and responsibilities are shared between the jobs being compared.

Finally, information on wages and salaries is collected. In addition, full information on benefits should also be included. This is especially important for public sector jobs. Because politics has cast a cold shadow over "high" pay for public employees, benefits form a larger proportion of the total compensation package than is usually the case in the private sector.

Unfortunately, benefits information is not easily gathered and, more important, is quite difficult to interpret. The value of differing packages and their options poses infinite calculation problems. Differing coverage, deductibles, co-payments, and options paid for entirely by the employee (but benefiting from the organization's group status) make the benefits field one of exceeding complexity.

Although comparing jobs filled from local markets is rather easy (all one needs to do is to contact the organizations or the employment security office), comparability for professional positions poses some more serious challenges. With the growing dependence of organizations on the knowledge possessed by their workers, this is a challenge that will only increase in importance.

In some instances, national (and international) wage and salary information (including benefits) may be available from governmental sources or professional associations. For others, further searching is required. Because it is costly and impractical to seek out complete information from all similar jobs, a set of "peer institutions" or similar geographic areas is focused on. In this way, comparisons are limited to jobs that are drawing their talent from the same or similar labor pools (and are the institutions and areas most likely to appeal or attract those you are seeking to hire or retain).

Even so, differing cost-of-living factors need to be taken into account. Housing and food costs vary. Quality-of-life issues (such as schools and cultural activities) can also matter. A growing use of locality pay options by many organizations assists in calculating some of these adjustments.

Pay Scales

Traditionally, organizations calculate a pay scale that encompasses all positions within the organization. Job evaluation (based on the individual job analyses) is used to weave positions into an organizational fabric. Symbolically, this one pay scale serves to indicate the unity of purpose and contractual rights that all share. It is a vivid picture of the organization as a community.

The widespread use of pay scales originates with the Classification Act of 1923. The federal government adopted the use of job analysis and the classification or grading job evaluation technique (the term *classification* is still used to refer to the entire field). Jobs were studied and assigned to classes or sorted into grades. While these grades involve other matters, their primary association is with pay scales such as are displayed in Figure 6.1 for the federal General Schedule.

Figure 6.1
U.S. General Schedule

OPM U.S. Office of Personnel Management
2000 General Schedule*
(Not Including Locality rates of Pay)
Effective January 2000

Grade	Annual Rates for Steps (in dollars)									
	1	2	3	4	5	6	7	8	9	10
1	13,870	14,332	14,794	15,252	15,715	15,986	16,440	16,900	16,918	17,251
2	15,594	15,964	16,481	16,918	17,107	17,610	18,113	18,616	19,119	19,622
3	17,015	17,582	18,149	18,716	19,233	19,850	20,417	20,984	21,551	22,118
4	19,100	19,737	20,374	21,011	21,648	22,285	22,922	23,559	24,196	24,833
5	21,370	22,082	22,794	23,506	24,218	24,930	25,642	26,354	27,066	27,778
6	23,820	24,614	25,408	26,202	26,996	27,790	28,584	29,378	30,172	30,966
7	26,470	27,352	28,234	29,116	29,998	30,880	31,762	32,644	33,526	34,408
8	29,315	30,292	31,269	32,246	33,223	34,200	35,177	36,154	37,131	38,108
9	32,380	33,459	34,538	35,617	36,696	37,775	38,854	39,933	41,012	42,091
10	35,658	36,847	38,036	39,225	40,414	41,603	42,792	43,981	45,170	46,359
11	39,178	40,484	41,790	43,096	44,402	45,708	47,014	48,320	49,626	50,932
12	46,955	48,520	50,085	51,650	53,215	54,780	56,345	57,910	59,475	61,040
13	55,837	57,698	59,559	61,420	63,281	65;142	67,003	68,864	70,725	72,586
14	65,983	68,182	70,381	72,580	74,779	76,978	79,177	81,376	83,575	85,774
15	77,614	80,201	82,788	85,375	87,962	90,549	93,136	95,723	98,310	100,897

*Incorporating a 3.80% general increase.

A pay scale will have anywhere from five to a hundred distinct pay grades. Although the federal General Schedule uses fifteen grades, some such as that in North Carolina (see Figure 6.2) can have around fifty active grades. The minimum, starting salary in each grade should be from 10 to 15 percent above that in the immediately lower grade. In each grade, the range from minimum, starting salary to maximum pay level is between 25 and 30 percent. Each pay range is divided into ten to fifteen "merit" steps.

Because governments lacked provisions for cost-of-living adjustments, merit steps that were originally meant to reward performance very quickly became automatic, annual increases. The first four increments are granted at six-month intervals, and the last two at two-year intervals. Hence, it would take an individual twelve years to work his or her way through a pay range. Because employees were expected to receive promotions into similar, but more responsible jobs, an entire career could be encompassed in two or three grade levels. The

Figure 6.2
North Carolina State Government Salary Schedule

Viewed by Grade Ranges:
50–54, 55–59, 60–64, 65–69, 70–74, 75–79, 80–84, 85–90

Grade Range 50–54

Grade	Hiring Rate	Minimum	Midpoint	Maximum
50	$16,332	$17,067	$18,659	$20,986
51	$16,370	$17,103	$19,105	$21,839
52	$16,414	$17,150	$19,576	$22,738
53	$16,458	$17,196	$20,048	$23,637
54	$16,502	$17,242	$20,554	$24,606

Grade Range 55–59

Grade	Hiring Rate	Minimum	Midpoint	Maximum
55	$16,787	$17,446	$21,176	$25,564
56	$17,440	$17,793	$22,047	$26,653
57	$17,854	$18,480	$22,828	$27,801
58	$18,268	$19,181	$23,623	$28,978
59	$19,001	$19,951	$24,608	$30,214

Grade Range 60–64

Grade	Hiring Rate	Minimum	Midpoint	Maximum
60	$19,764	$20,752	$25,660	$31,555
61	$20,594	$21,626	$26,766	$32,937
62	$21,412	$22,483	$27,875	$34,337
63	$22,296	$23,411	$29,059	$35,822
64	$23,194	$24,355	$30,311	$37,427

Grade Range 65–69

Grade	Hiring Rate	Minimum	Midpoint	Maximum
65	$24,136	$25,343	$31,650	$39,164
66	$25,156	$26,413	$33,050	$40,944
67	$26,257	$27,570	$34,558	$42,859
68	$27,362	$28,729	$36,126	$44,890
69	$28,531	$29,957	$37,748	$46,964

Grade Range 70–74

Grade	Hiring Rate	Minimum	Midpoint	Maximum
70	$29,826	$31,315	$39,500	$49,174
71	$31,104	$32,659	$41,270	$51,436
72	$32,425	$34,046	$43,117	$53,809
73	$33,827	$35,519	$45,084	$56,340
74	$35,378	$37,148	$47,206	$59,033

Figure 6.2
(continued)

Grade Range 75–79				
Grade	**Hiring Rate**	**Minimum**	**Midpoint**	**Maximum**
75	$37,040	$38,891	$49,428	$61,816
76	$38,713	$40,650	$51,729	$64,745
77	$40,565	$42,594	$54,186	$67,806
78	$42,430	$44,552	$56,744	$71,058
79	$44,432	$46,652	$59,445	$74,458

Grade Range 80–84				
Grade	**Hiring Rate**	**Minimum**	**Midpoint**	**Maximum**
80	$46,486	$48,812	$62,232	$77,978
81	$48,664	$51,098	$65,175	$81,685
82	$50,872	$53,415	$68,266	$85,660
83	$53,322	$55,987	$71,596	$89,870
84	$55,852	$58,645	$75,046	$94,240

Grade Range 85–90				
Grade	**Hiring Rate**	**Minimum**	**Midpoint**	**Maximum**
85	$58,493	$61,418	$78,648	$98,803
86	$61,243	$64,306	$82,431	$103,618
87	$64,157	$67,365	$86,418	$108,679
88	$67,273	$70,639	$90,611	$113,949
89	$70,446	$73,971	$94,964	$119,481
90	$73,797	$77,485	$99,569	$125,341

overlapping of pay rates in the adjoining grade levels acted to facilitate such transitions.

The interlocking of jobs and pay implied by pay scales makes them a complex device. They can easily unravel under the impact of inflation or changing market conditions. The supply and demand for particular skills or a change in the tasks and responsibilities of a particular job can easily alter its validity. Unfortunately, the commitment to the "integrity" of the overall system itself and its symbolism (along with a desire to keep costs down) has often lead to this failure.

Broadbanding

The "triumph of technique over purpose" is also evident here. The rigidity invested in the use of pay scales (and the concomitant job analyses upon which they are based) denies organizations the flexibility to adjust to and meet change. Individuals cannot readily be reassigned duties. This is especially a problem if those duties are from jobs officially designated as having lower grades. Even if pay remains constant, a lower grade assignment might be seen psychologically as a career setback. Reward for exceptional performance is thwarted by the formal attachment of pay ceilings or maximum salaries to specific job grades.

Broadbanding has been introduced as a means to cut through the Gordian knot of classification. Broadbanding helps redesign jobs and the workplace. It introduces greater flexibility into the organization. Tasks and responsibilities can more easily be gathered together around the individuals who perform them rather than fit into a somewhat arbitrary positional box. In addition, this allows for an easier linkage of those jobs with pay-for-performance.

However, broadbanding is not without its disadvantages. Because it gives managers greater flexibility in assigning and rewarding job tasks and responsibilities, broadbanding weakens the control over wages and salaries that a more formal position classification system imposes. Furthermore, total salaries are likely to rise as individuals are freed from zero-sum reward systems. Pay equity perceptions may also suffer under broadbanding (especially where supervisory trust is insufficient). Finally, the elimination of many small grade levels reduces the opportunity for "promotions." Even when economic incentives are not affected or even when enhanced, the loss of this form of recognition may negatively affect motivation.

Broadbanding can occur in either of two forms: (1) an incremental, "broad grades" approach or (2) a more dynamic, "career bands" version. Whether "broad grades" or "career bands" are used, management obtains greater flexibility. The employee is seen to benefit from both more challenging and meaningful work assignments and the possibility of pay increases (Risher and Schay, 1994; Risher, 1999).

The hypothetical pay grades used in Exercise 7, Collective Bargaining, can be restructured into broadbanding scale as displayed in Figure 6.3. In this example, ten

Figure 6.3
Broadbanding

Grades	Min	Mid	Max	Broadbands
I	15	18	20	
II	17	20	22	A
III	19	22	24	
IV	20	22	25	
V	21	24	27	B
VI	22	25	28	
VII	23	26	29	
VIII	25	28	32	
IX	28	32	35	C
X	32	36	40	

pay grades (which are each divided into ten steps at 2.5 percent for a 25 percent range) are collapsed into three bands. Under a "broad grades" approach these three new bands could each be sorted into ten steps (the resultant step increments would vary between 5 and 10 percent). A "career band" approach would allow for supervisory discretion on salary determination within the entire band range.

Broad grades are simply a recalibration of the existing pay scales. Under broad grades, a system of, say, fifty pay grades is collapsed into one of ten or twelve grades. The range for each broad grade is from 50 to 100 percent of the minimum, starting salary. These new grades are subsequently divided into steps. The advantage of this simple, incremental approach is twofold. First, within each broad grade individuals can take on any of the previously lower-grade duties without loss of pay or prestige. Second, for all but the formerly top-rung employees in each of the broad grades, there is now more "headroom" between them and the pay ceilings. However, this flexibility introduces a higher degree of uncertainty or fussiness in the calculation of appropriate pay.

Career bands are more innovative and dynamic. Although career bands also reduce the number of pay grades from, for example, fifty to ten or twelve, they do not impose any internal step structure onto this new system. Managers are given the flexibility to freely assign (and reassign) duties and salaries (limited only by overall budget figures). Individuals need not begin at the minimum, starting salary nor serve their time prior to receiving increases. Managers are often permitted to hire at any salary between the minimum and range midpoint; offers above the midpoint would be permitted but require approval. Ideally, salary determination within broadbanding is calculated from a midpoint base. The base is set by the market or competitive salary, which should be the median or average salary.

PAY POLICIES

Pay policies are the specific options used to reward employees (and, thereby, reinforce desired work behaviors). They may be inflexible, across-the-board incentives designed to attract and retain, or they can be flexible, individual prizes encouraging motivation. Although the emphasis here is on extrinsic, monetary rewards, one must remember that intrinsic rewards are also important. Many of the inflexible pay and benefits policies help create the intrinsic worklife quality that is essential for a successful organization.

In American society monetary rewards are valued, in part, because they are a meaningful social statement recognizing an individual's worth and contributions. Because money by definition is a medium of exchange, it is translatable into numerous extrinsic and intrinsic rewards valued by the employee (the basis for Frederick Taylor's focus on money as the motivator under his scientific management theory).

While pay structure outlines the linkage of pay to organizational strategy, pay policies are the specific tools that are used in implementation. Pay policies close the circuit and provide the energy that makes things work.

Pay-for-Performance

Pay-for-performance incentives take numerous forms. While mostly focused at providing individual incentives (merit pay, bonuses, and skill-based pay), they are readily adaptable to group situations (gain sharing and team/group incentives). Although it can be argued that the public sector greatly benefits from emphasizing its intrinsic, public interest or ethos aspects (Perry and Wise, 1990; Naff and Crum, 1999), extrinsic pay-for-performance schemes for enhancing productivity are quite appealing.

The added benefits that can be derived from pay-for-performance are predicated on the existence of an adequate base pay rate that rewards job performance (and is adjusted for inflation and other cost-of-living factors). Failure to maintain this foundation erodes organizational trust and undermines the effectiveness of pay-for-performance incentives (Carnevale, 1995).

Pay-for-performance is also predicated on rewarding employees for desired, productive performance. The pay-for-performance "reward" works because it reinforces desirable employee behaviors. Inasmuch as the organization fails to identify and reward the "correct" behaviors, its pay-for-performance scheme will be less than effective (Luthans and Stajkovic, 1999).

Merit pay and bonuses are closely related, individual incentives. Both are awarded for exceptional performance (measured through a performance appraisal process); in fact, they are based on the same exceptional performance. Merit pay is a merit annuity. It is added to an individual's base pay and is retained there in future years (where it also benefits from the compounding effects of any future percentage pay increases). On the other hand, bonuses are awarded as an extra, one-time compensation. They are not added to an individual's base salary. Pay-for-performance is more effective if the payment is actually separate from the regular salary base. This creates a psychological distinction that identifies merit pay or bonuses as special.

To be effective motivators, merit pay and bonuses must exceed a psychological threshold. Each individual must see what is offered as a significant increment worth the added effort required. Even if an individual is predisposed toward the effort, an inconsequential offer (chump change) can discourage it. The amounts and percentages necessary vary with economic and social circumstances (Lawler, 1990: 57–69). However, merit pay calls for a minimum increase of 2.5 percent while the one-time bonuses require double that, 5 percent. To be fully effective, however, both merit increases and bonuses should be double, triple, or quadruple these figures (Prinz and Waldman, 1985; Kanter, 1987).

Merit pay and bonuses can be awarded using a merit matrix or guide chart that varies the percent awarded with an individual's performance rating and position in the pay range. Although awarding differing merit and bonus rates as an individual's performance rating exceeds a standard competence or fully satisfactory level is straightforward, adjustments for an individual's pay range position are less well publicized. Under this approach, higher percentage rates are associated with the same performance rating in the lower pay range quintiles than in the higher. For example, where a rating of "3" might merit an increase of 5 percent for an employee in the lowest quintile, it would only earn a 3 percent increase for one in the highest quintile (Scott, Markham, and Vest, 1996).

The use of pay guide charts for merit and bonus decisions helps stretch out a finite pay pool. Although employees in the lower quintiles benefit from higher percentage increases (for comparable performance), those in the higher quintiles remain satisfied in that the dollar amount of their increases tend to be higher.

Merit pay is especially in vogue with many public sector jurisdictions seeing it as a means for enhancing productivity and, at the same time, cutting costs. However, the reality of merit pay in the public sector is somewhat different (Gabris, 1986; Halachmi and Holzer, 1987; Lovrich, 1987; Perry, Petrakis, and Miller, 1989).

The federal experience with pay-for-performance is illustrative of this problem. The difficulties faced in implementing the Civil Service Reform Act (CSRA) were noted from the beginning. As Kramer (1982) outlined, the policy development process set the stage for implementation. Although the solutions proposed by the CSRA were primarily in the nature of structural reforms, extensive behavioral changes were also required for successful implementation. Hence, continued follow-up and reinforcement are necessary (Bellone 1982). Given that federal employees approached the civil service reforms with a great deal of skepticism and indifference (Lynn and Vaden, 1979, 1980), successful reform, while not improbable, was problematic.

The federal merit pay experience actually began optimistically. Employees were aware of the real problems that had previously plagued the federal performance appraisal and pay systems and held hopes for improvement under the new CSRA provisions (Nigro, 1981). Given federal employees' prior experiences with other administrative fads and schemes, early indications also showed a healthy "wait and see" or "give it a chance" attitude (Nigro, 1982).

The Senior Executive Service (SES) was established in an uncertain environment (Huddleston 1987; Newland 1987). The top-level civil servants who joined the SES (the alternative of remaining at the GS-16 to GS-18 grade but without the policymaking responsibilities inherent in SES positions was an unappealing choice) were concerned about political interference and bureaucrat-bashing reforms. The pay-for-performance incentives (e.g., merit pay and various bonuses) included in the original CSRA were rather quickly limited by Congress and the Office of Personnel Management (which felt them too generous and awarded to too many); there were also concerns with regard to how fairly the performance appraisal and incentive systems had been administered (Colby and Ingraham 1981; Ingraham and Colby 1982; Nigro 1981, 1982; Pagano 1984).

In spite of these early drawbacks, the federal service proceeded with the continued implementation of the CSRA proposals. Efforts were made to correct or, at least, work around the earlier mistakes. Later evaluations of the CSRA efforts are necessary to assess the success of these adjusted reforms. Various government reports and a growing and increasingly critical academic literature (Ingraham and Ban 1984; Marzotto 1986; Rosen 1986; Huddleston 1988–1989; Daley 1987b, 1990a; Ingraham and Rosenbloom 1992; Hammond 1993; Kellough and Lu 1993; Ingraham 1993; Lane 1994; Marzotto 1993) address this issue.

Pay-for-performance was provided for the SES and a merit pay system was also introduced for middle managers in 1981. Implementation difficulties (appraisal development, payout pool construction, revenue neutrality, etc.), followed by a severe cutback in the financial incentive payouts (the reduction of the number of awards), quickly undermined these pay-for-performance systems. When initial payouts under the pay-for-performance provisions fully utilized the pay options available under CSRA, political leaders were surprised and shocked.

Because it was required that payouts be linked to objective appraisal instruments (Milkovich and Wigdor 1991), it should not have come as a surprise that significant awards were made. Agencies already possessed of objective appraisal systems (along with other progressive features) were more likely to be dynamic, high-performing organizations with employees of a like nature. These conditions meant that initial use would be skewed to the more effective agencies.

Implementation of the pay-for-performance system among GS-13 to GS-15 middle managers, however, quickly exposed serious problems. There were questions with regard to the effectiveness of the causal theory underlying the pay-for-performance concept itself. How much of this is attributable to the learning and implementation problems is debatable. In addition, the expectations for relatively quick and substantial changes were probably unrealistic. However, these early negative experiences certainly cast doubts on the entire effort's chances of ever succeeding.

Merit pay implementation exposed a number of other, more serious problems. The establishment of payout mechanisms, that is, the constituting of merit pay pools, proved difficult (Perry, Hanzlik, and Peace, 1982; Peace and Perry, 1983). To ensure that the distribution of merit payouts occurs across the entire organization—thereby supporting perceptions of equity and legitimacy among employees—it is necessary to group employees into clusters of comparison pools. However, the practical mechanics of constructing organizational groups of comparative employees is extraordinarily intractable. Similar problems existed in the Biloxi, Mississippi, bonus pay scheme. Even though this was a smaller organization, there were initial problems of a perceived bias favoring managerial employees (Gabris, Mitchell, and McLemore, 1985).

Federal employees were anxious not only over the composition of merit pay pools but also with regard to the new objectives-based performance appraisal system that was simultaneously being introduced. This anxiety was coupled with the traditional learning problems faced whenever new systems are introduced (O'Toole and Churchill, 1982; Pearce and Perry, 1983).

Similar problems were recorded with SES awards and bonuses. The Civil Service Reform Act combined the old GS-16 to GS-18 supergrades with the executive level IV and V ranks into an American version of the British administrative class. As part of this more flexible arrangement, SESers were eligible for substantial monetary rewards and bonuses. Determination of awards and bonuses was based on an objective, MBO-based performance appraisal system. However, early evidence raised concerns about the continuing influence of previous rank in the determination of awards (Pagano, 1984). Well-publicized reductions in the number of employees eligible for and the size of SES awards and bonuses, in addition to rapid and repeated changes in the performance appraisal instrument, undermined confidence in the integrity and fairness of the system.

Beginning with President Carter and continuing through the Reagan, Bush, and Clinton administrations, there has been a reassertion of the executive-focused administrative presidency. Reminiscent of the original administrative presidency under Franklin D. Roosevelt when public administration took on an executive advocacy role, administrative theory once again has highlighted the managerial agenda outlined by the Brownlow Committee on Administrative Management—an agenda that is also focused on enhancing the power of the executive branch over the administrative structure. Administrative processes have been put to the service of political agendas (Carroll, 1995; Ingraham, Thompson, and Eisenberg, 1995).

Of a more substantive nature were the concerns expressed in regard to merit pay's effects. Early studies came up empty-handed. Merit pay was not found to influence motivation, nor did it enhance organizational performance (Daley, 1987c; Pearce and Perry, 1983; Pearce, Stevenson, and Perry, 1985). In addition, the managers responsible for its implementation often failed to see its purported usefulness (Gaertner and Gaertner, 1985; Milkovich and Wigdor, 1991: 21–33, 151–158). These doubts not only lingered but grew. The federal system appears to have failed to achieve its CSRA goals (Pearce, Stevenson, and Perry, 1985; Perry, 1986; Perry, Petrakis, and Miller, 1989; Daley, 1990a; Kellough and Lu, 1993; Ingraham, 1993; Lane, 1994).

This soon led to the replacement of the Merit Pay System by the Performance Management and Recognition System (PMRS) in 1984. Even with these revisions the federal system appears to have failed to achieve its CSRA goals (Pearce, Stevenson, and Perry, 1985; Perry, 1986, 1988–1989; Perry, Petrakis, and Miller, 1989). Doubts not only lingered but grew. Well-publicized reductions in the number of employees eligible for SES awards and bonuses, along with rapid and repeated changes in the performance appraisal instrument, did little to instill confidence in the integrity and fairness of the federal performance appraisal system. These finally led to the PMRS being terminated in 1993.

However, hope is expressed (U.S. Merit Systems Protection Board, 1988; although Daley, 1990a questions this). Further analysis suggests the presence of complex, indirect effects. Drawing upon SES attitudes expressed in the 1986 Merit Principles Survey, the anticipated effects of the CSRA changes were analyzed (Perry and Miller, 1991). Previous work failed to discover substantial direct relationships involving performance appraisal and organizational effectiveness. However, this study hints at the existence of substantial, indirect effects between performance appraisal systems and employee perceptions of organizational outcomes.

In addition, the federal demonstration project experiments—China Lake, National Institute of Standards and Technology (NIST), and Pacer Share—conducted under the aegis of the CSRA show definite benefits from pay-for-performance systems. In the

Navy's China Lake experiment, focusing on the scientific and engineering personnel, contrasts between employees at experimental and control sites noted that pay-for-performance led to enhanced job satisfaction, lower turnover, and greater supervisory authority. Of course, the experimental sites benefited from higher average salaries in that their merit pay systems had been fully funded in contrast to the control sites, which had often been subjected to underfunded merit pay pools (Schay, 1988). Similar results were found in the NIST experiment, whereas the Pacer Share project, a gain-sharing experiment, suffered the consequences of the general Department of Defense downsizing (Siegal, 1994; Schay, 1997).

Another problem that seriously faces merit pay systems occurs somewhat more clearly among state and local governments that remain proponents of pay-for-performance (Kellough and Selden, 1997). The ability or willingness to pay is a matter of much controversy. Pay-for-performance is an aspect of expectancy motivation theory under which an individual in deciding whether to undertake a task calculates the value of the reward offered, the difficulty of the task, their respective cost-benefit formulation, and the likelihood of actually being rewarded for accomplishing the task.

This last item—the actual payoff for work done—is rather taken for granted in private sector systems. This is not so in the public sector. Financial exigencies are too much a normal part of public sector budgeting for the payoff provision of any scheme to be taken for granted. Even in the 1960s and 1970s, state and local governments were more likely to be under regimes governed by revenue budgeting rather than incremental formats. The economic and political changes of the 1980s and 1990s have, if anything, made things even more precarious. State and local governments exist with budgets that are structurally weak.

Whereas the 1960s through the 1980s was an era of incremental and even rational program budgeting, the 1990s and beyond are more likely to reflect the traditional revenue and perhaps repetitive budgeting that is characteristic of the public sector. This is especially true with regard to state and local governments. Under these structural conditions, governments are unlikely to possess the certainty with which to guarantee the ongoing financing of programs (Wildavsky, 1988).

This structural limitation applies to popular, substantive projects as well as to administrative and managerial endeavors. When the basic provision of public services is itself in question, it is difficult to foresee the will for maintaining pay-for-performance schemes.

Constitutional requirements for balanced budgets and the federal dominance of personal income taxes as a revenue source mean that most state and local governments function under revenue-budgeting systems. Revenue budgeting ties expenditures tightly to the preexisting sources of revenue. These state and local government revenue sources are not as dynamic as those possessed by the federal government. In addition, any natural expansion is just as likely to trigger calls for tax cuts as for new programs.

Economic instability can also contribute additional problems. Faced with program expectations born in the growth era of the 1960s to 1970s and antitax attitudes from the 1980s, state and local governments exist today with very little of the budgetary slack that previously handled emergencies and new endeavors. An economic recession, no matter how mild, can easily throw a government into repetitive budgeting. Previously approved programs can quickly find their appropriations clawed back. In such circumstances an extra-pay provision, as indeed pay-for-performance is, is unlikely to receive a great deal of political or public support.

North Carolina is typical in this respect. Twice—in the 1970s and again in the 1990s—the state attempted to implement pay-for-performance systems. In both cases, the financial circumstances that enabled political leaders to fund these programs were soon subject to change. Recessions swept away the state's financial security and foundered the pay-for-performance systems. In fact, fear of just such an event led state administrators to cast the 1990 system not as one of pay-for-performance (although this was the state legislature's preference) but as a performance management system (focusing on the concept's proven strengths) with an incidental scheme for monetary incentive attached (Daley, 1990b).

Similar problems arose in the implementation of pay-for-performance among various Australian governments. Even though they were aware of the difficulties that U.S. governments had encountered, they made the same mistakes. Interestingly, these failed efforts were sponsored by both liberal (Labor Party) and conservative (Liberal Party) governments. Inadequate or nonexisting training was coupled with an unwillingness to actually deliver on the promise of paying for performance. Victoria, in fact, repeated the North Carolina example in unsuccessfully implementing pay-for-performance in the late 1980s, early 1990s, and again in the late 1990s. Problems were compounded in Australia in that most governments lacked any experience with performance appraisal systems for measuring performance (Marshall, 1998; Renfrow, Hede, and Lamond, 1998).

Unless a record of continued payouts for performance is established, the motivational and productivity effects envisioned in a pay-for-performance system will just not occur. In the public sector, the expectancy theory calculation on the odds that the organization will deliver on its promise of reward is neither trivial nor necessarily favorable.

The demise of many of these pay-for-performance schemes under the pressures of economic recession is typical of public sector behavior. In such economic circumstances, even public employees grant and often insist that the provision of ongoing and needed public services take priority over pay increases. The preservation of jobs is also accorded a higher priority.

Although state governments remain advocates of pay-for-performance, Kellough and Selden (1997) note that support diminishes wherever those involved have experience with such systems. The public sector reality is a shallow image of pay-for-performance's promise.

Pay-for-performance's strengths lie in its ability to provide structure and enhance goal setting. Other than its ability to focus workers on the task, pay-for-performance (especially under its popular merit pay option) is not a major force in increasing motivation or productivity. Added to this are the numerous interpersonal conflicts that it engenders. Alfie Kohn (1993) argues that any system that relies on an extrinsic reward structure, as pay-for-performance most certainly does, will fail. Even if the extrinsic rewards are delivered as promised, they undermine long-term, intrinsic motivation and refocus effort away from performing the job. In fact, Kohn argues that the added concern for obtaining the reward actually lessens individuals' abilities to accomplish the task. The fear of loosing a desired reward inhibits action. Individuals behave more conservatively and incrementally; they forgo considering options they otherwise would. The rationally based, calculated risk is discounted not on its own merits but on its perceived affect on obtaining the extrinsic reward.

Skill-Based Pay

Reminiscent of rank-in-person systems, skill- or competency-based pay rewards individuals for possessing specific skills (through professional certifications and academic degrees) and wider competencies (developed characteristics such as problem solving, oral communication, or critical thinking). The organization (based on its strategic plan) chooses skills and competencies that it has a projected need for. Employees who have these (and meet the test established for verification) are awarded extra pay for a specific time period (two to three years). Reverification of individual skills and competencies as well as the renewal, addition, and deletion of those required by the organization are undertaken periodically (Lawler, 1990: 153–178; Shareef, 1994, 1998; Gupta, 1997; Risher, 1997, 1999).

Skill-based pay is designed to enhance motivation by instilling a learning framework among employees. The organization benefits in two ways. First, it gains flexibility in assigning people to jobs. With more individuals cross-trained in the performance of necessary tasks, downtime or lessened productivity due to orienting new hires can be avoided. Second, as individuals gain more skills they can redesign and enrich their jobs, thereby adding to overall productivity (Murray and Gerhart, 1998).

Under skill-based pay, the organization periodically, usually in conjunction with its strategic planning process, establishes a set of skills and competencies it desires and, hence, will reward. Each skill or competency can also be subdivided into proficiency levels or units (where feasible). This helps to encourage the obtainment of skills by providing the individual with intermediate reward points. The organization can also facilitate skill obtainment (and confidence in the program) by offering or supporting employee training. Skill-based pay also serves to financially recognize individual contributions or value added due to the impact of employees' different levels of performance (Murray and Gerhart, 1998).

To be successful, Shareef (1998) notes that a skill-based pay scheme must follow some basic principles. First, an open, participative culture fosters and encourages employee–supervisor trust. Because the narrower traditional job descriptions are replaced under skill-based pay, employees must be assured that they are being treated fairly and not being manipulated or exploited.

A second, public sector consideration is that skill-based pay must recognize and support the public ethos (Naff and Crum, 1999). Individuals seek employment in the public sector because it is indeed different. The importance of serving civil society (and the team-based organization this necessitates) must be factored in.

Implementation also requires that the administrative support structure be compatible. Rules and regulations governing the workplace must be compatible with skill-based pay. Primarily, the position classification system must be altered to accept the flexibility of such concepts as broadbanding. Although skill-based pay is independent of other pay-for-performance, its financial "payoff" must be substantial enough to motivate employee interest. Finally, the skills rewarded must fit in with the organization's strategic objectives. This is especially true with respect to public organizations because employees obtain a great deal of their intrinsic motivation and reward from the public mission (Shareef, 1998).

An important aspect of skill-based pay is that it is a form of "on-call" pay. The individual regularly receives the extra compensation associated with that skill for the entire planning period regardless of whether he or she is ever called upon to perform any task or function with it.

The organization is buying insurance that a critical skill will be available when and if needed. By cross-training employees, a smaller workforce can be employed more effectively. It develops a more flexible workforce that can readily be reassigned to various tasks. Because this also minimizes the need to replace existing, "obsolete" workers or the risk of hiring new people, it has the added advantage of encouraging organizational trust and commitment. Skill- and competency-based pay is often integrated into broadbanding concepts. Retention bonuses are another use of the skill-based notion.

Gain Sharing

Where productivity is derived from the interdependent work of a team, individual incentive pay can be detrimental and divisive. Where success is based on multiple efforts, substantial pay differentials among individuals may not appropriately reflect (and reward) actual accomplishments. Individuals whose efforts are slighted in such an accounting may also harbor ill will toward those unduly/unjustly compensated for the work of others. In such circumstances, a team-based incentive system is more appropriate (Bloom, 1999).

Gain sharing, an instrument for implementing pay-for-performance, is a synthesis of participatory management and profit sharing (Greiner, Hatry, Koss, Millar, and Woodward 1981; Graham-Moore and Ross, 1990; Markowich, 1993; Sanders, 1997; Patton and Daley, 1998; Risher, 1999). With the advent of interest in both pay-for-performance and total quality management (TQM), gain-sharing programs have attracted the attention of public sector organizations. Gain sharing is a means for encouraging or motivating employees through extrinsic expectancy rewards, yet staying within a group or organizational framework. Hence, it combines TQM's emphasis on the advantages derived from teamwork (and away from the distractions of individual competition) with the motivational effect of a strong individual reward system (Swiss, 1992; Cohen and Brand, 1993; Durant and Wilson, 1993; Wilson and Durant, 1994).

The private sector uses gain sharing to reward employees for increases in production and/or profit. Gain sharing focuses primarily on financial or budget figures.

The term *goal sharing* is used when the focus on goal attainment is combined with a system of rewards. In contrast with private sector organizations, public sector gains are often difficult to measure in terms of direct production or profit. In the public sector, budgetary savings and the attainment of specified, organizational goals are used as performance measurements for the gain-sharing award. Public sector budget savings may not have the same, clear linkage to "profit" found in the private sector. Although budget savings are indeed still a good measure, they need to be complemented with goal-sharing approaches in order to assure that organizational missions are being achieved.

Private sector gain-sharing research focuses primarily on profit-sharing plans (e.g., Scanlon, Rucker, and Improshare). These packages can be readily modified to fit each organization's particular situation or need. All the plans have a common factor—overall productivity—as the basis for calculating the gain-sharing award.

For a successful gain-sharing plan, management must be committed to and involved in the plan. This will require the organizational culture to be one of respect, cooperation, and communication with employees (Paulsen, 1991; Pfeffer, 1998). Employees must be comfortable enough with managers to bring suggestions or ideas about process or quality improvement to their manager's attention.

Even with employee involvement, the gain-sharing plan must be simple. Too many factors or complex formulas can cause confusion or mistrust among the employees (Paulsen 1991). Employees need to know the "numbers side" of the gain-sharing plan (Markowich 1993); otherwise, they may perceive that the plan is unfair or its measurements unrealistic or unreachable. Full communication and involvement of employees in the design and implementation can alleviate much of this.

Gain sharing or goal sharing is a group-level application of pay-for-performance. Instead of rewarding individual competition, it attempts to harness it into organizational cooperation. As such, the expectancy theory notions that undergird individual pay-for-performance schemes are still operative in gain sharing or goal sharing. Where employees work in an interdependent environment, individual pay-for-performance incentives can be counterproductive (i.e., they can actually demotivate employees and result in a loss of productivity). However, in gain sharing the incentive is attached to efforts or performance that fosters teamwork. Although this results in a more egalitarian pay distribution (and pay compression), it also contributes to enhanced productivity both overall and individually (Bloom, 1999).

Gain sharing focuses on several organizational aspects—employee involvement, pay-for-performance, and the development of specific and hard measurements in relation to performance. In the public sector with its service environment, the employment of hard, quantitative measures can pose added difficulties. A department may reach its quantitative goals but have the quality of service or department effectiveness actually decrease (defects). For this reason, the local government council or manager should set an objective to reduce the number of complaints received or define acceptable levels of customer (citizen) satisfaction, as measured by customer surveys. These surveys would ask customers to rate the local government's or individual department's quality of service (see, e.g., Parasuraman, Zeithaml, and Berry, 1985, 1988; Parasuraman, Berry, and Zeithaml, 1991, 1993). Swiss (1991) states that surveys have just recently been used to evaluate programs. The local government would need to set a customer satisfaction rating for the initial measurement for the gain-sharing reward.

Gain-sharing research highlights the basic themes of employee involvement, fair distribution, employee control of the criteria/factors measured, and employee–management collaboration to improve productivity. Although efforts at reinventing government and introducing TQM are beginning, little research has empirically addressed the roles of customer service and quality (issues paramount to public sector service applications). Without the inclusion of quality or good customer service, gain-sharing plans are apt to fail.

Employees may exceed the quantitative production target, yet the quality of the products may be so poor that they don't sell. Similarly, we all have probably had a bad customer service experience, and vowed not to do business with that organization again. There are very few types of organizations that do not rely on repeat business of current customers or picking up new customers by word of mouth.

Bullock and Tubbs (1990) performed a case meta-analysis on thirty-three gain-sharing plans. The factors studied included employee involvement, financial formula used, and award percentage split between employees and company. Organizations using a formal involvement structure had better success with gain sharing. "Involvement can occur without formal structures, but formal involvement structures provide clearer mechanisms by which participation can occur" (Bullock and Tubbs, 1990).

The meta-analysis also tested whether a plan that has award factors or criteria that an employee can control had any relation to the success of the program. Although Bullock and Tubbs (1990) believe that the controllable gain-sharing factors should act to further employee involvement (rather than uncontrollable factors) and, consequently, would have a strong effect on the success of gain sharing, this hypothesis was not fully supported in the findings of the meta-analysis. However, control was linked to employee innovation. It was also hypothesized that the higher the share of gain sharing, the greater the extent of employee involvement and collaboration. The meta-analysis's findings did not support this (Bullock and Tubbs, 1990).

In the public sector, it is difficult to link performance to specific productivity. A pilot program on gain sharing was performed in the San Francisco Region of the Office of Personnel Management's Federal Investigations Division. It implemented a productivity gain-sharing system (PGS) from the first quarter of FY85 to the last quarter of FY86 (Naff and Pomerleau, 1988). The PGS gave investigators $20 for each percentage point above 110 percent of productivity expectations, while deficient investigations reduced the production statistic for an investigator by 10 percent.

The result was that productivity increased and deficiencies decreased during the first year; however, these results were not sustained during the second year. In another project, the impetus in the Pacer Share experiment also wasn't sustained, in this case due to Department of Defense downsizing.

Two important factors come to light from these studies. First, gain-sharing awards must be based on variables that employees perceive themselves having control over. Second, the gain-sharing award should be based on productivity measurements that are equitable (Naff and Pomerleau, 1988; Bullock and Tubbs, 1990).

Gain-sharing measures have to be based on factors controlled by employees (Bullock and Tubbs, 1990). One area employees have control over is how tasks are performed. If an employee believes a task can be performed differently, resulting in saving time or money, and makes such a recommendation to his or her supervisor, this is employee involvement. Because the organization also benefits by the use of less resources, monetary measures can be used. These monetary measures are usually centered on the organization's budget.

An area that would require a different technique than the private sector is quality and customer service (Swiss, 1992). Most public sector organizations do not lose customers to competition. However, customer satisfaction and quality of service is important. Public organizations have, for the most part, a relatively captive customer/client base because the public organization is the only one providing the service (Swiss, 1992). This can hinder the quality of service by public organizations by the absence of competition.

However, the support for service delivery through privatization or nonprofit organizations represents a significant reaction to this captive-customer problem. Privatization redefines who delivers public services to the public; public programs need not be governmental programs. Furthermore, potential customers—both businesses and individual citizens—may choose another city in which to relocate (e.g., many real estate ads emphasize that "only county taxes" will be paid). The customer service and quality measurement problem can be alleviated by the use of surveys or focus groups.

The distribution of awards can cause problems in the public sector. Any type of award or bonus that is distributed in the public sector may be seen as a waste of tax money by citizens or favoritism by employees. An argument for gain sharing is that even though the employees receive a portion of savings, the local public organization receives a usually larger portion (plus all of the future savings) that may not have been actualized without gain sharing. Whether new programs are funded, resources reallocated to cover existing increases in demand, or tax cuts voted is a decision left to the city council's discretion.

BENEFITS

Benefits are a major component of compensation. They can compose from 20 to 40 percent of the total compensation package. Yet, benefits are a hodgepodge. Mainly composed of health care and retirement pension programs, benefits also include a vast array of miscellaneous services. Further complicating matters is the fact that not all benefits are tangible; many offer intrinsic incentives that are difficult to place a dollar value on. Furthermore, the value of benefits, even those with clear price tags, actually will vary from individual to individual. However, benefits still serve the same set of purposes that pay does—to attract, retain, and motivate employees.

Benefits distort the market-based approach found in Frederick Taylor's simple notion of paying workers and letting them choose how to use their money. As an organizational matter, benefits arise from the vagaries of governmental tax laws and market economies of scale. The organization can tap into these more economically than an individual can. In essence, the organization pays wholesale while the individual must purchase at retail prices. Hence, the organization can provide benefits that are highly valued by individuals at reduced costs.

However, these cost differentials also distort the market. Individuals who receive a subsidized or discounted benefit will prefer it over one that is not. Hence, two "benefits" or consumer needs of equal use will not be treated equally in their preference calculations. This can lead to the overpurchase of subsidized benefits and the underutilization of those not subsidized. The introduction of cafeteria benefit plans is meant to partially adjust for this problem.

Because benefits compose a growing proportion of the total compensation package, it is necessary to treat benefits with the same strategic pay considerations that wage and salary decisions are subjected to. Although benefits are more likely to satisfy attraction and retention needs than to be motivational, this latter role should not be overlooked. Hence, organizationally specific information on benefits desired by employees, whether public and private, is important (Moore, 1991; Bergmann, Bergmann, and Grahn, 1994; Davis and Ward, 1995; Streib, 1996).

Because benefits are paid for in pretax dollars, the employee obtains them for less than it would cost if taxable wages and salaries were used. The organization also derives tax savings. Tax deductions are allowed for those in the private sector. Yet, even public sector organizations receive tax breaks; the salary upon which social security and other employment taxes is calculated is often lower, thereby reducing the payments due from the organization.

Because of the size of their workforces, organizations can also negotiate favorable rates under group plans. In most cases, a single individual would be required to pay more. The organization, thereby, satisfies workers' needs at a bargain rate. This can occur even when the organization is not paying for the benefit itself but merely serving as a conduit for employees to purchase optional services.

These "savings" need not all be passed on to the individual consumer. It should be noted that the public sector organizations have often suffered from this problem. Benefits contracts are awarded on the basis of patronage. Vendors may be political players who make campaign contributions or underwrite the organization by providing it with professional equipment and services. To cover the costs of obtaining this patronage, the plans may not be as generous as those found in similar, private sector organizations or require larger deductibles and co-payments. These problems can exist even when only optional benefits entirely paid for by the employee are being provided.

Because the major benefits that organizations provide deal with health and retirement, employees are forced to take care of these long-term requirements. A healthy worker might see no urgent need for health insurance, and retirement is a lifetime away. If individuals are allowed to make their own choices in these matters, they are likely to prefer present pressing needs and discount future uncertainties. Will society be content to idly sit by when the negative consequences of poor choices occur? From the organizational perspective, will its workforce "blame" it and judge it harshly for allowing these poor choices? Will employees themselves be more worried and less motivated? Forcing employees to make decisions that adequately take into account the long term may be authoritarian or paternalistic, but it is also insurance for the organization's future well-being.

Health Care

One of the two primary benefits sought by employees is health insurance (Perry and Cayer, 1997). With the growing importance of professionalism (i.e., the knowledge worker) as the key organizational asset, maintaining a healthy workforce takes on an added importance. The skilled knowledge worker is not an interchangeable part that can be easily replaced. Their loss or even their reduced attention (Napoleon suffered illnesses in his last few, active years, including on the day of Waterloo; Franklin D. Roosevelt was seriously ill during the latter years of World War II) can be critical to organization performance (Buchmueller and Valletta, 1996).

Modern medical costs for hospital care will run into the thousands of dollars in a matter of a few days for even a minor illness. Something that requires intensive care indeed truly merits the name *catastrophic* not only in terms of its life-threatening nature but in respect to its exponential costs. Fears of illness and the subsequent devastating financial burdens that they can impose is quite disquieting.

Health Insurance

Health insurance is the means by which these fears can be, to some extent, allayed. In addition to major medical expenses, health insurance can also inexpensively aid in alleviating other health-related threats to motivation and productivity. Health insurance plans may include additional provisions for prescription drug, mental health, dental, and eye care benefits. What is included and the extent of that coverage varies substantially from plan to plan.

Deductible ($200 per individual annually with a $500 family cap) and co-payment (20 percent of charges) cost containment provisions also alter the real value and costs of these benefits (Cayer, 1997). These plans may also limit exposure through a total out-of-pocket provision ($1,500 per individual with a $3,000 family cap). It is because of this extensive variability among plans that it is extremely difficult to do cost comparisons on health benefits.

The basic health care covered under insurance plans is likely to be separated into segments requiring different levels of co-payments. Preventive care such as is found in an annual physical examination and periodic eye and dental checkups is often fully reimbursed (directly paid by the insurance company to reduce paperwork and delays) and exempt from any deductible provisions. Relatively common, minor medical procedures may be reimbursed at a 90 percent level. More serious or long-term (but not catastrophic, life threatening in nature) illnesses may require a 50/50 match. Catastrophic care (e.g., cancer and heart disease), whether as part of the general policy or as an additional or optional benefit, again provides something on the order of 80 or 90 percent reimbursement. Because the cost of catastrophic care quickly escalates into the hundreds of thousands of dollars, even at these reimbursement levels the co-payment requirements are substantial.

Employer-provided health plans usually provide options for family coverage (paid in full or part by the organization or entirely at the employee's expense). Concerns about the health of family members can adversely affect an employee's productivity. Hence, the extension of health benefits to family members is essential.

Family coverage is two fold. It provides health insurance for the spouse and for the children. Spouse coverage is actually the more expensive part. Because it is coverage for an adult, it has an adult risk exposure profile. Importantly, it extends insurance coverage for pregnancy (which is one of the major insurance costs). A spouse is also at risk for other adult illnesses, including the costly cancer and heart disease risks. Proposals for domestic partners' benefits address the same concern (Gossett, 1994; Hostetler and Pynes, 1995).

Child coverage is a relatively less costly component. After the first few years, children are surprisingly healthy and resilient. Most efforts are devoted to preventive medicine. Some plans, in fact, authorize employee-parent and children coverage, excluding the spouse. These options assume that the spouse is covered under another organization's health plan. This saves the organization and employee from paying for unneeded, duplicate insurance.

With dual-income families being more and more the norm, another concern arises vis-à-vis children's health coverage. When dual-income parents are given the choice of two health plans, they will gravitate to the better plan. Providing better child care benefits can lead to increased insurance costs for the organization. Of course, such a family-friendly policy is also going to be a major attraction for job candidates (Osterman, 1995; Durst, 1999; Newman and Matthews, 1999).

To pay for uncovered aspects of the health plans, tax laws allow for employees to establish medical and dependent care (a legal option is also available) accounts. Pretax dollars from their salary are deposited into these accounts by the employees according to a salary reduction agreement. These "trust funds" are then used to pay the medical, dependent, or legal expenses incurred. Unfortunately, unexpended funds revert to the federal government at the end of the year. However, it is quite easy to budget for anticipated, ongoing expenses or to plan some less serious operations.

Organizations can facilitate medical, dental, and eye care by arranging for onsite or nearby services. To avoid liability, these are set up as independent businesses. The organization often provides space and equips an office that is leased or sold on favorable terms. It also informally guarantees employee use of these services. This not only ensures readily available medical facilities for employees but often reduces time lost from work. Instead of waiting at a doctor's office, the employee can remain at work until actually seen by the physician, dentist, or optometrist.

Although health insurance covers the costs of obtaining medical care, it does not itself address the loss of income that also occurs due to illness. Workmen's compensation legally covers employees for job-related accidents. Sick leave also serves to continue an employee's income for short periods of illness (Garcia, 1987; Kroesser, Meckley, and Ransom, 1991).

Although part of the social security program covers long-term disability, the amounts may not be enough to fully or adequately replace lost wages and salaries. Disability insurance for replacing the lost income (enabling one to continue paying for the ongoing expenses which that level of income was financing) is often provided. Short-term disability policies can often provide 100 percent of pay replacement for up to a month and replace 50 percent of pay over the next six months. Long-term disability (often integrated with, i.e., reduced by, social security) can replace two-thirds of pay until the disabled employee reaches age 65. In case of permanent disability, long-term medical care insurance for home health care and nursing homes may be necessary (albeit this is quite expensive and seldom provided as an organization-paid benefit).

The Family Medical Leave Act (FMLA) mandates up to three months unpaid leave for employees who desire to take care of or assist sick relatives and for maternity/paternity leave (Allred, 1995; Crampton and Mishra, 1995). Dependent care accounts (for elders and children) can be used to help pay for these costs (Kossek, DeMarr, Backman, and Kollar, 1993). Although the FMLA guarantees an employee job security, it does place a burden on organizations for finding qualified temporary replacements. In addition, this "job guarantee" has been relaxed through court interpretations. *Lempres v. CBS, Inc.* (1996) does not guarantee permanent job security. *Patterson v. Alltell Information Services, Inc.* (1996) does not prevent job loss through general, "ordinary" business activities such as downsizing. In *Clay v. City of Chicago* (1997) and *Beckendorf v. Schwegmann Giant Super Markets, Inc.* (1997) poor job performance excludes reinstatement. The FMLA has also been constrained through interpretations as to the seriousness of an employee's or family member's illness, eligibility, and the provision of sufficient notification (Wisensale, 1999). The Consolidated Omnibus Reconciliation Act of 1986 (COBRA) mandates the continuation of group-rate employee benefits for up to eighteen months after leaving (up to three years for families of divorced or dead employees).

Sick leave, which can be accumulated at a rate of four to eight hours per month, provides an employee with pay during short-term illness. This encourages employees to take care of themselves when necessary, instead of attempting to "gut it out" only to lapse into a more long-term illness. It also removes potentially infectious individuals from the workplace. In addition, sick leave can be used for medical appointments and caring for ill family members.

Sick leave is used and thereby costs an organization. Patterns of use should be examined with thought for the introduction of cost-effective preventive action. Unfortunately, sick leave abuse also occurs. This needs to be treated. However, it must be first established that there is indeed a case of abuse. Anti-abuse policies where there is no abuse or only a few cases can undermine employee morale and trust.

In order to prevent sick leave abuse, programs allow for sick leave to be accumulated and applied toward service requirements in calculating retirement benefits. Alternatively, employees may be paid for unused sick leave. While meant as a protection against loss of income due to illness, it is often treated as just another form of paid leave. The incidence of Monday and Friday illnesses can be somewhat staggering. Monthly or quarterly incentives are often provided employees for not using their sick leave. Unused sick leave is a liability redeemed at the time of separation or retirement. Leave banks have been introduced to solve this problem.

Annual, paid leave or vacation time (one to four weeks per year depending on seniority) is another health benefit. It benefits the individual to step back from the day-to-day stresses in an organization. Vacations refresh and renew. As is the case with sick leave, this time can often be accumulated and applied toward retirement. Because this can create a substantial liability, the amount of leave that can be accumulated may be capped.

Concerns on health policies lead to mandating the annual usage of some leave. Because the purpose of leave is to refresh and renew the individual employee, it does no one any good if it is not used. Leave also benefits an individual's family relationships. Although one-day leaves (a Friday or Monday added to a weekend) are conveniently permitted, a required one-week block (five vacation days) is considered minimal. Short minivacations, as enjoyable as they can be, are intensive. An individual needs one to two days of leisured leave to "decompress" from the job and begin shedding its stress. The added days beneficially add to this.

All types of leave—vacation, sick, and paid holiday (secular and religious)—may be lumped together in a leave bank. A leave bank eliminates concerns about sick leave abuse. This reduces the organization's accounting and monitoring requirements. It also avoids the political questions that can arise regarding which holidays are observed and which are not.

Wellness programs focus on preventive health care. They undertake to encourage behaviors that lead to good health and ease stress. They encourage individuals to exercise, eat healthily, and give up hazardous habits. Many of these activities are geared to behaviors that are associated with the risk of cancer and heart disease—two of the costliest insured illnesses (Erfurt, Foote, and Heirich, 1992).

As part of such efforts, organizations may actually establish gyms or health spas for their employees or, alternatively, subsidize memberships (with reimbursement linked to actual spa/club attendance). Many large organizations construct walking trails around and build their parking lots at the edge of their "campuses." As a social activity, employee sports teams may be encouraged.

Cafeterias help ensure that employees eat a proper diet. They also ensure that employees are readily available for lunchtime emergencies. Vending machines can be stocked with fruits and other acceptable snacks. Nutritional information is made available to employees. Because obesity is a major problem among Americans (and contributes to heart disease and stroke), weight loss programs are also sponsored.

Stress reduction is also the focus of wellness efforts. Psychological stress can adversely affect productivity and lead to job burnout (Golembiewski, 1988; Cordes and Dougherty, 1993). Stress can also contribute to physical illnesses, including stroke and heart disease.

Uncertainty and a sense of helplessness are two conditions that contribute to job stress that are readily dealt with through communication and participation. The simple policy of keeping employees informed about what is occurring in an organization reduces stress. Goal setting and related TQM and MBO approaches also provide the employee with information on what is expected of or from them, thereby, reducing job stress. Because America is a highly individualistic society, control over the basic aspects of the job is highly desired. Hence, a lack of autonomy will place an employee under stress. This will even occur in team environments. Depending on others (which is really what organizations are all about) is perceived as a stressful loss of control. The more extensive employee participation is, the more individuals will feel that they are in control of their jobs.

In addition to communication and participation, wellness programs focus on a number of stress reduction techniques. Stress is an individual phenomenon. It affects people differently. The same event can trigger different responses. In fact, these responses can be both good and bad. For example, approaching project deadlines may turn one individual into a babbling basket case while another is turned on by the challenge. One individual meticulously plans and works on projects so they are completed well before they are due; the other only starts the "night before."

Stress reduction techniques are often surprisingly simple. Because of this, it is first necessary that stress and the body's physical, emotional, and behavioral reactions to it be described. This helps establish the importance of stress reduction for the employee and the organization. Stress can originate on the job or from events in an individual's life. Awareness of the sources of stress in an individual's life can be used in preparing to cope with it.

Relaxation techniques—deep breathing, muscle relaxation, breaks, massage, and imagery—are simple coping mechanisms. They temporarily break the stressor's grip on the individual; pleasant experiences or thoughts can be introduced to assist in this. More complex techniques—personality profiles, conflict resolution, diet and exercise regimes, and time management—can be employed in developing long-term stress strategies.

Stress and turmoil can also aggravate mental health problems. Public organizations with their constant state of flux, resource scarcity, and crisis management heighten such problems. Because of the stigma still attached to mental illnesses, people are reluctant to admit to or seek treatment for such problems. Mood disorders, anxiety disorders, and substance abuse/dependence (which account for the bulk of mental disorders) have a negative impact on organizational productivity (sick-leave abuse, absenteeism, poor performance, etc.). As with any other illness that affects employees, it is important for supervisors to recognize mental illness and help the employee regain his or her health (Schott, 1999).

The provision of adequate mental health benefits and their inclusion in employee assistance programs (EAPs) greatly aids in this endeavor. The confidentiality afforded by EAPs provides a secure framework in which individuals can seek out treatment for mental illnesses. Also important is supervisory training in recognizing potential mental health problems (Schott, 1999).

Health concerns may also lead to the organization becoming more intrusive. Lifestyle behaviors that increase health risks (and potential costs) may be targeted for modification—"lose the habit or the organization loses you." The exercise, diet, and stress reduction options may become required.

Growing concerns are also evident in regard to the use of medical records and genetic testing. Illness is not neutral; it is viewed as "deserving" or "undeserving." Individuals attach social stigmas to illnesses that are the consequences of lifestyle choices and, therefore, perceived as preventable. Whether the dissemination and use of such information is deemed to be relevant and job-related is still a subject of debate. Clearly, information regarding these stigmatized illnesses can exert a negative effect on careers.

A more sinister concern adheres to the use of genetic testing. Advances in medical science (the discovery of DNA markers) are allowing us to identify and monitor individuals who may possess a propensity for developing certain hereditary diseases and illnesses. In many cases, this can lead to early intervention and treatment. Minimally, it aids in the further study of these diseases. However, this information can also exert a negative effect on careers. Organizations may choose not to hire, develop, or promote individuals who may develop costly illnesses at some future date. Of course, this is a matter over which the individual has no control; socially the disease is "undeserved." In fact, the genetic test may represent only a probability and not a certainty.

Employee Assistance Programs

For individual employees the availability of counseling, drug and alcohol treatment, and other aspects of employee assistance programs can be quite encouraging (Johnson, 1986; Johnson and O'Neill, 1989; Mani, 1991; Perry and Cayer, 1992). Employee assistance programs represent the personnel function in its most positive, humanistic mode. The initial success with alcohol treatment led to the expansion of EAPs. Today they deal not only with other serious illnesses such as drug dependency and psychological disorders but with family and financial problems as well. In addition, some EAPs include career counseling, weight control, and related wellness activities.

Employee assistance programs treat the whole person. Organizations are cognizant that nonwork behaviors and personal problems can adversely effect an employee's work. They also recognize that their individual employees are valuable resources. Each employee represents a substantial human investment in job training and organizational socialization. Although termination and replacement is an option, it is often the least preferred and last resort. Hence, efforts spent in helping employees solve their problems are worthwhile for the organization.

Employee assistance programs are usually contracted for from other groups and organizations in the community. A nonprofit, umbrella organization may serve as an overall contact agency and coordinator. The independent EAP can provide excellent services due to its community-wide economy of scale. Its independence also assures employees of confidentially in what are still personal problems. This allows the employee's organization to make the EAP available and, in some instances due to job-related concerns, to make referrals. Yet, the organization stops short of actually meddling in an individual's private life (and the potential liability problems associated with that).

Employee assistance programs have also been the source of economical personnel functions. Family and marriage counseling services have formed the nucleus for alternate dispute resolution and mediation processes. Their very independence and confidentiality has helped in resolving conflicts. Family finances and budget planning has opened the door to financial planning for retirement (and other major life goals).

Cost Containment

Cost containment is also an organizational concern (Moore, 1989; Cayer and Perry, 1998). Without some effort at managing care, health insurance itself would cease to be affordable even under group rates. In most cases, the employee is subject only to a small, preliminary deductible payment. This discourages frivolous benefit abuse while not endangering its serious application. Cost shifting also takes place through varying partial co-payments that are often required depending on the nature of the procedure. Because living a more healthy lifestyle can reduce the use of expensive treatments for illnesses, there is a growing focus on prevention and employee wellness. With the importance of wellness issues, most health insurance plans also include fully reimbursable preventive physical (as well as dental and eye) examinations as a standard feature.

Cost containment has lead to the creation of various managed care options as alternatives to the traditional fee-for-services physician. The preferred provider organization (PPO) lists doctors who accept patients under a set payment schedule (analogous to medicare provisions). The health maintenance organization (HMO) is a business that provides full medical care for a preset fee. Each of these options, more or less, introduces financial incentives in balance to the provision of medical services.

Under HMO plans, doctors are usually on salary rather than "commission" as is the case under fee-for-service arrangements. In addition, there is usually some form of gain sharing or bonus incentive included as an added inducement against overmedication. It is assumed that the doctors' intrinsic desire to professionally serve their patients will counterbalance these financial incentives to ensure adequate patient health care.

A utilization review is conducted prior to authorizing a procedure. The purpose is to assure that necessary medical services are provided while "what if" and "wouldn't it be nice" are discouraged. These utilization review procedures often raise the spectre of individuals being denied needed services for the sake of corporate profits. Without a doubt, some of this occurs, especially where reviewers lack the relevant professional expertise of either physicians or registered nurses. Even so, the traditional fee-for-service approach often profited by ordered unneeded tests. Because there is an added danger in overmedication and from unnecessary procedures, utilization review is also likely to protect an individual's health and well-being.

A major danger inherent in cost containment efforts is the shifting of costs to the employee-patient. As a safeguard against such financial concerns coming at the expense of patient care, HMOs and PPOs are, albeit on a voluntary basis, subject to accreditation by the nonprofit National Committee for Quality Assurance (NCQA). Many organizations and employees will only do business with accredited plans. Although cost remains the most important factor in the determination of health care providers, quality is rapidly becoming a close second consideration. This is especially true for large organizations and for those considered as innovative leaders in their field.

Although traditional indemnity plans are still the most prevalent form of health insurance offered employees, the use of HMOs and PPOs is rapidly growing. This is especially true in regard to health maintenance organizations, which tend to offer a wider array of medical services and generate fewer customer complaints. Interestingly, in the public sector, HMO and PPO cost savings are apparently "reinvested" into added services. Although PPOs are a bit less expensive, the amounts spent on traditional indemnity plans hardly differ from the costs incurred by HMOs (Perry and Cayer, 1997; Cayer and Perry, 1998). Given the importance of health care to employees, reinvestment may indeed be wise use of cost containment's savings (Lust and Danehower, 1990).

RETIREMENT AND PENSIONS

Modern medicine has for the first time created a world in which there are truly substantial numbers of older people. This is actually a relatively new phenomenon. Until the twentieth century, old age was a rarity and an exceedingly short affair. Today, not only are more people living into their sixties and seventies, but life expectancies well into the eighties and nineties are not at all uncommon. In fact, the baby boom generation (those born between 1946 and 1964) is actually creating a permanent age shift in the population demographics.

This is far different from when social security was established in the 1930s; at that time, five-year payout periods were envisioned as the maximum that would be required. Individuals can no longer be expected to "die at their desks" or go into the hereafter shortly thereafter. Hence, the dilemma.

Although psychological perceptions are slowly adjusting (over age 50 is still seen as old), today's healthier individuals are quite capable of productive work for far longer than those of a generation or so ago. The magic age of 65 established by Bismarckian Prussia over a century ago (so workers could retire after fifty years of employment) is with today's health standards and life expectancies now somewhere between 75 and 85 years.

However, many individuals will not want to work that long. If they can afford to, they will want to seek new challenges and experiences. These may be in the pursuit of "leisure" activities or in other jobs. In addition, military and paramilitary organizations (e.g., police and firefighters), which require a physically fit workforce for the demanding tasks they may be called upon to perform, will still require retirement at an earlier age.

Not to provide the individual with some form of postemployment financial security would cause the same worries and resultant adverse effects on productivity as failing to provide for health insurance. To ensure employees' current commitment and attention on productivity, future security must be guaranteed.

Retirement Income

Retirement from employment need not mean that an individual ceases to work. Although many individuals must continue working to supplement their "retirement" income, many also undertake new employment for the enjoyment or activity it affords them. Voluntary and nonprofit organizations become the focus of attention for many active older people. Dynamic, public service careers are often the result. However, to engage in such pursuits requires financial security.

Although it is assumed that prior major expenses (e.g., home mortgages and children's education) reduce future needs, retirement income is still a substantial requirement. Although all projections are subject to the vagaries of individual preferences and inflationary changes, general estimates suggest that a minimum figure of from 80 to 85 percent of preretirement income is necessary to maintain one's lifestyle during retirement.

The money to provide this future stream of income during retirement is derived from social security, pensions, and individual savings. It is highly unlikely that any individual will be able to enjoy a financially secure retirement without contributions from all three sources.

The social security system provides a foundation for retirement. Social security guarantees a basic pension to virtually every American worker. Social security is a defined benefit plan with redistributive provisions for poorer workers. Although social security was not designed to be the sole source of retirement income, it is for some individuals. On average, social security replaces 40 percent of preretirement income. This will vary from 50 percent of preretirement income for salaries under $20,000 to 25 percent of preretirement income for salaries over $50,000). Under social security's redistributive formula, those who are financially better off (as are most professional workers) can see this proportion (but not the actual amount of the benefit) "erode."

Payroll taxes (combining employee and employer contributions) are used to fund fictitious individual accounts within the social security "trust fund." In actuality, current taxes from employees and employers are used to pay benefits to current retirees.

Perhaps more important, the related medicare (along with private medicare supplemental insurance) program offers some degree of insurance against the remaining major life expense that individuals face: health care. Medicaid, a program for providing medical care for the poor, is extensively used for nursing home care by older people. This is not limited to poor people but includes many who are not so poor. Many older people engage in activities designed to pass on their assets to their children (and grandchildren) rather than see them eaten up in paying for long-term care.

Government retirement benefits may also include added health care provisions for the retired employees. Although these benefits will be coordinated with those under medicare, they can provide added financial and psychological security. Long-term care provisions alleviate the fears associated with losing the legacy of a "lifetime's work" or one's independence.

Contrary to its trust fund language, social security and medicare are pay-as-you-go programs. The taxes dedicated to these programs are not really invested in trust funds but used to pay for current expenses. Any surplus is used to cover other governmental expenses (albeit the funds receive Treasury bond IOUs). Unfortunately, the tax rates funding social security and medicare are inadequate for the growing demand being placed on them. Escalating retirement (due to increased life expectancy) and health care (due to better but more expensive services) costs, on the one hand, and low tax rates and fewer taxpayers, on the other, are rapidly undermining the financial solvency of both these programs. This is a long-term problem. The current payroll tax will cover expenses until after 2010. The trust fund "surplus" won't be exhausted until sometime after 2030. Because this surplus is actually made up of Treasury bills, it can only be drawn on by imposing new taxes.

Somewhat unfortunately (but understandable in a pluralist society), the self-interest of older recipients and their role as active voters has hindered necessary reforms. However, ultimately adjustments will be made. Taxes supporting both social security and medicare will be raised. The retirement age for receiving social security benefits will also be raised. Medicare will be modified to include more managed care, including added deductibles and co-payments. Both programs may be subjected to means testing that reduces benefits or eligibility for those financially well-off.

This makes the pension and savings components of the retirement equation all the more important. These will be expected to assume an even greater role in underwriting future retirement benefits.

Pensions provide the structure built upon the social security foundation. Although social security sustains life, it is the pension that will make that life worth sustaining. Social security alone can only provide an individual with a retirement of "genteel poverty" at best (at worst, it can be a quite miserable existence).

Pensions are categorized either as defined-benefit or defined-contribution plans. Pensions are funded through salary reduction contributions from the employee and matching payments from the employer. The Employee Retirement Income Security Act of 1974 (ERISA) establishes a ten-year vesting requirement for private sector organizations (five years is more common); in general, its procedures have been voluntarily adopted among public organizations.

Employees are entitled to a refund on their contributions upon leaving employment prior to vesting but forfeit the employer match. However, upon being vested the employer's match is legally theirs, and they are entitled to retirement benefits. Most plans require that the employee obtain the age of 65 (earlier retirement beginning at age 55 or 62 at a reduced benefit level may be available) before receiving benefits. Police and firefighters are commonly required to retire at age 55 due to the physical (and psychological) demands involved in their jobs. The Tax Reform Act of 1976 requires that pensions begin paying out by age 70 1/2 (even if the employee is not formally retired).

Early retirement (prior to age 65) may be encouraged when organizations are trying to downsize. In such instances, added "bridge" benefits, including part-time employment or consultant work, are often provided that compensate the individual for any reduced social security or pension effects. Early retirement may also appeal to individuals for various personal reasons (Feldman, 1994).

Equally important in many cases is the need to retain employees past "retirement" or to have a phased retirement option. Critical shortages and higher salaries can pose serious barriers. Deferred retirement option plans (DROPs) are being introduced to address this concern. In the DROP, an employee continues working. However, his or her retirement is now calculated differently. Instead of continuing in the regular pension plan (whose benefits may be capped or minimal), the employee is provided a "new, defined-contribution plan" into which the organizations "drops" what would have been the regular plan's retirement payouts. Hence, on retirement the employee receives both the regular payments (calculated on the basis of years of service and salary prior to entering the DROP; i.e., the same amount that has been dropped into the new account) and the DROP account. The deferred retirement option plan can be paid out either as a lump sum or as an additional pension (Calhoun and Tepfer, 1999a, 1999b).

Traditionally, pensions were defined-benefit plans. Under a defined-benefit plan individuals are guaranteed from 50 to 75 percent of their highest salary upon retirement. Alternatively, their retirement benefit may be calculated on the basis of 2 to 3 percent of the highest salary multiplied by the number of years of service. Most systems also define "highest salary" in terms of a three- to five-year average.

Defined-benefit plans are not readily portable from one employer to another. Hence, they can somewhat discourage job changes that might otherwise be beneficial to both the individual and the organization. Under a uniform system that provided pensions calculated on 2 percent of highest salary multiplied by years of service, two individuals who shared identical salary histories would receive different pensions if one had changed jobs. Assume two individuals were paid $20,000 at the end of ten years, $40,000 after twenty years, and $60,000 on the completion of thirty years. An individual who had been employed for the entire thirty years by one organization would be eligible for a pension of $36,000. An individual who changed jobs every ten years, on the other hand, would for qualify for three separate pensions of $4,000, $8,000, and $12,000—a total pension of only $24,000 (Hegji, 1993).

The defined-contribution plan does not suffer from a portability problem. It is based entirely on each year's employee and employer contribution. These funds are invested, and their growth and accumulation is the basis for future retirement income. The defined-contribution plans are less generous to long-term employees as they dispense with the multiplier effect found in the defined-benefit plans.

Although cash-balance plans combine features from both defined-benefit and defined-contribution plans, they are closer to the latter in their overall effect. Like defined-benefit plans, the money (made up entirely of the employer's contribution; a separate employee 401(k) may also be available) placed in the pension fund is guaranteed to return a predetermined benefit regardless of actual performance. If the fund (which is theoretically invested) fails to achieve this growth, the organization "makes up the difference." Because cash-balance plans usually set their rate of return at a conservative money market level (4 to 5 percent), a shortfall is unlikely. In fact, most cash-balance plans earn a substantial return on investment (often in double digits). These extra earnings revert back to the organization. Organizations see cash-balance plans as a source of revenue. Because pension plans can be changed, a downturn in the economy (which would trigger extra contributions) could thereby be sidestepped. Cash-balance, like defined-contribution, plans avoid the longevity bonus that a defined-benefit plan entails.

The impact of inflation on retirement income is serious. Even at low 2 or 3 percent rates, inflation will erode the purchasing power of a pension rather quickly. Defined-contribution plans contain no provisions for dealing with inflation other than the aggressive investment strategies that individuals pursue. Defined-benefit plans may benefit from legislative enactment of cost-of-living adjustments (similar to those in social security).

If social security and pensions provide the "retirement home," it is individual savings that "furnishes" it. For most individuals, individual savings may, in fact, be their home. Although this is an asset, it is not readily available for use in meeting retirement expenses. The introduction of "reverse mortgages," which allow individuals to borrow against their home's equity, does meet some of these needs.

Yet, these homes may not be a sufficient source of savings. The immense appreciation in the real estate market makes the value of these houses appear large. Adjusting the value of a house for inflation provides perspective on its real worth. Retirement needs additional savings sources.

The major retirement arena for individual savings is the 401(k) and 403(b) tax-sheltered, supplemental retirement accounts. The tax code (from whence the 401(k) and 403(b) terminology is derived) encourages this form of retirement savings. In addition to employee–employer funded retirement pensions, individuals may also make tax-deferred contributions to a retirement account. Income tax on the principle (and the interest it earns) is deferred until it is withdrawn from the account during retirement (when the individual is usually in a lower tax bracket). At age 70 1/2 the distribution of retirement benefits must begin.

Defined-benefit plans primarily relied upon the taxing power of government as their guarantee. They often create an unfunded liability because these retirement systems operate on a pay-as-you-go approach. On the other hand, defined-contribution plans are totally dependent upon the investment of their funds. This has moved pension management to the forefront. Whereas in the past state treasurers placed pension funds (i.e., the employee contributions) into government securities and other very safe investments merely to protect the principle, more aggressive strategies are called for today. The growth and interest that totally safe investments can earn seldom meet the projections as to what the employee will need in retirement (Cayer, 1995).

Investment risk has changed the way in which pension funds are managed. Because a defined-contribution plan doesn't protect the individual from loss in the way that a defined-benefit plan does, the fiduciary responsibility of pension administrators becomes quite important (Ferris, 1987).

The political management of these pension funds has come under intense scrutiny. Proposals to use pensions as funding sources for socially desirable projects or to encourage local venture capital activities raise serious questions (Cayer, Martin, and Ifflander, 1986). Public pensions have (through loans to their own governments) also been diverted to pay for ongoing budgetary expenses.

In fact, this is what happens with the social security trust fund. By law it is invested in Treasury bonds. Because these bonds must eventually be redeemed by the federal government, the purpose of a fiscally responsible investment fund is subverted into pay-as-you-go burden. By law, these transactions are also off-budget so as to disguise the real size of the deficit.

More and more, the trend is to allow employees to choose how to manage their retirement funds. Unfortunately, public sector agencies lag behind those in the private sector (which really isn't doing all that well itself) on providing employees with proper preretirement planning. Employee productivity can suffer when employees are plagued by nagging questions and uncertainties over their future (Siegal and Rees, 1992; Siegal, 1994). Even where employees have full control over their pension investments, the provision of financial planning services is becoming an essential employee benefit. If employees are to make decisions regarding the investment of their retirement funds, they must receive expert advice from a certified financial planner (CFP) or a CPA who is a personal financial specialist (PFS) to assist and guide them.

Funds for retirement are invested in a combination of fixed assets (bonds, certificates of deposit, and other money market accounts) and stocks. Stocks, because of their equity in a company, are the dynamic part of these investment portfolios. Risk is involved—for great gains and large losses. Stock investments may range from the relatively safe blue chips to bets on emerging growth companies. Even more risky are international ventures (the U.S. stock market is the most regulated and consumer-friendly in the world). Although the developed nations are safer investments than the developing, all such investments must contend not only with currency fluctuations but with political risk.

Health and Family Considerations

Providing income for the individual employee in retirement is not the sole concern of pensions. With retirement projected to last from ten to twenty years, health care is also a concern. Many individuals see medicare as a basic, minimum level of service.

Supplemental health insurance and long-term care insurance (home health care and nursing home coverage) may be included in ongoing employee benefits packages.

Family concerns prior to and during retirement are also important matters. Many organizations provide employees with life insurance (in multiples of their salary, usually about 1 1/2 times earnings). Optional group life insurance policies may also be available for purchase (with a benefit of from 1 to 3 times earnings). In the event of their early death, the life insurance will provide for their families. Although the family would receive some benefits from the accumulated pension fund, these might not yet amount to much (or become available only later). Hence, life insurance serves as a financial bridge. Terminally ill employees may also be provided with the option for a "living benefit." A living benefit allows employees to borrow against (or sell the rights to) the policy's death benefit to cover expenses during their terminal illness. Such options assume that the surviving family, if any, is not denied support.

Adequate retirement income is not usually the concern of just one person; in many cases, there is a spouse and perhaps dependent children involved. Although many spouses will have pension rights of their own, others will not. Benefits to take care of the survivor in his or her retirement are also an issue (Nielson and Beehr, 1994). Under the Retirement Equity Act of 1984, pensions must include provisions for a joint-and-survivor annuity within the plan itself or through an insurance option.

OTHER REWARDS

Organizations may use a wide array of other benefits—special pay, employee development, business expenses, living expenses, and social activities—to induce employees to attract, retain, and motivate.

Special pay options can be used. Most organizations operate on the basis of a forty-hour work week. When employees are needed for longer periods, they will be offered overtime (time and a half or double time) or compensatory time (allowing for longer vacation periods). On-call pay can be used to reduce overtime. As long as individuals are not prevented from beneficially using their own time, the more costly expenses associated with overtime can be avoided. One should also note here the flextime programs that partially adjust work hours for the convenience of the employee (McGuire and Liro, 1986, 1987; Harrick, Vanek, and Michlitsch, 1986; Buckley, Kicza, and Crane, 1987; Vega and Gilbert, 1997).

Moonlighting or second-job opportunities may also be tolerated or encouraged. This is especially true with regard to public sector jobs. Unfortunately, this practice stems more from an inability or unwillingness to pay employees adequately than from a purposive policy. Hence, individuals are allowed to supplement their income with outside, secondary jobs. Although this somewhat eases the financial pressure on both employee and employer, it raises a number of other, potentially serious questions.

Moonlighting at a second job draws upon an individual's physical and mental energies. A second job may reduce employees' capacity or willingness to fully perform in their first job. For some reason, the public sector job is always thought of as being the first or primary job; it may not be. The public job may become secondary and be treated as such.

More seriously, second jobs may give rise to concerns about or perceptions of conflict of interest. Police and regulatory officials must clearly be prohibited or separated from employment by the people and organizations over which they enforce rules. Even ordinary administrators should be separated from organizations with which their governmental entities do business. If moonlighting is allowed, an organization should monitor this activity carefully.

There are organizational advantages to moonlighting beyond the financial. When employees such as police officers or research consultants are legitimately employed by private firms, this lessens the demand for free public services. This also helps to build support for the public sector. Private businesses not only appreciate the special services that they can receive (because of the governmental economy of scale) but also come to know those who work for government as people rather than "bureaucrats."

Organizations pay people for time not worked. Paid leave (vacations and holidays) are the most well known, but they may also pay for "coffee" breaks and travel time. Unemployment compensation, advanced termination notice, transition, and severance packages are another form of pay for time not worked. These, again, are benefits designed to take an employee's mind away from future fears (by providing a financial bridge between jobs or assistance in securing alternative employment) and concentrate it on current productivity (Woska, 1988; Ting, 1996).

While clearly designed to make the organization better able to cope with its environment, employee development is also a major individual benefit. The knowledge-based organization must invest in its people if it is to exist. Yet, that very investment in people improves and adds value to those people. Education, training, and professional conferences are all means of enhancing organizational productivity. Because it's more economical to hold conferences in major locations, they also serve the social benefit of providing the employee with a "paid vacation."

Employee development has the added advantage of not only enhancing technical skills but psychologically motivating the individuals involved. The organizational investment is a recognition of the employee's worth. The added skill, though paid for by the organization, belong to the individual. For the organization to fully obtain the benefits of its education and training programs, it must keep the individual. This implies a long-term relationship and fosters organizational commitment and loyalty.

Tuition reimbursement and educational leave are two means of encouraging employees to add to their knowledge and skills. Prior approval of course work is required in tuition reimbursement programs. They also usually stipulate that courses are job-related and that the minimum of a "B" letter grade (or equivalent) be earned. Educational leave may vary from a flextime arrangement (with work hours made up) to granting paid time-off for courses. A few public organizations (such as the military) even send employees to school as their duty assignment.

Business expenses are also paid for or provided by the organization. Employee equipment, parking, transportation, and vehicles can be furnished or subsidized. Uniform or clothing allowances can be included. On-site child-care (including sick-baby care) facilities may be available (Suntrup, 1989; Kossek and Nichol, 1992). All of these items help defray the direct costs of going to work.

Indirectly, organizations can subsidize living expenses. They can provide housing allowances and underwrite mortgages. They may actually provide the housing itself (in locations convenient to the organization's offices). Commissaries and cafeterias can reduce food costs. Other retail services may also be made available to employees at discounted rates. In recruitment, relocation and temporary housing expenses are often paid. In some cases, the organization may even assist in the sale (including buying) of an existing house.

Social activities designed to build teamwork and a sense of "family" loyalty can also be undertaken. The organization can create clubs (and even build or help the community build various sport facilities); it can organize parties and outings. Even a newsletter can be used to allow employees to place short ads.

Family-friendly benefits recognize the demographic changes that have made women a permanent part of the modern workforce. Because women in the workforce still bear the major brunt of family responsibilities, organizations are finding that they must make adjustments to accommodate these requirements. Flextime schedules (geared to school hours) and day care are only two of the most well known benefits. Educational assistance (tutoring, scholarships, school matching, etc.) for dependents may be offered. Trailing spouse programs are used in recruitment ranging from assisting in job searches to actually creating a job for the spouse.

Although family-friendly benefits are much in vogue, their actual existence is rather sparse. Most organizations go little beyond health care assistance and flexible work schedules (Osterman, 1995; Durst, 1999; Newman and Matthews, 1999). Because benefit packages are primarily designed by the mostly male upper-level managers, the need for family-friendly options has not registered as a priority. In part, this is also due to the lack of empirical evidence supporting the benefits of family-friendly benefits. Samantha Durst (1999) notes that personnel managers perceive a relationship between family-friendly benefits and an organization's recruitment (albeit the causal direction of this relationship remains uncertain). These personnel managers also see the provision of family-friendly options as successfully affecting employee satisfaction and organization results. However, they are unable to produce concrete, empirical evidence in support of these contentions.

Motivation can be further enhanced through cafeteria benefit plans. These attempt to fine-tune the benefits offered by allowing individuals to allocate their benefit dollars among those options that they themselves deem most useful. Some benefit programs are obviously mandatory for all employees. However, many others are merely in the desirable category. While many employees may desire them, for others they are clearly inappropriate. To provide these benefits to all employees is a waste of resources both in terms of the money spent and in the motivation they fail to elicit; in fact, they may result in a Herzbergian dissatisfier (Barber, Dunham, and Formisano, 1992).

The motivational value of extrinsic rewards can be enhanced by incorporating intrinsic recognition and growth aspects into these awards. By turning a tangible reward into a special prize, it takes on added trophy value. As a trophy, a clock or television set constantly reminds the individual and others of the recipient's accomplishments.

COMMUNICATION

Benefits compose a large portion of the compensation package. Their worth should be communicated to the employee. For an organization to leave them out of the picture is to grossly undervalue what it's willing to pay for an employee's productivity. The inclusion of benefits information states the true wage-and-effort bargain.

Employees need to be clearly informed of what benefits are provided. This is especially important in the recruitment of new employees. Understanding is improved if generic descriptions are replaced by individualized reports. This can readily and inexpensively be done with available computer technology. These computer programs also incorporate spreadsheet "what if" analysis provisions that can project the implications of different choices.

The complexity of benefits makes training all that more important. Mistakes in providing benefits information and counseling are not only costly but often tragic. Because these mistakes only come to light when a "crisis" calls for their use, they quickly can undermine employee confidence and trust in the organization. Although benefits liability insurance can cover the organization for the financial risks involved, only the adequate training of the benefits specialists can offer "insurance" against an erosion in trust.

Benefit statements must be provided annually and provide a good opportunity for highlighting this area. Employees are presented with the value of the benefits they receive. Organizations can magnify the value of the benefit package by calculating their cost not in terms of the actual dollars spent (at group rates) but as what the equivalent, individual benefit would have cost. When benefit use results in costs even greater than this, these real savings to the individual can be pointed out. Finally, the intangible benefits can be listed.

SUMMARY

Traditionally, public organizations have employed a pay structure that treats all employees occupying similar positions the same. Paying the position was designed to avoid favoritism and inequities. However, this traditional approach also ignores individual differences and contributions. While recognizing the equity dangers inherent in strategic pay, strategic human resource management focuses on rewarding individual (or group) performance and results. In balancing equity concerns with performance needs, strategic pay can be used to attract and retain employees and, especially, to motivate their efforts.

Pay structures can be redesigned around organizational goals and objectives to offer more rewards for individuals and teams willing to excel. Concepts such as broadbanding allow supervisors more flexibility in both work assignments and rewards. Pay-for-performance itself can take many forms. Individuals can be offered merit increases or bonuses for achieving results. Organizations can encourage the development of needed skills and competencies. Gain-sharing and goal-sharing programs allow incentive rewards for team efforts.

Although for the most part the availability of benefits remains a standard feature for all employees, benefits are themselves an important part of the compensation package and serve strategic attraction and retention functions. Benefits are designed to ease employee concerns over possible (illness) and future (retirement) events. With these concerns put at rest, the employee is free to concentrate on the work at hand. Understanding and being able to explain the benefits options is an important supervisory task.

Health care and retirement issues are the most crucial of benefits options. The adequacy and affordability of health care for individual employees and their families is a major concern affecting productivity. Although not "used" by all employees, the provision of health insurance and employee assistance program services addresses fears of devastating financial emergencies. Retirement systems assuage future fears. By driving out these fears, the employee is free to focus on achieving the organization's mission.

chapter 7

Performance Appraisal

Performance appraisal systems require a specific appraisal instrument; there are no generic appraisal processes. Each performance appraisal process is intricately involved with and dependent upon the instrument it employs (as well as with the organizational and individual behavior entailed). Focusing on the traditional question of what appraisal type or instrument to use (even if other factors are also now considered to be important) remains a central issue of concern among performance appraisal scholars and advocates.

This chapter provides:

1. An overview of the legal and practical factors and options used in designing appraisal systems
2. Knowledge of subjective and interpersonal comparison techniques
3. Knowledge of objective behaviorally anchored rating scales and management-by-objectives techniques
4. An overview of potential problems arising from organizational, structural, and rater error

In appraising individual performance, the search for specific performance appraisal instruments runs the gamut from the subjective (essay, graphic rating scale, and checklists) through interpersonal (rankings and forced distribution) to the objective (behaviorally anchored rating scales and management by objectives). Although history has, more or less, passed the subjective and interpersonal approaches by as meaningful solutions to the appraisal dilemma, reality still sees them employed quite extensively. So, an examination of these types of appraisals not only outlines the intellectual development that has led to the introduction of objective appraisal systems but, rather unfortunately, also is a look at systems—however inadequate they may be—that are still in use.

DESIGNING APPRAISAL SYSTEMS

In order to correctly employ the performance appraisal process, the answers to a series of five questions need to be explored. This chapter examines these questions—Why do we appraise? What do we appraise? When do we appraise? Who does the appraising? and How do we appraise? These questions focus on the fundamental elements that make up the performance appraisal process.

The answers to these questions provide the basis upon which the design for a successful appraisal system rests. In each instance it is important to note, however, that the answers to these questions do not point out the one best way to construct an appraisal system but rather serve to provide the questioner with a series of choices. Matching these choices or alternatives to the needs of an organization and its employees is the foundation upon which a successful performance appraisal system is built.

Performance Appraisal Criteria

Since the passage of the Civil Rights Act of 1964, American courts have mandated objective personnel practices. Although advocated prior to the Civil Rights Act of 1964, in enforcing the civil rights legislation the courts provided strong and compelling legal support for their employment. Performance appraisal has benefited greatly from this legal intervention. The net result is a synthesis of legal and objective criteria for the employment of performance appraisal.

Although the employment of objective performance appraisal techniques and processes should be a most ordinary occurrence, it has, unfortunately, all too often taken legal intervention with its implied threats of negative sanctions to introduce their practice. American management practices, especially when applied to the public sector, are notorious in their seeking out of shortcuts and short circuits. Unfortunately, little effort is often expended on validating many of these easier alternatives. The extension of the *Griggs v. Duke Power Company* (1971) decision to clearly include performance appraisal systems (*Connecticut v. Teal,* 1982) changed all this.

Performance appraisal benefits from the application of the system-designing process. Job elements, interpersonal relations, and organizational purposes all need to fit together (Mohrman, Resnick-West, and Lawler, 1989; Daley, 1992b). Case law outlines six criteria for constructing performance appraisal systems. According to Shelley P. Burchett and Kenneth DeMeuse (1985), attention to job analysis, work behaviors, communications, training, documentation, and monitoring combine to guide in the development of systems capable of appraising performance.

Derived from the scientific management movement, job analysis is the foundation for a number of personnel practices, including performance appraisal. It is viewed as essential that the performance on which an individual is to be appraised is clearly understood (*Albemarle Paper Company v. Moody,* 1975; *Wade v. Mississippi*

Cooperative Extension Service, 1976; *Patterson v. American Tobacco Company,* 1978; *Carpenter v. Stephen F. Austin State University,* 1983). Both employee and supervisor need to understand the job requirements that the employee is expected to fulfill. Without this mutual understanding, it is impossible to either perform or evaluate an employee's work.

Up-to-date job analyses delineate the job duties and responsibilities required of an employee; hence, they are the appropriate basis upon which to assess an individual. A job analysis informs employees of what is expected from them and reminds supervisors what it is their employees are being asked to do. The specific evaluation factors used in an appraisal instrument are designed to measure the performance of the tasks indicated by the job analysis.

Related to this criterion is the focus on work behaviors. According to court rulings (*Brito v. Zia Company,* 1973; *Zell v. United States,* 1979), job-specific work behaviors are to serve as the basis for the evaluation of an employee's performance.

Although vaguer, subjective notions may offer certain theoretical insights, the courts are reluctant to fully sanction their use (*Zell v. United States,* 1979; *Ramirez v. Hofheinz,* 1980). The employment of subjective assessments requires careful consideration and is best done in conjunction with the more objective aspects of performance appraisal.

Communication is essential to performance appraisal. American notions of due process and fairness are clearly evident here. Individuals must be aware of the performance standards used to evaluate them (*Rowe v. General Motors,* 1972; *Zell v. United States,* 1979). As a management tool, communication is also important. Feedback is essential for the improvement of performance. Research has long demonstrated the important role feedback plays in improving individual performance and enhancing productivity (Ammons, 1956; Vroom, 1964; Ilgen, Fisher, and Taylor, 1979). Government employees are just as influenced by feedback as are their private sector counterparts (Yeager, Rabin, and Vocino, 1985). Individuals seek out feedback on their performance.

Supervisory training focuses on another behavioral criterion. One of the great limitations that performance appraisal faces is the apparent reluctance of organizations to properly train employees in its use. Hence, court mandates appear necessary to overcome this hesitation. Supervisors cannot be left without any guidance in the application of the performance appraisal processes (*Rowe v. General Motors,* 1972; *Harper v. Mayor and City Council of Baltimore,* 1972; *Carpenter v. Stephen F. Austin State University,* 1983). As with any tool, performance appraisal requires instruction in its proper and safe use.

Documentation addresses the somewhat more negative issue of legal defensibility. Public trials in which the accused can both confront and cross-examine the witnesses and evidence against him or her are an integral element in the American way of life. These principles are seen to adhere in court rulings on performance appraisal (*Marquez v. Omaha District Sales Office, Ford Division of the Ford Motor Company,* 1971; *Turner v. State Highway Commission of Missouri,* 1982). The importance attached to an individual's job is such that the courts have extended the rules of evidence to cover the employment of performance appraisal systems. Organizations must be able to produce evidence in support of their personnel decisions, especially in those incidences wherein severe sanctions and job loss are imposed.

Due process considerations also underlie the requirement for monitoring. Organizations must check to see not only that their appraisal systems are up-to-date (*Carpenter v. Stephen F. Austin State University,* 1983) but also that they are not being abused (*Rowe v. General Motors,* 1972). Performance appraisal standards based on out-of-date job analyses fail to reflect current job requirements. The employee is often left with the unenviable, Catch-22 task of either doing the job right or correctly following procedure. In addition, liability litigation documents numerous cases involving the abuse of authority. Grievance and discipline appeal provisions can build in safeguards against the abuse of the performance appraisal process.

Why Do We Appraise?

Performance appraisal is a conscientious effort at formally, rationally, and objectively organizing our assessments of others. In doing so, it is focused on the task of enhancing job-relatedness. Eliminating measurement and rating errors and structuring the decision-making process itself in order to accomplish this are the dual foci of appraisal research.

As a decision-making tool, performance appraisal is designed to positively structure the assessment process. By formally focusing attention solely on the objective, job-related criteria for assessing performance, the manager is provided with the means for making appropriate decisions that rationally contribute to the organization's and individual's effectiveness and well-being.

The purposes for which performance appraisal can be employed are numerous. However, these can be grouped into two broad categories—judgmental and developmental (Cummings and Schwab, 1973: 5). Although both developmental and judgmental appraisals have enhanced productivity as their goal, they approach it in two quite distinct fashions.

Developmental methods take an employee's basic competence for granted (the coordination of recruitment and selection with position or job analysis techniques is deemed sufficient to handle this). Hence, developmental appraisals focus on adding value to the employee. Developmental approaches are humanistic in nature and operate on an intrinsic motivational level (albeit developmental opportunities may also entail substantial present or potential extrinsic rewards). More specifically, the performance appraisal serves as an action device or needs assessment instrument triggering employee training (Herbert and Doverspike, 1990). Linking appraisal to training can prove difficult even when used in conjunction with the most objective appraisal instrument (Daley, 1983a, 1987a).

Development focuses on an individual's potential rather than on his or her current level of skills and capabilities. Hence, it is essential in such assessments to consider the question of growth for what? Whether viewed from an organizational or from an individual perspective, the goal toward which this potential is directed needs examination.

Individually, it is important that developmental efforts take into account not only the employee's perceived capabilities but also what specific career opportunities are desired. A proactive effort at informing an employee about what is indeed possible should be included here. For example, managers can suggest that employees think about differing options and even provide for "exploratory" assignments and training. Training and development should be focused on obtaining the knowledge, skills, and abilities that qualify an employee for career advancement and promotion.

Organizationally, the need for developing this potential must be determined. Basically, will the organization accrue some benefit from developing an individual's potential? The human resources aspects of an organization's strategic planning process should serve to provide the answers to these questions. If an organization is to provide an employee with enhanced skills and abilities, it is important that the organization perceive what reward it expects to receive from this.

Judgmental purposes follow the management systems or command-and-control model of authority. Yet there are serious questions regarding the cognitive validity entailed in judgmental appraisals (Bowman, 1999). Judgmental appraisals are also quite explicitly linked to extrinsic rewards and punishments. In fact, the existence and adequacy of the reward structure is an important subsidiary question with regard to their effectiveness (Perry, 1986). This has proved an important limitation in their use among public sector agencies.

Promotion and merit pay decisions are the two most widely known and used of the judgmental appraisal purposes. Merit pay is especially in vogue with many public sector jurisdictions seeing it as a means for enhancing productivity and, at the same time, cutting costs. However, the reality of merit pay in the public sector is somewhat different (Gabris, 1986; Halachmi and Holzer, 1987; Lovrich, 1987; Perry, Petrakis, and Miller, 1989).

Promotion entails both developmental (what additional competencies does this individual need and how can they be provided for?) and pay considerations. Yet, it is a distinct decision. While the criteria used in assessing performance for pay and those involved in promotional considerations overlap, they also differ. It is even suggested that a separate promotability appraisal may be appropriate (Cederblom, 1991).

Performance appraisal can play a significant role in other career moves (reassignment and demotion) as well as in retention, reinstatement, and dismissal decisions. These negative tasks are key ingredients in the practice of cutback management (Levine, 1978, 1979; Lewis and Logalbo, 1980; Levine, Rubin, and Wolohojian, 1982). Either standing alone or in conjunction with other criteria such as seniority and education, performance appraisals are used in calculating the formulas used in determining employee bumping rights for positions.

In addition to all these purposes, performance appraisal plays a role in the validation of personnel techniques. Tests used in the staffing and selection process are often statistically validated in terms of their ability to predict job performance. That job performance is, in turn, measured by a performance appraisal instrument.

Individuals hope to receive feedback for improving their performance from the appraisal process. They also do not generally perceive an objective assessment as threatening. To a great extent, this latter attitude can be attributed to the relatively high opinion individuals tend to hold with regard to their own abilities. There is even some evidence for managers seeking out negative comments (Ashford and Tsui, 1991).

This desire for objective appraisal is, however, intricately tied to an individual's sense of self-identity. In addition, individuals are keenly aware that most appraisals are used for allocating highly desired extrinsic rewards. All of these factors combine to set the stage for an array of potentially divisive individual–organization conflicts (Mohrman, Resnick-West, and Lawler, 1989: 5–11; Murphy and Cleveland, 1995: 106–109).

Individuals desire development and rewards; organizations desire to develop and reward their employees. Unfortunately, the information necessary for achieving one of these goals may hinder the achieving of the other. If individuals detail their weaknesses so that they can receive needed training in order to improve their performance, they may in the process lose out on valued rewards. Obversely, in order to efficiently allocate rewards among employees, organizations may miss out on important considerations that vitally affect their future (Longenecker and Nykodym, 1996).

Where a substantial degree of employee loyalty and trust exists, appraisal systems may successfully merge judgmental and developmental purposes. Such appraisal systems rely on objective measures chosen through a highly participative, almost consensual, supervisor–employee understanding (Mikkelsen, Ogaard, and Lovrich, 1997).

Clearly, it may not be possible to mix judgmental and developmental purposes in the same appraisal process (Cascio, 1982; Hyde and Smith, 1982). Cognitive research has long indicated that managers are influenced by the purpose of the appraisal in making their judgments (Landy and Farr, 1980; Meyer, Kay, and French, 1965; Mohrman and Lawler, 1983; Murphy and Cleveland, 1995: 241–266; Daley, 1992b: 114–119; Bowman, 1999). The purpose for which an appraisal is to be used shapes and frames how a manager assesses an individual. Even with the most objective appraisal instruments, the criteria take on a more subtle and specific perspective.

The validity of appraisals completed with one goal in mind is questionable when they are subsequently used in the assessment of another. Even if the measurement factors employed were to remain identical, supervisors might assess them differently in light of a different purpose they were being asked to assess. In contrasting developmental and judgmental purposes with the extent of agency investment in the performance appraisal process, Balfour (1992) found few distinctions. Investment was found to make for virtually no significant difference among employee attitudes. The judgmental attitudes predominated regardless of whether an agency emphasized developmental purposes or not.

What Do We Appraise?

Job-relatedness is the chief standard by which the acceptability of a performance appraisal measurement is judged. Established through the Uniform Guidelines on Employee Selection Procedures (1978) in response to the Supreme Court's decision in *Griggs v. Duke Power Company* (1971), the courts have repeatedly reaffirmed and explained the requirement for job-relatedness in subsequent rulings (*Brito v. Zia Company,* 1973; *Ramirez v. Hofheinz,* 1980; *Zell v. United States,* 1979). Job-relatedness poses a twofold requirement for organizations—criteria must enable supervisors to discriminate between employees solely in terms of their job performance, and the organization must be able to prove or demonstrate the existence of that relationship.

In choosing performance measures, care must be taken to ensure that they are reliable, practical, and controllable. Reliability requires that performance measures be relatively stable over time such that they produce consistent readings vis-à-vis similar performance. For it to be practical, a measure must be readily available to those using it. In addition, it must be viewed as an appropriate measure and be accepted as such by those whose performance is being measured. Finally, controllability reminds us that the performance being measured should represent behaviors or results over which the individual actually exercises substantial influence (Smith, 1977; Gatewood and Feild, 1998).

The question of performance standards is an important one because the use of such standards is positively correlated with an intensified employment of the appraisal process itself. The purposes served by a performance appraisal process are intricately intertwined with the quality of the instruments or systems themselves. The technical systems and the concomitant efforts spent in developing and perfecting them are all directed at enhancing the effectiveness of the appraisal process in guiding organizational decisions. Inasmuch as this effort is successful, it serves to establish confidence in the appraisal process and encourage its employment for additional purposes.

Performance standards lie at the heart of all effective appraisal systems. What questions arise focus on the extent to which the performance standards are job-related and written to be consistent with the position's job description. It is only by adhering to such practices that an appraisal system can obtain objectivity and legality. This is also important because the performance being measured is the behavior that the organization reinforces (Luthans and Stajkovic, 1999). Performance standards are meant to anchor an appraisal system to specific, job-related tasks. Inasmuch as they are consistent with written position descriptions (which form the psychological contract or expectations basis upon which people are hired), they reinforce this. The failure to align a performance appraisal process with an organization's system of position descriptions introduces confusion and leads to ineffectiveness. Hence, written performance standards help to communicate to the workers a clearer understanding of their jobs. However, this is indeed a quite daunting endeavor. Most supervisors, even when benefiting from extensive training find it difficult to accomplish (U.S. Merit Systems Protection Board, 1999a).

Another related item is the concern for the appraisal process's participative aspect. The participation of employees and supervisors in the development of performance standards introduces a number of positive features. Employee acceptance of a performance appraisal system is a crucial element in determining if it will be successful. Participation helps to confer such legitimacy upon the appraisal system. It affords employees an opportunity to voice their concerns and assists in clarifying potential misunderstandings. The net result is to leave the employee with the sense of having a stake in the appraisal process. Without participation and the legitimacy it entails, the performance appraisal task is more difficult. In turn, supervisors become more reluctant users who themselves tend to undermine the appraisal process (Mohrman, Resnick-West, and Lawler, 1989: 11; Daley, 1992b: 86–87; Roberts, 1992).

Skills, knowledge, and abilities (SKAs), personal traits or characteristics, activities or work behaviors, and results all can serve as criteria for assessing performance (Milkovich and Boudreau, 1991: 94). However, behaviors and results are more likely to successfully meet the job-relatedness standard. SKAs traits are specific to individuals and not inherent in the jobs themselves. As such, they pose a serious problem with regard to satisfactorily establishing their validity. Although their use is not precluded, establishing the evidence of statistical validity necessary to support their use can be a difficult and costly task. Yet, it is these skills, knowledge, and abilities that constitute the core competencies that individuals bring with them to the job.

SKAs include such diverse characteristics as job knowledge, physical strength, eye-hand coordination, licenses, and business knowledge. These are the SKAs often included in position descriptions and used as a guide in recruitment and selection. Although they are clearly meant as a statement of competencies required to perform a given job, they are unlikely to sufficiently discriminate between different performance levels. Basically, SKAs represent the minimum qualifications necessary in order to perform a job adequately.

Traits encompass what are essentially the "boy scout virtues"—trustworthy, loyal, helpful, friendly, courteous, kind, obedient, cheerful, thrifty, brave, clean, and reverent. Although these characteristics are certainly key factors in the conduct of an effective life let alone in the performance of any job, the ability to validate the relationship between individual traits and the performance of specific jobs is extremely difficult.

Establishing validity is a serious legal challenge to the use of traits in personnel management. For the most part, organizations choose not to attempt it. Because traits are themselves rather general in nature, the methodological and cost barriers that organizations face in regard to demonstrating job-related validity are often seen as prohibitive.

Behaviors and results are the foundation upon which the two most objective performance appraisal instruments (behaviorally anchored rating scales and management by objectives) are built. Behaviors are the activities and tasks individuals engage in, in the performance of their jobs; results are the outcomes from those activities (Landy and Farr, 1983; Murphy and Cleveland, 1995: 112–115).

In general, the use of results is more preferred in the private sector whereas behaviors are favored in the public. This, however, is more an objective reflection on the individual versus group nature of the jobs in the public and private sectors.

The previously described conditions that make the public sector so distinctive also usually prevent any one individual from having complete control over the means necessary for actually accomplishing his or her job. In the public sector, individuals must work and cooperate with others in order to perform their tasks. Hence, behaviors—representing individual inputs—are often a more appropriate measure of performance than are outcomes. In the private sector, however, it is more likely that an individual can be given control over the essential factors affecting job performance. Under such conditions, it can be quite reasonable to focus on outcomes as measures of individual performance. Even so, such clear-cut distinctions between the nature of public and private sector jobs are seldom reflected in reality.

The exclusive concentration on either behaviors or results each has its disadvantages. An overemphasis on results can lead to the sacrifice of long-term advantages and interests for quickly won, short-term gains. In addition, an emphasis on results can lead to the ignoring of important, secondary functions whose contributions are not so clearly seen or easily measured, yet are nevertheless important to the organization's success. Furthermore, placing an overemphasis on results can also foster unethical conduct.

Equally, an exclusive focus on behaviors and processes is also to be avoided. Like Potemkin villages they may only give the appearance of economic prosperity and vitality. An overemphasis on correctly performing work behaviors can lead to excessive red tape. In many organizations, employees find that "working to rule" is a highly effective weapon for bringing management to the bargaining table. In fact, in both the public and private sectors it is proving to be more effective than threats of a strike. A mixture of behaviors and results tends to provide balance in the selection of performance standards.

Ultimately, organizational conditions and the nature of the job itself affect the choice of whether behaviors or results are employed for measuring performance. How the organizational culture views and supports performance appraisal is an important factor. The organizational climate in which employees must perform their duties is also an essential aspect (Milkovich and Wigdor, 1991: 110–111; Daley, 1992b: 38–41; Murphy and Cleveland, 1995: 82–84). Finally, the specific nature of the job itself plays a major role (Condrey, 1994). The appropriateness of behaviors or results as a performance measure stems from the individual job analyses.

Computer software (e.g., Austin-Hayne Employee Appraiser, Avantos ReviewWriter, KnowledgePoint Performance Now!, Insight Profiles, CompStar Appraiser Plus, 20/20 Insight Gold, Visual 360, and Intelligent Consensus) is widely available for use in performance appraisals. These computer packages are highly efficient; that is, they are easily installed and quickly mastered. For many, they are seen as improving both the performance appraisal process and performance itself (Nelson and Economy, 1997; Fried, 1999).

Unfortunately, most of these merely allow for the rapid creation of electronic versions of the subjective graphic rating scale. The packages provide "canned" narratives to "support" a supervisor's magic rating number (instead of the performance assessment leading to a summary number). Most of these packages have goal-based project management tracking options that can be added to the appraisal process.

When Do We Appraise?

In order to make judgments about an individual's performance, that performance has to be seen in its entirety. Hence, performance appraisals must be based on a time period sufficient for the accomplishment of the job responsibilities expected from an individual. As a practical matter, most appraisal systems operate on an annual cycle. However, critics of appraisal systems often focus on such short periods as contributing to the problems they see with their use. As Fred Thayer (1987) notes, an annual cycle leads to a short-term perspective with its concomitant sacrifice of long-range considerations. In matters such as promotion, a short appraisal cycle may be an inadequate time frame. Fred Thayer (1987) would argue for longer periods of up to six or seven years in which to adequately size up an employee.

In most circumstances where an annual cycle is indeed employed, the timing decision is reduced to a choice between the anniversary-date and focal-point methods (Mohrman, Resnick-West, and Lawler, 1989: 121–125; Daley, 1992b: 27–29). Under the anniversary-date approach, appraisals coincide with the anniversary of each individual's date of employment. The anniversary-date appraisal cycle spreads the supervisor's workload over the course of the entire year. Given the large number of employees for which an individual supervisor may hold appraisal responsible, this can be advantageous. Although the number of appraisals is the same under both approaches, the supervisor's ability to manage them is improved under the anniversary-date approach. With the supervisor no longer facing an avalanche of appraisals, the quality of individual appraisals should be improved.

An anniversary-date method also faces a number of shortcomings. Disadvantages may flow from a lack of timely measurement information. Up-to-date or appropriate measurements may just not be available for use in an anniversary-date appraisal. In addition, the anniversary-date method limits comparability. Supervisors find it more difficult to judge employee performances vis-à-vis one another. This is true even for employees who have virtually the same jobs.

Furthermore, organizations may find it more difficult to monitor the supervisor's handling of the appraisal process, including questions of fairness and equity. Because environmental or organizational conditions may be involved, anniversary-date appraisals can differ on what would otherwise be similar cases.

Although comparability along with equity and fairness concerns can be more adequately monitored with a focal-point approach to performance appraisal, the process itself may suffer from a lack of supervisory attention to detail. With too many employees to appraise, the individual appraisals may become perfunctory.

Because public organizations often operate with smaller spans of control and, consequently, with more supervisors than are typically found in the private sector, this need not be a serious problem.

Who Does the Appraising?

Traditionally, the immediate supervisor is most often the one responsible for appraising subordinates (Mohrman, Resnick-West, and Lawler, 1989: 95–96; Daley, 1992b: 29–36). Supervisory appraisal of subordinates is the predominate method and is widely suggested to occur in approximately 90 percent of the cases. This is the management individual deemed most knowledgeable about both the employee and the job. In fact, performance appraisal is often viewed as a key management system tool in establishing a supervisor's command-and-control authority. In contrast, from a more humanistic perspective, the appraisal process is also viewed as being designed to strengthen the employee–supervisor relationship through the encouragement of mutual understanding.

Yet, there are some potentially interesting answers to this question other than those found in supervisory-based appraisal. These proposals fall into two general categories—the use of agency insiders (e.g., self-appraisal, peer review, subordinate appraisal, and multiple raters) and the employment of outsiders (e.g., personnel officials, consultants and assessment centers, and clients and customers).

The self-appraisal calls upon employees to evaluate their own performance. Inasmuch as the employee is the individual who most accurately knows what his or her own performance is, this can be an extremely useful assessment. Self-appraisal is a technique well suited for use in developmental appraisals but questionable when employed in a judgmental setting (Campbell and Lee, 1988; Mohrman, Resnick-West, and Lawler, 1989: 98–100; Daley, 1992b: 29–30; Murphy and Cleveland, 1995: 137–140).

Research indicates that self-appraisals invariably produce higher ratings than those provided by supervisors. Although self-ratings move toward the ratings designated by supervisors when feedback is provided (Steel and Ovalle, 1984), research does not support any claim that one is a more accurate measure than the other. Employees may merely adjust their self-ratings because they recognize the realities of organizational power.

As a developmental tool, self-appraisals are invaluable. The self-appraisal provides the organization with firsthand knowledge of its employees' perceived needs for improvement. Self-appraisals do, however, require some mental adjustments in their employment. Basically, employees think about themselves more in terms of their competencies than in terms of their performance levels—what they can do rather than what they did (Latham, 1986). Hence, it is important to understand that framework when employing self-appraisals.

Peer review is most notably employed in both military and academic settings (Landy and Farr, 1983). Although it need not be limited to professionals, this is the venue in which it is most often employed. Research indicates that the assessments from peer ratings are just as accurate as those provided by supervisors (Love, 1983; Mohrman, Resnick-West, and Lawler, 1989: 100–101; Daley, 1992b: 31–32; Murphy and Cleveland, 1995: 140–142).

Peer review is an approach that uses multiple appraisers. Because peers have more extensive contacts with the employees being appraised than supervisors usually do, this often allows them to observe behaviors that would otherwise go unnoticed by a single supervisor. Peers are also able to base their rating on a comprehensive assessment of the employee's performance rather than on a sample of incidents as occurs with regard to supervisory evaluations. In addition, peers are better able to assess an employee's level of collegiality (Cederblom and Lounsbury, 1980).

Although objectivity is not a problem, peer ratings do face a number of subjective concerns. Basically, employees don't like them. Employees often are provided with little training to guide them in their application of the peer-rating process. With fears regarding what consequences ratings can have on individual careers and personal relationships, it is hardly surprising that employees are somewhat reluctant to participate in peer ratings. Supervisors and managers often share many of the same qualms when it comes to the performance appraisal process.

A developmental focus helps alleviate some of the hesitation surrounding peer review. Even so, the effect on employee interpersonal relationships still may tend to make individuals uneasy in such circumstances. Employees who regularly work with a colleague are in a far better position to discern another's behaviors. Hence, they can assist in the assessment of these individuals' needs for training and development. Furthermore, it is among these colleagues that the issue of collegiality is, in fact, determined. Although collegiality, like loyalty, is a rather intangible and difficult-to-validate trait, it is nevertheless an important factor in the composition of an effective organization.

Subordinate appraisal of supervisors and managers is antihierarchial. As such, it generates a high degree of unease from both managers and employees. Organizationally, it can undermine authority patterns founded on hierarchal status (Mohrman, Resnick-West, and Lawler, 1989: 101–102; Daley, 1992b: 32; Murphy and Cleveland, 1995: 136–137). The employment of subordinate appraisal is extremely infrequent; it draws mainly on the vast student–teacher evaluation research for its supporting evidence.

H. John Bernardin (1986) strongly advocates the employment of subordinate appraisal. Subordinates are especially capable of assessing those aspects of managerial job performance that focus on employee communications and development. Inasmuch as these are organizational goals, subordinate appraisals can actually support hierarchal structures. In such circumstances, the subordinate appraisal becomes an instrument for monitoring the supervisor or manager's implementation of the prescribed organizational policy.

Subordinate appraisals can provide managers feedback and serve to reinforce good behavioral practices (Ashford and Tsui, 1991). In addition, subordinate appraisals enhance the nonmanagerial work environment within an organization. They focus more attention on subordinate concerns. This can be quite important, especially among professional establishments as well as in the modern client- or customer-driven organizations.

As would be expected, a developmental focus for employing subordinate appraisal meets with more acceptance from managers than one used in a judgmental fashion (McEvoy, 1990; Roberts, 1995; Coggburn, 1998).

A number of different performance appraisal proposals employ upper-level managers (Mohrman, Resnick-West, and Lawler, 1989: 97–98; Murphy and Cleveland, 1995: 142–143) or team management concepts (Edwards, 1983, 1991; Edwards, Borman, and Sproull, 1985; Edwards and Sproull, 1985; Meyer, 1991; Daley, 1992b: 33-34). Both the superior and team management approaches are designed to encourage familiarity with an employee's work by managers other than an employee's immediate supervisor. Organizationally, participation by these superior or team managers results in their gaining a better understanding of the interrelationships and workings within their organization.

Team management employs multiple raters. Supervisors and managers drawn from cognate units serve together on an appraisal panel. Mark R. Edwards (1983, 1991) views this as a means for introducing multiple perspectives into the appraisal process, and thereby improving its overall objectivity and fairness.

A reduction in rater errors and biases is facilitated by a team management approach. Managers help to educate and guide one another, thereby supplementing their formal training. This informal training has the added advantage of fulfilling a continuing education function. It also entails an informal peer review of the team member supervisors inasmuch as their handling of the performance appraisal process is under observation of their fellow managers; this adds to their incentives to do it right.

The comparability of workers should also be enhanced under a team management approach to appraisal. Supervisors obtain knowledge about the skills and competencies of workers other than those they supervise. This expanded referent knowledge base can aid them not only in assessing their own subordinates but, potentially, in future employment decisions. Furthermore, the success derived from the appraisal task can contribute to building organizational trust among managers and lead to cooperation on other tasks.

Both Mark R. Edwards (1983, 1991) and Herbert H. Meyer (1991) see the employment of a multiple raters adaptation as a means for successfully integrating judgmental and developmental appraisals. For the most part, systems that attempt to incorporate both judgmental and developmental purposes fail. Under an application of Gresham's law to the performance appraisal process, it is usually the developmental function that is lost. However, on occasion dissatisfaction with the entire effort undermines the whole appraisal process.

Team management appraisal is the only method with a chance for achieving both development and judgment within the same appraisal process. In this approach, an employee's immediate supervisor performs the developmental role of advisor, coach, and advocate; the judgmental role is fulfilled by the other team managers. In turn, each supervisor presents and argues the cases of their subordinates before the panel. The other supervisors or managers hear the case. On the basis of these arguments and their personal knowledge of these individuals, the other panel members make the judgmental decisions. The team performs the judgment function for the organization while the individual supervisors play the developmental role for their employees. Supervisors reap the benefits from fulfilling a developmental purpose and the positive relationships that it helps foster. The onus of judgment is conveniently scapegoated onto the other managers.

Although such an approach might succeed in melding judgmental and developmental purposes within the same appraisal process, it entails a substantial effort on the part of both supervisors and employees. To work, a strong sense of supervisor–employee trust is required. Employees must not only trust in their own supervisor's developmental and advocacy capabilities but in the inherent objectivity and fairness of the other supervisors who sit in judgment. The organization needs to assure that communications, along with the appropriate supervisory training, fully support this appraisal process.

The participation of outsiders in the performance appraisal process is even rarer than that accorded to the other-insider approaches discussed above. Experts from the central personnel office and/or consultants can be brought in to assess employee performance. The performance appraisal process can be conducted in much the same manner that a job analysis is (Mohrman, Resnick-West, and Lawler, 1989: 103, 106). Instead of assessing job performance, another option evaluates employees on the basis of their participation in an assessment center. This is an indirect method of appraising performance and is analogous to the use of traits or characteristics. Hence, the job-relatedness of this approach is probably open to legal question.

In terms of external or outsider appraisals, an organization may also turn to its clients or customers (Mohrman, Resnick-West, and Lawler, 1989: 102–103). Because these customers and clients are also taxpayers and voters in addition to being recipients of services, public involvement is more commonplace among government agencies. In fact, it may be perceived as part of the definitional aspect of public organizations. What is perhaps not so readily seen or accorded to is a legitimate involvement by members of the public in the specific operations of agencies and in their personnel matters.

The combination of a number of these information sources (especially supervisor, subordinate, peer, and even self-ratings) is the basis for 360-degree feedback (Murphy and Cleveland, 1995: 144–146; Pollack and Pollack, 1996; Edwards and Ewen, 1996; DeLeon and Ewen, 1997; DeNisi and Kluger, 2000; Ghorpade, 2000). With its low hierarchy and professional staff the modern organization is, on the one hand, forced to seek out nonsupervisory sources for appraisal and, on the other, blessed with highly knowledgeable employees. Hence, 360-degree feedback promises to provide a more balanced form of appraisal. Of course, the 360-degree appraisal is designed to serve as a developmental instrument. When it is transformed into a judgmental appraisal, 360-degree appraisal loses its effectiveness (and often engenders employee distrust). A number of software packages (Insight Profiles, CompStar Appraiser Plus, 20/20 Insight Gold, Visual 360, and Intelligent Consensus) are available (Fried, 1999).

This technique is especially useful when employed for developmental purposes (Lepsinger and Lucia, 1997; DeNisi and Kluger, 2000; Ghorpade, 2000). However, it is somewhat problematic when incorporated into a judgmental system. Subordinates and peers are especially likely to be concerned with an appraisal that is used judgmentally. Such a transformation is viewed quite negatively and erodes employee loyalty. Depending on the purpose, individual ratings may change in up to a third of the cases (Waldman, Atwater, and Antonioni, 1998).

As with any performance appraisal system, 360-degree appraisals must be focused on job-related components. The training for raters (and the possible affects of rater error) is much more important. Because 360-degree appraisal is a highly participative technique, its success or failure has greater symbolic significance and implications (Waldman, Atwater, and Antonioni, 1998).

SUBJECTIVE TECHNIQUES

Subjective techniques are not in themselves inherently wrong. They are, after all, the foundation upon which the more objective techniques are developed. The problem with subjective appraisals centers on the basic vagueness or the idiosyncrasy that is their essence. Subjective appraisals are uniquely the assessment of a specific individual. It is the resultant possibilities for inter-rater differences and errors that creates the problem.

A subjective appraisal can, indeed, actually be more accurate than that provided for by the use of an objective technique. An individual using a holistic assessment may subconsciously factor in and weigh the relevant performance criteria much more accurately than would occur with a supposedly objective system (which may have inadvertently ignored or downplayed the importance of specific performance criteria). However, it is the a priori inability to sufficiently explain to others how this appraisal process works that is the crux of the problem.

Inasmuch as an individual can avoid vagueness and not succumb to the temptations for abuse, a subjective performance appraisal process can fulfill all of management's decision-making needs. The legal requirements undergirding performance appraisal systems are, of course, another matter. However, even here courts support the use of subjective appraisal when used in conjunction with other, objective instruments (*Ramirez v. Hofheinz,* 1980).

The Nonappraisal

The essence of performance appraisal is, in many ways, fully captured in Peter Drucker's subjective "nonappraisal" (1966: 86):

1. "What has he (or she) done well?"
2. "What, therefore, is he likely to be able to do well?"
3. "What does he have to learn or to acquire to be able to get the full benefit from his strength?"

4. "If I had a son or daughter, would I be willing to have him or her work under this person?"
   (a) "If yes, why?"
   (b) "If no, why?"

As subjective as this approach is, Peter Drucker's appraisal format has it all. It measures actual performance. It assesses an individual's potential for development and explicitly provides for a training plan to achieve it. Finally, in his fourth item Drucker focuses on the even more highly subjective dimension of ethics. This is an aspect of appraisal that objective systems, perhaps unfortunately, do not really adequately touch upon. In many instances, there are rather distinct differences between behavior that is legally permitted and that which is ethical. Although we often settle for the former, it is the latter that we prefer and need.

The Drucker performance appraisal is also interesting in terms of what it does not do. Peter Drucker warns against focusing on weaknesses. Too often, performance appraisals become part of a "Can'tian" philosophy of management. Weaknesses and shortcomings are focused on to the detriment of an individual's strengths and accomplishments. Individuals are not employed for what they cannot do, but for what they can do. Betraying their partial origin from the study of clinical psychology, many performance appraisals often seek out weaknesses rather than pointing out strengths. Although this may be good medicine, it is quite often bad management.

The Essay

Essays, graphic rating scales, and checklists are three of the formats that are basically subjective appraisals. The accuracy of the assessments derived when each of these formats is employed may prove exceedingly high. However, this accuracy flows more from the interactive combination of organization and individual rater than from the merits of the specific instrument being employed.

The essay appraisal format is a tabula rasa. Supervisors have a blank space on which they are free to write. Essay appraisals (along with the more modern audio or video log equivalents) are descended from the traditional duty or fitness report. Almost all appraisals, including today's objective techniques, include an essay component.

Both the essay's strengths and weaknesses are to be found in its written format. The essay is extremely dependent upon the individual communication skills of the supervisors using it. The talents of an extraordinary employee could easily go unnoticed because of a supervisor's inability to articulate them. Although communication skills are only one of the elements desired in a manager, it is rather unrealistic to assume that an organization would employ someone as a supervisor who was seriously deficient. Even so, marginal differences in supervisory ability may matter. Performance appraisal systems are used to basically magnify what are in reality the small differences that distinguish the various gradations of competent individuals from one another.

The essay's major drawback is the inability to use it for comparing employee appraisals. Most of the purposes in which performance appraisal is employed work by comparing employees with one another (on the basis of their job performance). This is the primary reason that organizations use appraisals.

Essays lack any easily or readily quantifiable component; there are simply no numbers involved. Although the supervisor–employee relationship is little affected by this, the ability of upper-level managers to compare employees' performance is. Upper-level managers just do not possess the time necessary to read and competently analyze written employee appraisals.

However, this weakness in the essay appraisal can also be viewed as a strength. The very lack of a numeric component prevents the essay appraisal from being reduced to a simplistic rating. Employee performance must be examined case by case, each on its own merits. It allows for the examination of both performance and circumstances in which that performance occurred. Consequently, as a management tool, the essay appraisal affords supervisors an extremely rich opportunity.

The essay's subjective nature and labor intensity limit its uses. In order to meet legal requirements, it must be used in conjunction with another, objective (i.e., valid and numeric) appraisal system. Otherwise, the organization must forego many of the judgmental applications to which performance appraisal is put. Furthermore, the essay format probably can only be fully used in smaller organizations or as a special managerial-level appraisal.

Although the topic of the essay appraisal is work performance, the lack of specific direction and guidance makes it a subjective assessment. The introduction of a structured essay format is a means for partially overcoming this problem. Personnel research indicates that the validity of reference letters and preemployment interviews can be improved by providing the examiners with guidelines and lists of questions to be asked of candidates. Interview questions can be specifically designed around obtaining candidate reactions to hypothetical job situations.

A similar structuring process can be employed to guide the use of essay appraisals. Supervisors can be provided with instructions about what is to be included in their essays. Supervisors can also be provided with sets of job situations. These can be accompanied by examples of expected behaviors, including examples of different performance levels. Although the essay appraisal still would lack numbers and a quantifiable dimension, it would now be more standardized.

The Graphic Rating Scale

The subjective graphic rating scale is perhaps still the most pervasive form of performance appraisal (Landy and Farr, 1980: 83; Murphy and Cleveland, 1995: 434; Milkovich and Wigdor, 1991: 55–56). Even though the trend is clearly toward the introduction of more objective systems, the graphic rating scale remains in widespread use. Rating scales remain popular because they give the illusion of objectivity while involving little in the way of monetary costs.

Basically, a graphic rating scale consists of a set of items addressing personal traits (trustworthy, loyal, helpful, friendly, courteous, kind, obedient, etc.) and job activities (communication skills, sets realistic goals, keeps files and records up-to-date, adheres to policies and procedures, knowledge of job, etc.). Figure 7.1 displays a typical graphic rating format. Employee "performance" on these items is then rated using another set of adjective evaluations (poor, acceptable, fair, good, exceptional, etc.) that are invariably linked to a system of numeric scores. This enables the calculation of an average or overall summary numeric evaluation or rating.

Graphic rating scales are subjective assessments. This is the case because neither the personal traits nor the job activities included in the appraisal are the result of a thorough job analysis. Graphic rating scales draw upon material such as that provided in the *Dictionary of Occupational Titles* (U.S. Department of Labor, 1977). Although these traits and behaviors are, in general, job-related, they are not specifically linked to the actual jobs being appraised. The less a specific job matches the ideal type from which the appraisal descriptions were copied, the less accurate the appraisal can become.

Similarly, the adjective evaluations are also loosely construed. The specific meanings or connotations attached to various terms can also remain quite vague and easily differ from supervisor to supervisor. Examples of different performance levels are also usually lacking.

Although supervisors often gather together and informally agree upon common meanings for the terms used in graphic rating scales, the appraisal process still remains subjective. These systems may or may not convey these agreed-upon meanings and definitions to the employees, and their use may or may not be binding on all supervisors. Even when employees are informed and all supervisors adhere to the common system, these oral traditions still suffer legally in that they lack the authoritative imprimatur of the organization.

Transforming a graphic rating scale into an objective system (in a process similar to that detailed above with regard to essay appraisals) is what occurs in creating a behaviorally anchored rating scale (BARS). The BARS format (more fully described below) is designed to address these validity and legal issues.

Checklists and Forced Choice

Checklist or forced-choice appraisals include sets of items that are linked to the performance of specific jobs; they also include items for which no established relationships have been previously documented (Landy and Farr, 1980: 85–86; Mohrman, Resnick-West, and Lawler, 1989: 52–54). In conducting a checklist performance appraisal, supervisors are asked to pick, from a series of lists of four items, those items in each set that are deemed to be most like and least like an employee. These are then compared against a code sheet and only those that match validated relationships are tabulated into a final score.

Figure 7.1
Employee Performance Evaluation

EMPLOYEE PERFORMANCE EVALUATION

EMPLOYEE'S NAME ______________________ CLASS TITLE ______________________

EVALUATION PERIOD: FROM __________ TO __________ DEPARTMENT ______________________

INSTRUCTIONS: PLACE A CHECK MARK IN BOX THAT MOST APPROPRIATELY INDICATES YOUR JUDGEMENT ON EACH CHARACTERISTIC. COMPLETE ALL ITEMS FOR ALL EMPLOYEES. DIFFERENCE BETWEEN RATINGS BY EMPLOYEE AND SUPERVISOR MUST BE DISCUSSED.	EMPLOYEE				SUPERVISOR			
	N/A	EXCEEDS EXPECTATIONS	MEETS EXPECTATIONS	NEEDS IMPROVEMENT	N/A	EXCEEDS EXPECTATIONS	MEETS EXPECTATIONS	NEEDS IMPROVEMENT
1. DEPENDABILITY:								
A. PUNCTUALITY								
B. DOES NOT ABUSE SICK LEAVE								
C. DOES NOT ABUSE OVERTIME								
D. ABSENTEEISM								
E. STARTS WORK TASKS ON A TIMELY BASIS								
F.								
2. ATTITUDE:								
A. INTEREST IN JOB								
B. COMMITMENT TO AND SUPPORT OF ORGANIZATION								
C. TOWARD OTHER EMPLOYEES								
D. COURTESY/TACT TOWARD PUBLIC								
E.								
3. QUALITY OF WORK:								
A. THOROUGH								
B. USEFUL AND EFFECTIVE								
C. COMPLETED IN TIMELY MANNER								
D. ACCURATE								
E. NEAT								
F.								
4. INITIATIVE:								
A. AWARE OF WHAT NEEDS TO BE DONE								
B. STARTS ASSIGNMENT WITHOUT SPECIFIC INSTRUCTIONS								
C. FOLLOWS THROUGH ON WORK ASSIGNMENT								
D.								
5. JUDGEMENT:								
A. USE OF COMMON SENSE AND LOGIC								
B. CAN MAKE APPROPRIATE DECISIONS UNDER STRESS								
C.								

Figure 7.1
(continued)

EMPLOYEE PERFORMANCE EVALUATION

EMPLOYEE'S NAME ______________________ CLASS TITLE ______________________

EVALUATION PERIOD: FROM __________ TO __________ DEPARTMENT ______________________

INSTRUCTIONS: PLACE A CHECK MARK IN BOX THAT MOST APPROPRIATELY INDICATES YOUR JUDGEMENT ON EACH CHARACTERISTIC. COMPLETE ALL ITEMS FOR ALL EMPLOYEES. DIFFERENCE BETWEEN RATINGS BY EMPLOYEE AND SUPERVISOR MUST BE DISCUSSED.	EMPLOYEE				SUPERVISOR			
	N/A	EXCEEDS EXPECTATIONS	MEETS EXPECTATIONS	NEEDS IMPROVEMENT	N/A	EXCEEDS EXPECTATIONS	MEETS EXPECTATIONS	NEEDS IMPROVEMENT
1. DEPENDABILITY:								
A. PUNCTUALITY								
B. DOES NOT ABUSE SICK LEAVE								
C. DOES NOT ABUSE OVERTIME								
D. ABSENTEEISM								
E. STARTS WORK TASKS ON A TIMELY BASIS								
F.								
2. ATTITUDE:								
A. INTEREST IN JOB								
B. COMMITMENT TO AND SUPPORT OF ORGANIZATION								
C. TOWARD OTHER EMPLOYEES								
D. COURTESY/TACT TOWARD PUBLIC								
E.								
3. QUALITY OF WORK:								
A. THOROUGH								
B. USEFUL AND EFFECTIVE								
C. COMPLETED IN TIMELY MANNER								
D. ACCURATE								
E. NEAT								
F.								
4. INITIATIVE:								
A. AWARE OF WHAT NEEDS TO BE DONE								
B. STARTS ASSIGNMENT WITHOUT SPECIFIC INSTRUCTIONS								
C. FOLLOWS THROUGH ON WORK ASSIGNMENT								
D.								
5. JUDGEMENT:								
A. USE OF COMMON SENSE AND LOGIC								
B. CAN MAKE APPROPRIATE DECISIONS UNDER STRESS								
C.								

Figure 7.1
(continued)

INSTRUCTIONS: PLACE A CHECK MARK IN BOX THAT MOST APPROPRIATELY INDICATES YOUR JUDGEMENT ON EACH CHARACTERISTIC. COMPLETE ALL ITEMS FOR ALL EMPLOYEES. DIFFERENCE BETWEEN RATINGS BY EMPLOYEE AND SUPERVISOR MUST BE DISCUSSED.	EMPLOYEE				SUPERVISOR			
	N/A	EXCEEDS EXPECTATIONS	MEETS EXPECTATIONS	NEEDS IMPROVEMENT	N/A	EXCEEDS EXPECTATIONS	MEETS EXPECTATIONS	NEEDS IMPROVEMENT
6. COOPERATION:								
A. WORKS WHEN AND WHERE REQUESTED								
B. WITHIN DEPARTMENT OR DIVISION								
C. WITH OTHER DEPARTMENTS OR DIVISIONS								
D. WITH MANAGEMENT (SUPERVISORS, ADMINISTRATION, DEPARTMENT HEADS)								
E.								
7. QUANTITY OF WORK:								
A. HOW MUCH IS ACCOMPLISHED								
B. EFFICIENT USE OF TIME								
C.								
8. SAFETY:								
A. OTHER EMPLOYEES/VISITORS								
B. PERSONAL WORK HABITS								
C. USE OF EQUIPMENT								
D.								
9. LEARNING AND SELF DEVELOPMENT:								
A. KNOWLEDGE OF JOB								
B. UPDATES AND INCREASES KNOWLEDGES, ABILITIES, AND SKILL LEVELS								
C.								
10. PERSONAL:								
A. APPROPRIATELY DRESSED								
B. HYGIENE								
C.								
11. LEADERSHIP:								
A. PLANNING								
B. ORGANIZING								
C. DIRECTING AND COORDINATING ACTIVITIES								
D. CONTROL								
E. ABILITY AND WILLINGNESS TO ASSUME RESPONSIBILITY								
F. ACCOUNTABILITY								
G. USE OF STAFF EFFECTIVELY AND EFFICIENTLY								
H.								
12. OVERALL EVALUATION:								

COMMENTS: ____

____

____

EMPLOYEE SIGNATURE ______________________ **DATE** ______________

SUPERVISOR SIGNATURE ______________________ **DATE** ______________

DEPARTMENT HEAD SIGNATURE ______________________ **DATE** ______________

THE ABOVE SIGNATURES INDICATE HAVING READ THE PERFORMANCE EVALUATION AND HAVING DISCUSSED DIFFERENCES.

Figure 7.1
(continued)

INSTRUCTIONS: PLACE A CHECK MARK IN BOX THAT MOST APPROPRIATELY INDICATES YOUR JUDGEMENT ON EACH CHARACTERISTIC. COMPLETE ALL ITEMS FOR ALL EMPLOYEES. DIFFERENCE BETWEEN RATINGS BY EMPLOYEE AND SUPERVISOR MUST BE DISCUSSED.	EMPLOYEE				SUPERVISOR			
	N/A	EXCEEDS EXPECTATIONS	MEETS EXPECTATIONS	NEEDS IMPROVEMENT	N/A	EXCEEDS EXPECTATIONS	MEETS EXPECTATIONS	NEEDS IMPROVEMENT
6. COOPERATION:								
A. WORKS WHEN AND WHERE REQUESTED								
B. WITHIN DEPARTMENT OR DIVISION								
C. WITH OTHER DEPARTMENTS OR DIVISIONS								
D. WITH MANAGEMENT (SUPERVISORS, ADMINISTRATION, DEPARTMENT HEADS)								
E.								
7. QUANTITY OF WORK:								
A. HOW MUCH IS ACCOMPLISHED								
B. EFFICIENT USE OF TIME								
C.								
8. SAFETY:								
A. OTHER EMPLOYEES/VISITORS								
B. PERSONAL WORK HABITS								
C. USE OF EQUIPMENT								
D.								
9. LEARNING AND SELF DEVELOPMENT:								
A. KNOWLEDGE OF JOB								
B. UPDATES AND INCREASES KNOWLEDGES, ABILITIES, AND SKILL LEVELS								
C.								
10. PERSONAL:								
A. APPROPRIATELY DRESSED								
B. HYGIENE								
C.								
11. LEADERSHIP:								
A. PLANNING								
B. ORGANIZING								
C. DIRECTING AND COORDINATING ACTIVITIES								
D. CONTROL								
E. ABILITY AND WILLINGNESS TO ASSUME RESPONSIBILITY								
F. ACCOUNTABILITY								
G. USE OF STAFF EFFECTIVELY AND EFFICIENTLY								
H.								
12. OVERALL EVALUATION:								

COMMENTS: ______________________________

EMPLOYEE SIGNATURE ______________________ DATE ______________

SUPERVISOR SIGNATURE ______________________ DATE ______________

DEPARTMENT HEAD SIGNATURE ______________________ DATE ______________

THE ABOVE SIGNATURES INDICATE HAVING READ THE PERFORMANCE EVALUATION AND HAVING DISCUSSED DIFFERENCES.

Even though validated job relationships are often employed in this method, checklists are still included among the category of subjective appraisals. Although the items used in a checklist are often derived from rigorous job analyses, the secrecy employed in using this method negates that advantage. In employing a checklist, a supervisor is unaware of which items are validly job-related. Hence, neither supervisor nor employee is really apprised as to what performance is desired.

These forced-choice checklists also engender significant animosities among supervisors. The technique's secrecy implies a level of distrust in the supervisors themselves. It raises questions about both their professionalism and their role in the organization. It undermines their confidence in themselves.

The checklist's secrecy also contributes to a loss of confidence and trust in the supervisor on the part of employees. A basic tenet in the legitimacy of a supervisor's authority is derived from the mediating role played between employee and the rest of the organization. When the supervisor is removed from an important part of this system, as the performance appraisal process indeed is, the supervisor's overall acceptance and power base is damaged.

Furthermore, a checklist does not provide the supervisor with the information necessary to explain or justify the appraisal process to the employee. With so much riding on the outcome of a performance appraisal (developmental opportunities, pay increases, promotion, etc.), the inability to explain its underlying reasons and to provide guidance for improvement fractures the basic supervisory–employee relationship.

Mixed Standards

These problems can be somewhat alleviated with the use of a mixed–standard scale. Mixed–standard scales are checklists that are based on behaviorally anchored items. Specific job-related measures representing good, average, and poor levels of performance are constructed for each job responsibility or task. These items provide an added dimension and depth to the checklists. Mixed–standard scales add a degree of objectivity to the format of checklist appraisals (Blanz and Ghiselli, 1972; Saal and Landy, 1977; Saal, 1979; Dickinson and Zellinger, 1980).

However, a mixed standard format still retains all the features that instill distrust and undermine confidence. Although the job-relatedness of the items assures a greater degree of objectivity, the supervisor–employee relationship is still neglected. Employees and supervisors must have confidence in a performance appraisal system if it is to be at all effective. Checklists, mixed standards or not, fail to instill that sense of trust.

INTERPERSONAL COMPARISON TECHNIQUES

Interpersonal comparisons, such as rankings or forced distributions, may be based on either subjective or objective criteria. However, even when initially based solely on objective, job-related evidence, they experience serious shortcomings. Central to all interpersonal appraisal systems is the comparison or assessment of the individual against other individuals rather than with the specific job to be done.

There is no doubt that interpersonal comparison is a legitimate part of or occurs in the overall assessment process. The question here is more one of whether the performance appraisal process per se is the proper place for it. Interpersonal comparisons are certainly involved in promotional, pay, and even training decisions. When these rewards or opportunities are in scarce supply, their allocation must include considerations that require interpersonal comparisons.

Yet, such decisions are also among the purposes for which appraisals exist. What is required in these circumstances is a two-tiered process. First, individual performance is measured against job requirements, and only then is it compared specifically to the performance obtainments of others. The tasks of job performance and individual comparison are dealt with separately. In this way, the individual comparisons are themselves founded on objective performance measures.

The problem inherent in an interpersonal-comparison performance appraisal is that it may transform what should be objective, job-related performance measures into subjective, comparative personal assessments. Although this may entail no immediate harm, the resultant comparative data on employees quickly becomes the wrong basis for making further comparisons.

In essence, interpersonal comparisons mix together performance appraisals that are based on different norms. Although no organization would so cavalierly total the numeric value of their dollars, yen, francs, and marks together on their financial statement, that is precisely what occurs in conducting an interpersonal-comparison performance appraisal.

Ranking

One method for interpersonal comparisons is that of ranking. This is approached in a holistic manner wherein an organization's employees are graded from best to worst. This requires a complete knowledge and understanding of the entire organization—purpose and people. While perhaps feasible only in very small organizations, a number of gimmicks can be used in order to extend its application to larger units.

An alternative ranking process can be employed in which an organization's best employee and worst employee are designated. The process is then repeated ad finem with the remaining employees whereby the next best and next worst employees are so indicated. In the end, this peeling of the onion produces a composite list that ranks employees from best to worst.

Inasmuch as each employee is assessed on his or her job performance, this process is objective. However, such a holistic assessment is exceedingly difficult to perform and nearly impossible to document for legal purposes. Subjective assessments without the merit of any job-related relationship can easily intrude into this process.

Paired comparison can also be used to compile a single list ranking employees. Under a paired-comparison approach, the performance of each employee is, theoretically, judged against every other employee's performance or contribution to the organization. Instead of peeling the onion, comparisons are made between every possible combination.

This, as can be imagined, is a rather complex and quite time-consuming task in itself. It is also prone to a myriad of problems. Just as is the case with alternative ranking, non–job related, subjective assessments can be introduced into the process quite easily and relatively undetected. In addition, the complexity and tediousness of the comparisons can dull perceptions and lead to simple mistakes. Finally, human cognitive processes also introduce errors into this scheme.

Forced Distribution

Forced distributions are another means for making interpersonal comparisons (Mohrman, Resnick-West, and Lawler, 1989: 182–183). Grading on the curve is not a new notion and, unlike rankings, can easily be applied to large organizations. However, it is just as prone to error. Forced distributions assume that employee performance fits some external model or distribution, usually envisioned along the lines of something like a normally distributed, bell-shaped curve.

However, organizations do not randomly select their workers; there are elaborate selection processes designed to choose individuals who are already primed to succeed. This is often followed by extensive on-the-job training to further enhance those preexisting skills and to develop new ones. The conditions for assuming the existence of a population that would justify a forced distribution are simply not met in most organizations.

The U.S. Air Force briefly experimented with a forced-distribution appraisal in the mid-1970s (McBriarty, 1988). In a move designed to create more variance in the performance appraisal ratings, a forced-distribution formula was introduced. The results on morale and supervisory relations were devastating. Supervisors found it nearly impossible to build and maintain esprit de corps. Individuals responded by avoiding challenging assignments because they became viewed as career threatening rather than as career building. Commanding officers often found it necessary, in order to fill essential duty assignments and to protect their own "outstanding" performance ratings, to negotiate "outstanding" ratings in advance if they were to recruit individuals into their units. Fortunately, the Air Force soon abandoned this approach to performance appraisal.

OBJECTIVE TECHNIQUES

Behaviorally anchored rating scales (BARS) and management by objectives (MBO) essentially involve the same components but approach them with a slightly different focus in mind. Hence, the objective components that are common in both approaches are introduced into the appraisal process in a somewhat different order.

BARS appraisals work best with large groups and subgroups of individuals whose job descriptions can be standardized; MBO, on the other hand, can be tailored to each individual job. MBO is best when it is focused on the results to be expected from job performance; BARS handles behavioral processes where outputs are more identifiable and assurable than outcomes. Both employ variations on participative management to guarantee their effectiveness. A somewhat more passive approach to participation guides BARS, whereas a more proactive style is found in MBO.

Objective appraisal, regardless of which format is employed, is an expensive proposition (costing up to $2,000 per person when all time and resources are accounted for). It requires both the development of a complex instrument and the subsequent training of individuals in its use. In addition, these systems need constant attention. The instruments themselves require periodic updating and supervisory and employee training must be renewed, refreshed, and reinforced.

Although there are tremendous advantages to using objective systems, there are also some pitfalls. In a study of New Zealand professionals, the "average" employee benefits from the clear statement of goals under an objective appraisal with heightened levels of organizational commitment and job satisfaction. However, the "high performers" are likely to see this new system as an intrusion into their locus of control over their jobs (Taylor and Pierce, 1999).

Behaviorally Anchored Rating Scales

Behaviorally anchored rating scales are extensions of the subjective graphic rating scale. They are a clear attempt to translate the graphic rating scale into an objective appraisal system. They address and correct for many of the subjective issues that cloud the validity and inhibit the use of graphic rating scales (Bernardin and Beatty, 1984; Landy and Farr, 1980: 83–85; Latham and Wexley, 1981).

Although behaviorally anchored rating scales have received much attention in the private sector, they are also relevant to governmental settings. The emphasis BARS places on inputs and processes rather than on outputs and results is perhaps even more characteristic of the public sector organization than of the private. By the very nature of the tasks assigned or left to the public sector, employees in government agencies are even more likely to engage in group activities and operate under conditions of fragmented authority. These are all factors that are particular strengths in the BARS approach to performance appraisal.

Both the BARS and MBO approaches emphasize detailed job analyses. Ideally, performance appraisal should be able to work off the same job analysis system used in the development of an organization's position descriptions and position classification system (and employed as a guide in the selection process and for designing training programs). Unfortunately, many organizations, especially among those in the public sector, employ different systems of job analysis when it comes to selecting people to perform a job and when it comes to assessing their performance on that job.

The extent to which the jobs individuals were formally hired to fill and the jobs they are evaluated on overlap is not certain. Changing work environments, the time lags in the mechanics of updating systems, and the organizational units and rules governing the employment of job descriptions and performance appraisals all combine to create a situation prone to confusion.

The critical-incident technique (Flanagan, 1954) forms the central component in the BARS system. A job analysis, complete with questionnaires and confirmatory desk audits, is conducted on similar positions. Personnel analysts and subject matter experts (SMEs), (i.e., incumbent jobholders and supervisors), sift through the resultant job responsibilities, activities, or behaviors to identify those that are deemed most critical to its performance. It is assumed that these critical incidents will involve both quality and quantity considerations.

After the selection of a representative set of critical incidents for each job group has occurred, an overall or generalized scale is developed to allow for different job groups to be compared with one another. The previously identified individual job responsibilities are grouped into separate, independent dimensions or factors. Usually a half dozen to a dozen overall factors are identified in this manner. Although all need not be applicable to every job, most would be entailed or included in the analysis or evaluation of a specific job. Statistical analyses—correlations, factor analysis, or discriminate analysis—are performed to check that the factors are indeed independent of one another. The advantage of multiple measures can easily be lost if a halo effect leads the perceptions on one factor to unduly influence the assessment of other factors.

The BARS job analysis represents a passive application of participative management. Employee involvement and acceptance of the process's results compose its participative dimension. However, this can be sufficient to provide the employee with the sense of being a stakeholder in the organization. A thorough job analysis is the result of a fully collegial process in which employees and supervisors reach mutual understandings on the nature of the organization's jobs.

Following the selection of a representative set of critical incidents, the personnel analysts and SMEs then proceed to anchor these behaviors with a series of specific examples of acceptable and unacceptable performance. These examples are usually collected in conjunction with the job analysis itself, but they may also be assembled on a secondary basis. Although examples of exceptional and unacceptable performance levels are relatively easy to envision, examples of work levels that fall in between these two extremes (which are also essential to a BARS approach) often prove more difficult. Special effort must be made to assure that these "middle levels" are adequately anchored.

As a practical matter in order to save on costs, the courts require only that an organization formally anchor every other evaluation category. In a five-point system, only levels one, three, and five need to be anchored. Behavior that is, for example, better than that described for level three but less than that specified for level five can be assumed to be at level four. However, it is important to note that two adjacent levels cannot be left unanchored—for there would be no logical basis for allocating performance to one rather than the other.

The number of performance levels and whether the levels themselves are verbally labeled is optional. Courts are willing to allow systems with as little as two levels—acceptable/meets performance measures and unacceptable/fails to meet performance measures. The Pension Benefit Guaranty Corporation, the U.S. Department of Education, and the Food and Drug Administration have employed pass/fail appraisals (Skoien, 1997). Most systems use more and also tend to use some form of adjective descriptions—unsatisfactory, poor, acceptable, good, outstanding, and so on—with their ratings in addition to numeric values. However, there is a problem with using adjective descriptions. The descriptions can carry unintended connotations, especially if they have other, more common meanings. This danger must be taken into account in using and anchoring adjective labels.

In anchoring behaviors with specific examples, BARS has two major options to choose between—behaviorally expected scales (BES) and behaviorally observed scales (BOS). The BES approach represents a management judgment call as to what can be done; supervisors establish or designate the levels of performance to be expected from employees (Smith and Kendall, 1963). As such, it always involves some question about how realistic these expected performance levels are.

In a BES system, expectations are measured using a Thurstone scale wherein managers indicate behavior levels that they favor or find objectionable. However, studies often find that managers, at least initially, have overly simplistic views of what can be accomplished and concomitantly underrate the difficulties and obstacles employees face (Gabris and Giles, 1983a). However, BES objectives can serve to motivate employees by providing them with a goal worthy of accomplishing. Unfortunately, as that goal is stretched into unreality, motivation gives way to despair.

In order for BES objectives to work, they must be accompanied by "structural accommodation" and "bureaucratic immunity." Structural accommodation develops a high degree of worker autonomy (decision making) and empowerment (resource allocation) over how to accomplish the task. It instills the confidence and willingness to achieve the goals. Bureaucratic immunity preempts the organization's ordinary standard operating procedures and control processes that can thwart change and success (Thompson, Hochwarter, and Mathys, 1997).

In contrast to the Promethean "stretch objectives" that BES systems can introduce, a BOS approach anchors its behaviors firmly in the reality of the situation (Latham and Wexley, 1981). A Likert scale is used in measuring performance. The standards by which people are judged are based on performance levels that have actually been accomplished. This adds to their legitimacy and to the legitimacy of the performance appraisal process itself. Because they also instill confidence in the organization and its managers, they can serve to motivate individuals to strive harder. Because the outstanding levels (and the rewards attached to them) are not figments of someone else's imagination, they are seen as obtainable.

Management by Objectives Appraisal

Management by objectives is more focused on results; however, it obviously can also be adapted to situations in which outputs or processes are more involved than outcomes. MBO originated as a means for managers to translate their strategic plans into implementable programs (Drucker, 1954, 1974). It is a basic command-and-control management system for implementation and monitoring (Albrecht, 1978; Carroll and Tosi, 1973; Muczyk and Reimann, 1989; Odiorne, 1971, 1987; Swiss, 1991: 61–127).

Because private sector organizations tended to be overcentralized, MBO approaches often contributed to a decentralization of power to lower-level decision makers. In the public sector, however, the reverse experience often occurred. Public agencies are, perhaps somewhat surprisingly, relatively decentralized in terms of actual policymaking. The introduction of MBO systems led to a centralization of power as upper-level managers gained more control over the actual objectives and activities of their subordinate units. MBO, in documenting what is to be done, provides managers with a performance scorecard.

The step from MBO as an overall management system to its employment as one for appraisal by objectives is rather straightforward and simple. Although it has many advantages, the employment of an MBO approach is not without its limitations.

It is quite difficult for an MBO approach to assess performance and simultaneously identify potential. Although simply having subordinate "acceptance" of performance standards is often considered to be a workable approach, MBO actually assumes that objectives are arrived at through a more actively participative process. Supervisors and employees are envisioned as discussing and negotiating performance standards that are mutually acceptable. Standards are arrived at in an atmosphere of understanding and not in one of imposition. MBO, like the BARS approach, functions better in a more participative environment.

Finally, MBO may overstate the demand for results without focusing on or directly assisting with the means for achieving them. The conditions or resources necessary for successful implementation are assumed to be automatically provided for. Private sector organizations more readily assume that requisite resources will be forthcoming when goals and objectives are agreed upon than, unfortunately, is often the case in the public sector (Kearney, 1979; Odiorne, 1965: 180-181).

The specific focus on results can also lead to MBO systems in which quantifiable or easily achieved objectives subvert the process. Although this smooths out the immediate task of completing the MBO and the performance appraisal, it loses sight of its underlying purpose. MBO ceases to reflect the reality of the job and to focus attention on the important objectives. It becomes an "activity trap." MBO ceases to be a tool assisting in decision making and becomes an obstacle to effective management (Albrecht, 1978; Murphy and Cleveland, 1995: 438–439).

MBO is a means for setting priorities and allocating resources for achieving them. However, the political environment that predominates in the public sector often prefers to work in ambiguity. This has proven to be a major drawback in the implementation of public sector MBO.

Participation is central to MBO appraisal systems. Goals and objectives are meant to be worked out in a participative manner with emphasis on collegiality and mutual understanding. Although many MBO systems substitute an employee acceptance of imposed goals and objectives for this participative decision making, this weakens the process. A major element in an MBO system's strength is the team bonding it fosters.

In terms of the ultimate, "bottom line," participation leads to productivity. Employee participation in goal setting highlights this relationship with enhanced productivity (Locke, Shaw, Saari, and Latham, 1981; Roberts and Reed, 1996). Goal setting, or work agendas (which can be introduced as a distinct notion), is another key ingredient in objective systems of performance appraisal such as the BARS and MBO approaches (Latham and Yukl, 1975; Kotter, 1982; Barry, Cramton, and Carroll, 1997).

Goal setting is effective because it helps focus and direct individual efforts. It establishes priorities. Second, goal setting, more or less, allocates resources sufficient for achieving the designated goals. Unfortunately, this implicit effort–resources linkage often fails in the public sector. Finally, goal setting introduces persistence with regard to dealing with problems that prove difficult. Difficulty is highlighted by a formal system of goals. This enables the organization to be aware of such problems and to, subsequently, concentrate efforts on their solution (Latham and Wexley, 1981: 120–129).

In many instances, goal setting alone can prove sufficient to enhance productivity. The knowledge and psychological satisfaction that a sense of direction provides along with that attributable to the achievement of goals serve as intrinsic rewards. Employees detest wasting their time and effort. They prefer to work at meaningful tasks that provide them with a sense of accomplishment and craftsmanship.

Central to the task of goal setting is the development of objective performance standards. While easily described, this often proves a difficult job requiring extensive and repeated training (Burke, 1977: 46–53). Standards should take into consideration the conditions and circumstances under which they are to be achieved. They need to focus on results that are specific, measurable, and attainable. The importance and time aspect of individual results is also a factor (Daley, 1992b).

For illustrative purposes, a fuller description of the appraisal-by-objectives application of MBO warrants discussion. MBO appraisal approaches are similar to those used in Iowa, which is described here (see Figure 7.2). The introduction of this approach should be accompanied by a series of training sessions and supported with supervisory and employee handbooks.

The performance evaluation process is initiated with the joint completion of a "Responsibilities and Standards or Results Expected" section (also referred to as the job description) by the supervisor and employee. This is the first of three sections included in the performance appraisal process. The first section is completed at the beginning of the annual appraisal cycle, whereas sections two and three are written up at its conclusion.

The employee is given prior notice of and, ideally, participates in scheduling the preliminary conference. A worksheet and copies of previous evaluations are supplied to the employee for use as guides. The meeting between supervisor and employee specifies that their worksheets are to be filled out "in pencil" (other systems use the phrase "on the wordprocessor"). This is designed to remind both parties that no final decisions have been made and that the meeting is supposed to truly be participative.

Figure 7.2
Iowa Performance Appraisals

During the reviewing period, attach notes or comments here

State of Iowa
CONFIDENTIAL PERFORMANCE REVIEW/EVALUATION

RESPONSIBILITIES AND STANDARDS/RESULTS EXPECTED

NOTE: Please type or print

SECTION

1. EMPLOYEE NAME (LAST, FIRST, MIDDLE INITIAL)	2. SOC. SEC. NO.	3. JOB CLASSIFICATION	4. AGENCY/INSTITUTION	5. PAYROLL NUMBER (18 DIGIT)
6. PERIOD COVERED BY EVALUATION	7. PURPOSE OF EVALUATION	8. AGENCY DIVISION	9. UNIT	
10. WORK LOCATION	11. ENTRY DATE IN CLASSIFICATION	INSTRUCTIONS: Section A is to be completed at the beginning of the evaluation period. It must be discussed with and signed by the individual being evaluated. Employee's copy is given to the individual immediately following the conference. Other copies are held by the supervisor until the end of the evaluation period when they are attached to Section B. See separate instruction sheet and manual for detail.		

Number	Time	Conse-quence	%	12. MAJOR RESPONSIBILITIES: From job description, classification specification or other	13. STANDARDS AND RESULTS EXPECTED: Conditions, which will exist when the job is done satisfactorily. Several standards for each responsibility)

*NOTE: Weighted percentage expressed as a decimal (importance of a responsibility compared to others. Total 100%)

Figure 7.2
(continued)

During the reviewing period, attach notes or comments here

State of Iowa

CONFIDENTIAL PERFORMANCE REVIEW/EVALUATION

RESPONSIBILITIES AND STANDARDS/RESULTS EXPECTED

NOTE: Please type or print

SECTION

1. EMPLOYEE NAME (LAST, FIRST, MIDDLE INITIAL)	2. SOC. SEC. NO.	3. JOB CLASSIFICATION	4. AGENCY/INSTITUTION	5. PAYROLL NUMBER (18 DIGIT)
6. PERIOD COVERED BY EVALUATION	7. PURPOSE OF EVALUATION	8. AGENCY DIVISION	9. UNIT	
10. WORK LOCATION	11. ENTRY DATE IN CLASSIFICATION	INSTRUCTIONS: Section A is to be completed at the beginning of the evaluation period. It must be discussed with and signed by the individual being evaluated. Employee's copy is given to the individual immediately following the conference. Other copies are held by the supervisor until the end of the evaluation period when they are attached to Section B. See separate instruction sheet and manual for detail.		

Number	Time	Conse-quence	%	12. MAJOR RESPONSIBILITIES: From job description, classification specification or other	13. STANDARDS AND RESULTS EXPECTED: Conditions, which will exist when the job is done satisfactorily. Several standards for each responsibility)

*NOTE: Weighted percentage expressed as a decimal (importance of a responsibility compared to others. Total 100%)

Figure 7.2
(continued)

State of Iowa
CONFIDENTIAL JOB PERFORMANCE REVIEW/EVALUATION

PERFORMANCE REVIEW/RATING

NOTE: Please type or print

SECTION

1. EMPLOYEE NAME (LAST, FIRST, MIDDLE INITIAL)	2. SOC. SEC. NO.	3. JOB CLASSIFICATION	4. AGENCY/INSTITUTION	5. PAYROLL NUMBER (18 DIGIT)

6. PERIOD COVERED BY EVALUATION	7. PURPOSE OF EVALUATION

INSTRUCTIONS: At the end of the evaluation period the performance is to be reviewed against the responsibilities and expected results established on Section A. The number and weighted percentage of the responsibilities for Section B should correspond with those on Section A. See separate Instruction Sheet and Manual for details.

EXPLANATION OF RATINGS
1. UNACCEPTABLE—Does not meet standards and/or requirements
2. NEEDS SOME IMPROVEMENT
3. COMPETENT PERFORMANCE—Meets standards and/or requirements
4. VERY GOOD—Exceeds standards and/or requirements
5. OUTSTANDING—Far exceeds standards and/or requirements

8. Transfer from Section A		9. Rating: 'X' the Appropriate Column					10. Weighted Rating	11. COMMENTS OR EXPLANATION (FOR EACH STANDARD OR RESULT EXPECTED FROM SECTION A) (All ratings must be justified by comments or explanation)
Number	%	1	2	3	4	5	% Rating	
	100%						12.	Overall Sum of Job Performance Ratings (5.00 maximum)

DISTRIBUTION: Attach Section A to Section B and forward to:

WHITE—Employee's Copy—Given Immediately
CANARY—Supervisor's Copy
PINK—Merit Copy
GOLDENROD—Agency Copy

Figure 7.2
(continued)

SECTION C
SUMMARY OF TOTAL JOB PERFORMANCE & FUTURE PERFORMANCE PLANS

AREAS OF STRENGTH (Identify how these might be used more effectively)	AREAS NEEDING IMPROVEMENT (Identify how these might be strengthened)

ADDITIONAL COMMENTS In considering the total picture of work behavior and job performance, I would add these remarks (Exceptional accomplishments—suggestions—future performance goals—critical incidents—work behaviors affecting performance)

TRAINING AND DEVELOPMENTAL PLANS:

(The above information should be used in establishing responsibilities and standards for the next review period)

RECOMMENDATION: Based on this evaluation of total job performance, I recommend the following: Merit Increase: yes ☐ no ☐ (2.50 is the minimum level for consideration of a merit increase)

permanent status ☐ promotion ☐ demotion ☐ EMS ☐ Other (specify) ☐ ____________

SUM OF RATINGS ☐

TRANSFER FROM BOX 12

Supervisor's Signature: ____________ Date: ____________

If responsibilities and standards have not changed since previous evaluation, Section A does not need to be submitted to Merit Employment. Mark box at right if Section A is unchanged. ☐

EMPLOYEE COMMENTS: ATTACH ADDITIONAL SHEETS IF NECESSARY.

This performance evaluation has been discussed with me,
and I understand that my signature does not necessarily indicate agreement Signature: ____________ Date: ____________

I have reviewed and approve the job performance standards, evaluation & recommendation.

Signature: ____________ Title: ____________ Date: ____________

Up to eight or ten major responsibilities (with four to five as the norm) are to be selected and written down in a results-oriented format with specific performance standards against which the achievement of the results can be measured. Each responsibility may have more than one measurable standard associated with it. Supervisors and employees tend to find this a most difficult undertaking. Although they "know it when they see it," putting performance expectations into clear, written objective statements is quite challenging (U. S. Merit Systems Protection Board, 1999a).

Objective standards fall into three categories. Historical standards contrast one period in time with another (e.g., relating the upcoming year's "potholes filled" in relation to the previous year). Engineered standards focus on the numbers of things in specific time frames (e.g., the number of potholes to be filled in one year). Comparative standards measure expected results against a norm—for an industry, similar work unit, or employee performing the same duties (e.g., the turnover rate among municipal employees, generally or for specific types of jobs).

These individual responsibilities are weighted through the use of an additive (or multiplicative) formula that factors in the time spent on each task and the evaluation of its importance or the consequences of error. A five-point Likert scale is used for both measures. Time is calculated in either percentage terms or hours spent on a task. Consequences encompass financial loss, client dissatisfaction, time required to correct errors, broken equipment, or psychological stress.

Should these responsibilities require modification due to changing circumstances, a new first section can be prepared by the supervisor and employee. During the course of the evaluation period, the supervisor is also encouraged to use a critical-incident approach wherein noteworthy efforts are jotted down and placed in an evaluation file. Both formal (with a written copy inserted into the employee's file) and informal communications between employees and supervisors are encouraged. For negative incidents, it is important that a record of recommended corrective action be documented; employees must be notified if they are doing something wrong, and the supervisors must indicate how the employees can correct their behavior.

The MBO approach allows for tailoring the performance appraisal to each individual's job responsibilities. Although this is a tremendous advantage, it also entails certain difficulties. For large organizations, individual appraisals can be a time-consuming task. If, after all, the jobs are not all that different, then there is not much gained from this effort. Hence, most large organizations, even if they are using an MBO approach, resort to a BARS format for those position classes that involve multiple incumbents. As long as a full-scale job analysis is undertaken, this is not a problem. However, the MBO format's looser construction places less emphasis on this process, so it is more easily overlooked under an MBO approach than in the BARS system.

At the end of the evaluation period, another conference is scheduled at which the employee's formal "Performance Review or Rating" is discussed. As with the first conference, the employee has advance notice. The employee and supervisor meet to discuss the employee's job performance in light of the responsibilities and results expected that were outlined in the employee's first section. Again worksheets are used at this meeting with a formal, written evaluation prepared only afterward. Employees are also given the opportunity to comment formally on the final evaluation form.

The overall employee rating is the weighted average of the individual responsibility ratings. Each responsibility's weight is determined by dividing its time and importance raw score (varying from 2 to 10) by the total for all raw scores and converting this into a percentage figure. This percentage is then multiplied by the individual rating assigned by the supervisor to that responsibility. Each responsibility is rated on a five-point scale—(1) unacceptable, (2) needs some improvement, (3) competent performance, (4) very good, and (5) outstanding—assessing the degree to which its standards were achieved. The rounded-up tally of the weighted responsibility ratings is used as an overall measure, using the same five-point scale terminology.

Finally, a third, essay section devoted to a "Summary of Total Job Performance and Future Performance Plans" is also completed at this time. The supervisor is provided the opportunity to list the employee's "areas of strength" and those "areas needing improvement." In the latter instances, "training and developmental plans" for correcting these are also completed. Although this description is based on an older Iowa process, Figure 7.3 shows that it could just as equally have been applied to today's North Carolina Performance Appraisal process (or any number of other objective MBO systems).

APPRAISAL ERROR

Performance appraisal is a human process. Although the tendency to focus attention on the tools used in the appraisal process can draw attention away from this, it remains the essential aspect of performance evaluation. The development of psychometric accuracy has produced a performance appraisal instrument of complex sophistication. Yet, the resultant objective BARS and MBO appraisal systems are only as good as the people who use them. For all their advantages, they are still only tools for aiding us in making our decisions. Rater error is a topic which has been extensively treated in the performance appraisal literature (Daley, 1992b, pp. 119–131; Landy and Farr, 1980; Latham and Wexley, 1994; Murphy and Cleveland, 1995, pp. 275–285; Bowman, 1999).

Figure 7.3
North Carolina Performance Appraisal

NORTH CAROLINA STATE GOVERNMENT

Performance Management Program Work Plan

Employee's Name: ______________________ Position: ______________________

Supervisor's Name: ______________________ Position: ______________________

Date of Performance Planning: ______________________

Date of Interim Review Discussion: ______________________

Date of Performance Appraisal Discussion: ______________________

Appraisal is for period of: ______________________

Effective date: ______________________

(Provide photocopies of signed form to Employee, Manager, and the Personnel Office.)

Figure 7.3
(continued)

PERFORMANCE MANAGEMENT WORK PLAN

Combined KRR Rating ____________

Key Responsibilities/Results	Results Expectations	Tracking Source/Frequency	Actual Results	Rating

Figure 7.3
(continued)

PMP Development Plan

Development planning is a way of analyzing an employee's strengths and weaknesses to determine actions which can maintain or improve job performance and areas needing additional job training and education. After completing the overall summary rating and discussing the results with the employee, indicate below the knowledge skills and/or abilities needing development or strengthening. Then indicate the appropriate training and/or education that should improve the performance. The supervisor and employee should list their responsibilities to make sure the plan is completed before the appraisal occurs. This document should also include any specific improvement plans or activities identified during the interim review.

A. Knowledge, Skills, and Abilities:

B. Training and Education:

Supervisor's Responsibilities:	Employee's Responsibilities:

Employee's Signature ______________ *Date* ______ *Supervisor's Signature* ______________ *Date* ______ *Manager's Signature* ______________ *Date* ______

Figure 7.3
(continued)

Overall Performance Summary

Interim Review Comments:

Employee's Signature ____________ *Date* ______ *Supervisor's Signature* ____________ *Date* ______ *Manager's Signature* ____________ *Date* ______

Please summarize employee's overall job performance based on information for each expectation:

The letter which represents overall summary rating: ______

Supervisor's Comments:	Employee's Comments:

Employee's Signature: *(Does not mean you agree but that your performance has been reviewed with you.)*	Supervisor's Signature:	Manager's Signature:
Date ______	Date ______	Date ______

Organizational Error

Much of what passes under the rubric of rater error is in reality supervisory adjustments to organizational demands (Daley, 1992b, pp. 119–121; Longenecker, Sims, and Gioia, 1987; Murphy and Cleveland, 1995; Bowman, 1999). Although the impact of these adjustments may be deemed negative, they are neither accidental nor totally within the control of the supervisor to correct. Goals may be unclear or misunderstood due to communication problems. A hidden agenda may desire to use performance appraisals as means of controlling employees rather than for encouraging productivity. The expectations of what can be done can simply be unrealistic. Finally, results may be due to activity of groups rather than of individuals. The supervisors endeavor to coordinate workers and obtain productivity within this system. As such, the performance appraisal is part of the organization's overall management control system (Swiss, 1991; Longenecker and Nykodym, 1996).

Structural Error

Structural problems can also undermine the appraisal instruments themselves. The failure to develop objective appraisal systems can lead to inconsistent or unreliable appraisals. The failure to provide adequate supervisory training in the use of objective systems can also result in a loss of consistency and reliability.

An inability or neglect in goal setting produces similar faults in the appraisal process. Objective appraisal systems operate only if results can be compared against expectations. The failure to establish goals and objectives leaves the system with no expectations. Because managers and supervisors take an appraisal's specific purpose into consideration in making their evaluations, using the appraisal for another, unintended purpose only confounds the process.

The performance appraisal process can also be abused when the decision-making relationships are inverted. Instead of serving as an aid in decisions regarding employee promotion, pay, dismissal, or development, the appraisals are abused in order to justify predetermined decisions.

On a somewhat more technical level, problems arise wherein employees aim to match their behavior to the criteria used in the evaluation. It is difficult to fault employees for doing what is asked of them, yet, for organizations, sins of omission are just as deadly as the sins of commission. Ideally, the appraisal system is designed to objectively encompass all the needed tasks. However, in reality important tasks are often ignored or unforeseen. Redesigning the appraisal process is both essential and helpful in such circumstances.

Many organizations accord little priority to the job of administration per se or to the exercise of personnel practices in particular. An organization that is serious about its performance appraisal process incorporates numerous training and support services into its process. It also clearly indicates to its supervisors and employees that the supervisors are themselves evaluated on their use of the appraisal system (Mohrman, Resnick-West, and Lawler, 1989: 125–130; Daley, 1992b: 127–131; Longenecker and Nykodym, 1996).

Rater Error

Although employees may be the direct source for the introduction of errors and misperceptions into the performance appraisal process, these also remain an organizational problem. The organization should either prevent the misunderstandings from arising or prepare supervisors for dealing effectively with them.

Inasmuch as individuals' personal identity and sense of self-worth are closely associated with their jobs, appraisals evaluate not merely job performance but human worth itself. An organization and its supervisors need to be aware of and sensitive to these psychological dimensions and especially alert to their dangers.

Performance appraisal is highly dependent upon the skill of the appraiser. As with any tool, it is only as good as the individual wielding it. Hence, when things go wrong, it is often considered convenient to blame appraisal problems on rater error. Although such a ploy shifts attention from the appraisal system itself, it does not shift responsibility from the organization. Even when problems are indeed due to rater error rather than to environmental or organizational factors, the organization is still responsible for the lack of training or monitoring that led or contributed to the commitment of that error.

The topic of rater errors has been extensively treated in the performance appraisal literature (Landy and Farr, 1980; Latham and Wexley, 1981: 100–104; Murphy and Cleveland, 1995: 275–285). Their elimination or alleviation is the focus of most of the efforts at performance appraisal training.

Rater errors fall into four categories: (1) job responsibility errors, (2) contrast errors, (3) unidimensional errors, and (4) interpersonal errors. In many cases, these errors are corrected through the employment of objective appraisal instruments. In other instances, more thorough supervisory training is recommended. Even though supervisors strive to objectively evaluate employees, rater errors prey on the weaknesses inherent in the cognitive process. It is this readiness with which an organization can slip into error that calls for the constant monitoring of the appraisal process.

Errors are committed whenever the responsibilities inherent in the job itself are substituted for a measure of the incumbent's job performance (Robbins, 1978). An important and demanding job often implies, and certainly requires, an individual of like stature. Given the effort put into selecting individuals with such capabilities and the basic vagueness or qualitative aspect entailed in most managerial jobs, this is an error easily introduced into the appraisal process.

Similarly, individuals working in a critical unit may benefit from the perceived centrality or significance of their part of the organization. In this case, the importance of the unit to fulfilling the organization's mission is substituted for the job performance of the individual in that unit. In neither instance is the individual's job performance actually measured. Objective appraisals inasmuch as they are focused on job performance, especially in terms of results, are a good check on such errors.

Contrast errors arise through interpersonal comparisons. Individuals are not assessed on their job performance but on their performance compared to someone else's performance, or, as is more often the case, someone else's personal traits and characteristics. Personnel profiles tabulating the social and leadership traits, demographic characteristics, or social, ethnic, and gender differences of successful employees are compiled. These are then used as the norm against which others are compared (Wexley and Nemeroff, 1974; Pizam, 1975; Rand and Wexley, 1975; Bigoness, 1976; Mitchell and Liden, 1982; Mobley, 1982; DeNisi, Cafferty, and Meglino, 1984; Kraiger and Ford, 1985; Shore and Thorton, 1986).

These social differentiation or similar-to-me approaches suffer significant validity problems. Although the individuals upon which they are based may be examples of successful employees, the characteristics and traits chosen for the profile may not in any way be related to that success. Concomitantly, even if those traits and characteristics are valid indicators, they may not be the only such indicators. Contrast error excludes people who may be successful or potentially successful from receiving a fair and accurate evaluation. Again the validation of criteria used in assessing job performance is essential.

Unidimensional errors abound. In these instances, one item dominates the evaluation process to such an extent that other, critical factors are ignored. Unidimensional errors can stem from either substantive or mechanical concerns.

Such traits and characteristics as age, longevity, or loyalty can be the basis for an overall evaluation even when other factors are formally specified in the appraisal instrument. Admittedly, these are factors that in many instances are desirable. Age and seniority are viewed as indictors of experience (Prather, 1974; Robbins, 1978; Ferris, 1985). On the other hand, loyalty is the trait supervisors often value the most among employees.

The problem here occurs when these measures are used in conjunction with other, supposedly independent factors. The unidimensional response eliminates the sought-after balance that the intentional introduction of the other factors was designed to achieve. Correlational studies often show this as a problem in the employment of basic graphic rating scales.

Similarly, the vividness of one event can overshadow all other incidents. A halo effect occurs when a good performance in one aspect of a job becomes the basis for overall assessment; a horns effect indicates that an incident perceived as negative was the basis of the evaluation (Odiorne, 1965; Murphy and Cleveland, 1995: 277–281).

Unidimensional error also occurs with regard to appraisal mechanics. First-impression or recency error is introduced when early or late events are given extraordinary weight in the evaluation. The first-impression error leads later performance to be discounted. The recency error places emphasis on the time period nearest the decision at the expense of earlier contributions. Critical-incident files are often a means of countering this cognitive limitation.

Supervisors may also exhibit a central-tendency (i.e, awarding everyone middle-range or average ratings) or restricted-range (i.e., extremely good and bad ratings are not awarded) problem in which all employees receive the same rating or very close and similar ratings. This problem often emerges when supervisors are required only to justify high and low ratings. It is also likely where supervisors fear that employees would resent an individual who received a higher rating or themselves lose motivation from a lower rating (Glueck, 1978; Bernardin and Beatty, 1984; Murphy and Cleveland, 1995: 275–277).

Constant error also occurs when supervisors exhibit tendencies toward awarding consistently high or low ratings or are overly lenient or strict in their rating evaluations (Robbins, 1978). Although such errors are often applied equally to all employees within the work unit, they make interunit comparisons inaccurate. This poses a special problem when employee appraisals are used in determining rewards such as merit pay raises. If one supervisor's rating of a "three" is equivalent to another's "four," the latter employee could well be rewarded and the former not for what is objectively the same level of performance.

Interpersonal biases introduce intentional distortions into the appraisal process. The extent to which a supervisor's own performance and career is dependent upon a subordinate's performance may determine the likelihood that favorable ratings will be awarded. This interdependence creates a mutual need for maintaining a harmonious relationship (Brinkerhoff and Kanter, 1980; Larson, 1984; Tjosvold, 1985).

Squeaky wheels also benefit from interpersonal bias. They may receive higher ratings than they otherwise deserve in order to avoid any unpleasantness. However, employees deemed difficult as well as those who make use of the organization's grievance process are likely to receive more critical attention in future performance appraisals (Klaas and DeNisi, 1989).

Interpersonal biases are also often found as examples of abuse rather than of errors. They may entail worksite politics wherein ratings are adjusted in order to support or hinder an employee's opportunity for advancement and reward. Supervisors may be influenced by the desires of others—superiors, peers, or subordinates (Robinson, Fink, and Allen, 1996). Lower-than-deserved ratings can be awarded in an effort to selfishly retain a valued and productive employee. Lower-than-deserved ratings are also a means for taking out someone seen as a potential competitor (Teel, 1986; Longenecker, Sims, and Gioia, 1987).

Similarly, appraisal ratings can be affected by factors entirely extraneous to the working relationship. External preferences vis-à-vis politics, religion, and sex may be furthered through the manipulation of the performance appraisal process. Avoiding such abuses is one of the purposes underlying the recommendations for continuously monitoring the appraisal process. Requirements for the automatic review of appraisal by upper-level officials and an appeals process are designed with the intention to deter abuse.

Training individuals in the use of these tools is just as important as the development of objective appraisal techniques. Supervisory training requires care. Supervisory training can encompass organizational and employee considerations as well as those related to the appraisal process itself. Performance appraisal is part of an overall performance management system. As such, its interaction with the other systemic aspects is just as important a part of its functioning as are the mechanics of the appraisal process itself.

SUMMARY

Performance appraisal is the central instrument used for calibrating and monitoring employee behaviors and results. It is used to verify recruitment and selection techniques and the appropriateness of job analyses. Performance appraisal is used both in making judgments regarding pay and promotion and in exercising developmental options such as feedback and training.

In designing and using the performance appraisal process, an organization must be cognizant of both legal strictures and strategic objectives. Fortunately, these two sets of standards are really the same. By paying attention to job analyses centered on job-related work behaviors and results, by communicating these and providing training in their use to employees and supervisors, and by documenting and monitoring the process for accuracy and fairness an organization can achieve a valid appraisal system,

Although many organizations still rely upon subjective techniques or interpersonal comparisons, these fail to meet either legal or objective criterion sets or effective appraisal processes. Only through the employment of objective techniques such as found in behaviorally anchored rating scales and management-by-objectives approaches will the strategic benefits of the performance appraisal process be achieved.

Even objective systems are subject to appraisal error. Organizational and structural errors arising from a misalignment or uncertainty of strategic goals and objectives can lead to distortion. Rater errors originate in cognitive behaviors that evolved for making quick decisions in simpler hunter/gatherer societies. Vigilance and continuous training are required to overcome these limitations.

chapter 8

Training and Development

The modern organization is indeed its people and the knowledge they possess. We must recognize that this knowledge is, at best, only the beginning of the mystery. It can no longer be taken for granted that employees will arrive at work with all the requisite skills. Too much of what goes on in today's organization requires specific adaptation. The most knowledgeable and skilled worker still requires training to fit into the organization and become a valuable contributor to the team (Goldstein, 1993; Quinn, Anderson, and Finkelstein, 1996).

This chapter presents an overview of both the management of training and development and the techniques used. The chapter provides:

1. Knowledge of the importance of and the means for assessing training needs
2. An overview on the importance of adult learning theory for structuring training and development
3. A framework for evaluating the effectiveness of training programs
4. Knowledge of the various on-the-job, information presentation, and action-based training and development techniques

The chief function of the supervisor is the development of the people in his or her unit. Managers who have been promoted from a technical position must remember that they are now the coaches; others have the responsibility of carrying out the plays on the field. The manager/coach can have the greatest effect only by assuring that the employee/player is truly prepared for action.

Unfortunately, training and development is one of the most neglected aspects of government. Well into the 1950s and 1960s, governments denied the value of training and development. Individuals were hired for specific jobs and were assumed to already possess all the skills that would be needed. Although the importance of training and development is now recognized, it remains a neglected area.

Employees, like the buildings and equipment of government, are allowed to depreciate through an underinvestment in maintenance (Elmore, 1991; Gray, Hall, Miller, and Shasky, 1997).

MANAGING TRAINING AND DEVELOPMENT OPERATIONS

Is training indeed the appropriate response to the perceived problem? Donald Klingner and John Nalbandian (1985: 234) note that training is only one of the possible responses to performance problems. Training is inappropriate wherever problems are deemed bothersome but insignificant, are due to inadequate selection criteria, or arise because employees are unaware of what is expected of them or lack incentives for performance. These problems are dealt with by ignoring them, the application of job analysis, orientation and performance appraisal feedback, or an explicit performance reward system. Only when performance problems are attributable to inadequate employee skills does training become the appropriate response.

Even here, the interaction between training and organizational goals is critical. With regard to equal employment opportunity, affirmative action, and multicultural diversity, for instance, training programs may either diminish or perpetuate ethnic, racial, and sexual inequalities in the agency's workforce.

Poor training may also create "tunnel vision," whereby the organization focuses on existing operating procedures at the expense of consideration of alternatives. Training is related to goal setting in agency planning processes as well as in the making of career assignments, the appraisal on performance, and other aspects of job management. Without the setting of clear organizational goals for the training function, the common result is management failure to utilize training effectively and consistently in relation to other administrative systems.

Training is not a panacea. It should not be forced to serve in place of other forms of employee development and interest articulation. On the other hand, training can smooth organizational processes by increasing understanding of the rules of the game. Training may address needs perceived as affecting the entire organization or as applying to an individual employee. It can focus on adding to an organization's overall level of knowledge or on the treatment of specific deficiencies. Training is an important implementation tool in an organization's strategic planning.

There are many specific organizational objectives toward which training may be directed. Common training topical areas include management skills/development, supervisory skills, technical skills/knowledge, communication skills, basic computer skills, new methods/procedures, customer relations/services, clerical/secretarial skills, personal growth, executive development, employee/labor relations, wellness, sales skills, customer education, and even remedial basic education (Gerber, 1989b: 50). Really, almost any topic may be the object of training. The question is, is it worth the organization's efforts and resources to do it?

An organization must subject its training and development efforts to the same analysis it uses in determining its other functions. How does training and development support and further the organization's mission? Although training and development focuses on delivering a variety of programs, the organization needs a holistic view that integrates these components. Training efforts should be designed to reinforce one another.

In the knowledge organization, training should be focused less on the simpler cognitive (know what) and advanced (know how) skills. Employee development must be centered on the more complex system understanding (know why) and motivated-creativity (care why) forms of knowledge. It is these latter, complex knowledges that exponentially add value and advantage to the organization (Quinn, 1992a, 1992b; Quinn, Anderson, and Finkelstein, 1996).

In organizations with a mature training function, training objectives take into consideration two perspectives. First, objectives must be integrated with the organization's overall approach to career management and the reward structure. An organization that emphasizes training in managerial skills, for example, will not ordinarily base its career system solely on the outside recruitment of formally credentialed applicants. Such a system would thwart the career incentives motivating effective participation in the training process. Likewise, an organization whose reward structure is geared to daily output penalizes participation in training in broader or longer-range management competencies.

Second, training objectives must be set on the basis of individually assessed training needs (Steadham and Clay, 1985; Rummler, 1987). Not only does the needs assessment process afford an opportunity for employee participation (and hence self-investment in the training concept), it also assures a linkage between organizational objectives, task structures, supervisory perceptions, and employee desires. Furthermore, it is a great opportunity for establishing and nurturing a positive employee–supervisor relationship. With both parties focused on doing something "good" for the employee, the negative master–servant psychological relationship that inhibits much of Western management practices can be circumvented.

Assessing Training Needs

Comprehensive training or executive development efforts begin with a needs assessment (Steadman and Clay, 1985; Rummler, 1987; Goldstein, 1993: 29–82). Needs assessments draw information from analysis of individual employees, management plans and concerns, or environmental factors affecting the organization. Regardless of the type of assessment approach adopted, the general objective is to determine training and development needs and to translate those needs into learning tasks. The involvement of trainees and their supervisors in the needs assessment process also helps develop organizational trust and teamwork (Braun, 1979; Boyer and Pond, 1987; Schneier, Gutherie, and Olin, 1988; Haas, 1991).

McGehee and Thayer (1961) outline three levels to the analysis of training needs—organizational, operational/job, and individual/personal. Organizational analysis focuses on the general treatment needs necessary for implementing or carrying out the human resources planning process. It concentrates on those functions that help in maintenance of the existing organizational structure, enhancing its efficiency or updating operations, and in nurturing the organizational culture.

Job analysis is devoted to delineating the specific skills and competencies involved in the tasks that compose an individual job. Training is directed at ensuring that the individual possesses these skills and competencies. Personal analysis needs assessment focuses on the organization–person fit. The advantages of individual, technical competence can be dissipated if the individual fails to successfully integrate into the organization's social structure.

An organizational approach to needs assessment focuses on environmental factors. Assessment may be based on the discrepancy between organizational competencies and those prescribed by professional standards nationally. Likewise, simple awareness of trends in current affairs (e.g., affirmative action and diversity, collective bargaining, productivity, automation and Management Information Systems MIS) may clearly dictate externally imposed training needs on the organization (Goldstein, 1993: 29–82).

Many of these concerns are brought together in the efforts fostering total quality management (TQM). Most notably associated with the work of Philip B. Crosby (1979, 1984, 1986), W. Edwards Deming (1986), and Joseph Juran (1964, 1988) and recognized in the United States through the Malcolm Baldrige awards, these are efforts at crafting the effective organization through the empowerment and training of its members.

Organizational needs assessment is associated with career management and workforce planning. Training is greatly enhanced in an organization if career ladders have been established. Career ladders are job systems in which any rung (position) is obtainable by specified training and experience in a previous rung (position). Workforce planning based on service load projections can provide general estimates of growth and turnover. From this may be derived a projection of the needed flow through job pathways in the career management system and projections for determining the scope and substance of the organization's training function over time (Goldstein, 1993: 29–82).

Another organizational assessment approach is the organizational climate survey (Zemke, 1979). Though often used in early phases of organizational development efforts, such surveys are useful in identifying training and management development needs as well. Employee surveys are an efficient means of gathering data on commonly perceived organizational problems often not noticed in policy-centered management planning. Training in conflict management, communications, team building, job design, and similar "humanistic" content areas may well seem more salient to the organization's "bottom line" if surveys reveal a climate marked by discontent, low morale, or confusion about organizational goals. Though not ordinarily used in this manner, surveys could also serve as a means of identifying employee-perceived priorities regarding potential training topics.

Management-centered approaches to needs assessment present certain advantages. First, of course, such approaches help mesh the training program with organizational objectives as determined by management. These objectives may take into account a variety of needs about which the individual employee may be totally unaware. Second, by involving management more closely in the training planning process, legitimation of the training effort is gained that is instrumental to success. Third, management-centered approaches avoid confusing training assessment with judgmentally directed performance appraisal (Daley, 1992b).

From the employee viewpoint, individual-centered needs assessment may seem like a demand to "confess weaknesses" that may lower the employee's standing in the eyes of those who rate his or her performance (Meyer, Kay, and French, 1965; Meyer, 1991). Where such systems are employed, it becomes imperative that the employee-provided information not be used or appear to be used in any judgmental decisions (i.e., retention, dismissal, promotion, or pay). Hence, both Meyer (1991) and Daley (1992b) advocate the use of developmental appraisal processes in such circumstances.

Training needs are basically assessed by asking the employees (Graham and Mikal, 1986). Individual-centered approaches usually include measures designed to ascertain the organization–person fit. Besides including training programs primarily designed to aid in an individual's growth and development, they include assessments as to whether that specific individual matches the present or projected human resources needs of the organization.

These personal analyses can also be used to ascertain whether the individual employees in question actually possess the ability to learn (Fleishman and Mumford, 1989; Geber, 1989a). In addition to ability itself, the motivation to seek or participate in training (Hicks and Klimoski, 1987), as well as other personal attributes and attitudes, plays a role in determining trainability (Noe, 1986; Noe and Schmitt, 1984).

Often overlooked in our concern for equity and fairness is the fact that real people are indeed different. They bring with them not only different personalities but different and meaningful job potentials. An individual's ability to learn specific tasks and skills is an important consideration in the overall assessment of training needs (Robertson and Downs, 1989).

In individual-centered needs assessments, remedial training commonly utilizes skills testing and performance testing. Such tests may be by written or oral examination, simulation, peer evaluation, superior's evaluation, or self-rating. The simplest, least scientific, but perhaps most common method is to translate the job description into a list of task elements and corresponding skills. The potential trainee is then asked to rate him- or herself in terms of perceived proficiency in each of the skill areas. Training for advancement or for displacement is often assessed similarly, except that the new position to which the employee will be moving is used as the base. In training for growth, the individual-centered approach to needs assessment may utilize the interest inventory as well (Maslow, 1976: 10–4).

Organizational, job, and personal needs assessment approaches are not mutually exclusive. In fact, each serves to inform the training designer in a different way. Ideally, a multimethod approach to needs assessment would be the rule in learning design. Regardless of the approach used, the guiding principle in assessing training should be "How does this improve the organization?"

Although needs assessment is essential if training is to be linked to organizational, job, or personal needs, it is, unfortunately, little practiced. For the most part, governments rush to provide training solutions to their problems without adequately assessing their needs. What information they possess is mainly employee surveys (which may not distinguish wants from needs) and supervisory suggestions (which may reflect current fads more than specific analysis). So, even though quantitative data is desired in guiding training and development decisions, little is available (Gray, Hall, Miller, and Shasky, 1997).

A wide array of specific techniques are available for assessing training needs. Besides the obvious sources derived from management and employee requests for training (for themselves or others), information on training needs can be gathered through attitudinal surveys, focus groups, and advisory committees. Employee skill inventories and assessment centers can serve to point out areas needing attention. Performance measures such as those provided by performance appraisals, work samplings, critical incidents, output or result reports, as well as information from program evaluations and management audits can be used.

A crucial element in needs assessment is to focus on those who are to receive the training. Do they perceive a problem? Do they think the proposed training is likely to help solve that problem? From an organizational perspective, there is also the question of whether the "problem" is indeed significant enough to warrant solution. Individuals may perceive a problem and feel that the proposed training program is likely to solve it, yet the organization may not obtain any substantial productivity enhancement from these expenditures and efforts.

The term *problem* needs to be construed broadly here. Too often, training is focused solely on poor performers and performance discrepancies. A "problem" may also be one that deals with high performers and how to get the most out of their superior talent. Concomitantly, training must avoid any "dumbing down." A least-common-denominator approach to training (in order to economically encompass poor and high performers in the same training session) is a costly mistake. The money saved by the omnibus session is wasted in that the high performers not only are bored and discouraged but may become dissatisfied and less productive as a result.

Adult Learning Theory

The psychological aspects of human development indicate that adults pass through a series of life stages. These life stages influence their perceptions and relationships with themselves, the world at large, and their work lives. Career development, motivation, commitment, and job satisfaction are all affected by an individual's life stage (Schott, 1986).

What does the adult-student approach mean in practice for training? Training will be based ordinarily on student self-assessment of learning needs and self-determination of learning goals, often calling for an individualized approach. Learning will be related to life problems and will be based on a problem-solving orientation. Physical conditions of learning will treat adults as adults (e.g., provision for comfort and other amenities), usually in a coequal, seminar setting (e.g., no individuals sitting behind one another). Attention will be given by the trainer to trust-building activities and to downplaying competitive pressures. The teacher will expose his or her own assumptions, values, and needs as a colearner and will involve students as information providers, discussion leaders, and resources.

Adult learning recognizes the importance or responsibility that the employee or learner has for acquiring knowledge. The audience must be aware of its need and desire the change. In addition, individuals learn in different manners. The method in which information is presented—sight, sound, and motion—can affect learning. Yet, neither employee motivation to learn nor the learning styles of employees are incorporated even in the rudimentary needs assessment that occurs (Goldstein, 1993: 83–143; Gray, Hall, Miller, and Shasky, 1997).

Although students possess differing learning styles (visual, auditory, and kinesthetic) that better enable each of them to comprehend material, they should not be sorted into groups on this basis. Although this approach would certainly enhance the individual task of learning, it has some severe drawbacks. Besides being impractical in terms of costs, it misses an opportunity to expose an individual to diverse style—both in terms of the presentation of knowledge and, perhaps more important, in terms of individuals.

Students will participate in setting learning objectives. They will ordinarily learn through self-organized project groups at least part of the time, as well as through individualized study, learning–teaching teams, and other self-selected modes. The teacher often will function as a resource, assisting in arranging role-plays, discussion of cases, and application of learning to life problems. Criteria for measuring progress are developed on a mutually acceptable basis with students, and final assessment is by self-evaluation (Knowles, 1978:77–79).

Knowles's humanistic approach to adult education is not necessarily in contradiction with a second major theory used in adult learning, stimulus-response theory. This theory, associated with B. F. Skinner and behaviorism, holds that learning is primarily a function of reinforcement (this is also the foundation upon which the various motivational-reward theories, such as expectancy theory, are based). What is learned results not from stimulation toward learning but reward for learning (Skinner, 1971).

Stimulus-response (S-R) theory could be used to support the view that any method of instruction can be effective so long as the content is geared to the desired behavior, enables the individual to engage in the desired behavior, and then rewards the individual for it. Trainers have usually seen behaviorism as an adjunct to adult learning, not a contradiction of it (Knowles, 1978:61).

Behaviorism is also associated with the advocacy of behavioral learning objectives and competency-based testing in training and development. Behavioral objectives are stated learning goals that are concrete and specific with regard to (1) the desired, observable behavior to be learned, (2) how the behavior is to be demonstrated, and (3) the standards for evaluating the behavior. Behavioral objectives are said to improve teacher–student communication, establish clear goals, set the basis for evaluation, allow individualization of learning, improve accountability for learning, and increase efficiency.

General applications in the learning process help us in the design of specific training methods. The development of training programs focused on imparting skills or competencies need to include (1) goal setting, (2) behavioral modeling, (3) practice, and (4) feedback if they are to be effective (Wexley and Latham, 1991).

Training must be focused on specific goals. The general lessons learned with regard to the inherent value in goal setting are equally applicable in the training arena. Employees must know what it is they are expected to learn and why it is important for their future job performance.

Approaches that provide the employee with a model of what is actually desired are better able to achieve this. Behavioral models demonstrate the skills or competencies that are to be learned (Robinson, 1985). Computer tutorials and audiovisual presentations of correct procedures and methods are ideal examples; more so are the techniques that employ simulations and role-playing in which the employee actually experiences or goes through what is to be learned (Cascio, 1991).

Continuing in this vein, learning requires practice if the material is to be retained. The frequent repetition of tasks provides for familiarity and confidence (Cascio 1991). Repeated practice sessions enable the trainee to avoid fatigue and better manage and focus on what is to be learned. Repeated sessions also reinforce and strengthen the learning process.

Finally, employees need feedback on what their skill levels are and what they need to do in order to correct or improve their performance. Feedback must be both immediate and specific. It must be provided as soon as possible to the event while memories are fresh and vivid. Otherwise, good practices may be overlooked and bad practices repeated. Feedback must also be specific. When correcting mistakes, it must not only clearly identify what is wrong but also include guidance or instruction on what is desired.

Evaluating Training and Development

Professional education and training should be subject to rigorous cost-benefit analyses. It is perhaps the failure to subject personnel practices, in general, and education and training programs, in particular, to evaluations that has allowed them to languish (Ammons and Nietzielski-Eichner, 1985; Slack, 1990; Gray, Hall, Miller, and Shasky, 1997). The application of thorough evaluations to these and other personnel practices would help to assess their contributions and, thereby, to establish their value to the organization.

The impact of education and training is evaluated on the extent to which it produces satisfactory reactions, learning, behaviors, or effective results (McGehee and Thayer, 1961; Kirkpatrick, 1975, 1987; Ammons and Nietzielski-Eichner, 1985; Goldstein, 1993: 147–221). While progressively more demanding, each of these four categories contributes useful information on the overall effectiveness of training.

The most common type of evaluation (and almost the only one actually used) is the satisfaction or reaction survey (Gray, Hall, Miller, and Shasky, 1997). The trainee is simply asked to rate the course, the instructor, and various learning elements (exercises, readings, cases, speakers, films) on a Likert scale ranging from strong satisfaction to strong dissatisfaction. Usually, open-ended questions are also included to elicit more concrete criticisms and suggestions useful in redesigning curricula.

The satisfaction survey approach is direct and useful, involves learners in course feedback, and is easy and inexpensive to administer. It rests on the commonsense premise that if learners feel that the training was poor, that they didn't learn much, that the instructor was boring, that the readings were unrelated to the real world, then training probably is poor.

Even simple reactions to the education courses and training sessions—the hot-coffee-and-fresh-donuts school—can be important sources of information. Comments on the content, teacher/trainer styles and methods, and perceived utility can be quite helpful (Ammons and Nietzielski-Eichner, 1985). The social environment and opportunity to interact with others afforded by educational opportunities and training programs is an important, added ingredient in creating a highly motivated work group. In many circumstances, the informal dialogue between participants contributes more to the education and training than do the formal sessions (Sims and Sims, 1991).

There are any number of problems with the satisfaction survey approach when used as the sole evaluative method. First, it is biased by the "gratitude" effect. Learners tend to say kind things about the training because it seems more polite and because most people like to think of themselves as kind and nice. Second, the satisfaction survey is biased by the "Hawthorne effect." By this is meant that the extra management attention of the training and evaluation rather than the training itself may cause satisfied responses. Third, this approach is biased by the effects of psychological self-investment. Participants have invested their time, energy, and perhaps money in training, and this investment, like all forms of participation, fosters favorableness and acceptance. Failure to hold attitudes of acceptance creates cognitive dissonance with the fact of self-investment. Fourth, the satisfaction survey is biased by subjectivity. Learners often are not in a position to rate their own learning, or may be distracted by other values (enjoyment, for example), which may infuse all their responses. This is the problem of individuals who note several years later that their most hated high school teachers were the ones who taught them the most. It is also the problem of contamination of subjective surveys by environmental factors (e.g., comfortable surroundings, prestigious sponsorship, high-status colearners), favorable reaction to which confounds evaluation of the actual training delivered.

Because individuals are notoriously disinclined to admit skill weaknesses and because the gratitude effect and other biases of satisfaction surveys are still present, this method also tends to make training "look good." An improvement measures skill accomplishment by self-assessment both pre- and posttraining. This partially controls for the hiding of weaknesses but not for gratitude and other effects. Another improvement is to interview learners months after the learning experience. At this time, they may be asked not only whether they perceive the training to have increased capacity but also to identify specific instances of accomplishment they perceive to have resulted from training. Other refinements include asking respondents about amount learned in comparison with other training programs or if they would like to take an additional course of the same type or recommend the given course to fellow employees. Though still subjective, such items also help puncture glittering generalities and bring responses down to a more concrete level.

Learning the material presented in an educational or training program is an initial, necessary condition in an effective endeavor. Information not presented or not received and correctly understood by the individual is information that is not going to be used. Learning measurements assess the potential inherent in an educational process. Learning techniques can assess how well the basic fundamentals are understood (Ammons and Nietzielski-Eichner, 1985).

The objective learning approach to evaluation is, of course, the academic standard. This conventionally takes the form of written examinations. Other forms are "hands-on" demonstration of skills, successful completion of individual or team projects, simulations (e.g., in assessment centers), and interactive computer exercises. When this approach to evaluation is combined with pre- and posttest training measurement and with a curriculum with clear learning objectives in the first place, it results in stable, reliable estimates of knowledge, skill, and attitude transfer in the training process. Panel studies may be necessary, however, if learning attrition and decay is of concern, as when knowledge, though organizationally important, will not be reinforced through continuous practice on the job. Reliability can be further improved through multimethod testing and through averaging ratings of multiple assessors, though these refinements are probably not necessary for most applications. Highest reliability requires panel testing of the training and a matched control group.

The learning approach to evaluation, in spite of its advantages, is not without its drawbacks. In comparison with the satisfaction approach, it fails to tap the effect of training on morale and organizational climate. A training program could, for example, pound a great deal of knowledge into employees' skulls (satisfying the learning-oriented type of evaluation) in a way that creates deep resentments, entirely undermining the organizational changes toward which training was ostensibly directed. The most serious objection to the learning approach (and the satisfaction approach as well) is that it does not measure directly whether knowledge and attitude acquisition actually translates into behavior on the job and desired effect on the organization.

This last objection is important for two reasons. First, we are all aware that "head knowledge" does not necessarily mean that a person can accomplish tasks well. If this were true, academic credentials would be the only form of evaluation necessary. What is less understood, but equally important to recognize, is that just as knowledge does not necessarily translate into effective action, the same is true of attitudes.

Although adult learners will themselves endeavor to apply what they have learned, modern educational and training programs should focus on assisting them in this. Work behaviors and, ultimately, organizational results become measures of a successful training program. Learning needs to be applied in the workplace and, in turn, those behavioral applications should lead to the desired organizational outcomes. Follow-up to training through the use of coaching is one means that can effectively enhance success. Coaching provides individuals with both constructive feedback on their efforts and, perhaps just as important, encouragement in those efforts (Olivero, Bane, and Kopelman, 1997). Although they are perhaps more general in their focus, professional educational programs should be held to the same standards. Like training, education imparts substantive knowledge.

Subsequent assessments can measure the long-term continuance of learned behaviors. Monitoring should detect improvements in the quality. Employee attitudes should also be more favorable (Ammons and Nietzielski-Eichner, 1985).

Finally, organizational productivity should show signs of improvement. Although many factors—many of which are beyond our control or influence—contribute to these outcomes, this is, nevertheless, the sine qua non for any organizational activity.

The fourth and final approach to evaluation centers on the measurement of organizational effectiveness. Just as it is possible for learned knowledge and attitudes to fail to affect individual behavior, so it is possible that behavior will fail to affect the effectiveness of the organization in attaining its goals. To take an obvious and extreme case, training is wasted and no amount of learned behavior change is helpful to an organization seeking to achieve impossible goals. Though it is often true that the sum of improvements in individual behaviors will contribute to, if not equal, the magnitude of overall improvement in organizational effectiveness, this is an empirical question that will vary by circumstance.

This fourth approach calls on the training evaluator to assess the proportion of variance in organizational goal achievement attributable to factors that can be improved through training. If effectiveness is 90 percent determined by budgetary, political, and environmental factors that training cannot affect, then this must be taken into account. There may be two programs that equally improve individual behavior, but if one is in a 90 percent constrained system and the other is at the opposite end of the spectrum, the two programs must be evaluated very differently. This raises questions of organizational equity. In essence, the effectiveness approach holds the training function hostage to factors that may be beyond its control.

Accountability for what one may not control is a problem of all management-by-effects systems, not just those in training evaluations. In complex organizations, effectiveness-based evaluations may assume a state of the art of management science that does not exist. A complete approach would assume that a multivariate input–output model of the firm can be constructed that simulates organizational performance over time; that the input measures can include training investments; and that the output measures reflect organizational effectiveness (as opposed simply to client, paper, or materials turnover). In the public sector, effectiveness measurement has become more and more sophisticated, yet human resource accounting still remains in its infancy. Overall, the input side of the information base needed to construct the simulation model for effectiveness measurement is largely missing, and even the output side is still in great controversy and development.

The effectiveness or transfer of training can be enhanced by planning for its use. In choosing specific training programs and the individuals to receive that training, an organization needs to clearly indicate what is the expected application or outcome it hopes to achieve. The organization must plan to use those new skills it has invested in. Too often, successful training "fails" because no use is made of it. The development of expert systems not only can aid training but can provide an invaluable reference guide for employees back on the job.

METHODS OF TRAINING AND DEVELOPMENT

By combining adult learning theory with advances in communications technology, the modern training operation in a large organization is apt to be a telecommunications, multimedia production, using curriculum development center employing a permanent and contract staff with a variety of skills drawn from education, public and business administration, communications, graphics, engineering, and the arts. Behind the attention-getting glitter of such methods as videotape and interactive feedback are a very wide range of approaches to education and development, many of them quite traditional. Campbell, Dunnette, Lawler, and Weick (1970) divide these methods into three major divisions: (1) on-the-job training methods, (2) information presentation methods, and (3) simulation methods.

On-the-Job Methods

On-the-job training methods are the oldest forms of training. Apprenticeship is the classic example, traceable to ancient times. Other methods include off-line training, on-line training and coaching, job rotation, committee rotation, and internships. Though the methods of training are subject to intense faddism (Campbell, 1971: 565), there is great stability as well.

Apprenticeship is the oldest training model in America. In the United States, apprenticeship programs have usually not occurred in semiprofessional, professional, or managerial career tracks. Unlike Europe, American apprenticeship has been rare even in office skill areas. In the public sector it is almost unknown.

Nonetheless, there are training counterparts to apprenticeship in the public sector (Riccucci 1991). Under 10 percent of all apprenticeships take place in the public sector and nearly a third of these apprenticeships occur among the military and civilian employees of the Defense Department. Yet, apprenticeships are employed in numerous state and local governments.

Booth and Rhode (1988) note that apprentice programs for firefighters, police, and corrections are widespread means used for recruiting women and minority candidates. Other analogies to apprenticeship exist in cooperative education programs in which students alternate between work experience and academic training (Riccucci, 1991).

Though not under the label of apprenticeship, this type of training is likely to increase in the future. There is a great interest in the mentoring concept inherent in apprenticeship and internship, for example. Mentors provide practical, expert advice or a "listening post." They are available after formal training programs to answer questions that arise later. Second, partly for affirmative action reasons, the personnel profession has become far more attuned to the concept of entry-level semiprofessional or assistant job classifications, which are, in effect, apprenticeship-type positions. Such transitional classifications are also likely to spread as career management becomes more prevalent in the public sector. Though seemingly a nineteenth-century concept, apprenticeship is a surprisingly vital idea that may, on close inspection, seem to be a highly motivating, participative, and cost-efficient training method.

On-the-job training programs (OJT) are another training model. Off-line versions, sometimes called "vestibule training" (Strauss and Sayles, 1980: 411), are relatively rare in the public sector because most government agencies are willing to undertake the risks to service delivery that on-line OJT carries. There are exceptions, however. Strauss and Sales note that NASA "could not provide on-the-job training for astronauts and instead use a simulated moon environment." On-line OJT remains far more prevalent in the public sector, however.

OJT is attractive because it provides direct, realistic training in the specific methods actually required by the position. OJT also provides immediate performance feedback in most situations and the motivation of active involvement of peers and superiors in the training process. It has the added advantage of being a form of learning that can be utilized by many individuals for whom the intellectual skills required in classroom training would constitute a barrier to performance and employment/promotions, a barrier not always truly germane to the actual requirements of the job. Finally, OJT may allow an agency to provide compensation to the learner that it could not provide for traditional classroom learning. This compensation may be an additional motivator in the learning process and may remove a financial barrier having a discriminatory effect in the organization's intake process.

Job rotation, unlike apprenticeship and OJT, assumes that the organization derives a generalized benefit from training the employee in related jobs as well as his or her own. In the private sector, this has sometimes been carried quite far.

Job rotation is based on experiential learning. It is peer-assisted. It provides direct feedback and generally involves the employee's superiors in the training process. Rotating committee assignments are analogous in purpose and function. Through learning by doing, the employee gains competence in new areas, confidence in self increases, and useful networks of cooperating individuals are built up through formal and informal association.

Information Presentation Methods

If on-the-job methods are the classic industrial mode, information presentation is the traditional educational mode of instruction. Though the lecture format comes quickest to mind and is perhaps still the most popular information presentation method, this mode also includes use of small group discussions, case methods, audiovisual techniques, and computer-assisted instruction (CAI). Also, information presentation can be undertaken in a variety of formats: university credit courses, institutes, short courses and conferences, and correspondence courses.

Though associated with the university, classroom instruction has strong advocates in many quarters (Donaldson and Scannell, 1986; Broadwell, 1987). Moreover, classroom training need not displace the performance of needed jobs, can allow for more counseling and assessment, and can provide for program stability in the face of fluctuating employer interest. Finally, because most employers still expect those hired to come to the job already trained, classroom training avoids much of the "remedial" stereotyping associated with special on-the-job training efforts.

Classroom instruction is offered today by nearly everyone. Not only do universities and community colleges offer courses for public managers, but government institutes and research bureaus, extension services, professional associations, consulting firms, personnel departments, training divisions, and many line agencies also provide this training. The instruction explosion makes generalization difficult, but probably the most common format is the short course (Reith, 1987). Offered for one to five days, the short course provides training in a specialized area (e.g., communication skills, information management, environmental impact analysis, performance appraisal, sexual harassment, the Americans with Disabilities Act, employee assistance programs) in a "bite size" that can be taken out of the in-service learner's schedule with a minimum of disruption. Typically, the classroom lecture format is combined with small group discussion and brainstorming, audiovisual presentations, and the simulation of real-life situations.

Short-course formats are sometimes criticized for their "in-and-out" nature, which lacks follow-through. In contrast to academic courses, such instruction rarely leaves adequate time for the important gestation period needed by many learners. Short courses, generally not offered for college credit, may also dispense with the evaluation of the participants, because the sales of short courses to agencies discourages anything that lowers participant satisfaction (e.g., grades, difficult readings, time-consuming projects). For this reason, academics and others frequently raise questions about short-course quality. These questions exist, of course, because training evaluation is inadequate or absent.

Programmed or printed instruction is the most common companion of classroom instruction and is the mainstay of most self-instructional approaches. Correspondence instruction, for instance, is based mostly on printed materials. Correspondence instruction is also linked to video presentations. Many Public Broadcasting Stations air video courses as part of their Saturday morning lineup. These broadcasts are offered often in conjunction with means for the viewer to obtain college credit. The case study, the core of the Harvard Business School approach and that used in some public administration programs, is also based on printed materials (Pigors, 1987); so is nearly programmed instruction designed for self-study. Well-designed printed instruction is highly efficient and can result in impressive cost savings by reducing training time. It also allows home study and later refresher sessions at the convenience of the learner.

Printed and programmed instruction has other advantages as well. It allows the learner to pause, back up, or skip ahead in the learning sequence on an individualized basis. Far more branching options (specialized explanations or topics) are possible in this method than in other learning technologies. Also, self-diagnostic checks and self-scoring quizzes can be incorporated into printed instruction to provide immediate feedback on learning in a nonevaluative, low-pressure context.

The disadvantages of print are equally many. It is the wrong method for trainees deficient in verbal skills. It may further de facto discrimination in the intake process, which could be avoided by using other training methods. It is difficult to anticipate all learner needs and usually requires a more personal backup system to field additional questions. Also, it is difficult to find talented writers who are capable of presenting material in an interesting and clear manner. Perhaps most important, many skills, particularly those dealing with human relations, are difficult to learn without the experience of group interaction. Group discussion will also ordinarily enrich the learner's insights into the subject by bringing out points not considered, by creating a sense of "ownership" of the material through participation, and by allowing brainstorming and other creative learning techniques based on group methods.

More and more, programmed instruction is included as part of a computer-based learning package (King, 1986; Hart, 1987; Madlin, 1987). Computer-assisted instruction possesses all the advantages found in programmed instruction and, in addition, often allows for an interactive environment in which the trainee can practice the skill being taught. The "what if" aspect of many computer packages allows the trainee to explore the limitations and possibilities inherent in a new method.

Though classroom and print-based instruction have many advantages, the sad experience of so many students in suffering through boring lectures and even more boring required readings creates a strong attraction to audiovisual (A-V) techniques as an alternative. There is a natural tendency for the organization just beginning a training function to seek to compete with television. The high technology and the powerful impact of well-done audiovisual productions seems to many the ideal answer to training problems (Wallington, 1987).

Audiovisual methods include much more than motion pictures and videotape, of course. Also included are slide and slide-tape presentations, transparencies, opaque projection, audio tapes, flip charts and easel graphics, interactive computer videodisks, and the simple chalkboard. The high-technology end of audiovisual production is not necessarily the best medium for every occasion.

Good audiovisual production requires tremendous effort. Some of the costs are obvious: the need to develop a storyboard, to write a script, to employ actors or train staff, to pay music copyright fees, not to mention the costs of lighting, sound mixing, directing, editing, duplicating, and special effects and graphics. Unfortunately, many of the cost factors that inflate Hollywood costs are present in the humble organization A-V production as well. Worse, viewers may expect the organization to meet commercial standards of production.

However, there are indeed well-done training films that are well worth the cost. They combine the production techniques of the modern film industry with content focused on the most correct management practices. In delivering their message, the best are also entertaining (e.g., Video Arts markets the highly effective training films of John Cleese and of the Muppets).

There are indirect costs, too. Production takes a great deal of time, which may be disruptive to the organization. Once completed, an A-V production is difficult to change and may soon become outdated. In the classroom, it may isolate the instructor from communication with students or seem a "canned presentation" and a poor substitute for "live" and lively teaching. It is also nonparticipatory and allows no individualization and provides no feedback.

These problems have been somewhat overcome with the introduction of interactive videos in recent years. While sophisticated and, hence, costly, interactive videos are keyed to the trainee's responses to the information presented and the expected results therefrom (Packer 1988). Interactive videos have been especially useful in training police officers for crisis situations.

In fact, visual presentations are best used when the information to be presented is kept to simple levels, avoiding complexity and overcrowding of visual imagery. Better uses of the medium include multiuse, open-ended problem visuals in which a situation is presented on video. Analysis and discussion, however, are left to the classroom leader. Videotaping students themselves can also be a valuable form of instant feedback, allowing either self-evaluation or greater class insight into group process.

Action-Based Methods

Three broad categories of action-based methods are role-plays and simulations; laboratory and behavioral methods; and organization development activities. Although these are not necessarily mutually exclusive, they do represent different emphases within the training profession (Goldstein, 1993: 273–308).

Role-playing and simulation exercises are among the most common forms of training today. They basically encompass the important concept of behavioral modeling. Role-plays ordinarily involve breaking a larger class into smaller groups. Group research suggests that small groups (three to five members) are most satisfying to participants and reach consensus sooner, but medium-sized groups (six to eleven), though slower to organize, often make higher-quality decisions (Cooke, 1987). The problem with larger groups is their tendency to decompose into smaller informal subgroups. Also, large size may inhibit expression for some participants. Various other concerns raised by Janis (1972) as aspects of groupthink can also affect such processes.

The instructor in a role-play often circulates from one small group to another, not to participate but to answer process questions and to gather impressions useful in leading end-of-role-play class discussions. The instructor may also function as a rule keeper, intervening to establish or reestablish basic role-play facts. This may be needed when an occasional participant goes to extremes in improvisation, changing the nature of the simulation learning objectives. The instructor usually is also firm in discouraging "stepping out of role" in the middle of a role-play, as when students stop to explain how they would feel "in real life." These comments can be saved for later discussion. The instructor may also act as a process controller. For example, the instructor may intervene to discourage aggression and personalization of conflict. Role reversal, where participants exchange roles, is an empathy-creating technique used in this regard. Videotaping also improves role-play feedback and empathized insight in many situations.

Simulations need not be involved and complex. They are readily available from commercial suppliers, from professional associations, from adaptation of examples distributed through the training press, and from examples designed for academic use. Instructions also exist on preparing original role-plays.

Role-play and simulation have drawbacks as well as advantages. The advantages of providing ego-involving behavioral practice and reinforcement for learning objectives are so great that trainers sometimes rely on this approach almost exclusively. There are two major disadvantages, however. First, some people learn best in traditional ways. Training evaluations tend to show that whereas most participants value role-playing, there is almost always a significant minority who prefer information presentation techniques. Second, role-playing is very time-consuming. Hurrying role-playing experiences is unwise and creates learner dissatisfaction with the training experience. For instance, one role-play can easily fill up an entire three-hour training session; informational content might be decreased as the role-play component of training is increased. This makes role-playing most valuable when the content is interpersonal relations and least valuable when the content is technical information.

While more passive, case studies are another form of training. Concrete examples of behavior and situations help to provide a "reality anchorage" for the conceptual ideas being presented. Individuals often more readily relate to the familiarity of a case study. It also helps them recognize and establish the importance of the problem under discussion. Case studies can model desired behavior; hence, they can serve as the basis for creating expert systems that will serve as day-to-day guides and references.

Laboratory and behavioral methods of training are other action-based approaches that are commonly used (Shore, 1985). Popularized in the 1960s by the National Training Laboratories (NTL), the laboratory approach came to be associated with sensitivity training. In sensitivity training groups (T-groups), organization members, often middle management, seek to improve interpersonal skills through open communications, direct personal feedback, and confrontation. Though it may utilize role-playing, the emphasis is not on simulation of actual situations but rather on providing a vehicle for expression of emotions and beliefs. The NTL approach emphasizes personal development (Dupre, 1976), and the psychological techniques employed provide just that: powerful personal experiences from which many individuals claim benefit. Others charge that the encouragement of openness merely fosters conflict and even inflicts serious psychological damage on vulnerable group members.

Because of charges of this sort and because of the lack of clear linkage of sensitivity training to organizational goals, the T-group approach to training fell from favor in the 1970s, though it is still common. Instead, laboratory methods tended to evolve in the direction of organization development, discussed below, or were combined with more goal-oriented and problem-solving approaches. Gaming is an objectives-oriented laboratory adaptation of role-playing that started to become popular in this period, for example. Various approaches to instrumented team learning are another example of a behavioral approach that evolved at least in part from the laboratory tradition.

These approaches are often more familiarly known under the general rubric of assessment centers. The assessment center is a managerial tool noted for its usefulness in the selection process where it serves as a battery of tests measuring a candidate's abilities to perform job-related tasks. However, virtually the same assessment center can serve to introduce an individual to the nature and demands of a new job (Byhan, 1971; Ross, 1988; Sackett, 1982; Yeager, 1986; Moses, 1987).

Evolving from the laboratory approaches of the 1950s and 1960s, organization development (OD) has since become a field unto itself. Included in organization development are such techniques as team building (Dyer, 1977; Shaw, 1985; Christen, 1987), survey feedback (Nadler, 1977), and leadership development (Blake and Mouton, 1969; Reiner and Morris, 1987). Other techniques include role analysis, process consulting, conflict management, and various aspects of management development.

After dramatic, even revolutionary claims made for organization development, and after over a decade of practice, it is difficult to discern any great changes. However, meaningful, if not great, changes are indeed evident (Golembiewski, 1985). Partly, this is because most organization development efforts are not intended to be experiments in creating participatory organizational structures even though, as training methods, participation is encouraged. Moreover, the focus of organization development as training is on process (leadership styles, organizational climate, interpersonal communication and role clarification, goal setting) and not on structural change (power relationships, benefit flows, accountability). Indeed, the "team" ideology of OD-type training suggests that harmony can be achieved through teamwork (process) apart from structure. Also, there is much evidence that organization development techniques improve employee satisfaction.

SUMMARY

Training and development is a key tool in strategic human resource management. Through the application of training and development, current employees—an organization's human capital—are kept up-to-date. This enables the organization to address current needs while benefiting from historical experience and the teamwork that familiarity creates.

If the full benefits of training and development are to be obtained, an organization must draw upon its strategic planning. The goals and objectives derived from the strategic planning process establish the skills, knowledge, and abilities that an organization needs today and tomorrow.

A combination of organizational, job, and personal needs form the basis for conducting the training and development. Advances from educational research on adult learning enable training programs to be designed for maximizing learning. The adult learner's motivation can be coupled with delivery mechanisms best atuned to an individual's ability to learn.

In managing a training program, evaluation plays an important role in auditing and validating the process. It is necessary to establish that the training indeed has occurred and that it has been transferred to the workplace. Unfortunately, many organizations neglect evaluation and as a result waste money and time on ill-advised training programs.

Training and development methods encompass on-the-job techniques, information presentation, and action-based programs. Apprenticeships, job rotations, temporary assignments, and mentoring take advantage of in-house expertise to guide and nurture individuals as they engage in real activities. Information presentation from brochures and lectures to high-tech adaptations using videos, the Internet, and other self-paced modules serve to provide employees with basic knowledge on virtually any task. While more intensive and costly, action-based training assures that new skills and knowledge are applied and practiced prior to being put to a real-world test.

chapter 9

Employee Rights

The knowledge-based environment also heightens the importance attached to employee rights along with the instrumental grievance and discipline system. Employees are human beings and work better when their humanity is recognized and respected. The employer–employee relationship is not that of master and servant (although much of the legal system is based on that design). Foreshadowed by the work of Mary Parker Follett and commencing with the Hawthorne studies in the late 1920s, motivational research has clearly pointed this out. With the transformation of the organization into an entity based on the skills of its employees rather than the efficiency of its machinery, this lesson becomes even more important.

This chapter examines employee relations with special attention to legal rights and responsibilities. This chapter provides:

1. Knowledge of the grievance and discipline process with special emphasis on progressive disciplinary procedures and dealing with poor employees
2. An overview of employee job rights with a focus on the employment-at-will doctrine and its legal ramifications
3. A general examination of the application of citizens' constitutional rights in their status as government employees
4. An overview of the legal obligations or restrictions employees have to the larger civil society

Employee rights and the mechanism for enforcing them (i.e., the grievance process) serve as a safeguard for assuring that employees are accorded the basic dignity that every human being is entitled to. As with similar safety devices, we hope that we never will really need to use them. Even though most organizations would prefer to do without such legal and formal systems, reality requires them. If there were no past abuses, there would be no need for laws prohibiting such practices.

Although all employees possess legal rights vis-à-vis the employment relationship or "contract," those in the public sector are afforded even greater protections. Public employees are both employees and citizens. As citizens, they are extended the basic protections that the federal and state constitutions provide citizens against the abuse of government power. In essence, the Bill of Rights becomes part of the employment contract.

Counterpoised to these greater legal rights that public sector employees possess is a greater difficulty in using them. Legal rights and real rights are not the same thing. Public officials possess greater standing in the eyes of the courts than business managers, and the public coffers run deeper than those of a business. Because public officials are viewed as agents administering the public interest, American courts only reluctantly cast them in the role of the "villain." The evidence must indeed be quite substantial for the courts to overcome their presumption of official good conduct. Whereas a business must calculate the costs of litigation against company profits, litigation involving government officials draws on the general public purse. Because litigation is not charged against an agency's operating budget and a court "loss" could damage an official's career, the incentive is to pursue a Dickensian strategy of legal exhaustion.

GRIEVANCE AND DISCIPLINE

Grievance and discipline are interrelated topics. Both use a common organizational mediation/due process system. They differ in that grievances are employee-initiated while discipline is employer-initiated. Grievances allege that the employer has failed to adhere to organizational objectives and procedures; discipline is a claim that the employee has failed to follow these procedures for achieving the organization's objectives.

In addition, the exercise of disciplinary control often forms the basis for employee grievances. A closely related aspect is the use of performance appraisal systems that may both document the job-related effects of disciplinary problems and themselves lead to grievances.

Formal management control systems may affect employee motivation and job satisfaction beyond the extent warranted by individual cases. Employees obtain an image of the organization from how well it handles the grievance and disciplinary process. The sense of protection or fear that grievance and disciplinary systems engender can have a major impact.

Research indicates that employees place great store in the perceived fairness of the formal grievance and disciplinary procedures. In fact, perceptions arising from the types of procedures employed may be more important than the objective fairness of specific, substantive or distributive outcomes. Employees are more likely to know and understand the conditions that make the process "fair" than they are to fathom the circumstances underlying specific decisions (Folger and Greenberg, 1985; Greenberg, 1988; Folger and Konovsky, 1989; Fryxell and Gordon, 1989).

The emphasis here is on the existence of formal systems. Although a question with regard to whether small organizations objectively need such things arises, the subjective perception of equity and justice is an absolute. Justice should not be limited by the question of size. One of the purposes underlying such formal systems is that their existence will alleviate the need for their use.

The Grievance Process

The grievance process need not be perceived entirely as a system of negative punishments. Personnel management has over the years developed a series of positive, conflict resolution remedies designed to rehabilitate, correct, and prevent disciplinary problems (Bohlander, 1989). To a great extent, these reflect the humanistic concerns that undergird modern personnel management. Personnel management is especially concerned with the development and welfare of the individual. Yet that is not the only justification for the use of these programs. Underlying these conflict resolution efforts are two "hard" notions.

First, because the organization has a substantial investment in each of its employees, a conscientious effort should be made before writing off this investment as a loss. Inasmuch as problems are temporary afflictions, it is quite cost-effective to salvage an employee (Likert, 1967; Cascio, 1982).

Because grievances may reflect problems that are harmful not only from the employee's perspective but from that of the organization as well, the availability of remedies can help the organization remain effective. This factor has often been neglected in discussing grievance systems. A good grievance system is part of the organization's management information system. By pointing out problems, it can draw attention to systemic oversights. Although grievances and disciplinary problems can be individual, they can also reflect job design, selection, orientation, training, performance appraisal, and compensation problems (Klingner and Nalbandian, 1985: 339–340).

Second, the presence of such conflict resolution programs reassures ordinary employees. Although it is unlikely most would ever need such programs, they provide a motivational safety net for employees worried about the "what if." They also provide the employee with a sense of voice in the organization (Hirschman, 1970). This, in itself, can be an important motivational factor.

Both cost-effective and humanistic concerns focus attention on the employment of conflict resolution efforts (suggestion systems, whistle-blower protection, counseling, and drug and alcohol assistance). To ignore these is both to risk serious morale or motivational problems and to introduce unneeded, added costs to the organization.

A small community may offer the argument that it does not need a formal system or that it does not suffer from such problems. First, that argument is wrong. Conflict exists at all levels of government, and formal systems help to constructively channel and manage it. Second, the purpose of these systems is primarily to act as a deterrent. By formally establishing grievance and disciplinary systems, a municipality defines in advance what are deemed to be prohibited behaviors and their punishments. Furthermore, it posts assurances that the system is not subject to abuse. Basically, grievance and discipline procedures extend the rule of law to the organization.

A grievance process establishes order. It identifies what are grievable matters and helps in the implementation of the employment contract by interpreting its provisions. Conflict resolution is thereby institutionalized.

Informal grievance procedures have the advantage of not producing a permanent record. This prevents anyone from formally being blamed or declared at fault. Without these career-negative factors to contend with, attention can be focused on the grievance itself. Although this mainly entails employee and supervisor mediation, it can also involve a peer review or outside mediator. This is how an ombudsman successfully works.

The disadvantages of informal grievance processes are found in the uncertainty about what is being done and the fear of "command presence." Without a formal, written record no one knows what has happened or whether justice has been served. Systemwide mistakes are not likely to benefit from the corrective precedents emerging from a grievance process. Because informal systems rely heavily on organizational structure, they are of little use when the complaints are directed toward the same organizational personnel.

A formal grievance process assures employees and employers that grievances meet the standards set in the contract or public personnel laws. Requiring grievances to be put into writing while creating a permanent record focuses attention on the real issue from the beginning. Without this requirement, one is liable to find that the alleged grievance (or disciplinary matter) shifts as time goes by (Duane, 1991).

Because formal grievances serve as precedents for guiding future behavior, care must be taken in deciding which "cases" to push. Both employee organizations and employers must know when to cut their losses. First, a case must be thoroughly investigated as to the documented facts. The consequences on long-term relationships and organizational trust must be factored into the individual case. Second, is the case indeed winnable? As important as they may be, symbolic and moral victories are still losses. Finally, is the case really important?

Formal grievance processes may also suffer from perceptions of command presence. When those who hear the grievance are, in fact, the same individuals responsible for carrying out or executing the matter that gives rise to the grievance, the fairness of the process may be challenged (Cozzetto, 1991).

Many organizations find that separate, independent quasi-judicial structures better serve their interests. The mediation and counseling services (along with another alternate dispute resolution process) provided by many employee assistance programs have proven quite useful in this respect. Alternatively, an internal panel composed of employees and managers can serve to hear grievances. An employee appeal and review system (EARS) constitutes a separate panel composed equally of peers and managers to hear each grievance. An outside facilitator often is brought in to chair the panel. The employee-grievant and management each present their cases followed by a secret ballot by the panel (Kalish, 1996).

A formal grievance process also focuses attention on the importance of training supervisors, employees, and mediators in interpersonal skills, conflict resolution techniques, and mediation.

The Disciplinary Process

Although disciplinary actions only involve a very small portion of the workforce, the repercussions can be explosive. Because discipline affects the individual's basic existence either through the imposition of financial punishments or by termination, it is a highly emotional phenomenon that psychologically ripples out across the entire workforce. It is this greater, shadow effect that an organization must be careful about. Like the criminal justice system upon which it is modeled, the disciplinary process must place its first emphasis on the overall perception of justice. The outcome of the specific case is, to a great extent, only a secondary concern.

In contrast to the criminal justice process, an organization's disciplinary process is voluntarily accepted by the employee. The employee is always free to quit (or, as the case may be, pursue countercharges in the legal system).

Disciplinary systems exist to enforce work rules that the organization deems necessary for its proper functioning. The organization also has a disciplinary system because its focus is not to savage but to salvage the employee. Although some offenses are so severe that termination is the only recourse, most are minor infractions by otherwise valuable employees. Hence, the purpose of discipline is not to punish but to modify behavior (Odiorne, 1987: 141–164).

Because of this, it is necessary that all disciplinary cases be based on well-documented incidents. The standards of evidence used must be objective and specific. Needless to say, they must also be work-related. Just as important, a disciplinary infraction should be accompanied by a statement outlining the appropriate corrective action. This prevents discipline from being imposed when the problems being dealt with are really remedial through training or coaching. The adherence to such standards helps establish the fairness of the disciplinary process.

The fairness of a disciplinary process is attested to more by the procedural safeguards that exist than by the substantive cases it deals with. Hence, it is important that a review or appellate process also be included (see Figure 9.1). Because individual cases may include special circumstances and be subject to privacy restrictions, employees will focus on the due process accorded in determining their acceptance of the process. Hence, consistency in rule application and uniformity of treatment are essential. Equity is the key.

As a practical matter, enforcement should occur as soon after a disciplinary event as possible. The rule violated should be clearly identified along with the reason the rule exists. This clearly reinforces the importance of the relationship between the undesired behavior and the disciplinary consequences. Otherwise, intervening events may serve to mute this relationship or even be seen as moderating it. This will result in a weakening of the disciplinary process.

Similarly, the work rules must apply to all. There cannot be separate, more lax standards for high performers. Geniuses and stars may indeed be different from us mere mortals, but as long as they live and work with us they need to abide by the common rules. High performers serve as role models. We want their best attributes and successes emulated rather than their worst.

Figure 9.1
Petition for a Contested Case

PLEASE PRINT CLEARLY OR TYPE

STATE OF NORTH CAROLINA IN THE OFFICE OF
COUNTY OF (1) ______________ ADMINISTRATIVE HEARINGS

(2) ______________________________ ______________________________ (your name) PETITIONER, v. (3) ______________________________ ______________________________ RESPONDENT-EMPLOYER State or Local agency or Board about which you are complaining	PETITION FOR A CONTESTED CASE HEARING (N.C. Gen. Stat. § 126)

I hereby ask for a contested case hearing as provided for by North Carolina General Statutes §§ 126-34.1 and 126-37 because the Respondent has acted as follows:

(4) MY APPEAL IS BASED ON: (check all that apply)

____ discharge without just cause ____ suspension without just cause ____ demotion without just cause
____ failure to receive priority consideration ____ other (explain) ______________________

- The following occurred due to discrimination and/or retaliation for opposition to alleged discrimination:

____ employment
____ promotion
____ training
____ transfer
} was denied me; AND/OR

____ demotion
____ layoff
____ termination
} was forced upon me

____ other (explain) ______________________

- If your appeal is based upon alleged discrimination and/or retaliation for opposition to alleged discrimination, you must specify the type of discrimination: ____ Race ____ Religion ____ Color ____ Creed ____ National Origin ____ Sex ____ Age ____ Handicapping Condition ____ Political Affiliation

(5) Briefly state facts showing how you believe you have been harmed by the State/local agency or board:

____

____

(If more space is needed, attach additional pages.)

Paygrade: ________ Months of continuous State employment: ____ Job title: ____________

If applicant, I applied for: ______________________

(6) Date: ______________ (7) Your phone number ( ) ______________

(8) Print your address: ______________________
(street address/p.o. box) (city) (state) (zip)

(9) Print your name: ______________ (10) Your signature: ______________

You must mail or deliver a COPY of this Petition to the agency or board named on line (3) of this form. You should contact the agency or board to determine the name of the person to be served.

CERTIFICATE OF SERVICE

I certify that this Petition has been served on the agency or board named below by depositing a copy of it with the United States Postal Service with sufficient postage affixed OR by delivering it to the named agency or board:

(11) ______________________ (12) ______________________
(name of person served) (agency or board listed on line 3)

(13) ____
(address)

(11) This the ____ day of ____________ ,19____. (15) ______________________
(your signature)

When you have completed this form, you MUST mail or deliver the ORIGINAL AND ONE COPY to the Office of Administrative Hearings, P.O. Drawer 27447, Raleigh, NC 27611-7447.

Filing a Petition for a Contested Case Hearing does not constitute the filing of a discrimination charge with the EEOC or the Civil Rights Division of the Office of Administrative Hearings. Should you decide to file such a charge, you should contact the Office of Administrative Hearings, Civil Rights Division or the EEOC office nearest you; EEOC offices are located in the following cities: Charlotte, Raleigh, and Greensboro.

H-06A(9.96)

Source: North Carolina Office of State Personnel.

Effective disciplinary processes usually incorporate a strategy of progressive discipline. In essence, a code of work rules is promulgated. Potential infractions dealing with undesired work behaviors in such matters as attendance, performance, personal conduct, safety and security, and general abuse are identified along with the penalty (or range of penalties) that will be imposed for first, second, and subsequent incidents. Although some serious infractions lead to automatic termination, most focus on remedial efforts to salvage the employee and change his or her undesirable work behavior. Figure 9.2 displays a hypothetical Progressive Discipline Schedule. Penalties for repeated offenses of even minor infractions merit progressive, harsher disciplinary action (Odiorne, 1987: 141–164; Finkle, 1995).

The conduct covered under the work rules may vary from minor irritants such as tardiness and absenteeism (which becomes a substantial problem when repeated) to breeches of safety procedures that place the lives of employees and the public at risk. It is this variation that requires the introduction of progressive or graduated responses.

Where progressive disciplinary systems are employed, each offense includes a "statute of limitations" in order to prevent earlier incidents from being used to harm salvaged employees. These "expiration dates" can vary depending on the seriousness of each individual infraction. In essence, such a system functions similarly to insurance points for car drivers. Because of the threat from liability suits, "expired" offenses are not destroyed but stored in a protective inactive file. As such, it can serve

Figure 9.2
Progressive Discipline Schedule

Type of Offense	1st–2nd Min–Max		3rd Min–Max		4th Min–Max	
Group 1: Unexcused tardiness, unauthorized absence, excessive absences, abusive language	V	W	PS	US	US	T
Group 2: Insubordination, violation of safety rules, unauthorized use of property, neglect of duty	W	US	PS	D	D	T
Group 3: Falsification of records, use of threat of physical violence, unauthorized possession of deadly weapons, criminal conviction of felony while employed, theft on the job	US	T	—	—	—	—

V=Verbal Warning W=Written Warning PS=Paid Suspension
US=Unpaid Suspension D=Demotion T=Termination

in the event of a liability suit to demonstrate that the organization took the appropriate actions. Otherwise, the inactive file is not used in any other fashion; its contents cease to exist for all internal personnel matters.

Progressive discipline often starts with an informal warning or verbal counseling. With an informal warning the employee is told what needs correction, but no record is put into the employee's file. Verbal counseling places a written notice that an oral warning was made into the employee's file. It documents the nature of the violation discussed and the date of the occurrence. It should also include the employee's response—acceptance or denial of the action (Finkle, 1995; Knierim, 1997).

More serious or repeat offenses can result in a formal, written warning that is included in the employee's personnel file. This would document the full nature of the violation, counseling that has occurred, and expected behavioral improvements. It would also outline the consequences for the employees if they fail to correct their behavior (see Figure 9.3). For more serious situations, suspension with pay (a strong indication that the organization still values the employee) is designed to force the employee to take time out and think about the situation (Finkle, 1995; Knierim, 1997).

Ultimately, the disciplinary process may involve the use of either suspension without pay or termination. Suspension without pay imposes a financial penalty. The loss of pay is designed to remind the employee of the hurt and seriousness that failure to reform can bring. Finally, termination may be necessary where reform has failed or the transgression is so egregious (Finkle, 1995).

Even in such justifiable cases, termination is an awkward phenomenon. As with all disciplinary matters, care should be taken. By handling terminations with civility and courtesy the chances for workplace violence can be minimized. Termination should be delivered by the immediate supervisor with another official in attendance to act as a witness (even though the presence of a third party may increase the likelihood of emotional outbursts or violence). While not followed in practice to the extent recommended, terminations should occur early in the week (thereby allowing the employee to start looking for another job and avoiding a weekend devoted to brooding). However, the likelihood for workplace violence may increase inasmuch as a Monday or Tuesday termination disrupts an employee's routine. Terminations should also take place late in the afternoon (so the employee can avoid others, yet have time to clear out his or her things). A neutral space or the employee's office is recommended as the venue (Karl and Hancock, 1999).

Progressive discipline is applied to specific behaviors and is designed to correct them. When an employee who has been subjected to progressive discipline for one behavior exhibits a new disciplinary problem, it is necessary to begin the process anew. Each type of infraction is dealt with separately. To lump all disciplinary infractions together creates an "out to get me" impression among employees and negates any successful or good-faith efforts.

Organizations often develop or negotiate "price lists" or "sentencing guidelines" that detail each infraction and the range of appropriate penalties. This both provides supervisors with guidelines and employees with prior notice.

Figure 9.3
Corrective Counseling Report

CORRECTIVE COUNSELING REPORT

LOCATION ____ *EMPLOYEE'S NAME (PLEASE PRINT)* ____ *DATE* ____

POSITION ____ *SOCIAL SECURITY NUMBER* ____ *TIME* ____

1. Reason for corrective counseling:

____ *ATTENDANCE* ____ *CARELESSNESS* ____ *INSUBORDINATION*
____ *TARDINESS* ____ *WORK QUALITY/QUANTITY* ____ *DOES NOT FOLLOW PROCEDURE*
____ *OTHER:* ____

DESCRIBE FACTS IN DETAIL: ____

2. Possible consequences if performance and behavior are not corrected:

____ *TERMINATION* ____ *LOSS OF POSITION* ____ *OTHER: PLEASE EXPLAIN* ____

3. To avoid the consequences of further discipline, the employee must take the following action:
(Explain in specific detail so the employee can measure their progress.)

4. Manager will determine if employee's progress is acceptable by: ____ / ____ / ____
MONTH DAY YEAR

5. Date the required performance must be accomplished by: ____ / ____ / ____
MONTH DAY YEAR

I acknowledge that I have received a copy of this report: ____
Employee's Signature Date

____
Manager's Signature Date

Employee is encouraged to make any comments on separate attached sheet.

COPIES: EMPLOYEE PERSONNEL FILE MANAGER'S FILE

Finally, all disciplinary systems should be monitored and periodically reviewed. The organization must monitor its imposition of disciplinary penalties in order to assure itself and its employees that they are being correctly implemented. Supervisors must be trained in the use of the disciplinary system and monitored in its use. In addition, the system needs a periodic review of the work rules to be sure they still serve a meaningful, work-related purpose (Finkle, 1995).

In administering disciplinary penalties, a supervisor should be aware of how it fits into the organizational culture for similar offenses and its fairness. As an aid, supervisors may maintain an informal record that is not a part of an employee's official file. This record can include memos of discussions and proposed solutions. If such notes are kept, the employee should be aware of exactly what they are and what they include. These are not secret dossiers (Knierim, 1997).

Computer technology allows for the construction of expert systems to aid and guide supervisors in making disciplinary decisions. An expert system consists of a series of menus linked together in the form of a decision tree. At each step, the supervisor is prompted with a set of questions and real-world, job-related examples of their meaning. The supervisor's decision generates the next computer screen menu and its set of appropriate options.

The Florida Department of Highway Safety and Motor Vehicles employs an expert system in its disciplinary process. Many positive effects are noted in this respect. The expert system gives the supervisors a much more useful and user-friendly "manual." Because the system has the support of top management and helps document the supervisor's actions, it fosters greater confidence. Finally, it also assures more consistent and appropriate responses to specific cases (Berry, Berry, and Foster, 1998).

On these grievance and discipline issues, employees in the public sector are afforded more protections than their private sector counterparts. The public sector requires well-documented evidence in support of managerial actions; hence, a case is not likely to succeed unless it is well founded. This, in turn, leads to a higher rate of management being sustained when grievances are later arbitrated. However, the severity of sanctions being imposed are often less in public sector cases. Because of employee safeguards, the public sector is likely to have more cases focusing on lesser matters (e.g., suspension and reprimand). Public employees are less fearful of management retaliation (Mesch, 1995).

Grievance and discipline systems can be augmented through the use of support services. Suggestion systems as well as quality circles and exit interviews can serve to detect problems in the making. Protections afforded to whistle-blowers or "official channels" guaranteeing confidentiality can direct complaints to appropriate officials and thereby avoid liability problems.

Suggestion systems are designed to detect problems before they get out of hand. They are common introductory devices in the implementation of organizational development and participative management. They are also an effective productivity tool for calling upon employees for help in spotting problems.

Protection of whistle-blowers is a controversial question. Whistle-blowing problems are not only major organizational concerns, but invariably represent serious damage. Whistle-blowers are often exercising a moral or ethical imperative that benefits society far more than it does any specific organization. In fact, the specific organization upon which the whistle is blown is likely to suffer. As a practical matter, whistle-blower protections are more a symbolic statement of ethical concerns than they are an attempt to address a perceived real problem. They are meant more as a deterrent to the conduct that would give rise to such needs rather than as a protection for the individual.

In addition, for individual employees the availability of counseling, drug and alcohol treatment, and other aspects of employee assistance programs (EAP) can be quite encouraging (Johnson, 1986; Elliott, 1989; Johnson and O'Neill,1989). Employee assistance programs represent the personnel function in its most positive, humanistic mode. The initial success with alcohol treatment led to the expansion of EAPs. Today, they deal not only with other serious illnesses such as drug dependency and psychological disorders but with family and financial problems. In addition, some EAPs include career counseling, weight control, and related wellness activities.

Missed opportunities abound here. Suggestion systems, even the most rudimentary, have great potential for enhancing motivation and productivity. In addition to these general benefits, employee assistance programs focusing on the costly health care area can represent long-term financial savings.

Although the vast majority of public employees are covered by basic grievance and discipline procedures, coverage should be total. At the very least, concern for legal liability should have motivated such universal coverage. That numerous towns lack such formal safeguards, including some with large workforces, is disheartening. A further flaw exists in that conflict resolution efforts are so widely ignored. Because personnel management represents a positive factor contributing to motivation and productivity, this is a serious shortcoming.

Problem Employees

The uninvolved worker can pose a serious organizational problem. The uninvolved worker is not "merely" less productive than her or she could be (for information on the uninvolved worker, see Crawford, Thomas, and Fink, 1980; Daley, 1988a; Gabris, 1988; Gabris, Mitchell, and Giles, 1988; Soden and Lovrich, 1988; and U.S. Merit Systems Protection Board, 1999a), the uninvolved worker's reduced productivity infects the entire organization as an example of the level of performance tolerated or accepted. Uninvolved workers, in that they set a bad example for their peers, make management difficult.

Replacement, however, may not be the solution. Although uninvolved workers are a problem, they are not necessarily total failures. Rather, though they may represent an underutilized resource, these employees still possess the potential as well as the real knowledge, skills, and abilities that prompted their initial hiring or promotion. In addition, it is more likely that the uninvolved worker's performance will be considered to be "satisfactory" rather than "marginal" or "unacceptable." In reality, involvement is primarily focused on obtaining that added extra commitment that registers as "superior" or "outstanding."

The interaction between employees and the various administrative techniques is crucial for determining whether, in reality, that technique or practice actually will help contribute to the goal of organizational success. For the manager, these techniques possess a dual nature. Not only are they the organization and management practices used to motivate employees, they are also the practices that motivate the manager.

Although factory-based notions were used earlier to define the terms, today *manager* and *employee* are not dichotomous categories. In most organizations, and especially among those in the public sector, the proportion of employees who also exercise supervisory and managerial responsibilities is quite large. Hence, most managers are also themselves "managed" by others.

Characteristically, greater importance and involvement is assigned to the tasks the employees deem themselves responsible for. Although this might lead to a narrower perspective (vis-à-vis their full role in the organization), it remains an important consideration. Hence, when others do not accord the job the importance they deem appropriate, uninvolvement may occur.

Uninvolved workers are often critical of the support they receive from others in the organization's hierarchy; they do not feel that they are receiving enough serious attention. They also tend to view disagreement as nonproductive; the subsequent competition for organizational resources (a means of obtaining information and setting priorities) is seen only as an unhealthy game of office politics. Ultimately, this can result in a lessening of the challenge and joy they derive from their job.

Among the common factors that influence uninvolvement are those related to the management practices of an organization. For workers and managers, involvement is affected by work group relationships, supervisory relationships, performance appraisal systems, and even the extent of job characteristics (a sense of mutual identity). More important, these are all factors that are well within the organization's sphere of control. Involvement need not be the result of some "luck of the draw" but is itself, at least in part, the product of good management.

The management practices that have in general registered the most impact tend to be precisely those with respect to the worker–manager team itself. This suggests, more generally, that productivity, while involving individuals, is perhaps more strongly influenced by group relations.

Specific recommendations abound. The literature is filled with proposals for team building, team management, task forces, self-management, participation management, and so on. In fact, most of the research on organizational development focuses on this issue. All of these techniques are designed to make the managers/employees aware of their place or role in the organization and to give them a "say" in what is done. These are precisely the attributes that the uninvolved employee lacks. Although these various techniques do not guarantee success, each, in its way, addresses the sense of alienation and frustration that hounds the uninvolved worker.

Because "managers" and "employees" appear to share common attitudes rather than being distinct groups, techniques specifically designed for uninvolved employees should also prove to have ready application among managers. Job enrichment (including rotation, redesign, and enlargement) as well as such notions as quality circles, labor–management committees, and training programs need not be limited to employees only. Supervisors, especially among middle management, may also suffer from jobs that are too narrow and routine. Job enrichment programs might demonstrate a positive impact in this respect. Supervisors could also benefit from training sessions and "get-togethers" that focus on their supervisory roles. Surprisingly, this is an often-neglected area (Wolf and Sherwood, 1981).

JOB RIGHTS

The central concern of employees is job security. Even though many would like to believe it possible, an absolute right to or property interest in a specific job (i.e., guaranteed employment) is an unrealistic chimera. Hence, job rights focus on establishing a wage–effort bargain that guarantees individuals employment as long as they successfully perform their tasks and the organization remains economically viable.

Given the inequality of the relationship between individual and organization, the burden of proof for terminating the employment relationship falls upon the organization. It must either demonstrate that the employee is unable to perform his or her duties (which requires an objective performance appraisal process and efforts at corrective action) or document its own financial exigencies.

Public Values

Public values should shape the public employment relationship. How the government manages its own workforce is a model for how society, in general, should treat its workers. Public employment values revolve around three concepts: the merit principle, political responsiveness, and the protection of individual rights.

The merit principle (with its struggle against prohibited practices and spoils politics) showcases the American belief in the individual and a career open to talent. Individual abilities rather than ascriptive characteristics are the hallmark of American society.

Political responsiveness emphasizes that democracy places government at the service of its people. Although government is expected to be staffed with talented individuals, they are professionals, not entrepreneurs or owners. Professionals, first and foremost, serve the needs of others.

The protection of individual rights emphasizes the importance and value attached by our social contract to each and every individual. The political responsiveness envisioned in the rule of a democratic majority is tempered and disciplined by a respect for individual differences. The majority is not allowed to tyrannize over a minority.

Blending these three values into a workable relationship that enables government to successfully function is a daunting task. Conflicts arise continuously. In fulfilling their professional responsibilities, merit-selected employees may fail to be responsive to political concerns; these political concerns can, of course, ignore the objective realities that professionals are required to deal with. Similarly, political responsiveness may threaten the exercise of constitutional rights by individual employees. Alternatively, the exercise of these rights may provide employees with added "political" advantages.

Political responsiveness is the preeminent value in this equation. Government is a social contract formed for the benefit of its citizens. Those citizens must have the ultimate say on whether or not the system is working correctly. Responsiveness need not mean that government must be a matter of either inefficiency or servitude. Merit and employee rights can exist and serve to complement responsiveness.

However, for most of the history of the American republic merit was ignored. The "fitness of character" standard introduced by George Washington encompassed both political responsiveness and merit (White, 1948). The Jacksonian era ushered in a reemphasis on responsiveness that ultimately degenerated into the meritless spoils system (White, 1954). It was not until the passage of the Pendleton Act in 1883 that merit again achieved a prominent role in the civil service.

Throughout this period and well into the middle of the twentieth century, this balance was also achieved by sacrificing the rights of individual employees. Only during the last few decades have employee rights received significant attention. For most of American history, government employment has legally existed under the doctrine of privilege (Rosenbloom, 1971, 1988; Rosenbloom and Carroll, 1995; Curtis, 1990).

Government employment was a special privilege rather than a contractual property right. The special needs of the government as an employer entitled it to readily impose such strictures as it deemed necessary to protect the freedom of its citizens and the Constitution. Under the tenets of the agrarian, night-watchman state, government was only a small aspect of society. Hence, only a few citizens had their rights imposed upon in contrast with the many who were afforded added protection from the dangers of an undemocratic administrative apparatus. Because government jobs were also viewed as being temporary rather than as part of a career system, the harmful aspects of these limitations were even further reduced.

As America has became an industrial nation with the need for a permanent, professional administration, the doctrine of privilege with its imposition of second-class citizenship upon government employees became less and less tenable. A larger government sector in continuing partnership with the business and agricultural communities is too important to have its members beyond the pale of protected rights. Over the past few decades, the doctrine of privilege has been replaced with a doctrine of substantial interest (Rosenbloom, 1971, 1988; Rosenbloom and Carroll, 1995;

Curtis, 1990). Government is now called upon to justify and prove the need for any infringement upon the rights of its citizens whom it employs.

Employment-at-Will

The employment-at-will doctrine is a newer version of the old doctrine of privilege. Employment-at-will does not deal directly with employees' rights as citizens but with the right of the government to decide what jobs it needs and who it wants to hire to carry out those jobs. As such, it is directly a matter of merit and efficiency. Because it is also a matter of job security from the employee's perspective, it is also concerned with rights.

Employees, whether government or private sector, want protection from unjust actions on the part of their employers. They want an employment contract that provides for due process protections requiring that dismissal be for documented cause.

This "contract" is, in fact, nothing more than the original medieval, common-law notion of employment. Prior to the industrial revolution and the introduction of the free-market revision of the common law (creating the "employment-at-will" doctrine, which entirely benefits the employer), employer and employee were bound, unless otherwise specified, to an annual contract. Neither party was free to abrogate this arrangement unless one party violated its performance terms. Employers could not hire others nor workers accept a better offer. Even the legitimate excuse of economic hardship itself was often limited by communal, social concerns.

Organizations see the employment-at-will doctrine as providing them with the flexibility to successfully adapt to their increasingly changing environment. It is an extension of the basic right of management to run the organization. The management perspective is that employment-at-will allows them to objectively and efficiently adjust their resources, including people, to meet the needs of their organization and guarantee its survival (Kellough, 1999).

The state of Georgia decentralized its personnel system in a reinvention effort, creating an employment-at-will model, when it abolished its civil service system in 1996. Although decentralized, many state agencies have reimposed the former merit system rules as their governing personnel policies. The "grandfather" protections afforded those formerly covered by the merit system (who have not changed jobs) has also slowed the implementation (and potential problems) of the new employment-at-will system.

Unfortunately, it is also a concept that greatly frightens employees. Divested of contractual protections under an employment-at-will arrangement, employees become subject to arbitrary and capricious actions. Managerial abuse is widely prevalent. Even in the federal government with its extensive civil service and merit protections, over a third of the employees have witnessed or experienced violations.

As long as organizations prefer to ignore such problems among their managers, the employment-at-will doctrine will generate avid opposition from employees. Contractual rights establishing dismissal for cause offer a small degree of protection from such practices.

Even though courts have enunciated their support for the employment-at-will doctrine since the nineteenth century, virtually all of their cases have in the very process of affirming the doctrine set aside exceptions to its use. Employees cannot be discharged for reasons specifically prohibited by federal or state law. An employee cannot be discharged for complying with a statutory duty. Of course, an employee cannot be discharged when an implied contractual right exists. The courts even leave the door open for matters of equity. They will examine discharges motivated by bad faith, malice, or retaliation to determine if they are also contrary to public policy (Tidwell, 1984).

In arguing against an employment-at-will discharge, an employee will endeavor to establish that he or she possessed a property interest (i.e., a contractual right) or a liberty interest (i.e., his or her ability to obtain future employment) that has been impaired. A property interest requires that a "legitimate claim of entitlement" be established (*Board of Regents v. Roth,* 1972; *Perry v. Sinderman,* 1972). On the other hand, a liberty interest focuses on an individual's standing and association in the community, specifically on how his or her ability to obtain future employment is affected.

The establishment of either a property or liberty interest results only in the requirement that a hearing be held (Goldman, 1981). The hearing does not mandate that an individual be reemployed; it only affords him or her the opportunity to set the record straight and clear his or her name. However, this can be the foundation for further civil or criminal actions. Because a hearing must be "on the record," the organization must present its evidence for the discharge. Lacking any cause for dismissal or unable to support its contentions with sufficient evidence exposes the organization to the threat of severe liability (Tidwell, 1984).

Statutory tenure, a specific contractual commitment, a collective bargaining agreement, and civil service status are all methods by which employees are afforded a property interest in their jobs (*Nicolletta v. North Jersey District Water Supply Commission,* 1978). Property interests can be denied wherever the government or agency lacks the explicit legal authority to confer them. Hence, employee handbooks and supervisory letters may not be legally binding. Neither is longevity sufficient to prove entitlement (Tidwell, 1984).

A liberty interest focuses on the issue of defamation of character. Defamation encompasses slander (transitory oral communication) and libel (permanent written communication) wherein an untrue statement is disseminated to others and thereby harms an individual's reputation. In such circumstances, the firing so stigmatizes the individual that he or she is unable to obtain employment (a clear case of harm). Of course, dismissal for job-related causes as well as for an inability to get along with supervisors and others (i.e., questions of organizational fit), which most certainly contribute to the failure to obtain future employment, are not considered as a justification for ordering a due process hearing (truth is an absolute defense). Defamation alone (without the accompanying loss of government employment) is in itself insufficient grounds for requiring a hearing (*Paul v. Davis,* 1976; *Wisconsin v. Contantineau,* 1971). With discharge, defamation occurs only if the reasons are false and publicly distributed (*Bishop v. Wood,* 1976; *Codd v. Velger,* 1977). The organization can avoid or reduce the threat from defamation if it is willing to correct employee files, rehire or retain the employee, or even place the employee in another, including lesser, job (Tidwell, 1984; Baskin, 1998b).

PERSONAL RIGHTS

The Constitution of the United States establishes a limited government "of the people, by the people, and for the people." The Constitution enunciates a set of civil liberties that government is prohibited from interfering with as well as individual civil rights it is charged with protecting. These restrictions and duties place added responsibilities on governments as employers. A dual relationship of employer–employee and government–citizen must be observed. The management rights of an organization must be balanced with the fundamental rights of citizens.

To ensure that elected and appointed officials are responsive to the people, the people must be able to observe and assess their activities. This requires that the people be informed of and able to deliberate on the government's activities. The freedoms of the press and of speech explicitly included in the Bill of Rights' First Amendment address the basic mechanisms for retaining citizen control over their government. In order to preserve this marketplace of ideas, the courts have tended to broadly define these rights. Hence, many matters that are hardly political are afforded protection.

Political Activity and Patronage

Political, especially partisan, activity is subject to regulation. The paramount political rights of other citizens justify placing some degree of restriction on the political rights of government employees. The civil service idea of merit assumes a neutral-competent public service serving the nation's political leaders (who are responsive to the public). This concept of overhead democracy requires that public employees not be engaged in or interfere with the partisan policymaking process. Without these restrictions, it is feared that public employees would use their positional advantage to distort public policies for their personal benefit.

Originally, rules governing political participation were designed to protect public employees from being pressured by political parties for contributions or "volunteer" work. They still serve that purpose today. In general, rules and regulations protect public employees from coercion. They also safeguard public property, including public employees, from being used in partisan activities. Restrictions on officeholding (or even candidacy) may be imposed in order to avoid appearances of "insider" influence or nonneutrality. Interestingly, many other countries deal with this problem by "partisanly balancing" their agencies. Hence, a transportation department would not merely have engineers on staff, but would have conservative engineers, liberal engineers, centralist engineers, religious-affiliated engineers, and so on.

The Hatch Acts passed in response to Franklin Roosevelt's attempt to use New Deal agency employees in the 1938 electoral campaign to "purge" Congress put these principles into law. They were originally designed to protect political leaders from an "electoral machine" reminiscent of the spoils era (the Democratic Party only reluctantly had accepted the Civil Service System).

The Hatch Acts have also served to protect civil servants from the pressures of partisanship. For most civil servants, this is a highly valued benefit. Participating as intimate observers in the political process has dampened their desires for more active roles. Relaxing Hatch Act restrictions in order to enable more political involvement is also seen as exposing public employees to the potential for partisan abuse.

As amended, the Hatch Acts restrict the Senior Executive Service, administrative law judges, and most career employees from engaging in political activities when on duty, on the premises, or recognizable as an employee (i.e., in uniform). Fund-raising activities are also carefully prescribed. Of course, the granting or withholding of governmental services, including personnel matters, for political considerations is also forbidden. Running for and holding partisan political office is prohibited. Off-duty political involvement, including holding a party office, is allowed.

These restrictions on the political involvement of federal workers (and state employees whose agencies receive federal funding for their positions) were sustained by the Supreme Court in *United Public Workers v. Mitchell* (1947). Efforts to overturn this decision have repeatedly been unsuccessful. The practice of patronage itself has been dealt even further setbacks in a series of cases (*Elrod v. Burns,* 1976; *Branti v. Finkel,* 1980; *Rutan v. Republican Party of Illinois,* 1990; Daniel, 1992; Roback and Vinzant, 1994). With the growing focus on privatization, these public employee protections from patronage are also being extended to those who provide contract services (*O'Hare Truck Service v. Northlake,* 1996; *Board of Commissioners v. Umbehr,* 1996).

Clearly, government possesses the right to restrict or protect itself from employees who are involved in subversive or antisystems groups. In the United States, subversion has been more a matter of hysteria than one of reality. Fueled by the excesses and abuses of the anticommunist red scares, the courts have put rules into place to safeguard citizens' rights (Rosenbloom, 1971; Rosenbloom and Carroll, 1995).

Restrictions on employees' rights must be based on clearly and narrowly defined "sources" of potential harm (*Cole v. Richardson,* 1972). The need for an informed citizenry calls for the separation of "speech" from action. Employees may hold beliefs, even those that are subversive, as long as they don't engage in activities (such as joining organizations actively working to overthrow the government) designed to implement those ideas (*Elfbrandt v. Russell,* 1966).

In determining the limitations placed on individual rights, the courts will take into consideration the nature of government work involved. Greater latitude or restrictions are allowed when jobs are seen as involving national security interests or involve safety-sensitive concerns for the public. Those responsible for enforcing specific laws will also be expected to obey them.

The Pursuit of Happiness

Interestingly, it is the nonpolitical ramifications of these rights that generate the most attention in terms of employee rights. Although these focus on off-duty activities, the organization can become involved if it is harmed by the actions. Individual or employee job performance must be adversely affected or the organization harmed. In either event, the organization must be able to provide documented proof.

Freedom of speech, even when it entails political commentary, is afforded most government employees. Most government employees are really no different from their private sector counterparts. As long as employees are not in policymaking positions (in which they are assumed to possess special knowledge) or in a position in which partisan affiliation is considered relevant to job performance (*Elrod v. Burns,* 1976; *Branti v. Finkel,* 1980), they are subject to few restraints on their nonpartisan speech whether serious or in jest (*Rankin v. McPherson,* 1987).

Balancing an employee's right to free speech and the government's interest in efficiency and public trust follows the preponderance-of-evidence rule (*Pickering v. Board of Education Township High School District,* 1968). The resultant *Pickering-Connick* rule establishes a two-step analysis. If an employee can demonstrate that he or she was fired on the basis of free speech on a matter of public concern (and not in the nature of a private grievance), the competing claims are then assessed. The government can overcome this infringement on free speech if it can establish a compelling interest (Koenig, 1997a).

These protections are required in order to prevent retaliation against an employee. Where an employee has demonstrated the involvement of an issue of free speech, the burden of proof switches to the employing government to demonstrate the legitimacy and importance of its other reasons (and the discipline or discharge associated with it). In fact, the government will most likely have to demonstrate that the other factors cited typically lead to the same result (disciplinary penalty or discharge) regardless of the question of free speech.

Freedom of association is an extension of the freedom-of-speech provision. It is designed to ensure the deliberation of political ideas. As a "nonpolitical" right, it has become the legal basis for union membership. Employees are free to join unions (*McLaughlin v. Tilendis,* 1967; *AFSCME v. Woodward,* 1969) or not join them (*Abood v. Detroit Board of Education,* 1977). Government cannot use belief in unionization or membership as a means of denying individuals employment (and, hence, avoiding unionization).

In addition to the important job security aspects discussed above under the employment-at-will doctrine, liberty interests are also found in a wide variety of other areas. These may involve the appropriateness of rules on appearance and dress codes (*Kelley v. Johnson,* 1976) or residency requirements for employees (*McCarthy v. Philadelphia Civil Service Commission,* 1976). Dress is an important form of social communication that can convey impressions about an organization (Bowman and Lavater, 1992; Easterling, Leslie, and Jones, 1992). Yet the imposition of overly detailed dress codes can be seen as an infringement on personal liberty. Like other matters, dress codes must be based on business necessity or job-relatedness. The imposition of any restrictions beyond those everyone in the community is subjected to are difficult to justify.

However, restrictions may be imposed on police, firefighters, and other paramilitary or safety-sensitive organizations for purposes of morale or the enhancement of their professional image. The dress codes or uniforms as well as rules on physical appearance are all intended to foster the work team's esprit d'corp and enhance overall effectiveness.

Interference with individuals' personal lives raises many concerns and is extremely hard to justify. Although the Family Medical Leave Act allows for leaves of absence for pregnancy and child care, regulations requiring mandatory leaves of absence from work due to pregnancy have not been supported (*Cleveland Board of Education v. La Fleur,* 1974). Similarly, the real or imagined moral diversity or sexual conduct of employees is not seen as a work-related matter (*Thorne v. City of El Segunda,* 1983).

Harassment

Although sexual (and nonsexual) harassment also focuses on many of these lifestyle issues, it does legitimately involve the organization. Harassment introduces questions of organizational misconduct (through the actions of its agents or by condoning the activities of others) in the efforts to influence private lifestyle issues (Lindenberg and Reese, 1995).

Organizations have a responsibility to provide their employees with a safe workplace. This safety extends beyond the physical to include an atmosphere free of psychological abuse and a positive moral climate. Sexual harassment entails two parts. First, it involves relationships between supervisors and employees. Second, it concerns relationships between one employee and another employee (Ross and England, 1987; Stringer, Remick, Salisbury, and Ginorio, 1990; Spann, 1990; Robinson, Allen, Franklin, and Duhon, 1993; Strickland, 1995; Eberhardt, Moser, and McFadden, 1999).

Although the formal or official incidence of sexual harassment tends to remain low, surveys consistently reveal much higher rates. Even though complaints are registered by under 5 percent of employees, from a fifth to a third of all employees are likely to have been subjected to some form of sexual harassment. The difference between the extent of the problem and the filing of formal complaints is attributed to a fear of retaliation as well as a reluctance to recognize or admit having been harassed (Reese and Lindenberg, 1997; Eberhardt, Moser, and McFadden, 1999).

Supervisor–employee relationships are strictly prohibited. Anyone in a position that exercises power (or is perceived to) over another is in a position to coerce. By granting an individual that sort of power (in order to accomplish organizational missions), an organization also assumes the responsibility for assuring its employees that that power is properly used. There is no legal defense when the existence of such a quid pro quo harassment is found (Lee and Greenlaw, 1996).

The matter of relationships among employees is more difficult to address. The modern workplace is not only a place of work but a forum in which people meet one another. Relationships, romantic and otherwise, may develop. It is not the job of the organization to interfere in these personal, consensual matters; in fact, such relationships may actually benefit the organization. Inasmuch as they serve to create a heightened commitment to the work group, the organization benefits (Baskin, 1998a).

However, in any case where one individual exercises formal professional responsibility over another, even a consensual relationship is, unfortunately, a conflict of interest. Others may perceive such relationships as unduly influencing professional decisions and disturbing appropriate workplace relationships.

Similarly, not all of these relationships are or remain consensual. When romantic relationships end, the parties may find their workplace situation awkward and somewhat strained. Where the end of a romantic relationship is unilateral, one party may be subject to continued, now unwanted attention or even subject to possible reprisals. In such cases where involvement or attention becomes unwanted, then the organization must enter the picture.

In this, as in any matter where the physical and psychological safety of its employees are involved, the organization has an obligation to protect them. Its duty to preserve the workplace as a safe environment justifies organizational involvement into what might otherwise be an entirely, if unpleasant, private matter. Hence, unwanted sexual advances or even a "hostile environment" that reduces or deters an individual's concentration and productivity become organizational problems.

Once notified or made aware of a potential problem, it is incumbent on an organization to investigate and to take remedial action wherever indicated. This is a thorny situation because, in many instances, there is insufficient collaborative evidence to support a conclusion one way or another.

An organization must have a clearly written policy stating its opposition to sexual harassment. Furthermore, employees must be made aware of this policy, and it must unambiguously define what is meant by sexual harassment. Finally, reporting procedures should be straightforward and easy to use. Employees must be assured of confidentiality, prompt investigation, and protection against retaliation. Employee and management training greatly assists in awareness and prevention (Peirce, Smolinski, and Rosen, 1998).

In addition to these policies, an organization must be alert to "defensive" reactions and rationalizations. Bruce J. Eberhardt, Steven B. Moser, and David McFadden's (1999) survey of North Dakota city and county governments is probably typical. Many governments still lack a formal policy prohibiting sexual harassment. Even those with a policy often fail to post it, inform employees of its existence, or outline how complaints will be handled. Similarly, training of supervisors or employees is limited. It is often quite easy to deny the existence of a harassment claim; however, investigation is mandatory even for the most "absurd" charge. Complacency can be lethal. When a harassment incident is recognized, it can still be "ignored" by blaming the victim or minimizing its seriousness. Valued employees may be protected. However, is the "value" they bring to the organization worth the indirect and real losses to productivity and reputation that they and their imitators bring to the organization (Peirce, Smolinski, and Rosen, 1998)?

Sexual harassment training should include both supervisors and employees; it should also be repeated on a regular schedule in order to reinforce the policy. Training should be included for new employees as part of their initial organizational orientation. Offering training programs is not enough; the organization must document that its employees have indeed received the training.

The purpose of sexual harassment training is not to fulfill an obligation for legal compliance. Like all training, it is designed to develop desired performance behaviors. An effective training program consists of more than a verbalization of the official (and legalistic) policy. Lessons are best learned when case studies, scenarios, or examples can be provided that translate abstract concepts into concrete situations (Eberhardt, Moser, and McFadden, 1999).

Workplace Violence

Workplace violence (with customers, clients, coworkers, family members, and intruders) is a growing concern in the public sector. Workplace violence encompasses both actual physical assaults and threats of assault. Although not seen as an organizational problem or a serious problem among large local governments, many human resources directors indicate having witnessed or experienced incidents (Nigro and Waugh, 1998a, 1998b).

Workplace violence may involve altercations between employees and clients/customers. These can be initiated by either the employee or the customer. Employees who are stressed out or burned out from long-term, downsized "doing more with less" can "snap." This is especially likely when customers or clients emphasize the "servant" and forget the "civil." Furthermore, regulatory and public safety agencies deal with anything but a cooperative clientele. Family disputes (related to drug and alcohol abuse or domestic violence) may spill over into the workplace. Work is one of the most likely places to find a specific individual (Johnson and Indvik, 1999). Domestic or international terrorists pose an additional threat (Nigro and Waugh, 1998a, 1998b; Smith, 1998d).

Lloyd Nigro and William Waugh (1998a) indicate that organizations can respond to the potential for violence in four ways. First, they can ignore it. Although this is not really a response, it remains the response of roughly half the local governments they surveyed. Target hardening, information and training, and employee support offer three sets of proactive programs.

Target hardening encompasses various measures to enhance the security of facilities. Protective barriers, security guards, and locked doors control access to facilities. Access is restricted to employees with ID badges (which often are needed to activate locks) and escorted guests. Outside grounds and parking lots are cleared of hiding places (eliminating aesthetic shrubbery and trees) and well lighted (Nigro and Waugh, 1998a).

Information is provided to employees making them aware of (and alert to) potential threats. Employees are also warned about the disciplinary (as well as the civil and criminal) penalties for committing acts of violence. Supervisors and employees are informed of procedures for the documenting and reporting of violence (Nigro and Waugh, 1998a).

Employee support is furnished immediately through response teams that secure outside law enforcement and medical support. Employee assistance programs are available both to deal with problems that may give rise to violence and to minister to the victims of violence. Training programs can emphasize interpersonal relations and conflict management as means of diffusing or avoiding violence (Nigro and Waugh, 1998a).

Domestic violence represents a growing concern. Previously ignored out of a false sense of privacy or efforts to avoid charges of "paternalism," organizations are taking a more active role in supporting their employees who are victims of domestic abuse. Physical and psychological abuse (along with efforts at sabotaging the employee's ability to work) all adversely affect individual productivity. In addition, other employees are aware of what is occurring and also suffer morale and productivity loss (Johnson and Indvik, 1999).

It is necessary for organizations to take a proactive approach in protecting their employees. This should entail training programs for recognizing the warning signs and encouraging the disclosure of domestic abuse. An organization needs to invoke both legal protections (restraining orders and small claims court actions) and the offer of help through employee assistance programs (Johnson and Indvik, 1999).

Privacy

Privacy is a growing area of concern among public employees. Constitutionally, the arguments are related to the Fourth Amendment's prohibition against illegal search and seizure rather than the Tenth Amendment's more general but unspecified rights left to the states and people. In addition, a number of state constitutions (Alaska, Arizona, California, Florida, Massachusetts, Montana, and Rhode Island) have specific provisions protecting their citizens' privacy (Roberts and Dass, 1991; Richman, 1994; Cozzetto and Pedeliski, 1997).

Drug testing has received the most publicity (*National Treasury Employees Union v. Von Raab,* 1989). Yet drug testing poses a serious dilemma for administrators. The proliferation of drug use in American society along with the recognition of its harmful effects—to the user, to others, and to the system of law itself—clearly establishes the need for action. Concomitantly, the rights of public employees as American citizens to be free from unreasonable searches and seizures is at issue. Drug testing is also a political issue. Balancing the needs of society with those for preserving individual rights has always required a delicate touch (Thompson, Riccucci, and Ban, 1991; Fine, Reeves, and Harney, 1996; Arthur and Doverspike, 1997).

Establishing policies and procedures implementing drug-screening programs that meld these concerns presents the public administrator with a gargantuan task.

Should only applicants and those seeking transfer or promotion be tested or should all employees occupying safety-sensitive positions undergo tests? How have the courts ruled on drug testing? Is "reasonable suspicion" required or can testing be performed on a random basis? What drugs should be screened? Should procedural guidelines address "chain of custody," lab, medical review, and other collection issues? What about confidentiality, confirmatory tests, disciplinary and dismissal issues? Should employee assistance or rehabilitation/counseling programs be established? What about liability issues? What are the direct and indirect costs (Daley and Ellis, 1994)?

Employers in both the public and private sector are beginning to address this problem with policies designed to detect substance abuse and rehabilitate abusers. Management policies must balance the public's right to be provided efficient services, the government's need to maintain national security, and the employee's right to be protected from unreasonable violations of basic constitutional protections in the workplace. It should be kept in mind that there is a fundamental difference in the employee–employer relationship in the public and private sectors. Most dealings between private business and their employees are not directly influenced by constitutional provisions; however, public sector employees are granted certain privacy rights through the Fourth and Fourteenth Amendments, which afford protection in the areas of search and seizure and due process. Public sector employers, therefore, have greater constitutional restraints imposed in any drug-testing policies (Elliott, 1989, 1990).

Executive Order 12564 required the federal government, as the nation's largest employer, to "show the way in achieving drug-free workplaces." It called for each "executive agency" to prepare a plan that would "(1) state policy regarding the agency's reaction to drug use; (2) specify the role of employee assistance programs in helping drug users; (3) provide for supervisory training to assist in identifying and addressing illegal drug use by agency employees; (4) articulate a process for treatment referrals; and (5) provide for the identification of illegal drug users through testing" (U.S. White House, 1989). The order devoted three pages to describing drug-testing programs and procedures as well as "personnel actions" to be taken in response to employee drug use.

Drug screening through urinanalysis and other biological tests measures characteristics of the body, especially its internal composition and processes. They tests typically do not rely on the observable—what people say or write, or how they perform. Biological probes draw samples from the body or otherwise monitor structure and physiology. They frequently aim "to discover the truth behind appearances" (Neikin and Tancredi, 1989).

Drug urinanalysis screens are the most effective types of drug tests. The positive results of a urine screen cannot be used to prove intoxication or impairment as does a blood alcohol test. A urinanalysis can only prove recent drug use. The drugs may appear in the urine for several days, even weeks, depending on the drug, without any noticeable impairment (U.S. Public Health Service, 1986; Rosen, 1987). Those employed in sensitive and public safety classifications are the most likely to be subjected to drug testing (Klingner, O'Neill, and Sabet, 1989, 1990).

Because of the special place held by the law enforcement community in our society, the effects of drug abuse by any officer or official are magnified. In addition to the obvious injuries that may stem from drug use, illegal drug use by law enforcement officers would create disrespect for law enforcement and diminish public trust in our system of government. Winning the support and trust of the community is an ongoing endeavor and is undermined if police officers themselves are breaking the law. The challenge for law enforcement is to prevent the disintegration of public trust and respect for law enforcement and to develop a viable mechanism to identify and deal with those officers who abuse drugs (Higginbotham, 1987).

Public administrators should always be cognizant of liability issues. What are the potential liability issues associated with mandatory applicant drug screening?

Applicants are not protected by civil service regulations nor collective bargaining agreements. An applicant generally has no expectation of employment and no property right in the job he or she is applying for. The employer also has the right to hire whomever he or she wishes to hire. There is no contract to enforce. In addition, there are no damages available when a person is denied the job.

The court divides public sector employees into two distinct groups in rendering its decisions regarding drug testing: those in sensitive positions—that is, jobs that have great impact on the efficient use of agency resources—and those where performance failure would endanger public health or national security (U.S. General Accounting Office, 1989).

Agency heads possess great discretion in designating positions for drug testing. An executive agency could test any employee where "reasonable suspicion" existed, that is, where there "is an articulable belief that an employee uses illegal drugs drawn from specific particularized facts and reasonable emphasis from those facts" (U.S. Office of Personnel Management, 1989).

National Treasury Employees Union v. Von Raab (1989) involved generalized drug testing of Customs Service employees who handled classified materials, who are required to carry firearms, or who seek transfers or promotions to jobs directly involved in the interdiction of drugs. In reaching this decision, the court made it clear that the standard of individualized suspicion is not necessary for measuring the reasonableness of a drug-testing program. Instead, the court confirmed that governmental interest in minimizing safety and security hazards for the general public justified the testing. Other court decisions have also upheld testing for these reasons (Thompson, Riccucci, and Ban, 1990; Riccucci, 1990).

In *Skinner v. Railway Labor Executives' Association (1989),* the court upheld the use of drug and alcohol tests mandated by the Federal Railway Administration. The court ruled that the government's interest in regulating the conduct of railroad employees engaged in safety or sensitive tasks, in order to ensure the safety of the traveling public and of the employees themselves, plainly justifies prohibiting such employees from using alcohol or drugs while on duty or on call for duty and the exercise of supervision to ensure that the restrictions are in fact observed. That interest in safety presents "special needs" beyond normal law enforcement that may exempt departments from the usual warrant and probable-cause requirements.

In both the Von Rabb and the Skinner case, random testing of those in safety or sensitive positions was upheld. The court ruled that random testing was constitutional and upheld suspicionless testing of employees who carried firearms and enforced drug laws. The court noted that the plan apparently applied to other members of the police department who might not carry firearms or enforce drug laws (Weeks, 1990).

Regarding applicants, the few court cases where this issue has arisen have uniformly concluded that drug testing of law enforcement applicants through urinanalysis is lawful (Higginbotham, 1987).

Procedural issues concerning drug screening through urinanalysis are of paramount importance to the public personnel manager. Similar concerns apply in the use of chemical analysis of hair samples (Stevenson and Williamson, 1995). Due to the nature of drug-screening tests, it is important that such a program be conducted in a manner so as to minimize the invasion of employees' privacy. The employer should ensure that a proper chain of custody is maintained for the drug sample to ensure that it is not tampered with while being shipped to the laboratory, and in the case of a legal challenge, the employer could establish who had control of the specimen at any given time. Because the drug-testing issue is such a recent development, and because many legal issues relative to the rights and responsibilities of employers in this area are not well defined, it is suggested that employers rely heavily on standards set by professional organizations (Elliott, 1989, 1990).

The International Personnel Management Association and the American Society for Public Administration both published their model drug-testing guidelines in 1987, as did the National Institute on Drug Abuse. The guidelines established by the National Institute on Drug Abuse specified detailed accountability procedures. These procedures require that an approved agency chain-of-custody form be used from the time of collection to receipt by the laboratory. "Chain of custody forms shall include an entry documenting the date and purpose each time the specimen is handled or transferred and identifying every individual in the chain of custody."

Although requirements for employee drug testing are almost universal, provisions for laboratory safeguards and procedures are often neglected. Drug-testing laboratories are expensive and the political commitment to the "drug war" is thin. This is a serious shortcoming that compromises employee privacy rights and erodes organizational trust (Nice, 1991; Daley and Ellis, 1994).

The National Institute on Drug Abuse stresses the need for a medical review officer (MRO) to interpret laboratory findings. The MRO assesses and determines whether an alternate medical explanation can account for a drug test result. Additional important functions of the MRO are to review fairness and credibility of test results and provide for the privacy and confidentiality of the employee's personal medical history during the course of reviewing drug tests. Clearly, an MRO must be a licensed doctor of medicine and have a strong professional interest and experience in drug abuse programs, and in the role of urine testing as part of these programs. The MRO is the linchpin between the client and the laboratory, and therefore carries a responsibility that requires diplomacy, understanding technical and social issues, and being able to ensure that all aspects of a urine test result are valid (Finkle, Blanke, and Walsh, 1990).

Personnel administrators must not only decide who will be tested and how to implement tests; they must decide what drugs should be tested. The number of controlled substances is endless, and selecting certain illegal drugs for screening requires guidelines. The U.S. Department of Health and Human Services (HHS) recommends that drug-testing policy focus on five primary groups: marijuana, cocaine, opiates, amphetamines, and phencyclidine. Agencies must test for marijuana and cocaine and have the option of probing for the other three (U.S. Department of Health and Human Services, 1988).

The exact dynamics that led to the selection of the five drugs targeted for testing by the federal government are unclear. Without doubt, however, the suspected prevalence of a drug's use by employees or the more general population loomed large. For instance, HHS justified the requirement that all agencies screen for cocaine and marijuana on grounds of "incidents and prevalence of their abuse in the general population and the experience of the Department of Defense and Department of Transportation in screening their work forces. Marijuana and cocaine are where you get your maximum bang for your bucks in terms of the testing program" (U.S. House Committee on Post Office and Civil Service, 1988).

The public personnel administrator must use extreme caution after an employee has tested positive. Employers should not take any action concerning a positive drug test result without undertaking a second confirmatory test (Elliott, 1989). Federal policy requires that all specimens identified as positive in the initial test be subject to a confirmatory test—gas chromatography/mass spectrometry. Double or triple testing of samples can cost as much as $80 per sample, but it is recommended by a host of authorities, including the National Institute on Drug Abuse (Finkle, Blanke, and Walsh, 1990).

Laboratory equipment for a gas chromatography/mass spectrometry system can cost between $100,000 and $150,000 to acquire, and technicians earn about $50 per hour. If these services are contracted out, the costs range from $30 to $100 per sample depending on the laboratory and the volume of work submitted by the organization (Strickland and Whicker, 1989). Chemical analysis of hair samples, while more accurate, is twice as costly (Stevenson and Williamson, 1995).

Both direct and indirect costs associated with drug testing are difficult to measure. Prior to exploring direct costs it may be more appropriate to examine indirect costs.

Testing can affect the level of trust among employees, their job satisfaction, their organizational involvement, their willingness to side with unions rather than management, and more. To the degree that drug testing makes the federal government a less attractive place for the best and brightest to work, problems multiply. Two major factors could confound calculations about the benefits and costs of drug testing—deterrence and diffusion. If knowledge that federal agencies test for drugs causes many of their job applicants and employees to abandon the habit, then a low hit rate need not indicate a poor benefit-cost ratio. It could even signal enormous success. Little evidence exists concerning the deterrent effect of workplace drug testing on employees' substance abuse (National Commission on the Public Service, 1989).

The public personnel manager is faced with a two-pronged dilemma after an employee has tested positive. Should the employee be referred to rehabilitation/assistance or is disciplinary action or dismissal appropriate? The option chosen depends on whether the agency has an employee assistance program in effect or if the employee maintains a safety-sensitive position such as a law enforcement officer.

The primary objective of any drug-testing program should be to ensure that public safety is not endangered as a result of drug use by public employees. A secondary objective is providing those employees who have a drug problem with the opportunity for rehabilitation. It is recommended that no disciplinary action be taken unless an employee (not in a safety-sensitive position) refuses the offer of rehabilitation, fails to complete a rehabilitation program successfully, or tests positive for drug use following the completion of a rehabilitation program (Daley and Ellis, 1994).

Test sensitivity and validity questions (as well as the concern for privacy) suggest alternative tests that focus on the employee's ability to perform. Various performance-based "fitness for duty" simulations, reaction time tests, rapid eye testing, and attitudinal integrity tests can often substitute for clinical examinations. Many of these readiness-for-duty tests can be administered quickly and inexpensively on a daily basis. The advantage of such a test is that it makes no attribution of why someone is not fit-for-duty. Failure can just as equally be due to drug and alcohol abuse or tending to a sick child. These tests also focus on what indeed counts—the ability to safely perform the job.

Although concerns over drug use receive most of the attention, privacy questions are raised in a number of other areas. The use of psychological and genetic testing along with other health issues such as smoking are of concern (Timmins, 1987; Cozzetto and Pedeliski, 1996). The Americans with Disabilities Act of 1991 affords added protection for the privacy of medical records. Even employees' off-the-job recreational activities are a subject for debate. All of these matters share potential sickness and accident liabilities that affect health insurance costs. They pit an employer's legitimate interest in maintaining affordable health benefits for its employees against personal interference on the basis of potential, probabilistic incidents.

There is added concern with regard to information in desks and lockers as well as various electronic communications (phone and e-mail). That these may entail questions of criminal activity and/or violations of legitimate organizational policies (*O'Connor v. Ortega,* 1987) is the justification for organizational concern. On the other hand, they may merely be an intrusion by overzealous individuals. Can information gathered from searches of employees' files and personal belongings that happen to be physically located at the workplace be used against them? Similarly, can employees be compelled to "incriminate" themselves, or is invoking constitutional rights under the Fifth Amendment grounds for immediate dismissal (Cozzetto and Pedeliski, 1996, 1997)?

The Fourth Amendment protection against unreasonable search and seizure and the Electronic Communications Privacy Act afford protection for e-mail. This protection hinges on whether there is a reasonable expectation of privacy. Organizational policies on e-mail use can help specify (or curtail) these expectations (Baskin, 1998a, 1998b; Cozetto, 1998; Smith, 1998a).

Employees do not have the same expectation of privacy in the workplace as they would at home. However, even under these circumstances privacy rights may exist. In *O'Connor v. Ortega* (1987) the Supreme Court raised questions relative to privacy expectations. Exclusive use of a workplace, allowing the placement and display of personal items, and setting aside secured facilities for employee use all give rise to an expectation of privacy. An e-mail policy limiting this expectation would notify employees of the exclusive business purpose of the e-mail system and remind them that all e-mail is stored and subject to review. An e-mail policy would also specify appropriate disciplinary action for misuse. Similarly, appropriate Internet use should also be defined (Baskin, 1998a, 1998b; Cozetto, 1998; Smith, 1998a).

The confidentiality of organizational information on employees is also of growing concern. The vast employee databases that have been so casually assembled contain information that is often quite personal. Health records, including HIV/Aids and genetic testing, are only the most well known (Elliott and Wilson, 1987; Cozzetto and Pedeliski, 1996).

CIVIL SOCIETY

Individual rights are always balanced by reciprocal responsibilities for protecting the rights of others. This is no less true for public sector employees. Employee rights represent limitations on the employer because the employee is also a citizen. Employers and their employees are also limited because other citizens must be guaranteed protection. In some instances, this leads to additional protections for public employees as in the case of whistle-blower provisions; in others, it leads to further restrictions on employees as occurs with matters of liability.

Dissent and Whistle-blowing

The abuse of power by public officials, elected and appointed, is the consummate fear emanating from the modern administrative state. That the reality of abuse, intentional and unintentional, is comparatively minuscule in America in no way lessens this concern. The federal government as well as various states have passed whistle-blower laws designed to protect those who come forward to denounce abuses. We recognize that in taking an oath of office to serve the public, employees possess a constitutional duty to disobey unlawful orders from their superiors (*Harley v. Schuylkill County,* 1979). Public employers themselves are part of the constitutional safety net protecting us from the abuses of power.

Although whistle-blower protection laws exist in many jurisdictions, they often prove ineffective. Regardless of the merits of the case, a whistle-blower is seen as denigrating the organization and harming its mission. Even when later evidence documents and supports the whistle-blower's contentions, many still feel that it would have been better to ignore the abuses. This, unfortunately, subjects potential whistle-blowers to extensive psychological pressures from their peers. Added to this are the almost inevitable attempts by those covering up their mistakes to use the "system" to punish the whistle-blower (Bowman, 1980; Miceli, Roach, and Near, 1988; Jus, Tompkins, and Hayes, 1989).

Public Employee Liability

With the exception of legislators, prosecutors, and judges, most public officials no longer possess absolute or sovereign immunity from civil liability for the manner in which they conduct or perform their duties. In most matters, both the governmental organization and the officials themselves are open to tort liability. The more lenient "preponderance of evidence" and "substantial evidence" rules that govern in civil suits along with the dynamics of a "bureaucrat in the dock" can make such cases volatile (Hildreth, Miller, and Rabin, 1980; Rosenblom, 1992; Rosenbloom and O'Leary, 1996).

Tort liability exists because democratic societies demand accountability from their public officials. Yet it can wreck havoc on innocent individuals. An investigation or suit will receive public attention and full media coverage. Many, including coworkers and friends, will assume that the allegations are indeed true. The organization will be weakened by this and vulnerable to attacks from its enemies. An individual (and his or her family) may be shunned by friends and suffer financially (legal expenses, leave without pay, the loss of business, etc.). All of these work to put added pressure on the individual and organization to settle the matter quickly.

The spectre of tort liability adds emphasis to the importance of training and development. Mistakes stemming from the failure to adequately train public officials for their official functions and the responsibilities that they have to the people in conducting public affairs can now result in costly lessons (Leazes, 1995).

Absolute or sovereign immunity still exists and applies to a substantial number of situations in which rulemaking and adjudication functions are performed. Because those who legislate and judge must be free from external pressures, those exercising these functions are still extended absolute immunity. Legislators are immune for their decisions in crafting the laws. Judges and prosecutors when exercising their judicial functions are also immune. However, activities and behaviors outside of these official functions can expose a legislator, judge, or prosecutor to suit. The lawmaking and judicial functions and not the offices are the subject of absolute immunity. Similarly, other administrative officials (e.g., legislative staff involved in bill drafting, administrative law judges, hearing officers, arbitrators, parole and probation officers, and those carrying out a direct court order) who engage in quasi-legislative and quasi-judicial activities can benefit from absolute immunity (White, 1997).

Qualified immunity for public officials rests upon the performance of their jobs within constitutional parameters. While acting in good faith, officials must believe they are acting within the scope of their authority and possess a reasonable understanding of the rights of those affected (Harlow v. Fitzgerald, 1982). Judicial intervention (and monitoring or oversight) occurs in the determination of what an official should have reasonably known (Koenig, 1997b).

Public officials who use the powers of their office to further personal agendas will find themselves held personally liable for their actions (*Hafer v. Melo,* 1991). Because these behaviors are clearly beyond the scope of their duties, they lose the partial immunity and often the tort liability insurance coverage provided by federal, state, and local governments for their employees' protection.

Because the threat of tort liability can discourage employees from enforcing the law, most governments have passed laws under which they assume the personal legal liability for their employees' acts. However, these laws often allow the government (through the federal or state attorney general) to opt out of the most egregious suits. Liability protection may cover only limited areas, such as fiscal matters. Because the actions are clearly outside the course of official duties, liability protection may not extend to matters pertaining to discrimination and sexual harassment suits. Hence, obtaining supplemental, private liability insurance is often necessitated (Singer, 1997).

The interests of the political jurisdiction (to minimize adverse publicity) need not correspond with those of the individual employee (for vindication). Unfortunately, these options create another gray area, albeit one that is indeed much smaller than that engendered by the possibility of exposure to a tort liability suit (Lee, 1996).

Even where liability protection is afforded, the individual employee can face substantial financial dilemmas. The jurisdiction may simply lack the funds (or refuse to vote them) to cover the costs of indemnification. There may also be requirements for the employee to cooperate with the jurisdiction, thereby subordinating the individual's interest to that of the political entity. In such instances, an assertion of constitutional rights afforded to individual citizens not only relieves the jurisdiction of any financial obligation to the employee but can also be considered as an act of insubordination (grounds for dismissal).

In other instances, the legal costs associated with investigating and defending a liability suit are either not covered in full or are covered on a reimbursable format (on completion of adjudication). Because these can result in substantial out-of-pocket expenses, they can pressure an individual to settle a claim in order to make it go away. Liability protection that includes both "duty to defend" and "pay on behalf" provisions afford the individual greater security (Singer, 1997).

SUMMARY

Although strategic human resource management focuses on creating a more responsive and flexible organization, concerns for the abuse of discretionary authority cannot be ignored. Safeguards are found in the provision of employee rights. By assuaging such fears, employee loyalty is enhanced and greater confidence is placed in the workings of strategic human resource management.

Central to this is the existence of a creditable grievance and discipline system. Employees need to be assured that perceived violations of work rules and processes can easily and fairly be corrected. Similarly, managerial invocation of disciplinary penalties must be seen as occurring within a framework of "law." A progressive disciplinary policy (with sanctions weighted for the severity and repetitiveness of the behavior) helps create such an atmosphere. The grievance and disciplinary process is an arena for due process.

Job security is a central factor in strategic human resource management. Although grievance and disciplinary processes help, more formal job rights limiting dismissal to "for cause" or financial exigencies provide greater protection. However, many organizations are enamored with the managerial flexibility envisioned in an employment-at-will doctrine. Unfortunately, the perceived loss of job security that this doctrine fosters wreaks great losses on organizational productivity. Strategic human resource management focuses on long-term relations—for both the organization and its employees.

An artifact of the American Constitutional system is that citizens are protected from governmental abuse through federal and state "Bills of Rights." In the latter twentieth century, the courts have found it difficult to separate the citizen from the employee. Hence, government employees possess added protections that limit managerial discretion that might interfere with their rights as citizens. Life, liberty, and the pursuit of happiness does not end at the office door. Government must establish compelling reasons for any imposition.

Finally, public purpose employees enjoy obligations and protections as part of civil society. Whistle-blower protection is afforded employees who challenge the abuse of power by higher authority; liability protection is provided to employees who inadvertently cause harm to other individuals while carrying out their lawful duties.

chapter 10

Labor Relations and Negotiations

Employee relations focuses on motivating and maintaining the workforce through communication and discipline while respecting employees' civil and organizational rights. Labor relations is an extension of the employee relations process. For the most part, labor relations is devoted to resolving the conflict that arises in these circumstances. While employee relations consists primarily of unilateral management operations for effectively encouraging and motivating the workforce, labor relations focuses on those operations that require bilateral management and union support.

This chapter explores labor–management relations and uses it as a focus for a discussion of negotiations and mediation. This chapter provides:

1. An overview of the collective bargaining process that has developed in the public sector
2. Knowledge of the basic issues negotiated over and included in a collective bargaining agreement or contract
3. An examination of the important issues that distinguish public sector collective bargaining from the similar private sector process
4. Knowledge of the process and techniques used in negotiations with an emphasis on the transformative, principled negotiation process
5. Knowledge of impasse resolution options such as strikes and lockouts, mediation, and arbitration

The substantive operations in employee relations can occur with union cooperation, and labor relations may transpire in a unionless environment. In fact, the extent and nature of (or need for) the union–management relationship is one of the things that is subject to negotiation. Conflict resolution is the major task of labor relations. Conflict management may occur through strikes, negotiations, or the use of mediation and arbitration techniques. Because unions are the agent of choice for employees in these endeavors, there is, of course, an avid secondary interest in them and their activities.

UNIONS

The American public has from the Boston police strike in 1919 to the air traffic controller's strike in 1981 been wary of public sector unionization. Even though they would agree with the arguments put forth by the unions and fully deplore the working conditions that were exposed, the public balked at recognizing the legitimacy of a strike that challenged government itself (Coleman, 1990; Kearney, 1992).

Unionization in the public sector has always been complex. Government is more than simply an ordinary employer negotiating a wage-and-effort bargain with labor to build its products or deliver its services. It is the repository and symbol of society's shared, public values. More important, it is the legitimate possessor of power with which those values are to be fulfilled. Any decisions, even those apparently as ordinary as an employment contract, affect the allocation and use of that power.

Americans have always been hypersensitive when it comes to the exercise of power and its potential to infringe on their freedom. The formation of the American constitutional system between the twilight of the medieval world and the dawn of the industrial era placed special attention on the public arena. Medieval theories showed that it was here that power could be concentrated while the emerging industrial society raised the stakes as to what it could purchase.

In such a setting, unionization is readily perceived as a conspiracy. Even though unions are more objectively similar to associations of apprentices and journeymen than of master craftsmen, they invoke images of the medieval guilds that restrained trade and hindered development for the benefit of their members. The American colonies and those who emigrated to them especially suffered from the latter stages of the guild movement. Because the initial unions were formed around crafts, they were a vivid reminder of the Old World. Hence, American common law with its pro-industrial focus saw unions as criminal conspiracies *(Commonwealth v. Pullis, Philadelphia Cordwainers, Pennsylvania,* 1806).

Hence, early efforts such as the Knights of Labor under Terence V. Powderly, which originated as a secret society only contributed to these perceptions. Later, radical unions such as the Industrial Workers of the World (Wobblies) or intellectual groups, while small, were highly vocal. The political agendas that they advanced were also suspect, in part due to the ethnic and religious composition of many of these groups.

However, American unions have focused primarily on the "bread and butter" issues of most concern to their members' well-being. Although these economic issues have often spilled over into the political arena, they have still remained pragmatic rather than ideological concerns. Even though American unions have traditionally sponsored little in the way of ideological or political programs, they have been politically suspect ever since those failed, earlier efforts.

Although public sector unions are historically among the earliest in the United States, current unionization stems from efforts begun in the 1960s. Earlier efforts failed due to antistrike prohibitions, pro-management courts, and the application of antitrust provisions against unions (Kearney, 1992). Without the strike weapon (or binding arbitration as a compensation), unions are unable to threaten "harm" to their employer. Furthermore, the judicial system, not a bastion of labor sentiment to start with, refused to believe the public managers would violate their trust by engaging in unethical acts against union members.

Hence, the gains made by private sector unions, especially in the National Labor Relations (Wagner) Act of 1935, became the model for public sector activities. The Wagner Act created the National Labor Relations Board (NLRB), which acts as the United States' Labor Court. The NLRB adjudicates case law under the Wagner Act and the rules added by the Labor Management Relation (Taft-Hartley) Act of 1947. Hence, the NLRB has created a series of precedents governing labor–management relations in the United States (Coleman, 1990: 34–78).

Collective Bargaining

Public sector collective bargaining is governed by law. In fact, it is more dependent upon the legitimacy conferred by law than is its private sector counterpart. The various legal structures or Public Employee Relations Acts are often the source of serious unionization within the public sector. Without the approval conferred by these laws, many efforts at unionization and collective bargaining would not even be attempted.

The Public Employee Relations Act that governs a specific public jurisdiction is indeed quite important. It not only encourages collective bargaining but also establishes the rules and the "prizes." All collective bargaining requires that negotiations proceed in "good faith." Although this does not require that an agreement be reached, it does mandate that both parties continue to listen and reason with one another. Hence, what matters are negotiable is an important determination.

The Public Employee Relations Acts will designate the scope of collective bargaining. They determine which topics are mandatory and must be negotiated as well as those that are permitted if both labor and management agree to negotiate on them (management usually chooses not to negotiate). They also specify which topics it is illegal to negotiate. The impact or implementation of public laws is also excluded from negotiation.

The issuance of Executive Order 10988 by President John F. Kennedy in 1962 marks the modern beginning of public sector unionization in the United States. These provisions were later refined by Executive Orders 11491 in 1969 and 11616 in 1971 under President Richard M. Nixon and ultimately included in Title VII of the Civil Service Reform Act of 1978 under President Jimmy Carter.

President Kennedy reaffirmed the right of federal employees to organize and established procedures for recognizing their right to collectively bargain. Following the success of these procedures in fostering unionization, President Nixon dispensed with some of the provisions no longer needed. President Nixon's reforms also addressed new problems through the creation of impasse panels and by permitting arbitration. In addition, President Nixon mandated that all agreements include a negotiated grievance procedure (Coleman, 1990: 34–78; Kearney, 1992: 51–67).

A major distinction between public and private sector collective bargaining was the "management rights" restrictions included in the original Kennedy Executive

Order 10988. Because an executive order applies only to the executive branch and the powers exercised by the president, powers that constitutionally belong to Congress cannot be affected. Hence, excluded from the negotiation table in public sector collective bargaining were all questions dealing with the mission of an agency, its budget, its organization, and the assignment of its personnel. In essence, all the really important issues were excluded from negotiation. These congressional restrictions renewed interest among businesses in their management rights.

Public sector employees were allowed to negotiate on working conditions and personnel policies within the scope of an individual agency. Although other matters were permitted if agencies consented to include them in the negotiation, these government agencies, as a matter of course, never grant their consent. Although courts refuse to weaken an organization's management rights (which are also a political question involving the fundamental issue of the separation of powers), they will interpret statutes to expand the list of issues subject to mandatory collective bargaining (Pynes, 1993).

This transformation of collective bargaining greatly weakens its public sector application. Because they are unable to "win" the big prizes, there is less incentive for public employees to join unions. Although unions are obligated to fairly represent all employees, the actual number who are union members may be substantially less than occurs in private sector unions. The exclusion of supervisors from union membership (or inclusion in separate unions) also reduces the proportion of actual employees who are union members (Douglas, 1987). Although this is not as significant a factor in the private sector, governments invest substantial numbers of their employees with supervisory responsibilities. This is also true in the case of any organization that is heavily dependent upon professional, knowledge workers.

This combination of reduced size due to small prizes and excluded supervisors means that public sector unions lack the clout to back up the threat to engage in a work stoppage or strike. A strike can only be effective if the workers stop working. In the public sector, unions seldom represent more than 60 percent of the total workforce and often far less than that. To this calculation must also be added the fact that seldom will the entire union membership actually participate in a strike. This is especially true in the public sector where many, many individuals care greatly about the public purposes and missions of their agencies. The result is unions who are unable to bargain effectively.

Because of this, public sector unions have focused their attention on obtaining mediation and, especially, arbitration provisions for resolving disputes and impasses. To assure themselves a role in making the major decisions that affect their members, public sector unions are proponents of participatory decision making (while managers and employees are even more enthusiastic) such as occurs under total quality management (Schwarz, 1990–1991; Kearney and Hays, 1994).

The Contract

Whether public or private, the labor–management contract focuses on four issues: (1) union security, (2) management rights, (3) employee security, and (4) the wage–effort bargain. The first three issues concern the protections afforded those in the process, and the last issue addresses all the substantive concerns over productivity and compensation.

Even after over half a century, private sector unions still struggle with efforts at organizing. The Wagner Act of 1935 established an electoral process for certifying unions as recognized agents for collective bargaining. Even so, many of the National Labor Relations Board's cases still deal with organizing and certification. American businesses remain to this day virulently antiunion. Union prevention and union busting often involves unethical conduct and illegal practices. Hence, union security remains a highly sensitive issue.

A union-organizing campaign is fraught with legal requirements, and, hence, the employment of labor attorneys is essential. Under the NLRA, employees representing 30 percent of the proposed bargaining unit can petition for a certification election. The union may also ask for direct recognition; however, organizations seldom grant that request. The NLRB will administer and observe the election to assure fairness (skills developed here are now used by the United States in observing foreign elections). Upon receipt of a majority in the subsequent election, a union is certified as the official representative of all the employees for the purposes of collective bargaining. No new election can be held for a year, thereby giving the union a secure period in which to prove itself.

The election process can also be used to decertify a union. However, this must be entirely an employee initiative (filing their petition between the ninetieth and sixtieth day prior to the contract's expiration. Any involvement by the organization will invalidate the process and bring further penalties. Although there only a few hundred private sector decertifying elections annually, dissatisfaction leads unions to lose around two-thirds of them. Other unions are free at this point to seek status as the employees' bargaining representative.

Public sector unionization has, since Kennedy Executive Order 10988, not faced such a hostile climate for organizing. In many states, it is the very existence of a Public Employees Relations Act that legitimizes and signals the go-ahead for unionization activities. Of course, there are a number of reasons for this public sector acceptance. As has been noted above, the stakes on the negotiating table are smaller. Second, employees are also voters. Finally, public unions provide organizations with valuable communications services (to both their employees and the public at large) and extend the organization's credibility.

To enhance its security, a union will seek to include in a contract favorable provisions on unit determination, recognition and dues, and duration and renewal. All of these will be designed to provide the union with a continuing role in the organization's labor–management process.

The boundaries of a bargaining unit only require that its members share in a "community of interest." Hence, private sector craft unions can seek to organize professional colleagues employed in the public sector. Similarly, a public organization (or subunit) can constitute itself as a community of interest and its members form a union. The latter organizational approach is preferred among governmental organizations.

Formal recognition requires the support of a majority of those to be included in the proposed bargaining unit. Although certification may be conferred upon presentation of authorization cards, an election (triggered when 30 percent of the employees sign the authorization cards) is usually required. Election campaigns are closely supervised and regulated for fairness. Management abuse can result in the certification of the union and the legal requirement to, in good faith, enter into collective bargaining. Unions can be decertified in a similar election upon loss of their majority.

Unions seek to define a bargaining unit that is most likely to support unionization while including components that are part of the core functions (i.e., include personnel essential to accomplishing the organization's mission as leverage in bargaining). Because unions may focus on small operations that they are sure of winning over, this can lead, from an organizational or managerial perspective, to fragmentation. It is preferable to negotiate with only one union. To undertake a negotiations gauntlet drains resources and leads to a lack of uniformity. Critical units can be held hostage in exchange for model settlements applicable to a wider organization.

Whether supervisors are included in the bargaining unit is an important question in the public sector. With up to a fifth of employees designated as supervisors, public organizations differ from businesses. If so many individuals are excluded from the bargaining unit, the union would automatically be in a weaker negotiating position. The exclusion of supervisors, therefore, reduces the threat of work stoppages and strikes as the organization retains the ability to field a meaningful workforce.

Although supervisors are usually excluded from a bargaining unit, the fact that many organizations promote from within means that sympathetic, former members often serve on the management bargaining teams. In addition, both employees and management in the public sector share a common purpose in supporting the agency's mission.

Although the public sector excludes closed shops (only union members can be hired) and union shops (employees must join the union), contracts may specify an agency shop (while an employee is not required to join the union, they are required to pay dues). Because an agency shop may be construed to interfere with a citizen-employee's constitutional right of association or nonassociation, a fair-share provision may be substituted for an agency shop requirement. Under a fair-share setup, an employee pays for the representational services that the union provides (Collins, 1986; Voltz and Costa, 1989).

The obligation to represent all employees, union and nonunion alike, is a serious charge. Union discrimination among employees can have substantial public policy implications (Riccucci, 1988).

Union security is further enhanced by requiring union members to maintain membership as a contractual provision. Because negotiating a collective bargaining agreement is costly, a union can only recoup its expenses and maintain its viability if it is guaranteed the future dues of the members it represented. Hence, maintaining union membership is included as a condition of continued employment. This prevents individuals from dropping out of the union following the successful completion of negotiations.

An extensive "free rider" problem exists for most federal unions, which cannot negotiate agency shop provisions. Because they cannot negotiate on the all-important "management rights" of Congress either, there is little incentive for individuals to join. Hence, federal unions remain relatively small and financially constrained (Masters and Atkin, 1989, 1995).

Dues are further safeguarded by including them as an automatic payroll deduction. This common payment practice, used widely among businesses and charities today, was pioneered by unions (the IRS even uses it for income taxes). Automatic deductions reduce nonpayment.

Contracts expire; hence, provision must be made for their renegotiation. A union wants to set the contract length (from two up to five years) so as to benefit its members. If the future looks to be strengthening the union and its members' bargaining hand, shorter contracts are preferred. If the future looks more uncertain, locking in a "good" deal may lead to longer contracts. In longer contracts, the ability to open the question of wage adjustments can be included as a hedge.

Termination provisions not only specify when the contract expires but may include the scheduling for its renegotiation. This, of course, gives the existing union an advantage as it presumes its continuation as the recognized bargaining agent. This gives a union a psychological advantage not only over the organization but also with its own members.

To be effective, management must maintain control over the running of an organization. It must determine an agency's mission and objectives. To achieve this it must be free to allocate the organization's resources—budget, staffing levels, and specific personnel assignments. It must also be allowed to discipline employees (for cause).

Unlike private sector collective bargaining where they are subject to negotiation, management rights are rather clearly protected in the public sector. Because "management rights" are basic, core legislative prerogatives under the separation-of-powers doctrine, they are excluded from negotiation (or severely constrained) by the legislature itself in authorizing collective bargaining.

The public employee relations act that the legislative body enacts either excludes these management rights from negotiation or allows the legislature, in addition to accepting or rejecting a negotiated contract, to "modify" it. This ability to unilaterally change the whole agreement (and still have it legally treated as a binding, negotiated agreement) trumps nearly everything. In addition, the courts decide heavily on the side of management in cases involving the question of management rights.

Individual security addresses the concerns of employees over their job rights and due process protections. A major aspect of individual security revolves around questions of seniority, or more specifically, the "rights" attached to seniority. Because the calculation of individual seniority is one of the few aspects of employment that is not readily manipulated, it is highly favored by employees and unions who are distrustful of management practices.

Employees see seniority as an indicator of loyalty and organizational commitment. They want that loyalty recognized and rewarded. Hence, contract provisions often accord rights or privileges to more senior workers. Seniority may be accorded a formal role in assignments and promotions. The approval of other practices used in promotion and merit pay decisions may also be requested.

Employees will also want seniority to be a factor if downsizing, reductions-in-force, or layoffs are required. While not necessarily a matter of seniority, employees would also like to be guaranteed preferences for reemployment or in the hiring for other government positions.

Individual security centers itself on the establishment of a due process system for adjudicating grievance and discipline. The grievance process is the centerpiece of contract administration. This is all the more important in that most contracts are written at a college graduate reading level (Scott and Suchan, 1987). Employees want a means of raising questions when the formal rules and procedures are violated at their expense. This also directly benefits an organization. A grievance process helps to monitor the behavior of supervisors and managers. Matters of discipline are also effectively handled in this manner. Because discipline is punishments or penalties imposed on an employee, it is important that it be seen as fair and just. Usually this requires that the infractions be made known or spelled out in advance of any violation and that they be deemed appropriate for the "crime."

Wage-and-Effort Bargain

The heart of the contract is the wage-and-effort bargain. It is here that the linkage between employee compensation and organizational productivity is forged. The contract outlines the basic pay and benefit systems, including all premium pay (overtime, shift differential, on-call, beeper pay, etc.) and pay for time not worked (holidays, vacations, breaks, bonuses, etc.) options. Public sector unions have been particularly effective in bargaining for fringe benefits (Kemp, 1989).

The central feature is the base pay and benefit scale along with the flexible pay and benefits incentives. These, especially the flexible incentives, are linked to productivity levels expected from employees.

In addition to the general pay grade or scale system, the contract can also specify the position classification system or techniques used in calculating job evaluations. Productivity may also be addressed through the establishment of rules for setting workload standards or time rates. In fact, the work rules themselves may be determined via negotiations. In this way, staffing tables or crew sizes can be set or the goals or results expected specified.

Public Sector Issues

Collective bargaining in the public sector differs from the simpler processes found in the private sector on four dimensions—public interest, politics, payments, and professionalism. These transform collective bargaining from a private, contractual relationship among two parties into a multiparty, value-laden phenomenon (Klingner, 1993).

Although the notion of sovereignty sometimes is used to argue against public sector collective bargaining, it is specious. In protecting the public interest, the concept of sovereignty denies the legitimacy of any government entering into a negotiated labor agreement with a "subordinate" entity. Yet public organizations have no difficulty in binding themselves when purchasing goods or services. Still, sovereignty does tap an unmet dimension.

The public interest is involved in all public sector collective bargaining. An agreement is not limited in its effects to the two parties that negotiated it. A private contract allows for those not party to the negotiation to basically opt out; they need not purchase the product or service. However, the public is not free to do this.

A two-party negotiation, especially when both of those parties share the same beliefs about the value and mission of an organization, can leave out the valid concerns of other public actors. How can these other interests or more general concerns be addressed? Various proposals for multilateral bargaining, sunshine bargaining, public hearings, and labor relations referenda are all designed to focus public attention on what are otherwise private, two-party agreements. Opening the negotiations in this manner is felt to be a method of assuring that the wider, community concerns are included.

The public arena is a political arena. This is true for labor negotiations just as much as it is for anything else. Two areas stand out in this respect. First, the executive–legislative relationship under the separation-of-powers doctrine is markedly different from its private sector corporate executive–board of directors equivalent. Second, electoral politics simply doesn't exist in private sector organizations.

Although the executive branch is most often responsible for carrying out the negotiations, the legislature (in the role of a board of directors) must ratify or accept the agreement. However, unlike the complementary relationship of corporate executives and boards of directors, the separation-of-powers doctrine is just as likely to make political executives and legislators adversaries. Add to this the political positions of the independent actors involved and one has a volatile mixture. Unions unable to get what they want through negotiations with executive officials can attempt to renegotiate with legislators. Similarly, contract negotiations can get caught up in executive–legislative struggles having nothing to do with their content.

Electoral politics is another major distinction. Union members are also citizens. As such, they have a vote in actually choosing those who will compose the executive management and legislative board of directors. American unions are quite active in electoral politics. They not only provide campaign funds through their voluntary political action committees but provide much needed campaign volunteers. Voter registration and other "soft money" educational campaigns can actually be financed with members' dues (Ball, 1993).

What cannot be gained through collective bargaining may be achieved through the legislative process. Campaign contributions to candidates predisposed to support union positions can create a favorable climate and access for achieving those results. Encouraging union members to participate actively in politics and to seek office themselves is an added way of assuring that the union presence is felt.

Individual campaign contributions from union members can be bundled together to emphasize their magnitude. Funds can also be directed to political parties and the money "tallied" to specific campaigns. Independent expenditures of "soft money" (that do everything but tell you who to vote for) can be used to inform the general public and to generate grassroots efforts. Unions can underwrite media campaigns to influence general public opinion and inform voters. This can also be used to create a favorable climate toward unions in general (Swanson, 1993).

Volunteers to staff phone banks (along with the phones themselves) and stuff envelopes can be made available to candidates. Audiences for campaign events and photo opportunities can be provided. The union can furnish people to watch the polls on election day for irregularities (which do indeed still occur in the United States) and to assist others in getting out to vote.

The importance of the "union vote" is dependent on a number of factors. The main one is, of course, just how much the union members share the same political perspective. By the 1970s, the solidarity of union voters began to fragment with the success of achieving most of their agenda. Today, the first task of a union is often to convince its own members of the importance of the political agenda. The impact of a union vote can be heightened in jurisdictions where employee residence is encouraged. Low voter turnout, as often occurs in primary elections, also magnifies union strength. Although many may see little of interest and hence contribute to a small turnout, public employees are not only concerned citizens but individuals "taking care of business."

Of course, as political players, the electoral arena can also be used to pillar unions and union activities. Because people's perceptions are often shaped by negative press, "big" unions and union "bosses" can be the target of political campaigns. Images of labor racketeering (still prevalent in old movies and many television dramas) can also be invoked.

The means by which the services provided by both management and union members are paid for—the budget —also separate the public and private sector. In the private sector, the financial realm is circumscribed by the organization's ability to make a profit and stay in business. This strategic factor sets a real limit on the scope of all negotiations.

In the public sector, however, this boundary does not exist. Because public programs are funded by budgetary expenditures, they are not dependent upon the value of the product or service provided or the "customer's" ability or willingness to pay. The budget process is a case of triangular trade. An agency's customers or clients "pay" for the products and services they receive by voting for political leaders. The political leaders assure their election and reelection by passing the budgets that the agencies need in order to do their jobs.

The ability or willingness of a particular set of customers or citizens to pay for those services is secondary. It is their votes that matter here. The money for programs can be found elsewhere in the tax coffers (or, even better, in the tax coffers of other political jurisdictions). Programs of immense value or use to a few will only cost pennies when the money is taken from the entire taxpaying public.

Lobbying executives and legislators (with campaign contributions assuring access) becomes another means of obtaining union ends. Coalitions of like-minded groups can be formed to push specific legislative agendas (Swanson, 1993).

The budget process also focuses on numerous questions involving public goods—from roads and schools to national security—that don't have a market aspect. Hence, we simply cannot put a cost on them (actually we can tote up the costs, it's just the benefits we cannot put a value on). So, even though we cannot deal with these matters in a straightforward business fashion, no one doubts their importance.

Public sector budgeting also places restraints on spending. Purchases must go through elaborate procedures designed to ensure fairness. Every citizen is given an equal chance at selling things to the government, and the spending of public money is done without waste or fraud. The very complexity of these rules can themselves alter the market. In addition, purchasing decisions can be influenced by secondary concerns such as "Buy American" provisions, local vendor preferences, or the political desirability of using the purchase to aid in the economic (or partisan political) development of an area. All of these nonmarket considerations can transform the rules of public collective bargaining.

Professionalism is the final distinction between public and private sector unions. The public sector has enjoyed the image of professional employees and civil service systems for over a century.

The very concept of professionalization carries with it an image of middle-class financial security and independence. That this image is far different from the reality has yet to undermine its hold on our minds. Professionals provide services that are both needed and clearly valued by those in society. Professionals possess knowledge; they are themselves the asset. This image is enhanced in the public sector through the public service ethos (which is itself a defining aspect of the notion of professionalism). Hence, professionals are seen to have no need to join together in "working class" unions. This has created a great reluctance on the part of public employees to join unions.

Added to the concept of professionalism has been the practical protection afforded by civil service systems. The establishment of merit systems designed to protect public employees specifically from political pressures also extended them many basic safeguards. Additional laws provide numerous safeguards and protections for public employees. It took union organizations to accomplish the same for private sector workers. Hence, many public employees view unions as unnecessary.

Of course, the image of civil service systems and their reality are quite different. Many public jobs are really not under civil service provisions. When they are, the enforcement of merit rules can be lax or nonexistent. The introduction of unions has been shown to regenerate semimoribund civil service systems that poorly protected public employees. However, the environment remains one of competition rather than of cooperation. Two, parallel systems—one civil service, the other collective bargaining—often come into existence. This generates additional, sometimes serious problems (Douglas, 1992).

CONFLICT RESOLUTION

"Conflict" is a word that invokes strong and often violent images. Yet, it is actually an ordinary, everyday occurrence. Every difference that arises between two people is a conflict. Although the overwhelming proportion of differences are relatively inconsequential matters, some do indeed take on significance. Because it is among these significant differences that violence may occur, the use of the term *conflict* becomes a relevant means for cautioning us to its hidden potential.

Differences may give rise to conflict because of individual characteristics, situational conditions, or organizational factors. Individuals may differ over values and ideology, needs and personality, or their perceptions of reality. A specific situation may require more or less interpersonal interaction, be a decision based on consensus, exhibit status or dependency distinctions among those involved, suffer from communication barriers, or lack goal clarity. Complex organizations introduce conflict in their very efforts at the coordination of work. Organization—the specialization of tasks, goal setting, resource allocation, rules and regulations, and reward structures—is conflict (Tosi, Rizzo, and Carroll, 1986: 473–482; Stephenson and Pops, 1989).

What is important is not that differences may lead to conflict but that these conflicts can be resolved. Assuming that the organization has developed means for dealing with the problems derived from its organizational structure and that the situational distinctions are addressed, conflict management focuses on working with individuals in search of mutually acceptable solutions (Tosi, Rizzo, and Carroll, 1986: 489–494; Lan, 1997).

Three general strategies are available for managing conflict: (1) violence; that is, the economic strike, (2) negotiation, and (3) impasse resolution; that is, the use of mediation and arbitration techniques. Of these, negotiation is the preferred option. The third strategy is, in fact, simply techniques for successfully "bootstrapping" the negotiation process.

Strikes and Lockouts

Violence is endemic. The problem is that most of this violence is unthinking violence. Very little thought is actually given to the use of violence and its consequences (and there are most definitely consequences). What is needed is not that we not think about resorting to violence but rather that we indeed think it out. Overwhelmingly, the well-thought-out answer is one that rejects violence as a viable solution.

In labor relations, "violence" is represented by the strike (or lockout). This is economic violence. Yet a strike may also lead to physical violence as well (both in terms of violence against opposing sides and in terms of domestic violence from the strain of conflict). Because of the intense emotional dimension entailed in all strikes, this analogy to or potential for physical violence must always be borne in mind.

Along with mediation and arbitration, the strike (or employer equivalent—the lockout) is an official impasse resolution technique. It is, of course, a much more serious means than the others for trying to resolve disputes when negotiations have stalled or failed. In contrast to mediation and arbitration, strikes (and lockouts) often take on a warlike atmosphere.

Whatever benefits they may bring or succeed in obtaining, strikes (and lockouts) always come with substantial costs. Employees, organizational managers, and the clientele/public all pay for strikes (Bent and Reeves, 1978: 212–261; Kearney, 1992: 267–315).

Rather surprisingly, the legal environment while fostering unionization has apparently little to do with the incidence of public sector strikes. States with favorable laws are no more likely to have strikes than those that prohibit them. "Right to work" laws show the same noneffect (Felker, 1986).

Employees lose both the income they would have received from being employed and the very important sense of identity that work gives. In meeting someone for the first time, one of the first questions asked is invariably "what do you do for a living?" or "what is your job?" This is equivalent to asking "who are you?" Yet it reduces that more general question to one dimension. For American workers, especially those in the public sector, their jobs are indeed who they are.

An organization and its management lose their purpose as well. They cease to provide the product or service that is their reason for being. In the private sector, this results in an immediate loss of the profit necessary to guarantee the organization's continued existence. Although public organizations continue to receive budgeted funds, ultimately they face the same fate if they cannot restore their operations.

The client or public suffers in the immediate loss of a valued product or service. Costs are incurred either in forgoing these or in finding substitutions. Because many of the products or services provided by governments are public goods, substitutions may not be available. Hence, the consequences can indeed be dire.

Because these clientele or public efforts in seeking substitutions may lead to permanent changes, the organization—both workers and managers—may continue to suffer even if they settle their own differences. It is not only businesses that need to worry about market loss. In the public sector, privatization is often seen as a viable alternative.

Because privatization delivers its lower primary costs through a combination of reduced wages and staffing, unions oppose it. To be successful in opposing privatization requires that a union possess political influence and harmonious labor–management relationships. Clearly, strikes can undermine both of these along with public support (Chandler and Feuille, 1991; Naff, 1991).

Although privatization is a potent threat in today's labor environment, it is not an automatic solution to management's perceived problems. Collective bargaining requirements and contractual rights (e.g., the duty to bargain or the fulfillment of obligations agreed to under bargaining) cannot simply be cast aside through unilateral decisions to privatize government services. Where efficiency is obtained through employee wages or layoffs, the courts (and unions) are vigilant in their demands that management adhere to legal contractual obligations and demonstrate well-thought-out proposals aimed at enhancing organizational effectiveness (Elam, 1997).

For strikes to be effective, they must deny one side a valuable resource. In a strike, the labor used to provide the product or service is withdrawn. Its effectiveness then depends on whether alternative products or services exist, whether replacement workers can be found and hired, and on how valued the product or service is in the first place. This denial of resources need not be direct. A third party can be held "hostage" if it is seen as having the ability to influence and convince the other side.

Negotiation Preparation

Negotiation is a team process. Although each side may be represented by a single spokesperson, the actual negotiations involve many players. Even when they are apparently limited to one-on-one negotiations, the agreement will need to be reviewed and accepted by others. Unions must have the agreement ratified by their members; management must obtain the approval of the legislative authority.

A negotiation team assembles individuals with different expertise needed for carrying on the negotiations. It is an ad hoc organization and, hence, requires someone to coordinate its performance. This is usually, but not necessarily, the chief negotiator. The chief negotiator is the team spokesperson and thereby serves to indicate that the communications are authoritative. Otherwise, the negotiation process quickly degenerates into the proverbial Tower of Babel.

A negotiation team can also represent differing factions within an organization. Not all the negotiations that take place are across the table. An organization's own bureaucratic politics can exert a strong influence on what is otherwise perceived as a rational debate between two opposing sides (Allison, 1971). The negotiations team is subject to all the viscidities inherent in group activity. To assure that their interests are voiced and pursued seriously, different elements within an organization will insist on observing and participating in the negotiations.

Negotiations in the public sector often involve management teams who are inexperienced with labor relations. This often proves a decided disadvantage when negotiating with a labor professional. Only as an organization gains experience in collective bargaining does it move to centralize and coordinate its labor relations. Smaller organizations (e.g., cities under 50,000 in population) will contract out this function to a labor attorney or specialist whereas larger organizations will have one on staff (Derber, 1988).

Negotiations are predicated on compromise. If the parties involved are unwilling to reach a compromise agreement, negotiations are futile. Unfortunately, many interpret the term *compromise* as introducing a note of suspicion and disrepute rather than as combining differing qualities. It is this latter meaning that is the focus of effective negotiations. However, suspicion and disrepute are certainly the result when one side enters the negotiations ill prepared.

Those engaged in negotiations must thoroughly prepare for them. They must obtain information, set goals and objectives, and plan for alternative outcomes. They must also be trained and understand the process of negotiation itself (Coleman, 1990).

Information on the current environment is the starting point for negotiation. Data on the numbers and status of present employees, the labor–management contract (or the organization's informal and formal civil service practices), and the budget situation define the psychological base against which all potential changes are compared. In addition, comparative knowledge of the area or industrial standards also serves as a negotiation reference.

This information helps define "what is"; just as important is information on "what will be." Although negotiations are undertaken by those in the "current" organization, they are always about relationships in the "future" organization. Knowledge of an organization's efforts at strategic planning are an intricate part of the negotiation process. The current budget will include fiscal and economic projections indicating the organization's financial capabilities, whereas its strategic plan will outline its future needs.

The ability to pay is often a central issue in many disputes. Because governments are public organizations, national unions can engage in budget searches and fiscal audits on behalf of their local units. In fact, these searches often end up providing local governments with a helpful, professional management audit (Toulmin, 1988). The private sector, which also suffers from some of the same "ability to pay" problems, is now addressing them similarly through notions such as open-book management.

Both management and labor must clearly formulate their goals and objectives prior to entering the negotiations. Proposals designed to achieve these must be ready for discussion and inclusion in the new contract. Because negotiations may lead to suggestions for alterations and compromises, it is important to understand what purpose is to be achieved by a specific proposal. Otherwise, one is left in doubt about the potential "success" or value of the new proposal.

Just as important as having a list of goals and objectives is to have prioritized that list. Seldom will anyone or any group obtain all that they desire. Equally, some goals and objectives are more important than others. Without a clear understanding of which items are more important, negotiating efforts can bog down on the inconsequential. The net result may be to unravel an agreement and the hard-won concessions that truly matter.

It is this setting of priorities that accounts for much of the intrateam, bureaucratic politics that occurs in negotiations. Neither labor nor management represents monolithic interests; they meld together disparate elements. Although each negotiating team shares a common purpose, they often disagree on how to best achieve that purpose. The struggle to assure that "your" proposals are given high priority and are included in the final agreement introduces added difficulties and complexities to the negotiations.

Negotiations suffer from their own "fog of war." The give-and-take of the battlefield can obscure the importance and meaning of individual actions. Scenario planning is a device that helps aid those involved in negotiations remain focused.

Assuming optimistic, realistic, and pessimistic situations, the negotiators outline what types of agreements would be "good" under each situation. Pessimistic scenarios may entail the granting of concessions even among public sector unions (Mitchell, 1986). Scenario planning provides a set of negotiation templates that can serve as referents during the actual negotiations. This helps to keep the negotiators on the track of their priorities while subjecting them to the harsh light of reality.

All of this material—information, goals and objectives, and contingency plans—is formally included in a bargaining book. The bargaining book serves as a convenient reference and guide to the negotiations.

The final steps preliminary to the beginning of negotiations are agreeing to the arena and the agenda. Although these are "housekeeping" matters, where the negotiations are to be held and what is to be discussed are important factors for properly setting the stage.

The actual physical setting itself can be an important aid or impediment to the negotiations. For this reason, mediators or facilitators often take charge of making these arrangements. It may be wise to employ a facilitator from the beginning of negotiations rather than calling in one as a mediator when difficulties arise. Obviously, the physical location where negotiations occur should not afford one side or the other an undue advantage (Moore, 1986; Schwarz, 1994; Slaikeu, 1996).

However, this question goes beyond a tactical concern. A comfortable locus well supplied with the appropriate creature comforts can keep tempers at bay and attention focused on the topic. Seating arrangements can be set up to encourage discussion and working together. Mediators and facilitators endeavor to physically foster communications and cooperation. The traditional, adversarial arrangement of two sides facing one another in competition across a table is often bypassed. By seating the parties at tables set up to form the shape of an "L" or a "V" (in the ultimate arrangement, the bend in the letter is straightened out and both sides sit together), they are physical less confrontation and more complementary. This nonverbal, physical relationship tends to influence how individuals verbally negotiate as well. In addition, the availability of separate rooms in which to hold private caucuses is a must (Moore, 1986; Schwarz, 1994; Slaikeu, 1996).

The initial agenda is also a matter to be agreed upon in advance. Basically, the first meeting is devoted to summarizing the issues under negotiation and establishing the ground rules under which the negotiations will be conducted. Although these have both been worked out in advance of the meeting, the presence of both parties at the meeting itself confirms and legitimizes the process.

An important purpose of the initial agenda is to formally define those issues remaining under dispute and the focus of negotiations. As such, it serves to limit the matters under negotiation and prevents the addition of new items and proposals (unless mutually consented to). This prevents one side from springing surprises on the other or piling on additional demands.

The issue of formally establishing ground rules has been introduced by mediators and facilitators. It cannot be taken for granted that those involved in the negotiations understand either how the negotiation process works or how they are expected to behave (Moore, 1986; Schwarz, 1994).

Negotiations rationally focus on interests and, hence, involve serious debate. They call into question virtually everything that each side is seeking. They focus on causal relationships and their underlying assumptions. In addition, questions are raised about the relevance and importance of information offered as supporting evidence. This is to be accepted and personal emotions reined in (Moore, 1986; Schwarz, 1994).

Negotiations require that all parties demonstrate courtesy and respect for one another. Negotiations, while involving conflict, are designed to resolve that conflict. The process is designed to bring the contending parties together as an effective working group. A formal agreement or legal contract is worthless if the parties to it refuse to honor it or carry out its provisions.

The Negotiation Process

The process of negotiation itself is a complex interplay in which the balance between substantive interests and long-term relationships is sought by two or more parties. The focus on substantive interests is a straightforward concern that has been at the center of most negotiation strategies. The importance attached to maintaining relationships is a more recent concern; however, it's also obvious.

Negotiations are not single, independent events. They are an intricate part of the tangled web we weave. In concluding a substantive negotiation we often envision similar, future negotiations. The agreement we have just concluded will also, most likely, require compliance and follow-up actions by the parties if it is to be implemented. Finally, our own conscience and sense of well-being benefits from knowing that we have behaved in an ethical manner.

As Savage, Blair, and Sorenson (1989) have indicated, this leads to sixteen possible combinations of substantive and relationship priorities. Depending on what each side to a negotiation wants and its assessment of what the other side's desires are, some nine negotiating strategies can be applied.

When no one is interested in anything, active avoidance (i.e., simply refusing to negotiate) can be pursued. When the other party is interested in either a substantive issue or a long-term relationship avoidance can be passive (i.e, delegating the negotiations to other, lower-level people in the organization; this serves to provide these individuals with practical training in negotiations) or responsive (i.e., applying the organization's regulations and policies to the situation). If the above roles are reversed with the other side uninterested, the organization needs to pursue a strategy of focused or even open subordination in order to elicit a response.

As interest is developed in carrying on negotiations (especially in terms of substantive outcomes) by both parties, strategies move forward into those of soft and firm competition. When a long-term relationship is also an important consideration, the negotiations call for strategies that emphasize principled or trusting collaboration.

It is this latter set of collaborative strategies that is the focus of the Harvard Negotiation Project and the various *Getting to Yes* works (Fisher and Ury, 1981; Fisher and Brown, 1988; Ury, 1991; Fisher, Ury, and Patton, 1991). Fisher and Ury argue that practicing principled negotiation leads to improved, win-win solutions. Most important, the solutions obtained through principled negotiation are better not only in general but for you specifically. They are superior to those that can be obtained through competitive strategies.

Fisher and Ury do, of course, recognize the need for caution. However, their emphasis is on helping the other side in a negotiation become aware of the benefits that it will obtain from the principled-negotiation strategy. Even though they see the advantages of Fisher and Ury's collaborative strategy, Savage, Blair, and Sorenson (1989) take a more cautious approach and advocate their nine strategies.

Principled negotiation is a strategy designed to build trust and collaboration. It is based on five steps: (1) separating the people from the problem, (2) focusing on interests, not positions, (3) inventing options for mutual gains, (4) using objective criteria, and (5) the best alternative to a negotiated agreement (BATNA). It inherently assumes that the negotiations both involve concerns for substantive outcomes and place value on the relationship between those conducting the negotiations (Fisher, Ury, and Patton, 1991).

Although relationships are an important factor in negotiations, the first step is to separate the people from the specific problem that is being addressed. The purpose behind this is not to ignore or denigrate the importance of the personal relationships but to concentrate attention on the substantive issue.

People are, in fact, the most important factor in the negotiation process. It is their perceptions that form the basis for all negotiations. Separating the people from the problem attempts to simplify negotiations by concentrating on a more manageable area—the substantive issue—and using its resolution to work out the more complex relationship issues.

Negotiations can quickly become imbued with emotional content. It is necessary to take this into consideration and recognize its meaningfulness. For example, you may be purchasing a house; however, the owner is selling a home. Although that may not increase the value of the property from your perspective, a callous disregard of the homeowner's emotional context can adversely impact the negotiations significantly.

The emotional side of any negotiation is one that calls for recognition and understanding. What is being asked in many cases is no more than an acknowledgment of its importance to the affected individual. Active listening skills extensively focus on addressing such problems.

The other danger of emotions to negotiations is confusing the "messenger" with the "message." This can lead to unnecessary and unproductive confrontation. In addition, substituting the person for the substantive issue does not help solve the problem at hand.

Only by focusing on the interests and not the positions is a problem likely to be solved. Positions are slogans. They are symbolic statements summarizing the desired outcomes. Meaning comes only when one examines the full intent or purpose that underlies the slogan. What is it that the position is meant to achieve or accomplish?

Positions are often proposed solutions to a problem. Yet the interest is in solving the problem and not in a specific solution. Other solutions that satisfy the interest would be as acceptable. However, this all-important distinction can be lost in arguments centered on positional slogans.

Only through understanding and acknowledging the interests of those engaged in the negotiations can an effort be made toward their resolution. Interests establish the parameters defining the conditions that a solution must meet. Even though an agreement may not be reached, interests serve to give the negotiations a task that is doable.

The focus on interests also allows for the invention of options. Instead of a single position being offered and debated as the solution to a problem, interests can serve to generate a series of options that can be analyzed for a mutual comparative advantage. Various brainstorming techniques help generate potential solutions. These are later subject to rational analysis based on the competing interests of the negotiators.

An important step in finding a mutually acceptable option is the use of objective criteria. Fair standards drawn from the geographic area or industry and fair procedures for arriving at decisions guide the choice among alternatives. This ensures the acceptance of the agreement both today and tomorrow. Fair agreements do not become a casus belli. One only need be reminded of the aftermath of the Versailles treaty's "settlement" of World War I.

Finally, those entering into negotiations need to be aware of their best alternative to a negotiated agreement (BATNA). What happens if the negotiations fail? One does not want to think of this, and certainly doesn't enter into negotiations with the thought of failure. Yet this is a realistic outcome, and, as such, it deserves serious consideration.

In American elections, only the Missouri-type judicial ballot allows the voter a "yes" or "no" decision on an individual candidate. All other elections pose the question as a choice of one candidate or another. Judgment is comparative. The individual decision must take into account the alternative. The same process governs the selection of the German chancellor and gives the multiparty, parliamentary system executive stability.

Negotiations must also face this reality. The BATNA, by clearly articulating each side's alternative, helps define the outer limits of the negotiations. No one need settle for less than their BATNA. Hence, only what lies in between is the subject for negotiation. In addition, a BATNA, especially a good one, can instill confidence in a negotiator. Even a "bad" BATNA provides the negotiator with added insight.

Mediation

Negotiations seldom run smoothly. In many instances, they need and benefit from outside assistance. Employing a facilitator from the beginning of the negotiations or bringing in a mediator when progress is stalled are viable approaches augmenting the chances for success.

Impasse resolution is most effectively addressed through both mediation and arbitration (Coleman, 1990: 213–233; Kearney, 1992: 317–365; Mareschal, 1998). There are also a slew of lesser techniques such as fact-finding/nonbinding arbitration/dispute panels/mini-trials (a public recommendation by an objective neutral), med-arb (mediation turns into arbitration at a set point), labor–management committees (issues are parceled out to quality circles for solution), sunshine bargaining (like fact-finding, public observation to impose reasonableness), and referendum (agreement decided by a vote of the people).

Mediation is an extremely flexible and adaptable technique. It maintains a degree of informality in the negotiation process while aiding those engaged in the bargaining to obtain a voluntary agreement. These strengths also expose mediation's chief weakness—there is no guarantee that an agreement will be reached.

Alternate dispute resolution in the terms of mediation is in growing demand. However, it is not a philosopher's stone for impasse resolution. Good mediators and facilitators remain scarce. Mediators are drawn from a wide array of backgrounds: educators, managers, counselors, therapists, social workers, and lawyers. For the most part, their occupational antecedents do not matter. However, attorneys often find it more difficult to shed their analytical, adversarial/judgmental training. The highly regarded Federal Mediation and Conciliation Service indicates that mediators should be knowledgeable about the general labor relations and collective bargaining environment (including its economic, political, and social aspects), skilled in negotiation and facilitation (including organizational development and communication techniques), and capable of assisting in the design and implementation of conflict resolution systems (Mareschal, 1998).

Using their knowledge of the conditions that contribute to the likeliness that dispute resolution will be successful, good mediators select the disputes that they will assist in. Mediators look for disputes where the parties are motivated to reach an agreement but separated by minor issues that have become bogged down due to an overcommitment to a position rather than an interest. They tend to avoid negotiations in large jurisdictions where strong constituent or political pressures exist. They also are distrustful of parties that repeatedly resort to mediation or arbitration rather than putting in the effort to work out their differences (McCabe, 1990).

In attempting to mediate a dispute, three general strategies are available depending upon the situation. The mediator can, in escalating order of involvement, be facilitative, conciliative, or directive. The intensity of the dispute often determines the extent to which a mediator involves him- or herself in the process. This is especially true in regard to federal mediators, whereas state-level mediators are often superseded by political actors in the more serious disputes (Rodgers, 1986). Although greater involvement on the part of the mediator helps assure that the parties will reach an agreement, it also may lessen their sense of ownership in that agreement (Kessel, 1972).

A facilitative or reflexive strategy introduces the mediator as little more than a neutral observer. The mediator serves to quiet the emotional turmoil that occurs in all impasses so that the parties can focus on negotiating an agreement that reflects their interests.

The mediator's first task is to establish that he or she is knowledgeable about disputes and dispute resolution. This proof of expertise helps assure both parties that external observation (and the threat of public disclosure) on the ultimate fairness of the negotiation procedure occurs.

The mediator then proceeds to demonstrate his or her empathy and understanding of the specific dispute (without appearing to take sides). This enables the mediator to play a secondary, but catalytic role in restarting the stalled negotiations. By diffusing emotions the mediator can help each side to see what the real issues involved are and to understand the importance of their mutual relationship (Kessel, 1972).

A conciliative or nondirective strategy registers an escalation of involvement on the part of the mediator. While still maintaining neutrality with regard to the specific issues of the dispute, the mediator actively undertakes to create a climate for settlement and to educate the disputants in negotiations.

The context or climate in which a negotiation takes place can be crucial to its success. A mediator will take over all the administrative details—both in terms of the logistics and physical arrangements and in terms of acting as the official record keeper.

In this latter, secretarial role the mediator finds the authority to assume control over the pacing of the negotiations. The agenda and length of individual negotiating sessions can be used to keep the parties on track toward a settlement. The mediator can focus attention on issues that, while small in themselves, can be used to begin a "record" of agreement. By discussing different issues at the same session, a mediator can ideally lead the parties to agree on a package deal.

In some instances, it becomes necessary for the mediator to teach one or both parties the negotiation process and how to bargain. The mediator may also need to assist a party in determining which issues are indeed significant to it (Kessel, 1972).

Directive mediation is the most active strategy in that the mediator attempts to honestly broker the negotiations. The search for an agreement and areas of compromise is far more wide-ranging than that which occurs under a conciliative strategy.

The mediator actively seeks out solutions, often offering suggestions of his or her own. This is quite useful in that it also enables the parties to a negotiation to float "trial balloons." Because it remains unknown whether the proposal is that of the mediator or of the other party, there is no indication that this item is valued less by one side or the other. The mediator may also engage in "shuttle diplomacy" when neither side wishes to directly talk with the other. In fact, the entire negotiation process may occur preliminary to the first, formal meeting (Kessel, 1972).

A directive mediator will also force both sides to face reality. He or she will be sure that each side is aware of its BATNA and the costs of a strike. Using his or her knowledge of similar disputes, a mediator will be able to indicate what has been the range of settlements. If need be, the mediator will focus each side on the priority issues (Kessel, 1972).

Finally, a mediator may be called upon to help sell the agreement to each side's constituents. Negotiators seldom possess unilateral authority. Union leaders must have their membership ratify the agreement; government negotiators must obtain legislative approval and appropriations. The mediator can assist in obtaining these approvals.

Although disputants may not trust one another, it is important for the mediator that they trust him or her and that they trust the mediation process itself. Mediators concentrate a great deal of their attention on creating and maintaining this trust (Moore, 1986; Slaikeu, 1996).

Karl Slaikeu (1996) builds the mediation process around analysis of the conflict grid. This is a stakeholder analysis technique that identifies each party to the dispute (or stakeholder) and categorizes their interests, the other facts affecting the dispute, each party's BATNA, and possible solutions. The conflict grid is used to guide the mediation process through five steps: (1) first contact, (2) the opening meeting, (3) the caucuses, (4) joint/shuttle meetings, and (5) closing.

First contact invokes science fiction images of encountering alien creatures. This is precisely the tone Karl Slaikeu wants to establish—the mediator must not assume that the disputants understand. First contact is designed to summarize the problem—to ensure that both (or all) parties are indeed arguing about the same thing. It is also used to explain and educate the disputants about what mediation is (and is not). If both parties commit to mediation, then an opening meeting is scheduled. Because the first contact usually is done separately with each party, the *opening meeting* repeats what has been agreed to and the explanation of mediation. This is to put the mediator in control of the process and establish the mediator as a confidential and neutral actor. Prior to adjourning this initial meeting, each party is allowed to make an opening statement.

The third step focuses on the mediator holding separate *caucuses* with each party to the dispute. Assurances of confidentiality enable the mediator using the conflict grid to analyze the disputants' interests. By melding the shared perspectives from these separate, confidential caucuses, a mediator can guide the negotiations toward resolution. The one-text approach outlined by Fisher and Ury is often ideal for this.

Step four focuses on the use of joint meetings or *shuttle diplomacy* to move the negotiations forward to a mutually acceptable conclusion. The mediator constantly summarizes where the parties are at to help frame or anchor the negotiations. More important, the mediator may be called upon to avoid obstacles that can cause impasses. This may require (1) starting over with a reanalysis of the conflict grid, (2) breaking the "timing" or "flow" of the process through humor, changed meeting formats, or bringing in outsiders, (3) forcing a "reality check" on the disputants, (4) supporting the negotiating parties with education or encouragement, (5) introducing alternative solutions, or (6) confronting the disputants with the spectre of failure.

The mediation process ends with the *closing*. An agreement must be tested or analyzed to assure that it indeed satisfies the interests of the disputants. Otherwise, it will fail (and generate additional ill will) as soon as the flaws become apparent (Moore, 1986; Slaikeu, 1996).

Facilitation is an extension of mediation techniques to group problem solving. Facilitation focuses on groups that share a unity of purpose rather than the formal adversarial relationship that underlies mediation and other impasse resolution procedures. Although the facilitator is still an outside, neutral broker, the focus is on group effectiveness. The facilitator concentrates on making the group process effective so that the group itself can better solve its problems. It is not the function of the facilitator to mediate or resolve differences among group team members. Of course, a facilitator may be called upon to engage in such mediation (Schwarz, 1994).

Facilitation demonstrates the wider application of the basic techniques employed in mediation. In examining group effectiveness, Roger Schwarz (1994) delineates three sets of nested criteria—organizational context, group structure, and group process. It is only in this last aspect—group process—that facilitation occurs. Hence, effectiveness may elude a group despite the best efforts of a facilitator if problems are located in the organizational context or group structure.

At the heart of Schwarz's (1994) approach are the sixteen principles of group effectiveness derived from the research literature. These become ground rules when formally adopted by the group itself. Regardless, the facilitator will use them in guiding and intervening in the group process. Of course, their acceptance by the group as ground rules will obviously strengthen the argument.

These sixteen principles are (1) test assumptions and inferences, (2) share all relevant information, (3) focus on interests, not positions, (4) be specific—use examples, (5) agree on what important words mean, (6) explain the reasons behind one's statements, questions, and comments, (7) disagree openly with any member of the group, (8) make statements, then invite questions and comments, (9) jointly design ways to test disagreements and solutions, (10) discuss indiscussible issues, (11) keep the discussion focused, (12) do not take cheap shots or otherwise distract the group, (13) all members are expected to participate, (14) exchange relevant information with nongroup members, (15) make decisions by consensus, and (16) do self-critiques (Schwarz, 1994).

Arbitration

Arbitration is an indicator that negotiations have indeed failed. In reality, it does not resolve an impasse but merely imposes a truce. Arbitration results in an agreement that is a legally binding contract, but this is an imposed solution. Hence, while a formal settlement may be in place, the willingness of both parties to abide by it and carry it out is not. This is the case regardless of whether the Public Employee Relations Act governing the negotiation process calls for mandatory arbitration after a set period or allows for either side to invoke it (or even when both parties voluntarily agree to arbitrate a matter).

A dependence on arbitrating disputes can chill negotiations (why seriously talk when the matter is going to be decided elsewhere?). Of course, the petty advantage here is that both the work and the onus for the final outcome are shifted from the negotiating parties to the arbitrator (Kessel, 1972).

Even with all these disadvantages, arbitration remains an important impasse resolution technique. Arbitration may be the only way out of a protracted and divisive dispute. It can buy time in which both parties can reevaluate their interests and preserve the long-term relationship that exists.

Arbitrators are extremely cautious about engaging in contract or interest arbitration. Because most of their own income is derived from grievance arbitrations, the high visibility and higher stakes of contract arbitrations can seriously jeopardize their very livelihood. This often leads arbitrators to work out settlements that give each side something and leave no one a "loser" (Helburn and Rogers, 1985; Vest, O'Brien, and Vest, 1990).

Final-offer arbitration is a variation in the technique designed to avoid this "splitting of the difference." Each side puts forward its best, final offer, and the arbitrator accepts one or the other. Arbitrators, of course, do not like this approach as it definitely makes one side a "loser." Final-offer arbitration is indeed a drastic solution. The intention is, in fact, that it will appear so drastic that it will force both parties to reach a negotiated agreement rather than resort to arbitration.

Med-arb is a technique that combines the mediation and arbitration processes. If mediation proves ineffective, the mediator is granted the authority to arbitrate the impasse. The chief advantage here is in the time and money saved in not having to bring a new person "up to speed." The disadvantage lies in this same singularity. Knowing that the mediator may metamorphose into an arbitrator can cause participants to hold back information and impede negotiations.

SUMMARY

Even though the contract issues dealt with by public and private sector unions are the same, public sector unionism remains a more sensitive topic. Here is popular evidence of one of the more visceral public–private distinctions.

Collective bargaining in the public sector is governed by law. Because it has lagged the development of private sector unionism, it also tends to follow the precedents worked out in that arena. The fact that they work so well is in itself an indicator of the great similarities shared. Contract negotiations in both public and private organizations center on issues of union security, management rights, employee security, and the wage–effort bargain.

Of course, there are differences. The public sector is indeed the "public" sector. Negotiations are not merely between two parts of an organization; they involve the interests of many others. Politics is also a factor. In the private sector, union members don't get to vote for management. Publicness affects funding as well. Contracts are funded from budgets and not profits on products and services. Finally, the organizations in the public sector demonstrate a sense of professionalism and public ethos not found among private enterprises.

Universally applicable, negotiation is the central "technique" displayed here. It is a complex and detailed process. The technique of "principled negotiation" made famous by Fisher and Ury forms the primary strategy. Its transformational, win-win approach is especially appealing to those in the public sector. The focus on objectivity, reason, and a common, shared interest complement normal public sector perceptions.

When negotiations stall or reach impasse, resort can be made to mediation or arbitration. Mediation can range from a gentle, nondirective facilitative approach through more involved conciliative efforts to an active, directive style. In all cases, however, mediation remains a persuasive instrument. On the other hand, arbitration "settles" disputes. Whereas mediators must obtain the agreement of the parties involved, arbitrators are empowered by those parties to decide for them.

Exercises

EXERCISE 1: JOB ANALYSIS

Job analysis is the basic building block in professional personnel/human resource management. It is the foundation upon which the other personnel activities are built. The job analysis results in a *job description* or *job specification,* which describes the most important aspects or duties performed in that specific job. The job description is used for attracting candidates in recruitment. It is the document upon which selection testing is based. It is a guide for orientating new employees. It serves as the benchmark for determining training needs and for establishing performance appraisal standards.

The individual job tasks or responsibilities that are identified in the job analysis process may be either narrowly or broadly defined. Narrowly defined job analyses focus on specific tasks that usually occur in a stable, routine environment (and allow for centralized administration). Broadly defined job analyses, such as are involved in broadbanding, emphasize the requirement for situational adjustments and flexibility in the performance of tasks (usually entailing decentralization).

JOB ANALYSIS EXERCISE

The class will be divided into groups of three to four students. In each group, one student will be selected to serve as the *job incumbent* (such students will use their current or past job experience as the basis for this exercise); the other students conduct a *desk audit* in which they will *interview* the job incumbent.

For each job analysis the students will develop from three to six task statements. Each task statement will encompass (1) the *activity*—what is to be done, (2) the *results*—why the task is to be performed, and (3) the *process*—how the individual is to go about accomplishing the task (including resources required, supervision given and received, and working conditions). A list of the skills (can do what is to be done), knowledge (understand what is to be done), and abilities (could do what is to be done) appropriate to each specific task statement will also be indicated.

In brainstorming, ideas (about job tasks) are thrown out willy-nilly. Analysis and judgment are suspended until later. After a substantial number of task statements have been developed, they can then be grouped together for similarities or separated for differences. The completeness and practicality of each individual task statement can then be judged and analyzed. Afterward, transfer the final task statements to the individual pages that follow.

When identifying major responsibilities, do not develop a laundry list that documents every minor task the employee performs. Instead, state in broad terms approximately eight to ten major segments or responsibilities involved in the job for which the employee is held accountable.

Responsibilities can be written as action statements starting with:

administers
advises
allocates
analyzes
answers
attends
classifies
cleans
codes
collects
compares
compiles
completes
conducts
controls
coordinates
delivers
determines
develops
disseminates
ensures
enters
establishes
explains
files
identifies
informs
interprets
interviews
keeps
maintains
makes
manages
monitors
motivates
obtains
operates
organizes
oversees
performs
plans
prepares
presents
processes
provides
purges
recommends
records
reports
represents
responds
reviews
searches
selects
sends
serves
submits
surveys
transcribes
types
verifies
writes

It is often helpful to complete task or responsibility statements by adding "so that." This clause explains why the task or responsibility is performed, usually by stating the results that are expected from that task.

Task Statement 1: ______________________________

____

Activity (What): ______________________________

____

____

____

Results (Why):

Process (How):

SKAs:

Task Statement 2:

Activity (What):

Results (Why):

Process (How):

SKAs:

Task Statement 3:

Activity (What):

Results (Why): ______

Process (How): ______

SKAs: ______

Task Statement 4: ______

Activity (What): ______

Results (Why): ______

Process (How): ______

SKAs: ______

Task Statement 5: ______

Activity (What): ______________________________

Results (Why): ______________________________

Process (How): ______________________________

SKAs: ______________________________

Task Statement 6: ______________________________

Activity (What): ______________________________

Results (Why): ______________________________

Process (How): ______________________________

SKAs: ______________________________

EXERCISE 2: JOB EVALUATION

Job evaluation allows an organization to compare individual jobs with one another. This enables the organization to develop an overall picture of how various positions are related to and support one another. It also enables the organization to assess the direct and indirect contribution each position makes to the organization's mission. In addition, job evaluation can be the basis for compensation systems.

Typically, an organization determines which factors are essential to carrying out its mission. Although anywhere from a dozen to twenty overall factors may be developed, specific jobs may only relate to three to six factors. Individual jobs are ranked or rated on the extent and degree to which they are involved in each factor. The composite score from these separate evaluations indicates the overall worth or contribution of the job to the organization.

The class will be divided into groups of three or four students. Each group will use the set of job analyses developed in the job analysis exercise or one of the sets provided here. These jobs will be evaluated on three factors—decision making, skill, and effort. Each student group will decide how to weight the overall factors; they will also decide the scale value (five-point scales are provided). Each student group will evaluate each position and assign points appropriate to it for each factor.

FACTORS

Decision Making

1. Carrying out defined, technical tasks
2. Choosing appropriate defined, technical tasks
3. Interpreting rules and guidelines for implementing tasks
4. Allocating resources to tasks
5. Overall, strategic choices regarding tasks

Effort

1. Repetitive (simple, single task repeated for each new case or client)
2. Patterned (set of interrelated tasks that follow a consistent path or procedure)
3. Interpretive (employee must determine which tasks are appropriate for each case or client)
4. Adaptive (although standard operating procedures govern the application of tasks, these are general guidelines that require "fine-tuning" or the exercise of judgment about which applies)
5. Uncharted (because tasks are unlikely to fit standardized categories, creative solutions are needed in order to fulfill organizational requirements)

Skill/Education

1. Basic skills in reading, writing, and arithmetic
2. Vocational abilities with regard to a specific set of equipment or processes
3. Technical skills in the application of sets of equipment or processes
4. Professional knowledge of a complex area of endeavor
5. Advanced analytical abilities

SAMPLE JOB ANALYSES

Department of Sustainable Environment

The Department of Sustainable Environment (DSE) administers programs designed to protect air quality, water quality, and land quality. The DSE also provides education and technical assistance to the public, aiding in their efforts to responsibly manage our natural resources. The DSE's mission is to protect the environment, protect human health from environmental hazards, manage our natural resources, and provide environmental education to the public. The DSE operates throughout the state. It is organized into Environmental Protection, Natural Resources, and Organization & Management divisions employing over 5,000 people.

POSITION: Environmental Engineer

DESCRIPTION OF WORK: Management of state-led leaking underground petroleum storage tank cleanups through coordination of assessment/remediation activities with preselected environmental contractors, including but not limited to initial assessments, corrective action, emergency response, and implementation of alternative drinking water sources; evaluate preapproval/reasonable rates data for updating of documentation for state trust fund reimbursement claims; assistance in the development of performance-based cleanups and reimbursement; assistance in the development of policies and amendments to rules and statutes; technical assistance to division of waste management, underground storage tank section regional and central office staff related to petroleum cleanups; limited supplemental technical evaluation of reimbursement claims; responses to verbal and written inquiries from consultants, tank owners/operators and the public related to the state trust fund and other leaking underground storage tank issues.

TRAINING AND EXPERIENCE REQUIREMENT: Graduation from a four-year college or university with a major in civil engineering, environmental engineering, mechanical engineering, chemical engineering, or a related engineering curriculum and two years of engineering experience including one year in an area related to environmental engineering; or an equivalent combination of education and experience.

Preferred: Experience with soil and groundwater assessment and remediation system design; knowledge of state trust fund statutes, regulations, and policies; EIT or PE; excellent written and verbal communication skills.

POSITION: Environmental Specialist

DESCRIPTION OF WORK: This position serves as one of three watershed coordinators for an organizational unit within the Division of Water Quality called the Special Watershed Project Unit. This unit consists of eleven (11) staff, including the project leader, hired with funding provided by the Clean Water Management Trust Fund. The objective of this unit is to identify the causes and sources of water quality problems for eleven (11) impaired watersheds across the state. The product of the unit is an assessment and restoration strategy for each watershed that can be funded by the

Clean Water Management Trust Fund. This position has primary responsibility for determining the causes and sources of impairment in project watersheds in the Wolf region and for developing watershed management strategies to restore water quality. This involves: conducting fieldwork in these watersheds to assess watershed condition and sources of water quality impairment; evaluating land use information, water quality data, and other sources of information; and developing management strategies to address identified causes and sources of pollution.

SKILLS, KNOWLEDGE, AND ABILITIES: Considerable knowledge of water quality programs with an emphasis on nonpoint source (NPS) programs. Knowledge of technical aspects of water quality management strategies, including interpretation of water quality data, best management practices for NPS pollution control, source reduction strategies, and stream restoration methods. Considerable knowledge of stream and watershed processes, including chemical, physical, and biological factors. Synthesize large amounts of technical information on water quality and controls and communicate effectively (technically and generally) in both the written and oral form. Computer skills in word processing and spreadsheets. Knowledge of simple water quality models and data analysis techniques.

TRAINING AND EXPERIENCE REQUIREMENTS: Graduation from a four-year college or university with a major in environmental science, ecology, or related natural science curriculum, plus three years of experience related to the work to be performed; or an equivalent combination of education and experience.

Preferred: Prefer that at least one year be directly related to water quality protection or watershed assessment. Experience or training in geomorphology and stream restoration would be helpful.

POSITION: Environmental Supervisor

DESCRIPTION OF WORK: This position is located in the Planning Branch of the Water Quality Section and is responsible for the Modeling/TMDL Unit. This unit develops regional and basinwide surface water quality modeling frameworks for use in Total Maximum Daily Loads (TMDL) and guiding major decisions in the basinwide planning process. The unit provides guidance to other water quality section staff on predicting the impact of point and nonpoint sources of a water body and the impact of various point and nonpoint management strategies on the water body. The position will develop unit goals and priorities that are consistent with division needs and state and federal requirements, plan and assign projects to meet the goals, provide technical guidance to the unit staff on model development, and technically review the unit's models, reports, and other products for consistency with state and federal regulations and guidance. The person in this position will interact regularly with other agencies within the department, the Environmental Protection Agency, the U.S. Geological Survey, university researchers, and the public about water quality and modeling issues.

SKILLS, KNOWLEDGE, AND ABILITIES: Considerable knowledge of physical, chemical, and biological principles as they relate to water quality. In addition, the individual should possess knowledge in the area of data management, statistics, and water quality modeling. The individual should have an understanding of the state and federal water quality programs and regulations. The individual must have strong leadership skills including the ability to communicate, motivate others, and promote teamwork. The individual will have contact with other agencies, the regulated community, and the public, in order to meet state and federal requirements concerning stakeholder involvement in environmental decision making. The individual must be able to interact effectively with a diversity of people. The individual must have strong written and oral communication skills.

TRAINING AND EXPERIENCE REQUIREMENTS: Graduation from a four-year college or university with a major in civil engineering, environmental engineering, chemistry, one of the natural sciences, one of the environmental sciences, or a closely related curriculum and five years of progressive experience in environmental work; or an equivalent combination of education and experience.

POSITION: Forester

DESCRIPTION OF WORK: This position is responsible for a variety of forest service programs including, but not limited to: forest management assistance to private landowners involving preparation of stewardship and management plans; overseeing reforestation projects; administering cost-share programs; ensuring compliance with federal/state BMP laws; development of urban forestry program and plans that incorporate nontraditional forestry techniques as required; fire control, including initial and extended attack on wildlands fires; enforcing state fire laws; fire prevention and training programs; supervision of assistant county ranger and other personnel as assigned; maintenance of fire-fighting apparatus and vehicles; must reside within county; valid driver's license; telephone required.

SKILLS, KNOWLEDGE, AND ABILITIES: Excellent verbal and written communication skills, self-starter with ability to actively influence outcomes to achieve goals. Ability to work with diverse groups of people and organizations.

TRAINING AND EXPERIENCE REQUIREMENTS: Graduation from a four-year college or university with a degree in forest management and two years of experience in technical forestry work; or equivalent combination of education and experience.

Preferred: Registered forester; pesticide license; urban forestry experience and/or training; completion of the following: basic L.E., prescribed burning, advanced water handling, instructor training.

POSITION: Hydrogeologist

DESCRIPTION OF WORK: This position is responsible for the technical review of comprehensive site assessment reports and corrective action plans prepared for sites that have soil and/or groundwater contamination resulting from underground storage tank releases. The purpose of these reviews is to determine if the environmental cleanup at the sites is consistent with the general statutes, rules, and guidelines. If deficiencies are identified in the reports or plan, the person in this position provides written responses to the responsible parties noting the actions needed to bring the site into compliance. If compliance is not achieved, the person in this position is responsible for preparing recommendations for enforcement action. This position has responsibility for review of claims for reimbursement from the state trust fund for environmental cleanup costs in current sites. Periodically, this position has responsibility for directing and conducting investigations to determine the source and party responsible for the subsurface contamination. This position requires that a high level of technical assistance and advice be provided to responsible parties, their representatives, and to the public in general.

SKILLS, KNOWLEDGE, AND ABILITIES: Thorough knowledge of theoretical hydrogeology and its practical applications. Knowledge of the fate and transport of petroleum hydrocarbons and other contaminants in soil and groundwater. Knowledge of state and federal rules and regulations pertaining to environmental cleanups. Ability to communicate well both orally and in writing. Very good people skills to be able to handle with tact, consistency, and sound judgment the diversity of public contacts encountered. Good analytical skills to apply to reviews and to problem solving at technically difficult sites. Good organizational and time-management skills to track compliance at sites. Ability to multitask in a high-energy, high-volume work environment.

TRAINING AND EXPERIENCE REQUIREMENTS: Graduation from a four-year college or university with a B.S. in geology and one year of experience in hyrdogeological work; or an M.S. degree in hydrogeology; or an equivalent combination of education and experience.

Preferred: Licensed geologist and either regulatory or environmental consulting experience in conducting subsurface investigations and cleanups of petroleum contamination within the state.

POSITION: Marine Fisheries Biologist

DESCRIPTION OF WORK: The biologist is responsible for the planning, coordinating, and statistical analysis of sampling conducted at commercial fisheries landing sites as part of the trip ticket program. Duties include: evaluate the validity of the data collection design, adequacy of sampling, and statistical relevance of resulting sampling and research activities; prepare sampling design and reports on fisheries landings; fishery landings' values, species composition, species conversion factors; maintain edit and code tables; analyze other features of commercial landings' data and value; supervise five Marine Fisheries Technicians who conduct field sampling. Supervisory duties include hiring, evaluation, work plan development, career growth, and work assignments. The biologist reviews and interprets possible errors in biological data, documents, and scientific reports. In addition, the biologist is responsible for identifying and developing computer edit programs for error detection and resolution; completing reports for federal aid grant; representing DMF on technical issues before the public, commercial fishing industry, division, state, and interstate fisheries forums. The biologist uses SAS, SQL, and DMF's FIN.

SKILLS, KNOWLEDGE, AND ABILITIES: Knowledge of commercial fisheries, fisheries management, and policy; good communications abilities including technical writing skills; must be able to work in a dynamic teamwork environment; good organizational skills; the ability to work with the public and technical staff; knowledge of a variety of statistical programming software packages including SAS; ability to multitask and handle competing priorities.

TRAINING AND EXPERIENCE REQUIREMENTS: Graduation from a four-year college or university with a major in marine biology, fisheries science, or a closely related curriculum and two years of experience in related environmental work; or equivalent combination of training and experience.

Factor: Decision Making **Weight:** ______

1. Carrying out defined, technical tasks
2. Choosing appropriate defined, technical tasks
3. Interpreting rules and guidelines for implementing tasks
4. Allocating resources to tasks
5. Overall, strategic choices regarding tasks

Job 1: ______________________ Factor Ranking _________
Job 2: ______________________ Factor Ranking _________
Job 3: ______________________ Factor Ranking _________
Job 4: ______________________ Factor Ranking _________
Job 5: ______________________ Factor Ranking _________
Job 6: ______________________ Factor Ranking _________

Factor: Effort **Weight:**______

1. Repetitive (simple, single task repeated for each new case or client)
2. Patterned (set of interrelated tasks that follow a consistent path or procedure)
3. Interpretive (employee must determine which tasks are appropriate for each case or client)
4. Adaptive (although standard operating procedures govern the application of tasks, these are general guidelines that require "fine-tuning" or the exercise of judgment about which applies)
5. Uncharted (because tasks are unlikely to fit standardized categories, creative solutions are needed in order to fulfill organizational requirements)

Job 1: ______________________ Factor Ranking _________
Job 2: ______________________ Factor Ranking _________
Job 3: ______________________ Factor Ranking _________
Job 4: ______________________ Factor Ranking _________
Job 5: ______________________ Factor Ranking _________
Job 6: ______________________ Factor Ranking _________

Factor: Skill/Education **Weight:_______**

1. Basic skills in reading, writing, and arithmetic
2. Vocational abilities with regard to a specific set of equipment or processes
3. Technical skills in the application of sets of equipment or processes
4. Professional knowledge of a complex area of endeavor
5. Advanced analytical abilities

Job 1: ________________________ Factor Ranking _________
Job 2: ________________________ Factor Ranking _________
Job 3: ________________________ Factor Ranking _________
Job 4: ________________________ Factor Ranking _________
Job 5: ________________________ Factor Ranking _________
Job 6: ________________________ Factor Ranking _________

Job/Factor Matrix

	Factor 1	Factor 2	Factor 3	Total
Weight	______	________	________	
Job 1:	________	________	________	_____
Job 2:	________	________	________	_____
Job 3:	________	________	________	_____
Job 4:	________	________	________	_____
Job 5:	________	________	________	_____
Job 6:	________	________	________	_____

EXERCISE 3: STRATEGIC PLANNING (Brainstorming)

1. Focusing on either a substantive problem or its possible solutions, have the students take five minutes to write down their thoughts. Because all students will have written down their ideas, this both encourages their participation and alleviates any reluctance with regard to "showing off."
2. Using large Post-it® notes and a magic marker™ (flip charts and magic marker™ or chalk and chalkboard), call on students one at a time to share one of their ideas (noting that the idea has already been mentioned by a previous student is acceptable). The instructor should call on each student in class at least once. Continue until a large number of suggestions have been obtained or the generation of new suggestions has been exhausted.
3. With class participation, the instructor can rearrange the Post-it® notes to reflect common problems or solutions. Ultimately, these can be grouped into a Ishikawa cause-and-effect or fishbone chart.
4. For problem solutions (if time permits), the class can engage in a Policy Spectrum extension to brainstorming. In Policy Spectrum, the individual solutions are examined. First, students list why each solution will likely work. Only then will students focus on the shortcomings evident in any proposed solution. However, it is incumbent on any student who identifies a shortcoming to suggest a means for correcting it.

SUGGESTED SUBSTANTIVE ISSUES FOR BRAINSTORMING:

1. Development of recruitment practices for police officers, nurses, information technology professionals, and so on
2. Development of intrinsic rewards for motivating productivity
3. Development of family-friendly practices
4. Development of sustainable-environment practices [note: examines the effects of piggybacking a valued outside task onto the organization]
5. Development of an orientation program for new employees and their families

EXERCISE 4: HUMAN RESOURCE PLANNING (Cutback Management)

Human resource planning translates the efforts devoted to strategic planning into operational road maps. Human resource planning focuses on the people and their need to make things happen. First, an environmental scan of the current situation—goals, organizations, people, resources, and legal strictures—is required. You need to know where you are and what is within the realm of the possible. Although you certainly want to conduct sensitivity analyses exploring differing options, the emphasis is upon their doability. The environmental scan is followed by a forecast of the desired future organization. What are the new goals and purposes, and what resources (especially people and skills) are necessary to make them happen? Third, an analysis of the current human resource inventory is performed. Always remember that people are the primary assets of any organization. After all, organizations are merely the informal and formal rules for enabling people to work together. What existing people fit into the new organization? This involves not only an assessment of already-existing skills but what can be accomplished through training and development efforts. Current employees possess tremendous organizational knowledge, which is just as essential as specific job skills for achieving organizational success.

Even under circumstances involving cutback management, the focus should be on the "new" organization. Although the immediate task may be the elimination of positions (and the people who occupy them), the manager needs to psychologically turn this into a focus on staffing the organization's future needs. Even though the situation is the same, cognitive heuristics demonstrate quite different decision-making strategies that come into play. Damage control, loss avoidance, and restoring the status quo focus attention on different elements from those involved in restructuring an organization's mission.

The uncertainty entailed even in the most positive of changes induces fears and anxieties. It is therefore extremely important to keep the employees informed, if not actively involved in the process. Otherwise, the organization will simultaneously suffer from countless rumors, mostly false and negative. How changes affect individuals should be clearly outlined. Job changes should be guided by objective criteria divorced of the influence from the single, vivid characteristics associated with specific individuals. Human resource plans often include the calculation of a "bumping rights" formula by which an individual accrues "points" that rank his or her entitlement for positions that he or she is qualified to fill.

Outplacement services for those to be let go are also important. These are, especially in the public sector, individuals who have provided loyal and valued service.

Failure to treat these individuals with courtesy and human dignity sends an extremely strong and negative message to all the employees you do want or are able to retain.

You are the vice president for human resources at Great Northern University (GNU). Great Northern is a state-assisted university serving 20,000 undergraduate and 5,000 graduate students with faculty and contract service (FCS) and Civil Service (CS) employees totaling over 7,000. A citizen-initiated tax referendum has recently been passed forcing cutbacks in nonmandated, discretionary spending. GNU falls into that category.

You have been ordered to reduce the forty-four position GNU Human Resources Department by 15 percent (seven positions). In addition, you are committed to creating a Financial Planning operation within the Human Resources Department. Certified financial planning staff would be provided to coordinate and advise employees on retirement and intermediate investments and assist with current family budgeting.

The current organization and functions of the Human Resources Department is provided below.

ADMINISTRATION (3) The vice president's office and immediate staff.

BENEFITS (7) Coordinates all retirement, health, sick leave, and workers compensation/disability

EMPLOYMENT AND COMPENSATION (2) Administrative office for units responsible for hiring and paying

Classification (6) Job analysis and evaluation
Employment (6) Oversees hiring and selection
Temporary Services (2) Oversees hiring and selection of contingent/temporary workers
Salary Administration (7) Payroll and data/records management

EMPLOYEE RELATIONS (5) Oversees civil service employees' grievance and discipline process

TRAINING (6) Oversees contractual and internal provision of staff development and computer training. Computer training focuses on supporting GNU's efforts at management decentralization.

A roster of current employees and vacant positions is provided. Information on position, seniority, education, party identification, performance rating, age, sex, and race is available.

first name	surname	position	years	degree	education	party
ADMINISTRATION						
Kathy	Meyers	Vice-President	2	MPA	PubAdm	D
Deborah	Bricker	Admin Asst	4	BA	Eng	I
Dick	Whitt	Pgm Consultant	1	BS	Econ	D
BENEFITS						
Alan	Appel	Director	1	MA	Eng	R
Enid	Murphy	Benefits Mgr	5	BA	BusAdm	D
Paula	Kure	Work Comp/Disability	4	HS		R
Corrinda	Chambers	Benefits Counselor	8	BA	PolSci	I
Barbara	Littler	Clerk-Typist	7	HS		D
Donna	Whalen	Receptionist	3	BA	PolSci	D
Adam	Keely	Benefits Counselor	5	MPA	PubAdm	I
EMPLOYMENT AND COMPENSATION						
Veronica	Jeffers	Director	9	MBA	BusAdm	D
Patricia	Pittman	Staff Asst	6	HS		D
CLASSIFICATION						
Jean	Johnson	Asst Director	7	MA	Eng	R
Elaine	DeWitt	Class Analyst	12	BA	BusAdm	D
Carol	Casey	Class Analyst	6	BA	Econ	D
Victoria	Komoroff	Per Analyst	7	BA	PubAdm	D
Lise	Dole	Class Analyst	2	BA	Hist	D
Kathey	Kincade	Class Analyst	2	BS	PolSci	D
EMPLOYMENT						
Maria	Schmidt	Manager	5	BA	Econ	R
Lee Ann	Aikens	Receptionist	4	BA	Eng	R
Louise	Green	Receptionist	2	HS	D	
Enrique	Obregon	Emp Spec	4	BA	Comm	D
Angela	Angell	Emp Spec	4	BA	Eng	I
Toni	Yong	Emp Spec	3	BS	CompSci	I
TEMPORARY SERVICES						
Mavis	Harris	Coordinator	7	MA	Hist	D
Susan	Kennedy	Acct Clerk	3	BS	Acct	I
SALARY ADMINISTRATION						
Robert	Cooper	Manager	10	BA	Urban	R
Eunice	McCloud	Per Asst	6	MPA	PubAdm	D
Jae Ho	Kim	Records/Policy Sup	3	BA	Comm	I
Annette	Esposito	Per Asst	5	BA	PolSci	R
Nicholas	Charles	Per Asst	4	BS	BusAdm	D
Becky	Walton	Data Proc Asst	3	BA	Eng	R
Lynn	Terzano	Computer Systems C	3	MS	CompSci	I
EMPLOYEE RELATIONS						
Dianne	Ireland	Director	13	MA	Eng	I
Laurie	Narsaki	Secretary	5	BA	Eng	I
Tina	Dunbar	Emp Rel Spec	7	BA	Psych	R
Lindsay	Brooks	Emp Rel Spec	4	BA	Psych	D
vacant		Emp Rel Spec	0			
TRAINING						
Michele	McAvoy	Manager	5	PhD	Ed	D
Daniel	Malone	Computer Train Mgr	3	MA	Ed	R
Morgana	Fay	Staff Dev Tech	1	HS	I	
Melissa	Hadar	Computer Train Spec	2	BA	PolSci	D
Jerome	Hall	Comm Spec	3	BA	Comm	D
vacant		Computer Train Spec	0			

perapp	age	sex	race	religion	marital	children	vet	dis
Out	43	F	W	Cat	M	3		
Esat	27	F	B	Cat	S			
Sat	35	M	W	Luth	S			
Sup	52	M	W		D	2	Y	
Esat	44	F	W	Mor	M	5		
Unsat	32	F	B	AME	M	3		
Unsat	28	F	W	SBAT	M	2		
Esat	25	F	B	AME	S	1		Y
Sup	24	F	W	Meth	M			
Out	37	M	W	Cat	M		Y	
Out	57	F	B	Cat	W	3		
Unsat	52	F	W	J	M	2		
Out	53	F	B	E	M	4		
Sat	62	F	W		M	2		
Sat	34	F	W	Gk O	S			
Sat	34	F	B	Muslim	M	3		
Sat	23	F	W	D Reform	M	1		
Sat	24	F	B	E	D	2		
Esat	42	F	H	Cat	D	3		
Out	23	F	W	Pre	M			
Out	20	F	W	Pre	S	1		Y
Esat	28	M	H	Cat	S		Y	
Sup	27	F	B	SBat	M	1		
Sup	28	F	A	Meth	W	2		
Sat	32	F	B	Pre	M			
Sat	27	F	B	Cat	S		Y	
Sup	49	M	W	Luth	M	2	Y	
Out	36	F	W	Pre	M			
Esat	43	M	A	Bud	M	1	Y	
Esat	42	F	H	J	M	2		
Out	38	M	W	GkO	S		Y	
Esat	26	F	B		D	2		
Esat	27	F	W	Cat	S			
Esat	48	F	B	Muslim	S			
Sup	37	F	W		S	1		
Out	45	F	W	E	M	4	Y	Y
Sat	39	M	NA	S	1			
Sup	32	F	W	E	M	1		
Esat	32	M	B	Cat	M	2		
Sat	19	F	W		M	1		
Unsat	24	F	B	Muslim	M	2		
Sat	25	M	W		M	1		

EXERCISE 5: HIRING

The Director of Benefits position is vacant at Great Northern University. Vice President for Human Resources Frederick Mosher has asked you to serve on the selection committee. Following the appropriate announcement of this position (see below), a substantial (and adequate) number of applications were received. The committee has winnowed through these and narrowed the choice to the remaining four finalists. Your job is to select of these individuals for the position of University Benefits Director.

OPTIONAL INTERVIEW

The exercise can be expanded to include the interview of candidates. Prior to the class in which the exercise is to be performed, students can be assigned roles as job candidates in order to familiarize themselves with the individual resumes. The remaining students would then serve as the selection committee conducting the interview. (You may wish to divide the remaining students into a number of selection groups and have the job candidates separately interview before each.) The selection committee should meet prior to the interviews and decide on how they will proceed. Although most texts approach applications and interviews as independent selection tests, they are most often used in conjunction. Hence, the application (cover letter and resume) provides information that helps shape the nature and direction of the interview. In addition to a standard set of questions to be asked of all candidates (some of which may have been answered in the application itself), the application may lead to or suggest unique questions or concerns.

GNU JOB DESCRIPTION

UNIVERSITY BENEFITS DIRECTOR

The University Benefits Director oversees the administration of State-legislated and university-based benefit programs for faculty and contract service (FCS) and for Civil Service (CS) employees totaling over 7,000. This includes analyzing and initiating new benefit plans through research and developing proposals and recommendations; developing, planning, and implementing workshops, training sessions, and seminars; analyzing, developing, documenting, and revising university benefit policies and benefit plans and insurance policies; developing and issueing communications concerning legislated and voluntary benefit plans; maintaining contact with federal and state regulating agencies, insurance and investment companies, financial planners, and consultants to ensure appropriate administration of benefit plans. Also, acts as benefit advisor to the GNU Compensation and Benefits Committee as well as the subcommittees. Represents Benefits Office on the State Public Administrators Liability Insurance Committee.

Mary Follett

1861 Magnolia Avenue
Jackson, Mississippi 39211
May 19, 2001

Dr. Frederick Mosher
Vice President for Human Resources
Great Northern University
Des Moines, Iowa 55102

Dear Dr. Mosher:

It is with great pride that I submit my resume to you for the position of Director of Benefits. I have worked in the human resources field for more than thirteen years with broad exposure to the overall administration and development of employee benefit plans. I have been directly involved in the administration of each plan, the development and dissemination of written communication (brochures, flyers, and news articles), advising and counseling employees, and the ongoing task of monitoring the day-to-day operation.

My personal qualifications include: the ability to communicate effectively with employees of varied economic and cultural backgrounds; attention to details; excellent organization skills; self-motivated; self-starter who is committed to a long-term career in the human resources field; and the ability to problem-solve and make decisions.

As a benefits specialist, I know the importance of keeping abreast of changes in the benefits area and having all the facts to help employees make informed decisions. I enjoy my work and would indeed welcome the opportunity to discuss the Director's position and the experience I have to offer in an interview.

For your review, I have enclosed two letters of recommendation. References are available upon request. If you should have any other questions, please call me at 601-555-4570.

Mary Follett
University Benefits Manager

ds enclosures

RESUME

MARY PARKER FOLLETT
1861 Magnolia Avenue
Jackson, Mississippi 39211
601-555-4570

OBJECTIVE: Director of Benefits

EDUCATION: Graduated 1989 from the University of Tennessee. Received Bachelor of Science Degree in Business Administration, with emphasis in Personnel Management.

PROFESSIONAL ACHIEVEMENTS:

Over ten years' experience in Personnel Administration. Skills developed in recruitment of nonexempt personnel, benefits administration, EEO compliance, and training.

Presently completing course requirements for Public Managers' Program.

EXPERIENCE:

May 2000–Present University Benefits Manager
June 1998–April 2000 Assistant Benefits Manager
Jackson State University
Jackson, Mississippi 39211

Responsibilities include overseeing and providing technical assistance for the administration of State-legislated and University-based benefit programs for over 3,000 JSU employees; interpreting and applying the Mississippi General Statutes that govern the State Retirement System, the optional retirement program, and the Comprehensive Health Care Program; interpreting and applying federal and state regulations that govern voluntary benefit plans; developing and disseminating information to University employees through written and oral communication; analyzing and recommending benefit plan and policy changes; maintaining contact with federal and state regulatory agencies, insurance, and investment companies to ensure appropriate administration of benefit plans; monitoring salary reduction agreements to ensure compliance with Internal Revenue Codes; developing, organizing, and facilitating orientation program for new employees, as well as pre-retirement planning workshops for employees approaching retirement; developing media announcements and course materials used in pre-retirement workshops; coordinating special projects such as the annual benefits statement, staff employee handbook, and creation or revision of benefit brochures and flyers; serving specifically as "personal counselor" for faculty and staff in the President's and Provost's areas and to other JSU employees in general; supervising and directing the work flow of three benefits counselors, a clerk-typist, and clerk-receptionist.

September 1993–March 1998 Personnel Specialist
Northern Telecom
Nashville, Tennessee

Responsibilities included recruiting, interviewing, and assisting in the selection of nonexempt personnel for the Corporate Headquarters and field projects; supervising the administration of benefit programs for all non-executive personnel, life and health insurance, the company's 401(k) investment plan, retirement, and tuition assistance programs; implementing the company's personnel policies and procedures; maintaining employee benefit records and departmental files; and the administration of the company's EEO and affirmative action programs to ensure federal compliance.

March 1990–September 1993 Administrative Clerk
Northern Telecom
Nashville, Tennessee

Implemented a training program for branch administrative staff (i.e., office managers) in personnel functions; coordinated and maintained employee records for multi-site location facilities (foreign and domestic); responsible for maintaining a log of all employee transactions such as hires, terminations, promotions, job transfers; scheduled salaried employees for performance appraisals; responsible for the in-processing of all new employees assigned to the Corporate Headquarters and foreign projects; provided clerical support to departmental managers as needed.

September 1989–December 1993 Part-time Instructor
Tennessee State University
Nashville, Tennessee

Responsibilities included instructing students in the fundamentals of typewriting and the manipulative parts of the typewriter; formatting letters, memos, manuscripts; setting up columnar copy; proofreading; care and maintenance of the typewriter.

May 17, 2001

Vice President
for Human Resources
Great Northern University
Des Moines, Iowa 55102

Dear Vice President:

I am responding to your May 3 advertisement in the *Des Moines Register* for a Director of Benefits. I believe my background in benefits administration closely matches your requirements. My qualifications for the position include:

—9 years of experience in managing employee benefit programs

—7 years in administration and development of benefit plans

—Extensive knowledge of Federal laws and taxes

—Customer service orientation and consulting skills

—Knowledge and utilization of on-line benefit systems

—MBA in Management

My resume is enclosed for your consideration. I look forward to discussing this excellent opportunity with you.

3232-K Hawkeye Drive
Des Moines, Iowa 55102

Enclosure

LOUIS BROWNLOW

3232-K Hawkeye Drive
Des Moines, Iowa 55102
(515)555-4321

SUMMARY

An experienced Administrator and Manager with a strong background in Employee Benefit Programs, Policy Formulation, Human Resources, Financial Planning and Management Information Systems. Ability to motivate employees, effectively communicate and provide innovative solutions.

EXPERIENCE

Rocket Popcorn, Inc., Ames, IA
1997 to Present
MANAGER, BENEFITS

Manage the health, welfare and retirement programs for 4,500 employees at three locations. Responsible for plan development and administration, policy formulation and interpretation, consulting services, benefit seminars and training.

Implemented service center concept to increase level of customer service. Expanded department's role in retirement counseling, administration of 401(k) hardship withdrawals, and review of policy interpretation. Coordinated conversion to a new health claims contractor. Established retiree club to increase awareness and knowledge of benefit programs for retirees and spouses. Restructured staff responsibilities to improve customer service on a proactive basis.

Brownlow, Merriam & Associates, Des Moines, IA.,
1994–1997
ADMINISTRATIVE and MANAGEMENT SERVICES

Founded business which provided managerial and technical employee benefit services to companies on a contract basis. Services included review and analysis of retirement and welfare benefit programs; recommendations for improved cost-effectiveness and plan administration; and coordination and implementation of program changes. Assignments involved:

- Coordinating a project to consolidate three 401(k) plans.
- Revising defined benefit pension plans to comply with Federal laws.
- Interim management of a branch office of a national HMO.
- Directing a survey to identify health insurance needs of small businesses.

State of Iowa, Des Moines, IA.
1987–1994
DEPUTY ADMINISTRATOR–DIRECTOR,
STATE HEALTH PLAN

Managed the health insurance program for the State of Iowa covering 630,000 members. Employed a professional staff, claims contractor, actuary, CPA's, attorneys and plan consultants. Responsible for expenditures exceeding $420 million for 2.1 million claims. Prepared legislation working with the General Assembly, State Departments and Universities, and employee groups.

- Established the State Health Plan Office to administer the self-insured health program and three Health Maintenance Organization (HMO) plans.
- Designed a monitoring system used to evaluate performance of the claims contractor.
- Converted an insured health program to a self-insured program.
- Provided ongoing training for over 300 health benefit representatives who coordinated the health insurance program for their departments. Reduced administrative costs to less than 3% of total health plan costs.

Hoover Foundation Health Plan, Inc., Palo Alto, CA.
1982 –1987
MANAGER, RETIREMENT ADMINISTRATION (1984–1987)

Managed the administration of 28 retirement plans covering 45,000 employees. Responsible for accounting, actuarial analysis, system design and benefits processing.

- Coordinated and monitored implementation of revised retirement system programs.
- Restructured the retirement plan unit improving retirement plan processing time frames.

EMPLOYEE BENEFITS ADMINISTRATOR (1982–1984)

- Planned and designed corporate employee benefit programs.
- Drafted plan documents and amendments to conform with ERISA.
- Negotiated with IRS for approval of retirement plans.

Brownlow, Gulick & Associates, San Jose, CA.
1981–1982
CONSULTANT–OWNER

Provided consulting services for compensation and benefit programs, performance evaluation systems and personnel policies.

Bankers' Trust Company, Des Moines, IA.
1978 - 1980
TRUST ADMINISTRATOR

Consulted with and advised corporations, attorneys and accountants regarding plan documents, laws, investments and administration.

USX Corporation, Newark, NJ.
1976 - 1978
SYSTEMS ANALYST - PROGRAMMER

Provided systems and programming support for personnel, accounting and payroll departments.

EDUCATION

MBA—Stanford, Management and Health Services

BS—University of South Florida, Business and Economics

CIVIC ACTIVITIES

- Councilman, District 4—City of Des Moines
- Public Works and Comprehensive Planning Committees
- Member Hawkeye Townhome Association—Board of Directors

OTHER

- State and Local Government Benefits Association—Board of Directors

ACTIVITIES

- Iowa Medical Database Commission—Advisor

1802 Jackson Avenue
Mankato, MN 56001
507-555-4299
May 20, 2001

Vice President for Human Resources
Great Northern University
Des Moines, IA 55102

Dear Sir or Madam:

Your recent advertisement for a Director of Benefits at GNU was of great interest to me.

As my resume indicates, I have eight years of experience as the director of benefits for the Green Giant Company. I also have six years experience in Operations Research working on a wide variety of problem-solving projects as indicated in my resume. Although these experiences are not in the public sector, the vast majority of skills should be transferable from the corporate world. My background includes all the qualifications mentioned in your advertisement, including a statistics minor. These skills should help me provide GNU with the leadership needed in this important and technical area.

Although Green Giant has been very good to me and it would be difficult for me to leave, I received two graduate degrees from GNU and have fond memories of the University and the Des Moines area. As a result, an opportunity to return to the area and work for GNU has great appeal to me. I look forward to talking with you about this position.

Please keep this application confidential.

Sincerely,

Charles Levine

CHARLES LEVINE

SUMMARY OF EXPERIENCE

I am currently Director of Benefits at the Green Giant Co. My prior experience at Green Giant was in the Operations Research Department where I served as an internal consultant on a wide variety of topics, some of which are highlighted below. In each position, I have successfully interacted with management at all levels of the company and with local and industry groups.

This experience was preceded by years at the University of Mississippi and Auburn University as an Instructor of Economics.

POSITIONS HELD
1995 to Present—Director of Benefits, Green Giant

Duties and accomplishments include:

- Developing, administering, and communicating insurance and retirement benefits at Green Giant in the U.S. and Canada.
- Managing the benefits department staff of 4 people and controlling the budget for the department.
- Structuring the requirements of a computer system for retirement plan administration and recordkeeping which includes real-time access to retirement benefit information. The computer system has automated most of the routine administrative functions.
- Coordinating the work of our outside legal counsel, actuary and consultants.
- Holding the company's medical insurance costs below the regional average, in both dollar and percent increase terms.
- Working with our investment manager to greatly increase member control of the investment of defined contribution plan account balances. Members can now change the investment of their account balances and/or the level of 401(k) contributions with a phone call. Also added a new investment option.
- Serving 6 years as a member of the Steering Committee for the food industry's annual compensation and benefits survey, chairing the Committee in three of those years.
- Participating in the process of selecting a new investment manager for all our defined contribution plan assets.
- Working with consultants to develop guidelines for measuring the performance of our retirement plan asset investment managers.
- Creating budget allowances for salary and bonus increases for various areas of the Company.

1989–1995—Operations Research Analyst, Green Giant

Activities in this position provided a broad exposure to many areas of Company responsibility. Details of some of my accomplishments are given below.

Manufacturing

- Guided the development and implementation of statistical quality control procedures at various locations.
- Worked on numerous other successful process improvement and quality improvement projects, including the development of computer simulations of manufacturing processes to eliminate bottlenecks, improve efficiency, and determine new machinery needs.

Marketing

- Developed a demonstration program on a portable computer which allowed marketers to illustrate to customers the importance of product quality and durability in determining true lifetime product cost and profitability.
- Developed a "billings analysis" program for one of our businesses which gave marketers detailed information on sales at each customer location so that problems and opportunities could be identified, quickly.
- Served as consultant for two customers on inventory control. Helped the customers restructure and reduce their inventories, improve their responsiveness to market demands, and lower costs.

Human Resources

- Developed a model to forecast the number of new managers needed monthly for the next three years and to identify where they will be needed. The program has been used successfully for the last six years.

1988–1989—Instructor of Economics, University of Mississippi

Taught Principles of Economics, U.S. Economic History, and Labor Economics and completed work on dissertation for Ph.D. degree.

1987–1988—Teaching Assistant, Great Northern University

Taught Principles of Economics and worked on dissertation for Ph.D. degree.

1986–1987—Instructor of Economics, Auburn University

Taught Statistics and Principles of Economics and worked on dissertation for Ph.D. degree.

1983–1986—Teaching Assistant, Great Northern University

Taught Principles of Economics while doing class work for my Masters and Ph.D. degrees in economics.

EDUCATION

B.A. in Economics, State University of New York at Binghamton, 1983
Masters in Economics, Great Northern University, 1985
Ph.D. in Economics, Great Northern University, 1990, minor in statistics

PERSONAL

Date of Birth: October 3, 1961
Residence: 1802 Jackson Avenue, Mankato, MN 56001
Telephone: Home - 507-555-1245
Office - 507-555-6310
Married with two children.

May 14, 2001

Vice President for Human Resources
Great Northern University
Des Moines, IA 55102

Dear Search Committee:

Please accept this letter and enclosed resume as application for the position, Director of Benefits at Great Northern University. I learned of the position from GinPA News 5/11/92.

More than fifteen years of progressively responsible experience in all aspects of employee benefits, in both the private and public sectors, has provided me with the skills and abilities necessary to the Director of Benefits.

As an experienced manager in Human Resources, I recognize the importance of our efforts to the mission of the university, and how those efforts must result in efficient and effective services to all constituencies. As a Native American, I understand the many sensitivities inherent in a culturally diverse community and have been able to incorporate this understanding into effective services. This combination of experience and sensitivity make me an ideal candidate.

I would welcome an opportunity to further explore this position and am looking forward to hearing from you.

Sincerely,

Joseph Nez Perce
125 Cherokee School Rd.
Raleigh, NC 27612
919-555-5689

Enclosure

JOSEPH NEZ PERCE
125 Cherokee School Rd.
Raleigh, NC 27612
(919)555-5689

SUMMARY OF QUALIFICATIONS

Comprehensive, service-oriented experience in Human Resources Management in both the public and private sectors.

Demonstrated effectiveness in planning and administration of compensation and benefits programs including program/plan design and implementation.

Proven ability to work independently and to provide the leadership and direction necessary to manage a pro-active Human Resources function.

Demonstrated understanding and knowledge of principles and practices, laws and regulations relating to Human Resources and ability to translate to organization policies and procedures.

Demonstrated proficiency in problem solving, supervision, and goal achievement.

Proven human relations and communication skills including the ability to work effectively with management and employees at all levels, in diverse environments.

PROFESSIONAL ACCOMPLISHMENTS

Installed compensation programs in both public and private sectors, including classification system for over 4,000 employees.

Supervised the selection and implementation of Human Resource Information Systems (Personnel and Payroll).

Designed, implemented and administered employee benefit plans for life, health, dental, auto and vision insurances.

Administered defined benefit and defined contribution retirement programs in public and private sector.

Administered U.S. Expatriate and TCN compensation program.

Administered Section 125 employee benefits plan including Flexible Spending accounts.

Managed compensation and benefits communication programs including design and production of Employee Benefits Statements.

Investigated and resolved EEOC charges.

Successfully recruited executive, supervisory and professional employees.

Participated in successful labor negotiations.

Designed and implemented standards-based performance appraisal system.

Planned and implemented video-based supervisory training and
HRD program.

WORK EXPERIENCE

1999 TO PRESENT —North Carolina State, University, Raleigh, NC 27695
ASSISTANT HUMAN RESOURCES DIRECTOR

Manage compensation and employee benefits departments serving 7,000 faculty and staff. Including job evaluation, classification, policy development, salary planning and budgeting, structure maintenance and employee benefits administration, including health, welfare and retirement programs.

1997 to 1999—City of Raleigh, Raleigh, North Carolina
HUMAN RESOURCES CONSULTANT

Administered pay-for-performance compensation program, designed and implemented salary planning and budgeting system, maintained salary structure, salary administration policies, data collections, analysis and operations budget analysis.

1992 to 1997—Family Health International, Durham, North Carolina
DIRECTOR HUMAN RESOURCES

Managed all Human Resources functions and services including policy development, recruitment, affirmative action, compensation, employee and management development, communications, employee benefits and HRIS for 1,500 employees in thirty-three facilities in seventeen states.

1989 to 1992—Glaxco Health Care Group, Raleigh, North Carolina
MANAGER, COMPENSATION AND BENEFITS

Designed, implemented and maintained total compensation systems (wages, salaries and benefits) and HRIS for 2,000 plus employees in four (4) business entities. Participated in labor negotiations.

1985 to 1989—Square D Company, Raleigh, North Carolina
CORPORATE MANAGER, COMPENSATION AND BENEFITS

Participated in labor negotiations and union avoidance campaigns. Developed personnel policies. Designed and implemented the company's first formal salary administration plan. Administered corporate employee benefits and implemented computerized Personnel information.

1982 to 1985—Rake and Hoe, Raleigh, North Carolina
MANAGER, PERSONNEL ADMINISTRATION

Supervised the Employment, Compensation, EEO and Records retention functions for 3,000 employee Manufacturing division. Responsible for Personnel Management Information System and U.S. Expatriate Compensation, labor contract negotiation, grievance handling, safety and hourly employment.

1981 to 1982—United States Steel Corporation, Cleveland, Ohio
STAFF ASSISTANT, PERSONNEL

Worked with the Training Department in administering apprenticeship program for over 100 apprentices in 18 different trades and crafts. Also held position of Safety Inspector for 2,000 employee Basic Steel division.

EDUCATION
Bachelor of Arts
Political Science Management
Cleveland State University, Cleveland, Ohio

MPA/Industrial Relations
Cleveland State University, Cleveland, Ohio

ACTIVE MEMBERSHIPS
American Compensation Association
American Society for Personnel Administration
Tri-University Personnel Association

References Furnished Upon Request

OTHER
Willing to travel
Able to relocate

COMMITTEES
Human Resources Information System Steering Committee
Human Resources Liaison Group
Native American Faculty/Staff Caucus
NCSU Board of Regents Benefits Steering Committee
Governor's ADA Task Force
Tri-University Job Evaluation Committee
Tri-University Employee Development Forum
University Insurance/Retirement Committee
NCSU Retirees Association Board Advisor
Minority Student Orientation Group
State of North Carolina Benefits Evaluation Panel

EXERCISE 6: PERFORMANCE APPRAISAL

The performance appraisal is used to assess the individual. It may measure separate or group-related activity. It can be focused on current performance, potential or future performance probabilities, or training and development needs. Performance appraisals can be invaluable as participative management tools for goal setting and feedback. They can also be used as aids for allocating rewards.

Objective appraisals are built around the job tasks individuals are asked to perform. They focus on measuring the extent to which (participative or mutually) predetermined goals and objectives have been achieved. Desired results can be stated in terms of either *expected* or *observed* standards.

The class will be divided into groups of three to four students. Each group shall choose one of the job analyses and construct a performance appraisal instrument for it. For each task statement in the job analysis, a list of behaviorally anchored performance standards that, at least, encompasses fully successful, intermediate, and unsuccessful performance levels will be constructed.

For each task statement, students should first *brainstorm* a list of performance examples. These examples should then be sorted out into different levels of expected or observed performance. Students may need to develop additional examples in order to ensure that all performance levels are included. Finally, the examples in each level are synthesized, integrated, and cuisinarted to produce a simplified, but concise, statement of the performance standard.

The Iowa *Performance Evaluation: Participant's Training Manual* (Burke, 1977; 49–50) illustrates typical approaches to writing objective performance standards.

> Objective standards fall into three categories or types and each of these types can be expressed in a way which best measures results expected.
>
> There are *Historical* standards which relate one period in time with another. For example: relating the upcoming year's gross earnings in relation to the previous year.
>
> There are *Engineered* standards which deal with numbers of things in specific time frames. For example: Forty-two (42) widgets made in one-half hour.
>
> There are *Comparative* standards which measure expected results in terms of a norm, for an industry, similar work unit, or employee performing the same duties. For example: The turnover rate among keypunch operators has been X percent. How does this compare with other employers in Iowa?
>
> To provide even greater clarity and flexibility, each of these Objective types of standards can be expressed in three different ways. The three ways of writing them are:
>
> Positive terms
> Negative terms
> Zero terms

For illustration three different expressions of each Objective standard follow:

Historical (Positive)—This year's gross revenues recovered from delinquent accounts will exceed last year's total by 4%.
(Negative)—There will be no more than a 1% increase in the number of complaints received this year.
(Zero)—There will be no increase in the hours dedicated to travel this year over last year.

Engineered (Positive)—The number of claims audited will be at least forty-two (42) each day.
(Negative)—No more than three (3) claims will be returned to you for a computation error in any week.
(Zero)—No client complaints about discourteous service will be received.

Comparative (Positive)—The average number of audits completed this year will be at least 50% of that of other field units.
(Negative)—The number of hours of downtime for your equipment will not exceed the department average by more than 1%.
(Zero)—No audit of either state or federal accounts will fail to meet published accounting guidelines of the State or Federal government.

PERCENTAGE WEIGHT—THE % COLUMN

Each major responsibility should be considered according to its importance to the total job. Here you are to first rank the major responsibilities in relation to each other.

Ranking your major responsibilities involves determining two factors:

Time spent.
Importance or consequence of error.

Consequence can include possible financial loss to the agency, physical injury, lost confidence on the part of a client, time required to correct the error, broken equipment, or psychological impact or stress on others.

Time simply refers to the number of hours involved in carrying out the particular responsibility. The two factors often go hand in hand, so the ranking is the result of a combined factoring. Use the following as a guide:

TIME

1. 0–5% of the time or 0–2 hours per week
2. 6–15% of the time or 2.5–6 hours per week
3. 16–25% of the time or 6.5–10 hours per week
4. 26–50% of the time or 10.5–20 hours per week
5. 50%+ of the time or 20+ hours per week

IMPORTANCE OF CONSEQUENCE

1. Virtually no damage
2. Very little damage
3. Moderate damage
4. Considerable damage
5. Extreme damage

A major responsibility could require only three hours per week time (2), but have the potential of causing considerable damage if an error is made (4) and would therefore have a combined factor ranking of 6.

When all the major responsibilities have been factored, then rank them on your worksheet by placing numbers alongside each major responsibility. Weighting major responsibilities involves determining the percentage or value of each major responsibility in proportion to all those major responsibilities being rated in this evaluation—not in terms of every duty.

It should be evident that those at the top of your list would normally receive the highest weighting. This weighting is expressed in terms of percent of 100, or its decimal equivalent. For example: If your highest ranked major responsibility represents 40% of the major responsibilities listed, then the figure 40% or .40 should be placed in the "%" column.

Requirement: Percentage Weights MUST total 100%.

For each task statement, indicate its importance to the overall job and the extent of time involved in carrying it out. The weighting formula can be either additive or multiplicative.

PERFORMANCE STANDARDS

Hard Data

Output

- Units produced
- Tons manufactured
- Items assembled
- Money collected
- Items sold
- Forms processed
- Loans approved
- Inventory turnover
- Patients visited
- Applications processed
- Students graduated
- Tasks completed
- Output per person-hour
- Productivity
- Work backlog
- Incentive bonus
- Shipments

Costs

- Budget variances
- Unit costs
- Cost by account
- Variable costs
- Fixed costs
- Overhead costs
- Operating costs
- Number of cost reductions
- Project cost savings
- Accident costs
- Program costs
- Sales expenses

Time

- Equipment downtime
- Overtime
- On-time shipments
- Time to project completion
- Processing time
- Supervisory time
- Break-in time for new employees
- Training time
- Meeting schedules
- Repair time
- Efficiency
- Work stoppages
- Order response
- Late reporting
- Lost-time days

Quality

- Scrap
- Waste
- Rejects
- Error rate
- Rework
- Shortages
- Product defects
- Deviation from standard
- Product failures
- Inventory adjustments
- Time card corrections
- Percentages of tasks completed properly
- Number of accidents

Performance Standards Soft Data

Work Habits

- Absenteeism
- Tardiness
- Visits to the dispensary
- First aid treatments
- Violations of safety rules
- Number of communication breakdowns
- Excessive breakage

Work Climate

- Number of grievances
- Number of discrimination charges
- Employee complaints
- Job satisfaction
- Unionization avoidance
- Employee turnover

Feelings/Attitudes

- Favorable reactions
- Attitude changes
- Perceptions of job responsibilities
- Perceived changes in performance
- Employee loyalty

New Skills

- Decisions made
- Problems solved
- Conflicts avoided
- Grievances resolved
- Counseling problems solved
- Listening skills
- Reading speed
- Discrimination charges resolved
- Intention to use new skill
- Frequency of use of new skill

Development/ Advancement

- Number of promotions
- Number of pay increases
- Number of training programs attended
- Requests for transfer
- Performance appraisal ratings
- Increases in job effectiveness

Initiative

- Implementation of new ideas
- Successful completion of projects
- Number of suggestions submitted
- Number of suggestions implemented

Task Statement 1: ______________________________

____

Students should first brainstorm a list of performance examples. These examples should then be sorted out into different levels of expected or observed performance.

Task Statement 2: ______________________________

____

Students should first brainstorm a list of performance examples. These examples should then be sorted out into different levels of expected or observed performance.

Task Statement 3: ______________________________

____

Students should first brainstorm a list of performance examples. These examples should then be sorted out into different levels of expected or observed performance.

Task Statement 4: ______________________________

____

Students should first brainstorm a list of performance examples. These examples should then be sorted out into different levels of expected or observed performance.

Task Statement 5: ______________________________

____

Students should first brainstorm a list of performance examples. These examples should then be sorted out into different levels of expected or observed performance.

Task Statement 6: ______________________________

____

Students should first brainstorm a list of performance examples. These examples should then be sorted out into different levels of expected or observed performance.

Performance Appraisal Task 1: ____________________
Performance Level Weight: ______

1. ______________________________
____
____
____

2. ______________________________
____
____
____

3. ____
____
____
____

4. ____
____
____
____

5. ____
____
____
____

Performance Appraisal Task 2: ______________________
Performance Level Weight: _____

1. ____
____
____
____

2. ____
____
____
____

3. ____
____
____
____

4. ____
____
____
____

5. ____
____
____
____

Performance Appraisal Task 3: ______________________
Performance Level Weight: _____

1. ____
____
____
____

2. ____
____
____
____

3. ______________________________

4. ______________________________

5. ______________________________

Performance Appraisal Task 4: ______________________________
Performance Level Weight: ______

1. ______________________________

2. ______________________________

3. ______________________________

4. ______________________________

5. ______________________________

Performance Appraisal Task 5: ______________________________
Performance Level Weight: ______

1. ______________________________

2. ____
____
____
____

3. ____
____
____
____

4. ____
____
____
____

5. ____
____
____
____

Performance Appraisal Task 6: ____________________
Performance Level Weight: ______

1. ____
____
____
____

2. ____
____
____
____

3. ____
____
____
____

4. ____
____
____
____

5. ____
____
____
____

EXERCISE 7: NEGOTIATION (COLLECTIVE BARGAINING)

Negotiation is central to the formulation and implementation of public policy. It is most clearly seen in the collective bargaining process between management and employees. As such, it can run the gamut from an adversarial tug-of-war (or even a scorched-earth confrontation) to the principled-negotiation ideal of win-win bargaining.

Principled negotiation advocates an objective approach in which the involved parties focus on the interests that underlie the negotiations rather than the positions taken. Why do people want what they're asking for? What do they hope to achieve by it? Principled negotiation also recognizes the intertwined emotional aspects and symbolic content and carefully works at addressing and diffusing them from the objective analysis of the interests. Principled negotiation strives for solutions that represent mutual gains. This process is assisted by insisting on the use of objective, measurable criteria.

Those involved in any negotiation must also contemplate what will happen if there is no agreement (or if it is less than they desire). What is your "best alternative to a negotiated agreement" (BATNA)? If realistically calculated, this is your "bottom line." You don't have to settle for anything less. In negotiating, you also have to assess both your intentions and the other party's intentions. How does each side view the agreement/relationship? Is the relationship a short-term, single event or part of a valued, long-term arrangement?

This exercise endeavors to involve as many students as possible in the actual negotiations. The class can be divided into sets of three-person management and three-person employee teams (with the addition of a mediator or arbitrator). Although only one individual per team participates in the formal negotiation sessions, the other team members are there to observe and participate in the recess discussions.

Negotiations formally begin with the employees presenting their proposals, directly followed by management's response (management may agree to employee proposals and introduce their own). Formally, only items introduced at this point are on the table for discussion. Formally, new items cannot be introduced later. Of course, one must remember that ultimately everything is negotiable. At this point, employees and management recess to consider each other's proposals. Following a prearranged time period, they meet again and respond to each other and begin to negotiate in earnest. The employment of a mediator greatly facilitates the administrative aspects of the negotiations. A mediator will keep a record of the negotiations and what was agreed to. A mediator will also manage the timing of negotiations and recesses. Mediators can also direct negotiations toward the items most likely to produce agreement.

COLLECTIVE BARGAINING EXERCISE

The City and the Waterworkers Association are involved in renegotiating the contract governing the employment conditions for employees working at the Water Pollution Control Plant. The Waterworkers Association includes all Water Department employees—maintenance, plant operators, maintenance truck drivers, and laboratory technicians.

The city has a rapidly growing population that has doubled in the past decade and is expected to double again in the next. This has provided a relatively good tax base for the city. However, the population is now composed largely of young people who are just starting families. Although their incomes are generally very good, most have hefty mortgage payments and upscale lifestyles. At the last election, the City Council shifted from two liberals (who support services and the taxes to pay for them, financed by economic development growth if need be), three moderates (who support services, are wishy-washy on taxes, and oppose growth), and one conservative (pro-growth and antitax) to three moderates and three conservatives. The moderate, weak-style mayor expects to face a conservative challenge in the next election. Economic development has been fueled, in part, by the plentiful, cheap, and reliable supply of water for industry and home. Any disruption of the Waterworks would have adverse consequences on future development. Although benefits are relatively good, waterworker salaries are now well below the median in the city. Few new employees can actually afford to live in the city itself.

A contract and list of issues is provided below. This exercise can be performed with three options. In larger classes, different groups can be assigned each option. Afterward, the concluding discussion can compare and contrast these differences. If only one option is used, the one involving mediation is preferred. The exercise may also be conducted with the students assigned specific roles to play.

Option 1: Negotiation

This option allows students to come to grips with the collective bargaining process all on their own. This often results in a great deal of floundering around and frustration. However, this reflects what happens quite often in real life. Given the time limits of in-class exercises, it is quite likely that students will be unable to reach an agreement or that under these artificial pressures they will reach an unsatisfactory agreement. Again, this reflects reality and points out the subsequent problems that carrying out or implementing the agreement may give rise to.

Option 2: Negotiation with Mediator

Mediators are the midwives of negotiation. Their role can vary from being a neutral observer to that of the crucial player who is really putting together the agreement. However, mediators are never able to order or impose decisions; they can only suggest and quietly coach. The mediator's task is to assist the parties in arriving at a mutually acceptable agreement. For neophytes, they help educate the parties in how to negotiate. For intransigents, they provide a forum for continued discussion and may even serve to float trial balloons for breaking impasses. Mediators keep a record of discussions and what was agreed to. Mediators will manage the timing of negotiations and recesses. Finally, mediators try to build confidence and trust among the parties. In doing this, they will attempt to focus on issues more likely to result in agreement and build upon these successes. In extreme cases, mediators may introduce their own trial balloons and steer the negotiations toward an agreement.

Option 3: Negotiation with Arbitration

Arbitrators decide. They impose their judgment onto the failed negotiations. They are an impartial third party who, depending on the arbitration format, may "mix and match" proposals or (as under final-offer arbitration) choose a "winner-takes-all." Because the arbitrator imposes a solution, this agreement may suffer added problems in the implementation stage.

Management Roles:

1. *Water Wizard:* The Water Wizard created the Water Pollution Control Plant. The Water Wizard is very paternalistic about this creation. While a strong advocate for the Waterworkers, the Water Wizard is rather antiunion (which is viewed as an indicator of disharmony and distrust). Specifically, the Water Wizard thinks that a grievance and discipline system insults his/her character and fairness. He/She also opposes merit pay as an unnecessary and divisive influence. However, the Water Wizard favors full funding of the family health care option.
2. *City Manager:* The City Manager wants to keep his/her job (after all, this is a truly wonderful place to live). Pleasing the City Council—encouraging economic development while avoiding tax increases—is paramount. Introducing a merit pay concept (as long as it doesn't cost too much) and controlling escalating health care costs are of major importance.
3. *Human Resources Director:* The HR Director is an advocate of progressive personnel practices. The broadbanding proposal is his/her "baby." The HR Director also favors the introduction of a grievance system. However, he/she opposes changes in vacation benefits due to cost. Similarly, the HR Director is concerned about health care costs.

Labor Roles:

1. *Waterworkers Association Chancellor:* The union head is a Lab Chemist II with over 16 years of experience. He/She favors changes in the vacation system and opposes the proposed retirement changes.
2. *Lab Technician II* (with 6–10 years of experience): With four young children he/she is a strong advocate for the family health care package. The Lab Technician II is the "spokesperson" for the younger workers and is considering a challenge to the Chancellor at the next union election.
3. *Plant Operator III* (with 11–15 years of experience): As a "maxed out" employee, he/she favors the change in pay increases. He/She also doesn't like the retirement changes proposed by management.
4. *Maintenance III* (with 0–5 years of experience): As a younger worker, he/she favors pay increases in any form and considers family health care an important factor.

CONTRACT

Article I: Recognition

The City recognizes the Waterworkers Association as the sole and exclusive bargaining agent for employees classified as maintenance, plant operator, maintenance truck driver, or laboratory technician. The City will deduct from each employee a monthly dues. Upon notification from an employee, his/her dues contribution will be redirected to an approved charitable organization. However, the Waterworkers Association shall be allowed to recover any general representational expenses.

Article II: Management Rights

The City retains the right to determine the mission and set the performance standards for the Water Pollution Control Plant Department. The City retains the right to plan and direct operations, to hire, transfer, suspend, demote, discipline or discharge for cause, and promote employees, subject to any provisions provided for in this agreement.

Article III: Grievance Procedure

Employees will verbally present any grievance to their immediate supervisor. If unresolved, a written appeal can be made to the Water Wizard. The Water Wizard's finding can be appealed to the City Manager.

Article IV: Wages and Benefits

Section 1: Salary Schedule (range: 25% in 10 steps)

Employees automatically receive an in-grade step increase annually until they reach the maximum salary.

	Min	Mid	Max
Maintenance Schedule			
Maintenance I	15	18	20
Maintenance II	17	20	22
Maintenance III	19	22	24
Maintenance Electrician I	21	24	27
Maintenance Electrician II	23	26	29
Maintenance Electrician III	25	28	32
Plant Operator Schedule			
Plant Operator I	17	20	22
Plant Operator II	19	22	24
Plant Operator III	21	24	27
Maintenance Truck Driver Schedule			
Maintenance Truck Driver I	17	20	22
Maintenance Truck Driver II	19	22	24
Maintenance Truck Driver III	21	24	27
Maintenance Truck Driver IV	23	26	29
Laboratory Technician Schedule			
Laboratory Technician I	20	22	25
Laboratory Technician II	22	25	28
Laboratory Chemist I	25	28	32
Laboratory Chemist II	28	32	35
Senior Laboratory Chemist	32	36	40

Section 2: Vacation

Vacation shall be accrued at the following rates:

Recruitment through fifth year:	1 week
Sixth through tenth year:	2 weeks
Eleventh through fifteenth year:	3 weeks
Sixteenth and later years:	4 weeks

Section 3: Group Insurance

The City participates in the State-Local Health Plan and shall pay the entire cost of the "employees only" option ($100/month). The City shall also pay half the cost of the "family" option (full cost = $150/month).

With ten years' service, Waterworkers are eligible to retire at age 60 or after 25 years' service with full pension (75% of last five-year salary average)

Section 4: Sick Leave

Each employee accrues six (6) days sick leave during his/her first year of employment and twelve (12) days every subsequent year. Unused sick leave can be converted to time-in-grade for purposes of retirement.

ISSUES FOR NEGOTIATION

Article I:

Management wants to introduce a positive dues checkoff where employee must formally designate that he/she wants the payroll deduction to be made.

Article III: Grievance Process

The Waterworkers Association wants the introduction of a mediation option, independent of the Water Pollution Control Plant Department's chain of command.

Article IV:

1. Salary Schedule
   Management wants to institute broadbanding job analyses. Management wants to eliminate the in-grade step system and automatic step increases. Supervisors are to have the flexibility to allocate pay levels within each category. All individual pay increases are to be determined on the basis of performance.

   Waterworkers Association wants a 10% increase. It wants pay increases for those who have "maxed out" at their grade-level equivalent to the regular step increase.

2. Vacation
   Waterworkers Association wants one week added to all employee vacation allotments. Unused vacation can be applied to time-served for purposes of retirement.
3. Group Insurance
   City wants to discontinue payment for "family" option. Waterworkers Association wants full payment for "family" option.
   City wants to change full retirement to age 65 (with ten years of service). City wants to eliminate retirement after twenty-five years of service regardless of age.
4. Sick Leave
   Management wants accumulated sick leave capped at 120 days. It wants formal program of approval on use of sick leave.

STAFFING ROSTER

	0–5	6–10	11–15	16+
Maintenance				
Maintenance I	10	12	–	–
Maintenance II	9	15	12	–
Maintenance III	2	13	21	4
Maintenance Electrician I	–	7	12	7
Maintenance Electrician II	–	5	12	9
Maintenance Electrician III	–	7	8	2
Plant Operator				
Plant Operator I	17	5	–	–
Plant Operator II	9	13	7	–
Plant Operator III	2	14	12	3
Maintenance Truck Driver				
Maintenance Truck Driver I	17	20	–	–
Maintenance Truck Driver II	19	22	12	–
Maintenance Truck Driver III	–	24	27	–
Maintenance Truck Driver IV	–	12	8	9
Laboratory Technician				
Laboratory Technician I	6	5	–	–
Laboratory Technician II	2	4	2	–
Laboratory Chemist I	1	2	4	–
Laboratory Chemist II	1	4	6	5
Senior Laboratory Chemist	–	–	3	2

References

Aamodt, Michael G., Devan A. Bryan, and Alan J. Whitcomb (1993) "Predicting Performance with Letters of Recommendation." *Public Personnel Mangement* 22, 1 (Spring): 81–90.

Abelson, Robert P. (1976) "Script Processing in Attitude Formuation and Decisionmaking," in J. Carroll and J. Payne, eds., *Cognitive and Social Behavior.* Hillsdale, NJ: Erlbaum.

Aberbach, Joel D., Robert D. Putnam, and Bert A. Rockman (1981) *Bureaucrats and Politicians in Western Democracy.* Cambridge, MA: Harvard University Press.

Aberbach, Joel D., and Bert Rockman (1976) "Clashing Beliefs Within the Executive Branch: The Nixon Administration Bureaucracy." *American Political Science Review* 70 (June): 456–468.

Aberbach, Joel, and Bert Rockman (1988) "Mandates or Mandarins? Control and Discretion in the Modern Administrative State." *Public Administration Review* 48, 2 (March/April): 606–612.

Abraham, Yohannan T., and Mary V. Moore (1995) "Comparable Worth: Is It a Moot Issue? Part III." *Public Personnel Management* 24, 3 (Fall): 291–313.

Adams, J. Stacy (1963) "Toward an Understanding of Inequity." *Journal of Abnormal and Social Psychology* 67 (November): 422–426.

Albrecht, Karl (1978) *Successful Management By Objectives: An Action Manual.* Englewood Cliffs, NJ: Prentice Hall.

Alderfer, Clayton (1972) *Existence, Relatedness, and Growth: Human Needs in Organizational Settings.* New York: Free Press.

Allen, Natalie J., and John P. Meyer (1990) "Organizational Socialization Tactics: A Longitudinal Analysis of Links to Newcomer's Commitment and Role Orientation." *Academy of Management Journal* 33, 4 (December): 847–858.

Alexander, L. R., Marilyn M. Helms, and Ronnie D. Wilkins (1984) "The Relationship Between Supervisory Communications and Subordinate Performance and Satisfaction." *Public Personnel Management* 18, 4 (Winter): 415–429.

Allison, Graham T., Jr. (1971) *Essence of Decision: Explaining the Cuban Missile Crisis.* Boston, MA: Little Brown.

Allison, Graham T., Jr. (1974) "Public and Private Management: Are They Alike in All Unimportant Respects?" in *Setting Public Management Research Agendas.* Proceedings of Public Management Research Conference. Washington, DC: U.S. Office of Personnel Management, November 19–20.

Allred, Stephen (1995) "An Overview of the Family and Medical Leave Act of 1993." *Public Personnel Management* 24, 1 (Spring): 67–73.

Ammons, David N. (1984) "Peer Participation in Local Government Employee Appraisal." *Administration and Society* 16, 2 (August): 239–256.

Ammons, David N., and James J. Glass (1988) "Headhunters in Local Government: Use of Executive Search Firms in Managerial Selection." *Public Administration Review* 48, 3 (May/June): 687–693.

Ammons, David N., and Phillip A. Nietzielski-Eichner (1985) "Evaluating Supervisory Training in Local Government: Moving Beyond Concept to a Practical Framework." *Public Personnel Management* 14, 3 (Fall): 211–230.

Ammons, R. B. (1956) "Effects of Knowledge of Performance: A Survey and Tentative Theoretic Formulations." *Journal of General Psychology* 54: 279–299.

Aplin, John C., and Peter P. Schoderbek (1976) "MBO: Requisites for Success in the Public Sector." *Human Resources Management* 15 (Summer): 30–36.

Appleby, Paul H. (1952) *Morality and Administration in Democratic Government.* Baton Rouge: Louisiana State University Press.

Armacost, Robert L., and Rolene L. Jauernig (1991) "Planning and Managing a Major Recruiting Project." *Public Personnel Management* 20, 2 (Summer): 115–126.

Arthur, Michael B., Priscilla H. Claman, and Robert J. DeFillippi (1995) "Intelligent Enterprise, Intelligent Careers." *Academy of Management Executive* 9, 4 (November): 7–20.

Arthur, Winfred, Jr., and Dennis Doverspike (1997) "Employment-Related Drug Testing: Idiosyncratic Characteristics and Issues." *Public Personnel Management* 26, 1 (Spring): 77–87.

Arvey, Richard D., Steven M. Nutting, and Timothy E. Landon (1992) "Validation Strategies for Physical Ability Testing in Police and Fire Settings." *Public Personnel Management* 21, 3 (Fall): 301–312.

Ashford, Susan J., and Anne S. Tsui (1991) "Self-Regulation for Managerial Effectiveness: The Role of Active Feedback Seeking." *Academy of Management Journal* 34, 2 (June): 251–280.

Axelrod, Robert (1976) *Structure of Decision.* Princeton, NJ: Princeton University Press.

Babbie, Earl (1995) *The Practice of Social Research.* Belmont, CA: Wadsworth.

Bailey, Stephen K. (1966) "Ethics in the Public Service," in Robert Golembiewski, Frank Gibson, and Geoffrey Y. Cornog, eds., *Public Administration.* Chicago: Rand McNally: 22–32.

Baker, Herbert George, and Morris S. Spier (1990) "The Employment Interview: Guaranteed Improvement in Reliability." *Public Personnel Management,* 19, 1 (Spring): 85–90.

Balfour, Danny L. (1992) "Impact of Agency Investment in the Implementation of Performance Appraisal." *Public Personnel Management* 21, 1 (Spring): 1–15.

Ball, Carolyn (1993) "Union Donations to Congressional Candidates: A Test of Exchange Theory." *Review of Public Personnel Administration* 13, 3 (Summer): 8–18.

Ban, Carolyn (1995) *How Do Public Managers Manage? Bureaucratic Constraints, Organizational Culture, and the Potential for Reform.* San Francisco: Jossey-Bass.

Ban, Carolyn (1997) "Hiring in the Public Sector: "Expediency Management" or Structural Reform?" in Carolyn Ban and Norma M. Riccucci, eds., *Public Personnel Management: Current Concerns, Future Challenges.* New York: Longman, pp. 189–203.

Barber, Alson E., Randall B. Dunham, and Roger A. Formisano (1992) "The Impact of Flexible Benefits on Employee Satisfaction: A Field Study." *Personnel Psychology* 45, 1 (Spring): 55–75.

Barnard, Chester (1938) *The Functions of the Executive.* Cambridge, MA: Harvard University Press.

Barney, Jay R. (1990) "The Debate Between Traditional Management Theory and Organization Economics: Substantive Differences or Intergroup Conflict." *Academy of Management Review* 15, 3 (July): 382–393.

Barrick, M. R., and M. K. Mount (1991) "The Big-Five Personality Dimensions and Job Performance: A Meta-Analysis." *Personnel Psychology* 44: 1–26.

Barry, David, Caterine Durnell Cramton, and Stephen J. Carroll (1997) "Navigating the Garbage Can: How Work Agendas Help Managers Cope with Job Realities." *Academy of Management Executive* 11, 2 (May): 26–42.

Baskin, Maurice (1998a) "Employee Privacy and Recordkeeping: The Legal Ground Rules—Part 1 of 2." *IPMA News* (August): 16–18.

Baskin, Maurice (1998b) "Employee Privacy and Recordkeeping: The Legal Ground Rules—Part 2 of 2." *IPMA News* (September): 17–19.

Becker, Brian, and Barry Gerhart (1996) "The Impact of Human Resource Management on Organizational Performance: Progress and Prospects." *Academy of Management Journal* 39, 4 (August): 779–801.

Becker, Thomas, Robert S. Billings, Daniel M. Eveleth, and Nicole L. Gilbert (1996) "Foci and Bases of Employee Commitment: Implications for Job Performance." *Academy of Management Journal* 39, 2 (April): 464–482.

Bellone, Carl J. (1982) "Structural vs. Behavioral Change: The Civil Service Reform Act of 1978." *Review of Public Personnel Administration* 2, 2 (Spring): 59–67.

Bent, Alan E., and T. Zane Reeves (1978) *Collective Bargaining in the Public Sector.* Menlo Park, CA: Benjamin/Cummings.

Bergmann, Thomas J., Marilyn A. Bergmann, and Joyce L. Grahn (1994) "How Important Are Employee Benefits to Public Sector Employees?" *Public Personnel Management* 23, 3 (Fall): 397–406.

Berman, Evan M., and Jonathan P. West (1995) "Municipal Commitment to Total Quality Management: A Survey of Recent Progress." *Public Administration Review* 55, 1 (January/February): 57–66.

Bernardin, H. John (1986) "Subordinate Appraisal: A Valuable Source of Information About Managers." *Human Resource Management* 25, 3 (Fall): 421–439.

Bernardin, H. John, and Richard W. Beatty (1984) *Performance Appraisal: Assessing Human Behavior at Work.* Boston: Kent.

Berry, Frances Stokes (1994) "Innovation in Public Management: The Adoption of Strategic Planning." *Public Administration Review* 54, 4 (July/August): 322–330.

Berry, Frances Stokes, William D. Berry, and Stephen K. Foster (1998) "The Determinants of Success in Implementing an Expert System in State Government." *Public Administration Review* 58, 4 (July/August): 293–305.

Berwick, D. M. (1989) "Continuous Improvement as an Ideal in Health Care." *New England Journal of Medicine* 320, 1: 53–57.

Bigoness, William J. (1976) "Effects of Applicant's Sex, Race, and Performance on Employer's Performance Rating: Some Additional Findings." *Journal of Applied Psychology* 61: 80–84.

Bishop, Peter C., and Augustus J. Jones, Jr. (1993) "Implementing the Americans with Disabilities Act of 1990: Assessing the Variables of Success." *Public Administration Review* 53, 2 (March/April): 121–128.

Blake, R. R. and J. S. Mouton (1969). *Building a Dynamic Corporation through Grid Organization Development.* Reading, MA: Addison-Wesley.

Blanz, F., and E. E. Ghiselli (1972) "The Mixed Standard Scale: A New Rating System." *Personnel Psychology* 25: 185–189.

Bloom, Matt (1999) "The Performance Effects of Pay Dispersion on Individuals and Organizations." *Academy of Management Journal* 42, 1 (February): 25–40.

Bohlander, George W. (1989) "Public Sector Independent Grievance Systems: Methods and Procedures." *Public Personnel Management* 18, 3 (Fall): 339–354.

Boller, Harvey R., and Douglas Massengill (1992) "Public Employers' Obligation to Reasonably Accommodate the Disabled Under the Rehabilitation and Americans with Disabilities Acts." *Public Personnel Management* 21, 3 (Fall): 273–300.

Bolton, Robert (1986) *People Skills: How to Assert Yourself, Listen to Others, and Resolve Conflicts.* New York: Simon and Schuster.

Booth, W. S., and Rohe, C. A. (1988). "Recruiting for Women and Minorities in the Fire Service: Solutions for Today's Challenges." *Public Personnel Management* 17 (Spring): 53–61.

Bowen, David E., Gerald E. Ledford, Jr., and Barry R. Nathan (1991) "Hiring for the Organization, Not the Job." *Academy of Management Executive* 5, 4 (November): 35–51.

Bowman, James S. (1980) "Whistle-Blowing in the Public Service: An Overview of the Issues." *Review of Public Personnel Administration* 1, 1 (Fall): 15–27.

Bowman, James (1999) "Performance Appraisal: Verisimilitude Trumps Veracity." *Public Personnel Management* 28, 4 (Winter): 557–576.

Bowman, James, and Ronald Lavater (1992) "Dress Standards in Government: A National Survey of State Administrators." *Review of Public Personnel Administration* 12, 2 (January–April): 35–51.

Boyer, C. E. and P. Pond (1987) "Employee Participation and Involvement," in R. L. Craig, ed., New York: McGraw Hill, pp. 771–784.

Bozeman, Barry (1987) *All Organizations Are Public: Bridging Public and Private Organization Theories.* San Francisco: Jossey-Bass.

Bradford, David (1998) "Police Officer Candidate Background Investigation: Law Enforcement Management's Most Effective Tool for Employing the Most Qualified Candidate." *Public Personnel Management* 27, 4 (Winter): 423–445.

Braun, A. (1979) "Assessing Supervisory Training Needs and Evaluating Effectiveness." *Training and Development Journal* 33: 3–10.

Brinkerhoff, D. W., and R. M. Kanter (1980) "Appraising the Performance of Performance Appraisal." *Sloan Management Review* 21 (Spring): 3–16.

Broadwell, M. M. (1987) "Classroom Instruction, Training and Development Handbook," in R. L. Craig, ed., New York: McGraw Hill, pp. 383–397.

Brumback, Gary B. (1996) "Getting the Right People Ethically." *Public Personnel Management* 25, 3 (Fall): 267–276.

Bryson, John M. (1996) *Strategic Planning for Public and Nonprofit Organizations.* San Francisco: Jossey-Bass.

Buchanan, Bruce, II (1974a) "Building Organizational Commitment: The Socialization of Managers in Work Organizations." *Administrative Science Quarterly* 19: 533–546.

Buchanan, Bruce, II (1974b) "Government Managers, Business Executives, and Organizational Commitment." *Public Administration Review* 32: 339–347.

Buchanan, Bruce, II (1975a) "Red Tape and the Service Ethic: Some Unexpected Differences Between Public and Private Managers." *Administration and Society* 6: 423–438.

Buchanan, Bruce, II (1975b) "To Walk an Extra Mile: The Whats, Whens, and Whys of Organizational Commitment." *Organizational Dynamics* 4: 67–80.

Buchmueller, Thomas C., and Robert G. Valletta (1996) "The Effects of Employee Provided Health Insurance on Worker-Mobility." *Industrial and Labor Relations Review* 49, 3 (April): 439–455.

Buckley, M. Ronald, Diane C. Kicza, and Nancy Crane (1987) "A Note on the Effectiveness of Flextime as an Organizational Intervention." *Public Personnel Management* 16, 3 (Fall): 259–267.

Bullock, R. J., and Mark E. Tubbs (1990) "A Case Meta-Analysis of Gainsharing Plans as Organizational Development Interventions." *Journal of Applied Behavioral Science* 26, 3: 383–404.

Burchett, Shelley P., and Kenneth DeMeuse (1985) "Performance Appraisal and the Law." *Personnel* 62 (July): 29–37.

Burke, Zona (1977) *Performance Evaluation: Participant's Training Manual.* Iowa City: University of Iowa Institute of Public Affairs (March 7).

Byhan, W. (1971) "The Assessment Center as an Aid in Management Development." *Training and Development Journal:* 10–21.

Caiden, Gerald (1981) "Ethics in the Public Service." *Public Personnel Management,* 10: 146–152.

Calhoun, Carol V., and Arthur H. Tepfer (1999a) "Deferred Retirement Option Plans ("DROP" Plans), part 1." *IPMA News* (August): 13, 15.

Calhoun, Carol V., and Arthur H. Tepfer (1999b) "Deferred Retirement Option Plans ("DROP" Plans), part 2." *IPMA News* (September): 13, 15.

Campbell, Donald J., and Cynthia Lee (1988) "Self-Appraisal in Performance Appraisal Evaluation: Development Versus Evaluation." *Academy of Management Review* 13, 2 (April): 302–314.

Campbell, Donald T., and Julian C. Stanley (1963) *Experimental and Quasi-Experimental Designs for Research.* Chicago: Rand McNally.

Campbell, J. P. (1971) "Personnel Training and Development." *Annual Review of Psychology* 22: 565–602.

Campbell, J. P., Dunnette, M. D., Lawler, E. E., and Weick, K. E. (1970) *Managerial Behavior, Performance, and Effectiveness.* New York: McGraw Hill.

Carnevale, David G. (1993) "The Old Employee Suggestion Box: An Undervalued Force for Productivity Improvement." *Review of Public Personnel Administration* 13, 2 (Spring): 82–93.

Carnevale, David G. (1995) *Trustworthy Government: Leadership and Management Strategies for Building Trust and High Performance.* San Francisco: Jossey-Bass.

Carnevale, David G., and Steven Housel (1995) "Recruitment of Personnel," in Jack Rabin, Thomas Vocino, W. Bartley Hildreth, and Gerald J. Miller, eds., *Handbook of Public Personnel Administration.* New York: Marcel Dekker, pp. 241–265.

Carnevale, David G., and Bart Wechsler (1992) "Organizational Trust in the Public Sector: A Model of Its Determinants." *Administration & Society* 23, 4 (February): 471–494.

Carr, David, and Ian Littman (1990) *Excellence in Government: Total Quality Management in the 1990s.* Arlington, VA: Coopers and Lyband.

Carroll, James D. (1995) "The Rhetoric of Reform and Political Reality in the National Performance Review." *Public Administration Review* 55, 3 (May/June): 302–312.

Carroll, Stephen, and Henry Tosi (1973) *Management by Objectives: Applications and Research.* New York: Macmillan.

Cascio, Wayne F. (1982) "Scientific, Legal, and Operative Imperatives of Workable Performance Appraisal Systems." *Public Personnel Management* 11, 4 (Winter): 367–375.

Cascio, Wayne F. (1991) *Costing Human Resources: The Financial Impact of Behavior in Organizations,* 3rd ed. Boston, MA: PWS-Kent.

Cayer, N. Joseph (1995) "Pension Fund Management," in Jack Rabin, Thomas Vocino, W. Bartley Hildeth, and Gerald Miller, eds., *Handbook of Public Personnel Administration.* New York: Marcel Dekker, pp. 377–389.

Cayer, N. Joseph (1997) "Issues in Compensation and Benefits," in Carolyn Ban and Norma M. Riccucci, eds., *Public Personnel Management: Current Concerns, Future Challenges.* New York: Longman, pp. 221–236.

Cayer, N. Joseph, Linda J. Martin, and A. James Ifflander (1986) "Public Pension Plans and Social Investing." *Public Personnel Management* 15, 1 (Spring): 75–78.

Cayer, N. Joseph, and Ronald W. Perry (1998) "Municipal Personnel Director Evaluations of HMO, PPO, and Indemnity Plans." *State and Local Government Review* 30, 1 (Winter): 17–25.

Cederblom, Douglas (1991) "Promotability Ratings: An Underused Promotion Method for Public Safety Organizations." *Public Personnel Management* 20, 1 (Spring): 27–34.

Cederblom, Douglas, and J. W. Lounsbury (1980) "An Investigation of Use and Acceptance of Peer Evaluations." *Personnel Psychology* 33 (Autumn): 567–579.

Cesare, Steven J. (1996) "Subjective Judgment and the Selection Interview: A Methodological Review." *Public Personnel Management* 25, 3 (Fall): 291–306.

Chandler, Timothy, and Peter Feuille (1991) "Municipal Unions and Privatization." *Public Administration Review* 51, 1 (January/February): 15–22.

Christen, J. C. (1987) "Team building." in R. L. Craig, ed., *Training and Development Handbook.* New York: McGraw Hill, pp. 442–455.

Clement, Ronald W. (1987) "Performance Appraisal: Nonverbal Influences on the Rating Process." *Review of Public Personnel Administration* 7, 2 (Spring): 14–27.

Clement, Ronald W., and George E. Stevens (1986) "The Performance Appraisal Interview: What, When, and How?" *Review of Public Personnel Administration* 6, 2 (Spring): 43–58.

Clifford, James P. (1994) "Job Analysis: Why Do It and How Should It Be Done?" *Public Personnel Management* 23, 2 (Summer): 321–340.

Clifford, James P. (1996) "Manage Work Better to Better Manage Human Resources: A Comparative Study of Two Approaches to Job Analysis." *Public Personnel Management* 25, 1 (Spring): 89–102.

Cluff, Gary A. (1999) "Computing Your Cost Per Hire." *IPMA News* (March): 18, 19.

Coff, Russell W. (1997) "Human Assets and Management Dilemmas: Coping with Hazards on the Road to Resource-Based Theory." *Academy of Management Review* 22, 2 (April): 374–402.

Coffee, Karen (1996) "To Fee, or Not to Fee, What a Question?" *Public Personnel Management* 25, 2 (Summer): 165–181.

Coffee, Karen (1998) "Candidate Reduction Strategies." *Public Personnel Management* 27, 4 (Winter): 459–473.

Coggburn, Jerrell D. (1998) "Subordinate Appraisals for Managers: Lessons from a State Agency." *Review of Public Personnel Administration* 18, 1 (Winter): 68–79.

Cohen, Steven, and Ronald Brand (1990) "Total Quality Management in the U.S. Environmental Protection Agency." *Public Productivity and Management Review* 14, 1 (Fall): 99–114.

Cohen, Steven, and Ronald Brand (1993) *Total Quality Management in Government: A Practical Guide for the Real World.* San Francisco: Jossey-Bass.

Colby, Peter W., and Patricia W. Ingraham (1981) "Civil Service Reform: The Views of the Senior Executive Service." *Review of Public Personnel Administration* 1, 3 (Summer): 75–89.

Coleman, Charles J. (1990) *Managing Labor Relations in the Public Sector.* San Francisco: Jossey-Bass.

Collins, R. Douglas (1986) "Agency Shop in Public Employment." *Public Personnel Management* 15, 2 (Summer): 171–179.

Condrey, Stephen E. (1994) "Qualitative vs. Quantitative Performance: Implications for Managerial Performance Appraisal Systems." *Review of Public Personnel Administration* 14, 3 (Summer): 45–59.

Cooke, P. (1987) "Role Playing," in R. L. Craig, ed., *Training and Development Handbook.* New York: McGraw-Hill, pp. 430–441.

Cordes, Cynthia L., and Thomas W. Dougherty (1993) "A Review and Integration of Research on Job Burnout." *Academy of Management Review* 18, 4 (October): 621–656.

Cotton, J. L., and J. M. Tuutle (1986) "Employee Turnover: A Meta-Analysis and Review with Implications for Research." *Academy of Management Review* 11, 1 (January): 55–70.

Coulton, Gary F., and Hubert S. Field (1995) "Using Assessment Centers in Selecting Entry-Level Police Officers: Extravagance or Justified Expense?" *Public Personnel Management* 24, 2 (Summer): 223–254.

Cozzetto, Don (1991) "Public Sector Grievances: The Case of North Dakota." *Review of Public Personnel Administration* 12, 1 (September–December): 5–13.

Cozzetto, Don A. (1994) "Implications of the ADA for State and Local Government: Judicial Activism Reincarnated." *Public Personnel Management* 23, 1 (Spring): 105–116.

Cozzetto, Don A. (1998) "Privacy and the Workplace: Technology and Public Employment." *IPMA News* (August): 14, 16.

Cozzetto, Don A., and Theodore B. Pedeliski (1996) "Privacy and the Workplace: Future Implications for Managers." *Review of Public Personnel Administration* 16, 2 (Spring): 21–31.

Cozzetto, Don A., and Theodore B. Pedeliski (1997) "Privacy and the Workplace: Technology and Public Employment." *Public Personnel Management* 26, 4 (Winter): 515–527.

Crampton, Suzanne M., and Jitendra M. Mishra (1995) "Family and Medical Leave Legislation: Organizational Policies & Strategies." *Public Personnel Management* 24, 3 (Fall): 271–289.

Crawford, K., E. Thomas, and J. Fink (1980) "Pygmalion at Sea: Improving Work Effectiveness of Low Performers." *Journal of Applied Behavioral Science* 16, 4: 482–505.

Crosby, Philip B. (1979) *Quality Is Free: The Art of Making Quality Certain.* New York: McGraw-Hill.

Crosby, Philip B. (1984) *Quality Without Tears: The Art of Hassle-Free Management.* New York: McGraw-Hill.

Crosby, Philip B. (1986) *Running Things: The Art of Making Things Happen.* New York: McGraw-Hill.

Cummings, Larry L., and Donald P. Schwab (1973) *Performance in Organizations: Determinants and Appraisal.* Glennview, IL: Scott, Foresman.

Curtis, Craig (1990) "In the Spirit of Rosenbloom's 'What Every Public Personnel Manager Should Know About the Constitution': An Updated Annotated Bibliography of Recent Caselaw." *Review of Public Personnel Administration* 10, 2 (Spring): 39–53.

Daley, Dennis M. (1982) "State Administrators and Public Policy: A Survey of Political Attitudes." Paper presented at the Southwestern Political Science Association.

Daley, Dennis M. (1983) "Performance Appraisal as a Guide for Training and Development: A Research Note on the Iowa Performance Evaluation System." *Public Personnel Management* 12, 2 (Summer): 159–166.

Daley, Dennis M. (1984a) "Controlling the Bureaucracy Among the States: An Examination of Administrative, Executive, and Legislative Attitudes." *Administration and Society* 15, 4 (February): 475–488.

Daley, Dennis M. (1984b) "Bureaucractic Responsiveness to Governmental Elites: State Administrative, Executive, and Legislative Opinion Concurrence Regarding Regime Values and Policy Priorities." Paper presented at the Southern Political Science Association.

Daley, Dennis M. (1987a) "Performance Appraisal and the Creation of Training and Development Expectations: A Weak Link in MBO-Based Appraisal Systems." *Review of Public Personnel Administration* 8, 1 (Fall): 1–10.

Daley, Dennis M. (1987b) "Merit Pay Enters with a Whimper: The Initial Federal Civil Service Reform Experience." *Review of Public Personnel Administration* 7, 2 (Spring): 72–79.

Daley, Dennis M. (1987c) "The Effect of Organizational Commitment on Motivation: Participative Management and the Organization." Paper presented at the American Society for Public Administration.

Daley, Dennis M. (1988a) "Profile of the Uninvolved Worker: The Affect of Administrative Attitudes on Organizational Behavior." *International Journal of Public Administration* 11, 1 (January): 65–90.

Daley, Dennis M. (1990a) "The Civil Service Reform Act and Performance Appraisal: A Research Note on Federal Employee Perceptions." *Public Personnel Management* 19, 3 (Fall): 245–251.

Daley, Dennis M. (1990b) "Performance Appraisal in North Carolina: A Profile of Municipal Personnel Practices." Paper presented at the Annual Meeting of the American Political Science Association.

Daley, Dennis M. (1992a) "When Bureaucrats Get the Blues: A Replication and Extension of the Rusbult and Lowery Analysis of Federal Employee Responses to Job Dissatisfaction." *Journal of Public Administration Research and Theory* 2, 3 (July): 233–246.

Daley, Dennis M. (1992b) *Performance Appraisal in the Public Sector: Techniques and Applications.* Westport, CT: Quorum.

Daley, Dennis M., and Curtis L. Ellis (1994) "Drug Screening in the Public Sector: A Focus on Law Enforcement." *Public Personnel Management* 23, 1 (Spring): 1–18.

Daniel, Christopher (1986) "Science, System, or Hunch: Alternative Approaches to Improving Employee Selection." *Public Personnel Management* 15, 1 (Spring): 1–10.

Daniel, Christopher (1992) "Constitutionalizing Merit? Practical Implications of *Elrod, Branti,* and *Rutan.*" *Review of Public Personnel Administration* 12, 2 (January–April): 26–34.

Daniel, Christopher, and Sergio Valencia (1991) "Structured Interviewing Simplified." *Public Personnel Management* 20, 2 (Summer): 127–134.

Davis, Elaine, and Ed Ward (1995) "Health Benefit Satisfaction in the Public and Private Sectors: The Role of Distributive and Procedural Justice." *Public Personnel Management* 24, 3 (Fall): 255–270.

Davis, Kenneth Culp (1969) *Discretionary Justice.* Chicago: University of Illinois Press.

Davis, Kermit R., Jr., and William I. Sauser, Jr. (1993) "A Comparison of Weighting Factor Methods in Job Evaluation: Implications for Compensation Systems." *Public Personnel Management* 22, 1 (Spring): 91–106.

DeCotiis, T., and A. Petit (1978) "The Performance Appraisal Process: A Model and Some Testable Propositions." *Academy of Management Review* 3: 635–646.

DeLeon, Linda, and Ann J. Ewen (1997) "Multi-Source Performance Appraisals: Employee Perceptions of Fairness." *Review of Public Personnel Administration* 17, 1 (Winter): 22–36.

Delery, John E., and D. Harold Doty (1996) "Modes of Theorizing in Strategic Human Resource Management: Tests of Universalistic, Contingency, and Configurational Performance Predictions." *Academy of Management Journal* 39, 4 (August): 802–835.

Deming, W. Edwards (1982) *Quality, Productivity, and Competitive Position.* Cambridge, MA: MIT Center for Advanced Engineering Study.

Deming, W. Edwards (1986) *Out of the Crisis.* Cambridge, MA: MIT Center for Advanced Engineering Study.

Denhardt, Robert (1991) *Public Administration: An Action Orientation.* Pacific Grove, CA: Brooks/Cole.

DeNisi, Angelo, Thomas Cafferty, and Bruce Meglino (1984) "A Cognitive View of the Performance Appraisal Process: A Model and Research Propositions." *Organizational Behavior and Human Performance* 33: 360–396.

DeNisi, Angelo, and Avraham N. Kluger (2000) "Feedback Effectiveness: Can 360-Degree Appraisals Be Improved?" *Academy of Management Executive* 14, 1 (February): 129–139.

Derber, Milton (1988) "Management Organization for Collective Bargaining in the Public Sector," in Benjamin Aaron, Joyce M. Najita, and James L. Stern, eds., *Public Sector Bargaining.* 2nd ed. Washington, DC: Bureau of National Affairs, pp. 90–123.

DeVader, Christian L., Allan G. Bateson, and Robert G. Lord (1986) "Attribution Theory: A Meta-Analysis of Attributional Hypotheses," in Edwin A. Locke, ed., *Generalizing from Laboratory to Field Studies.* Lexington, MA: Lexington Books, pp. 63–81.

Dickinson, T. L., and P. M. Zellinger (1980) "A Comparison of the Behaviorally Anchored Rating and Mixed Standard Scale Formats." *Journal of Applied Psychology* 65: 147–154.

Digman, J. M. (1989) "Five Robust Trait Dimensions: Development, Stability, and Utility." *Journal of Personality* 57: 195–214.

Digman, J. M. (1990) "Personality Structure: Emergence of the Five-Factor Model," in M. R. Rosenzweig and L. W. Porter, eds., *Annual Review of Psychology* 41: 417–440.

Donaldson, Lex (1990) "The Ethereal Hand: Organizational Economics and Management Theory." *Academy of Management Review* 15, 3 (July): 369–381.

Donaldson, Lex and Scannell, E. E., eds. (1986) *Human Resource Development: The New Trainer's Guide.* Reading, MA: Addison-Wesley.

Douglas, Joel M. (1987) "Collective Bargaining and Public Sector Supervisors: A Trend Toward Exclusion?" *Public Administration Review* 47, 6 (November/December): 485–497.

Douglas, Joel M. (1992) "State Civil Service and Collective Bargaining: Systems in Conflict." *Public Administration Review* 52, 2 (March/April): 162–172.

Drucker, Peter (1954) *The Practice of Management.* New York: Harper and Row.

Drucker, Peter (1964) *Managing for Results.* New York: Harper and Row.

Drucker, Peter (1966) *The Effective Executive.* New York: Harper and Row.

Drucker, Peter (1974) *Management: Tasks, Responsibilities, Practices.* New York: Harper and Row.

Duane, Michael J. (1991) "To Grieve or Not to Grieve: Why Reduce It to Writing?" *Public Personnel Management* 20, 1 (Spring): 83–90.

Dupre, V. A. (1976) "Human Relations Laboratory Training," in R. L. Craig, ed., *Training and Development Handbook,* 2nd ed. New York: McGraw Hill, pp. 37-1–37-15.

Durant, Robert F., and Laura A. Wilson (1993) "Public Management, TQM and Quality Improvement: Towards a Contingency Strategy." *American Review of Public Administration* 22, 3: 215–245.

Durst, Samantha (1999) "Assessing the Effect of Family Friendly Programs on Public Organizations." *Review of Public Personnel Administration* 19, 3 (Summer): 19–33.

Dyer, W. G. (1977) *Team Building.* Reading, MA: Addison-Wesley.

Earley, P. Christopher, Gregory B. Northcraft, Cynthia Lee, and Terri R. Lituchy (1990) "Impact of Process and Outcome Feedback on the Relation of Goal Setting to Task Performance." *Academy of Management Journal* 33, 1 (March): 87–105.

Easterling, Cynthia R., Judith E. Leslie, and Michael A. Jones (1992) "Perceived Importance and Usage of Dress Codes Among Organizations That Market Professional Services." *Public Personnel Management* 21, 2 (Summer): 211–219.

Eberhardt, Bruce J., Steven B. Moser, and David McFadden (1999) "Sexual Harassment in Small Government Units: An Investigation of Policies and Attitudes." *Public Personnel Management* 28, 3 (Fall): 351–364.

Eders, Robert W., and Gerald R. Ferris, eds. (1989) *The Employment Interview: Theory, Research and Practice.* Beverly Hills, CA: Sage.

Edwards, Jack E. (1982) "Format and Training Effects in the Control of Halo and Leniency." Paper presented at the Academy of Management Annual Meeting.

Edwards, Mark R. (1983) "Productivity Improvement Through Innovations in Performance Appraisal." *Public Personnel Management.* 12, 1 (Spring): 13–24.

Edwards, Mark R. (1991) "Accurate Performance Measurement Tools." *HR Magazine* 36, 6 (June): 95–96, 98.

Edwards, Mark R., Walter C. Borman, and J. Ruth Sproull (1985) "Solving the Double Bind in Performance Appraisal: A Saga of Wolves, Sloths, and Eagles." *Business Horizons* (May/June): 59–68.

Edwards, Mark, and Ann J. Ewen (1996) *360 Degree Feedback: The Powerful New Model for Employee Assessment and Performance Improvement.* New York: AMACOM Books.

Edwards, Mark R., and J. Ruth Sproull (1985) "Team Talent Assessment: Optimizing Assessee Visibility and Assessment Accuracy." *Human Resources Planning* 8, 3 (Autumn): 157–171.

Elam, L. B. (1997) "Reinventing Government Privatization-Style—Avoiding the Legal Pitfalls of Replacing Civil Servants with Contract Providers." *Public Personnel Management* 26, 1 (Spring): 15–33.

Elling, Richard (1997) "Slip-Slidin' Away? Patterns of Employee Turnover in American State Bureaucracies," Paper presented at the American Political Science Association. Washington, DC (August).

Elliott, Robert H. (1986) "The Fairness of Veterans' Preference in a State Merit System: The Employees' View." *Public Personnel Management* 15, 3 (Fall): 311–323.

Elliott, Robert H. (1989) "Drug Testing and Public Personnel Administration." *Review of Public Personnel Administration* 9, 3 (Summer): 15–31.

Elliott, Robert H. (1990) "Contemporary Health Care Dilemmas in Public Personnel Management." *Review of Public Personnel Administration* 9, 3 (Summer): 15–31.

Elliott, Robert H., and Allen L. Peaton (1994) "The Probationary Period in the Selection Process: A Survey of Its Use at the State Level." *Public Personnel Management* 23, 1 (Spring): 47–59.

Elliott, Robert H., and Thomas M. Wilson (1987) "AIDS in the Workplace: Public Personnel Management and the Law." *Public Personnel Management* 16, 3 (Fall): 209–219.

Elmore, Richard (1991) "Teaching, Learning, and Education for the Public Service." *Journal of Policy Analysis and Management* 10, 2: 167–180.

England, Paula, and Barbara Stenek Kilbourne (1991) "Using Job Evaluation to Achieve Pay Equity." *International Journal of Public Administration* 14, 5: 823–843.

Erfurt, John C., Andrea Foote, and Max A. Heirich (1992) "The Cost-Effectiveness of Work-site Wellness Programs for Hypertension Control, Weight Loss, Smoking Cessation, and Exercise." *Personnel Psychology* 45, 1 (Spring): 5–27.

Farrell, Dan (1983) "Exit, Voice, Loyalty, and Neglect as Responses to Job Dissatisfaction: A Multidimensional Scaling Study." *Academy of Management Journal* 26: 596–606.

Farrell, Dan, and Caryl E. Rusbult (1981) "Exchange Variables as Predictors of Job Satisfaction, Job Commitment, and Turnover: The Impact of Rewards, Costs, Alternatives, and Investments." *Organizational Behavior and Human Performance* 27: 78–95.

Fayol, Henri (1949 [1916]) *General and Industrial Management.* London: Pitman.

Feild, Hubert S., and Robert D. Gatewood (1989) "Development of a Selection Interview: A Job Content Strategy," in Robert W. Eders and Gerald R. Ferris, eds., *The Employment Interview: Theory, Research and Practice.* Beverly Hills, CA: Sage, pp. 145–157.

Feldman, Daniel C. (1994) "The Decision to Retire Early: A Review and Conceptualization," *Academy of Management Review* 19, 2 (April): 285–311.

Feldman, Jack M. (1981) "Beyond Attribution Theory: Cognitive Processes in Performance Appraisal." *Journal of Applied Psychology* 66: 127–148.

Felker, Lon (1986) "Public Sector Labor Relations in the States and Municipalities: The Impact of Union Legislative Environment." *Public Personnel Management* 15, 1 (Spring): 41–50.

Ferris, George (1985) "The Influence of Subordinate Age on Performance Ratings and Causal Attributions." *Personnel Psychology* 38 (Autumn): 545–547.

Ferris, James M. (1987) "Local Government Pensions and Their Funding: Policy Issues and Options." *Review of Public Personnel Administration* 7, 3 (Summer): 29–44.

Fesler, James W., and Donald F. Kettl (1991) *The Politics of the Administrative Process.* Chatham, NJ: Chatham House.

Fine, Cory R., T. Zane Reeves, and George P. Harney (1996) "Employee Drug Testing: Are Cities Complying with the Courts?" *Public Administration Review* 56, 1 (January/February): 30–37.

Fine, Sydney (1974) "Functional Job Analysis: An Approach to a Technology for Manpower Planning." *Personnel Journal* 53, 1 (November): 813–818.

Fine, Sydney, and S. F. Cronshaw (1999) *Functional Job Analysis.* Mahwah, NJ: Erlbaum.

Fine, Sydney, and W. W. Wiley (1971) *An Introduction to Functional Job Analysis.* Kalamazoo, MI: W. E. Upjohn Institute.

Finkle, Arthur L. (1995) "The Practice of Employee Discipline," in Jack Rabin, Thomas Vocino, W. Bartley Hildreth, and Gerald Miller, eds., *Handbook of Public Personnel Administration.* New York: Dekker, pp. 603–615.

Finkle, B. S., R. V. Blanke, and J. M. Walsh (1990) "Technical, Scientific and Procedural Issues of Employee Drug Testing." Rockville, Maryland: National Institute on Drug Abuse; U.S. Department of Health and Human Services.

Fischer, Frank (1995) *Evaluating Public Policy.* Chicago: Nelson Hall.

Fisher, Frank (1980) "Trade-Off Analyses," in Michael J. White, Ross Clayton, Robert Myrtle, Gilbert Siegal, and Aaron Rose, eds., *Managing Public Systems: Analytical Techniques for Public Administration.* North Scituate, MA: Duxbury Press, pp. 319–335.

Fisher, Roger, and Scott Brown (1988) *Getting Together: Building Relationships as We Negotiate.* New York: Houghton Mifflin.

Fisher, Roger, and William Ury (1981) *Getting to Yes: Negotiating Agreement Without Giving In.* New York: Houghton Mifflin.

Fisher, Roger, William Ury, and Bruce Patton (1991) *Getting to Yes: Negotiating Without Giving In.* 2nd ed. New York: Houghton Mifflin.

Fitz-enz, Jac (1990) *Human Value Management: The Value-Adding Human Resource Management Strategy for the 1990s.* San Francisco: Jossey-Bass.

Flanagan, J. C. (1954) "The Critical Incident Technique." *Psychological Bulletin* 51: 327–358.

Fleischman, E. A., and Mumford, M. A. (1989). "Causes of Individual Differences." Human Performance 2, 3: 201–223.

Folger, Robert, and Jerald Greenberg (1985) "Procedural Justice: An Interpretive Analysis of Personnel Systems," in K. Rowland and G. Ferris, eds., *Research in Personnel and Human Resources Management.* Vol. 3. Breenwich, CT: JAI Press, pp. 141–183.

Folger, Robert, and Mary A. Konovsky (1989) "Effects of Procedural and Distributive Justice on Reactions to Pay Raise Decisions." *Academy of Management Journal* 32, 1 (March): 115–130.

Fowler, Floyd J., Jr. (1993) *Survey Research Methods.* Thousand Oaks, CA: Sage.

Fox, Charles (1991) "Employee Performance Appraisal: The Keystone Made of Clay," in Carolyn Ban and Norma M. Riccucci, eds., *Public Personnel Management: Current Concerns—Future Challenges.* New York: Longman, pp. 58–72.

Frazure, Mike (1997) "Re-Employment." *HRNET@cornell.edu* listserve (June 18).

Fried, N. Elizabeth (1999) "360 Feedback Software—Vendor Feature Comparison." *IPMA News* (August): 21–23.

Fried, Robert (1976) *Performance in American Bureaucracy.* Boston: Little, Brown.

Fryxell, Gerald E., and Michael E. Gordon (1989) "Workplace Justice and Job Satisfaction as Predictors of Satisfaction with Union and Management." *Academy of Management Journal* 32, 4 (December): 851–866.

Gabris, Gerald (1986) "Can Merit Pay Systems Avoid Creating Discord Between Supervisors and Subordinates?—Another Uneasy Look at Performance Appraisal." *Review of Public Personnel Administration* 7, 1 (Fall): 70–89.

Gabris, G. T. (1988) "The Uninvolved Employee as a Unique Management Problem: A Symposium Introduction." *International Journal of Public Administration* 11, 1 (January): 1–26.

Gabris, Gerald, and William A. Giles (1983a) "Perceptions of Management Style and Employee Performance: Resurrecting A Diminishing Debate." *Public Personnel Management* 12, 2 (Summer): 167–180.

Gabris, Gerald, Kenneth Mitchell, and William A. Giles (1988) "Motivating the Uninvolved Worker: Some Conceptual and Empirical Observations." *International Journal of Public Administration* 11, 1 (January): 27–63.

Gabris, Gerald, Kenneth Mitchell, and Robert McLemore (1985) "Rewarding Individual and Team Productivity: The Biloxi Merit Bonus Plan." *Public Personnel Management* 14, 3 (Fall): 231–245.

Gabris, Gerald T., and Steven M. Rock (1991) "Situational Interviews and Job Performance: The Results in One Public Agency." *Public Personnel Management* 20, 4 (Winter): 469–484.

Gabris, Gerald T., and Gloria Simo (1995) "Public Sector Motivation as an Independent Variable." *Public Personnel Management* 24, 1 (Spring): 33–51.

Gael, S., ed. (1988) *The Job Analysis Handbook for Business, Industry, and Government.* New York: Wiley.
Gaertner, Karen N., and Gregory H. Gaertner (1985) "Performance Contingent Pay for Federal Managers." *Administration and Society* 17, 1 (May): 7–20.
Garcia, Richard L. (1987) "Sick-Time Usage by Management and Professional Employees in the Public Sector." *Review of Public Personnel Administration* 7, 3 (Summer): 45–59.
Gardner, Howard (1985) *The Mind's New Science: The History of the Cognitive Revolution.* New York: Basic Books.
Gatewood, Robert D., and Hubert Feild (1998) *Human Resource Selection.* Fort Worth, TX: Dryden Press.
Gerber, B. (1989a) "The Limits of HRD." *Training* (May): 25–33.
Gerber, B. (1989b) "Industry Report: Who, How, What." *Training* (October): 49–63.
Ghorpade, Jai (2000) "Managing Five Paradoxes of 360-Degree Feedback." *Academy of Management Executive* 14, 1 (February): 140–150.
Gilmore, Thomas N. (1988) *Making a Leadership Change: How Organizations and Leaders Can Handle Leadership Transition Successfully.* San Francisco: Jossey-Bass.
Gioia, Dennis, and Peter P. Poole (1984) "Scripts in Organizational Behavior." *Academy of Management Review* 9, 3: 449–459.
Glueck, William (1978) *Personnel: A Diagnostic Approach.* Dallas, TX: Business Publications.
Goldberg, L. R. (1993) "The Structure of Phenotypic Personality Traits." *American Psychologist* 48: 26–42.
Goldman, Deborah D. (1981) "Due Process and Public Personnel Management." *Review of Public Personnel Administration* 2, 1 (Fall): 19–27.
Goldstein, Irwin L. (1993) *Training in Organizations: Needs Assessment, Development, and Evaluation.* Pacific Grove, CA: Brooks/Cole.
Golembiewski, Robert T. (1985) *Humanizing Public Organizations.* Mt. Airy, MD: Lomond.
Golembiewski, Robert T. (1988) *Phases of Burnout: Developing Concepts and Applications.* New York: Praeger.
Golembiewski, Robert T., and M. L. McConkie (1975) "The Centrality of Interpersonal Trust in Group Processess," in C. L. Cooper, ed., *Theories of Group Processes.* New York: Wiley.
Goodale, James G. (1989) "Effective Employment Interviewing," in Robert W. Eders and Gerald R. Ferris, eds., *The Employment Interview: Theory, Research and Practice.* Beverly Hills, CA: Sage, pp. 307–323.
Goodnow, Frank (1900) *Politics and Administration.* New York: Macmillan.
Gortner, Harold F., Julianne Mahler, and Jeanne Bell Nicholson (1987) *Organization Theory: A Public Perspective.* Chicago: Dorsey Press.
Gossett, Charles W. (1994) "Domestic Partnership Benefits." *Review of Public Personnel Administration* 14, 1 (Winter): 64–84.
Graham, J. L., and Mikal, W. L. (1986) "Can Your Management Development Needs Surveys Be Trusted?" *Training and Development Journal* 40, 3: 38–42.
Graham-Moore, Brian, and Timothy L. Ross (1990) *Gainsharing: Plans for Improving Performance.* Washington, DC: Bureau of National Affairs.
Gratton, Lynda, and Michael Syrett (1990) "Heirs Apparent: Succession Strategies for the Future." *Personnel Management* (January): 34–38.
Graves, Laura M., and Ronald J. Karren (1996) "Employee Selection Interview: A Fresh Look at an Old Problem." *Human Resources Management* 35, 2 (Summer): 163–180.

Gray, George R., McKenzie E. Hall, Marianne Miller, and Charles Shasky (1997) "Training Practices in State Government Agencies." *Public Personnel Management* 26, 2 (Summer): 187–202.

Green, Samuel B., John G. Veres, and Wiley R. Boyles (1991) "Racial Differences on Job Analysis Questionnaires: An Empirical Study." *Public Personnel Management* 20, 2 (Summer): 135–144.

Green, Stephen G., and Terence R. Mitchell (1979) "Attributional Processes of Leaders in Leader-Member Interactions." *Organizational Behavior and Human Performance* 23, 3: 429–458.

Greenberg, Jerald (1988) "Cultivating an Image of Justice: Looking Fair on the Job." *Academy of Management Executive* 2, 2 (May): 155–158.

Greenlaw, Paul S., John P. Kohl, and Robert D. Lee, Jr. (1998) "Title VII Sex Discrimination in the Public Sector in the 1990s: The Courts' View." *Public Personnel Management* 27, 2 (Summer): 249–268.

Greenlaw, Paul S., and Robert D. Lee, Jr. (1993) "Three Decades Experience with the Equal Pay Act." *Review of Public Personnel Administration* 13, 4 (Fall): 43–58.

Greer, Charles R., Stuart A. Youngblood, and David A. Gray (1999) "Human Resource Management Outsourçing: The Make or Buy Decision." *Academy of Management Executive* 13, 3 (August): 85–96.

Greiner, John M., Harry P. Hatry, Margo P. Koss, Annie P. Millar, and Jane P. Woodward (1981) *Productivity and Motivation: A Review of State and Local Government Initiatives.* Washington, DC: Urban Institute.

Gulick, L. (1937) "Notes on the Theory of Organization," in L. Gulick and L. Lyndall, eds., *Papers on the Science of Administration.* New York: Institute of Public Administration.

Gupta, Nina (1997) "Rewarding Skills in the Public Sector," in Howard Risher and Charles Fay, eds., *New Strategies for Public Pay.* San Francisco: Jossey-Bass, pp. 125–144.

Haas, Peter J. (1991) "A Comparison of the Training Priorities of Local Government Employees and Their Supervisors." *Public Personnel Management* 20, 2 (Summer): 225–232.

Halachmi, Arie, and Marc Holzer (1987) "Merit Pay, Performance Targeting and Productivity." *Review of Public Personnel Administration* 7, 2 (Spring): 80–91.

Hammond, Barry R. (1993) "The Uneasy Partnership: The Senior Executive Service and Political Executives in American Public Agencies." Paper presented at the American Society for Public Administration National Training Conference, San Francisco, CA.

Harrick, Edward J., Gene R. Vanek, and Joseph F. Michlitsch (1986) "Alternate Work Schedules, Productivity, Leave Usage, and Employee Attitudes: A Field Study." *Public Personnel Management* 15, 2 (Summer): 159–169.

Hart, F. A. (1987) "Computer-Based Training," in R. L. Craig, ed., *Training and Development Handbook,* New York: McGraw-Hill, pp. 470–487.

Hays, Steven W., and Richard C. Kearney (1995) "Promotion of Personnel—Career Advancement," in Jack Rabin, Thomas Vocino, W. Bartley Hildreth, and Gerald Miller, eds., *Handbook of Public Personnel Administration.* New York: Dekker, pp. 499–529.

Heady, Ferrel (1995) *Public Administration: A Comparative Perspective.* New York: Dekker.

Heclo, Hugh (1977) *Government of Strangers.* Washington, DC: Brookings Institution.

Heffron, Florence (1989) *Public Organizations: The Political Connection.* Englewood Cliffs, NJ: Prentice Hall.

Hegji, Charles E. (1993) "A Note on Job Transfer, Pension Portability, and Compensating Salary Differentials." *Review of Public Personnel Administration* 13, 1 (Winter): 76–86.

Helburn, I. R., and Robert Rogers (1985) "Hestancy of Arbitrators to Accept Interest Arbitration Cases: A Test of Conventional Wisdom." *Public Administration Review* 45, 3 (May/June): 398–402.

Herbert, Glenn R., and Dennis Doverspike (1990) "Performance Appraisal in the Training Needs Analysis Process: A Review and Critique." *Public Personnel Management* 19, 3 (Fall): 253–270.

Herman, Susan J. (1994) *Hiring Right: A Practical Guide.* Thousand Oaks, CA: Sage.

Herzberg, Frederick (1966) *Work and the Nature of Man.* Cleveland, OH: World.

Hesterly, William S., Julia Liebeskind, and Todd R. Zenger (1990) "Organizational Economics: An Impending Revolution in Organizational Theory?" *Academy of Management Review* 15, 3 (July): 402–420.

Hicks, W. D., and Klimonski, R. J. (1987) "Entry into Training Programs and Its Effects on Training Outcomes: A Field Experiment." *Academy of Management Journal* 30: 542–551.

Higginbotham, Jeffrey (1986, 1987) "Urinanalysis Drug Testing Programs for Law Enforcement." FBI Law Enforcement Bulletin, U.S. Department of Justice, Washington, DC. October and November 1986, January 1987.

Hildreth, W. Bartley, Gerald J. Miller, and Jack Rabin (1980) "The Liability of Public Executives: Implications for Practice in Personnel Administration." *Review of Public Personnel Administration* 1, 1 (Fall): 45–56.

Hirschman, Albert (1970) *Exit, Voice, and Loyalty: Responses to Decline in Firms, Organizations and States.* Cambridge, MA: Harvard University Press.

Hogan, Joyce, and Ann Quigley (1994) "Effects of Preparing for Physical Ability Tests." *Public Personnel Management* 23, 1 (Spring): 85–104.

Hollwitz, John, Deborah F. Goodman, and Dean Bolte (1995) "Complying with the Americans with Disabilities Act: Assessing the Costs of Reasonable Accommodation." *Public Personnel Management* 24, 2 (Summer): 149–157.

Hoover, Larry T. (1992) "Trends in Police Physical Ability Selection Testing." *Public Personnel Management* 21, 1 (Spring): 29–40.

Hostetler, Dennis, and Joan E. Pynes (1995) "Domestic Partnership Benefits: Dispelling the Myths." *Review of Public Personnel Administration* 15, 1 (Winter): 41–59.

House, Robert J., and Terence R. Mitchell (1974) "Path-Goal Theory of Leadership." *Contemporary Business* 3 (Fall): 81–98.

Houston, David (1988) "The Availiability Heuristic: Implications of Behavioral Decision Theory for Public Administration." Paper presented at the Southeastern Conference on Public Administration.

Huddleston, Mark W. (1987) *The Government's Managers: Report of the Twentieth Century Fund Task Force on the Senior Executive Service.* Washington, DC: Brookings Institution.

Huddleston, Mark W. (1988–1989) "Is the SES a Higher Civil Service?" *Policy Studies Journal* 17, 2 (Winter): 406–419.

Hughes, Marie Adele, Ronald A. Ratliff, Jerry L. Purswell, and Joy Hadwiger (1989) "A Content Validation Methodology for Related Physical Performance Tests." *Public Personnel Management* 18, 4 (Winter): 487–504.

Hunter, William G., J. K. O'Neill, and C. Walter (1987) "Doing More with Less in the Public Sector." *Quality Progress* (July): 19–26.

Hyde, Albert C. (1982) "Performance Appraisal in the Post Reform Era." *Public Personnel Management* 11, 4 (Winter): 294–305.

Hyde, Albert C. (1990–1991) "Rescuing Quality Measurement from TQM." *The Bureaucrat* (Winter): 16–20.

Hyde, Albert C. (1995) "Placing the Individual into the Organization: Staffing and Classification in Human Resources Management." in Jack Rabin, Thomas Vocino, W. Bartley Hildreth, and Gerald Miller, eds., *Handbook of Public Personnel Administration.* New York: Dekker, pp. 285–320.

Hyde, Albert C., and Melanie A. Smith (1982) "Performance Appraisal Training: Objectives, A Model for Change and a Note of Rebuttal." *Public Personnel Management* 11, 4 (Winter): 358–366.

Ilgen, Daniel R., and Jack M. Feldman (1983) "Performance: A Process Focus," in B. M. Staw and L. Cummings, eds., *Research in Organizational Behavior.* Vol. 5. Greenwich, CT: JAI Press.

Ilgen, Daniel R., Cynthia D. Fisher, and M. Susan Taylor (1979) "Consequences of Individual Feedback on Behavior in Organizations." *Journal of Applied Psychology*, 64, 4 (August): 349–371.

Ingraham, Patricia (1993) "Of Pigs in Pokes and Policy Diffusion: Another Look at Pay-for-Performance." *Public Administration Review* 53, 4 (July/August): 348–356.

Ingraham, Patricia, and Carolyn Ban, eds. (1984) *Legislating Bureaucratic Change: The Civil Service Reform Act of 1978.* Albany: State University of New York Press.

Ingraham, Patricia, and Peter Colby (1982) "Individual Motivation and Institutional Changes Under the Senior Executive Service." *Review of Public Personnel Administration* 2, 2 (Spring): 101–118.

Ingraham, Patricia, and David Rosenbloom, eds. (1992) *The Promise and Paradox of Civil Service Reform.* Pittsburgh, PA: University of Pittsburgh Press.

Ingraham, Patricia, James R. Thompson, and Elliot F. Eisenberg (1995) "Political Management Strategies and Political/Career Relationships: Where Are We Now in the Federal Government." *Public Administration Review* 55, 3 (May/June): 263–272.

Ishikawa, Kaoru (1976) *Guide to Quality Control.* Asian Productivity Organization.

Janis, Irving L. (1972) *Victims of Group Think.* Boston: Houghton Mifflin.

John, O. P. (1990) "The 'Big-Five' Factor Taxonomy: Dimensions of Personality in the Natural Language and in Questionnaires," in L. A. Pervin, ed., *Handbook of Personality: Theory and Research.* New York: Guilford Press, pp. 66–100.

Johnson, Arthur (1986) "A Comparison of Employee Assistance Programs in Corporate and Government Organizational Contexts." *Review of Public Personnel Administration* 6, 2 (Spring): 28–42.

Johnson, Arthur, and Nancy O'Neill (1989) "Employee Assistance Programs and the Troubled Employee in the Public Sector Workplace." *Review of Public Personnel Administration* 9, 3 (Summer): 66–80.

Johnson, Pamela R., and Julie Indvik (1999) "The Organizational Benefits of Assisting Domestically Abused Employees." *Public Personnel Management* 28, 3 (Fall): 5–374.

Juran, Joseph M. (1964) *Managerial Breakthrough.* New York: McGraw-Hill.

Juran, Joseph M. (1988) *Juran on Leadership for Quality.* New York: McGraw-Hill.

Jus, Philip H., Mark E. Thompkins, and Stephen W. Hayes (1989) "In Praise of Difficult People: A Portrait of the Committed Whistleblower." *Public Administration Review* 49, 6 (November/December): 552–561.

Kahneman, Daniel, Paul Slovic, and Amos Tversky (1982) *Judgment Under Uncertainty: Heuristics and Biases.* New York: Cambridge University Press.

Kahneman, Daniel, and Amos Tversky (1979) "Prospect Theory: An Analysis of Decision Under Risk." *Econometrica* 47: 263–291.

Kalish, Doug (1996) "Employee Appeal and Review System." *HRNET@cornell.edu* listserve (November 12).

Kaman, Vicki S., and Cynthia Bentson (1988) "Roleplaying Simulations for Employee Selection: Design and Implementation." *Public Personnel Management* 17, 1 (Spring): 1–8.

Kamensky, John M. (1996) "Role of the "Reinventing Government" Movement in Federal Management Reform." *Public Administration Review* 56, 3 (May/June): 247–255.

Kanter, Rosabeth M. (1987) "From Status to Contribution: Some Organizational Implications of the Changing Basis for Pay." *Personnel Journal* (January).

Karl, Katherine A., and Barry W. Hancock (1999) "Expert Advice on Employment Termination Practices: How Expert Is It?" *Public Personnel Management* 28, 1 (Spring): 51–62.

Kaufman, Herbert (1960) *The Forest Ranger: A Study in Administrative Behavior.* Baltimore, MD: John Hopkins Press for Resources for the Future.

Kearney, Richard C. (1992) *Labor Relations in the Public Sector.* New York: Dekker.

Kearney, W. J. (1979) "Behaviorally Anchored Rating Scales—MBO's Missing Ingredient." *Personnel Journal* 58: 20–25.

Keen, Christine D. (1994) "Tips for Effective Strategic Planning." *HRMagazine* (August): 84–87.

Kellough, J. Edward (1999) "Reinventing Public Personnel Management: Ethical Implications for Managers and Public Personnel Systems." *Public Personnel Management* 28, 4 (Winter): 655–671.

Kellough, J. Edward, and Haoran Lu (1993) "The Paradox of Merit Pay in the Public Sector." *Review of Public Personnel Administration* 13, 2 (Spring): 45–64.

Kellough, J. Edward, and Will Osuna (1995) "Cross-Agency Comparisans of Quit Rates in the Federal Service." *Review of Public Personnel Administration* 15, 4 (Fall): 58–68.

Kellough, J. Edward, and Sally Coleman Selden (1997) "Pay-for-Performance Systems in State Government: Perceptions of State Agency Personnel Managers." *Review of Public Personnel Administration* 17, 1 (Winter): 5–21.

Kettl, Donald (1993) *Sharing Power.* Washington, DC: Brookings Institution.

Kettl, Donald F. (1994) *Reinventing Government? Appraising the National Performance Review.* Washington, DC: Brookings Institution (August).

Kettl, Donald F., and John J. DiIulio, Jr., eds., (1995) *Inside the Reinvention Machine: Appraising Government Reform.* Washington, DC: Brookings Institution.

Kemp, Donna R. (1989) "Major Unions and Collectively Bargained Fringe Benefits." *Public Personnel Management* 18, 4 (Winter): 505–510.

Kessel, Kenneth (1972) "Labor Mediation: An Exploratory Survey." in David Lewin, Peter Feuille, and Thomas A. Kochan, eds., *Public Sector Labor Relations: Analysis and Readings.* 2nd ed. Sun Lakes, AZ: Thomas Horton and Daughters, pp. 246–266.

Kiel, L. Douglas (1994) *Managing Chaos and Complexity in Government.* San Francisco: Jossey-Bass.

Kikoski, John F. (1998) "Effective Communication in the Performance Appraisal Interview: Face-to-Face Communication for Public Managers in the Culturally Diverse Workplace." *Public Personnel Management* 27, 4 (Winter): 491–513.

Kikoski, John F., and Joseph A. Litterer (1983) "Effective Communication in the Performance Appraisal Interview." *Public Personnel Management* 12, 1 (Spring): 33–42.

Kilpatrick, Franklin, Milton Cummings, and Kent Jennings (1964) *The Image of the Federal Service.* Washington, DC: Brookings Institution.

Kinard, Jerry, and Stanley Renas (1991) "Negligent Hiring: Are Hospitals Vulnerable?" *Public Personnel Management* 20, 3 (Fall): 263–270.

King, J. (1986) "Computer-based Instruction," in L. Donaldson and E. E. Scannell, eds., *Humam Resource Development: The New Trainer's Guide.* Reading, MA: Addison Wesley, pp. 79–85.

Kirkpatrick, D. L. (1975) "Evaluating Training Programs." *American Society for Training and Development.* Madison, WI.

Kirkpatrick, D. L. (1987) "Evaluation." in R. L. Craig, ed., *Training and Development Handbook.* New York: McGraw-Hill, pp. 301–319.

Klaas, Brian S., and Angelo S. DeNisi (1989) "Managerial Reactions to Employee Dissent: The Impact of Grievance Activity on Performance Ratings." *Academy of Management Journal* 32, 4 (December): 705–717.

Klaas, Brian S., and John A. McClendon (1996) "To Lead, Lag, or Match: Estimating the Financial Impact of Pay Level Policies." *Personnel Psychology* 49, 1 (Spring): 121–141.

Klingner, Donald (1993) "Developing a Strategic Human Resources Management Capability in Public Agencies." *Public Personnel Management* 22, 4 (Winter): 565–578.

Klingner, Donald, and Dahlia Bradshaw Lynn (1997) "Beyond Civil Service: The Changing Face of Public Personnel Management." *Public Personnel Management* 26, 2 (Summer): 157–174.

Klingner, Donald, and John Nalbandian (1985) *Public Personnel Management: Contexts and Strategies.* 2nd ed. Englewood Cliffs, NJ: Prentice Hall.

Klingner, Donald, Nancy G. O'Neill, and Mohamed G. Sabet (1989) "Drug Testing in Public Agencies: Public Policy Issues and Managerial Responses." *Review of Public Personnel Administration* 10, 1 (Fall): 1–10.

Klingner, Donald E., Nancy G. O'Neill, and Mohamed G. Sabet (1990) "Drug Testing in Public Agencies: Are Personnel Directors Doing Things Right?" *Public Personnel Management* 19, 4 (Winter): 391–397.

Knierim, Amy (1997) "Employee Discipline Troubleshooter." *HRNET@cornell.edu* listserve (June 10) Alexander Hamilton Institute.

Knowles, Malcolm (1978) *The Adult Learner: A Neglected Species.* 2nd ed. Houston: Gulf.

Knowlton, William A.,Jr., and Terence R. Mitchell (1980) "Effects of Causal Attributions on a Supervisor's Evaluation of Subordinate Performance." *Journal of Applied Psychology* 65, 4: 459–466.

Koenig, Heidi (1997a) "Free Speech: Government Employees and Government Contractors." *Public Administration Review* 57, 1 (January/February): 1–3.

Koenig, Heidi (1997b) "The Defense of Qualified Immunity in Employee Termination Suits: Four Cases from the Federal Courts of Appeal." *Public Administration Review* 57, 3 (May/June): 187–189.

Kohn, Alfie (1993) *Punishment by Rewards.* Boston: Houghton Mifflin.

Kossek, Ellen Ernst, Beverly J. DeMarr, Kirsten Backman, and Mark Kollar (1993) "Assessing Employees' Emerging Elder Care Needs and Reactions to Dependent Care Benefits." *Public Personnel Management* 22, 4 (Winter): 617–638.

Kossek, Ellen Ernst, and Victor Nichol (1992) "The Effect of On-Site Child Care on Employee Attitudes and Performance." *Personnel Psychology* 45, 3 (Autumn): 485–509.

Kotter, John P. (1982) *The General Managers.* New York: Free Press.

Kovalski, Toni (1997) "Test Security," *IPMA News* (February): 17–18.

Kraiger, Kurt, and J. Kevin Ford (1985) "A Meta Analysis of Ratee Effects in Performance Ratings." *Journal of Applied Psychology* 70: 56–65.

Kramer, Kenneth (1982) "Seeds of Success and Failure: Policy Development and Implementation of the 1978 Civil Service Reform Act." *Review of Public Personnel Administration* 2, 2 (Spring): 5–20.

Kroesser, Hazel L., Richard F. Meckley, and James T. Ranson (1991) "Selected Factors Affecting Employees' Sick Leave Use." *Public Personnel Management* 20, 2 (Summer): 171–180.

Krueger, Richard (1994) *Focus Groups: A Practical Guide for Applied Research.* Thousand Oaks, CA: Sage.

Lan, Zhiyong (1997) "A Conflict Resolution Approach to Public Administration." *Public Administration Review* 57, 1 (January/February): 27–35.

Landy, Frank J., and James L. Farr (1980) "Performance Rating." *Psychological Bulletin* 87: 72–107.

Landy, Frank J., and James L. Farr (1983) *The Measurement of Work Performance: Methods, Theories and Applications.* New York: Academic Press.

Lane, Larry M. (1994) "Public Sector Performance Management: Old Failures and New Opportunities." *Review of Public Personnel Administration* 14, 3 (Summer): 26–44.

Larson, J. R. (1984) "The Performance Feedback Process—A Preliminary Model." *Organizational Behavior and Human Performance* 33, 11: 42–76.

Latham, Gary P. (1986) "Job Performance and Appraisal," in C. L. Cooper and I. Robertson, eds., *International Review of Industrial and Organizational Psychology 1986.* New York: Wiley.

Latham, Gary P., and Kenneth Wexley (1994) *Increasing Productivity Through Performance Appraisal.* Reading, MA: Addison-Wesley.

Latham, Gary P., and Gary A. Yukl (1975) "A Review of Research on the Application of Goal Setting in Organizations." *Academy of Management Journal*, 18, 4 (December): 824–845.

Lavigna, Robert J. (1992) "Predicting Job Performance from Background Characteristics: More Evidence from the Public Sector." *Public Personnel Management* 21, 3 (Fall): 347–361.

Lawler, Edward E., III (1986) *High-Involvement Management: Participative Strategies for Improving Organizational Performance.* San Francisco: Jossey-Bass.

Lawler, Edward E., III (1990) *Strategic Pay: Aligning Organizational Strategies and Pay Systems.* San Francisco: Jossey-Bass.

Lawler, Edward E., III, Allan M. Mohrman, and Susan Resnick (1984) "Performance Appraisal Revisited." *Organizational Dynamics* (Summer): 20–35.

Lawler, Edward E., III, and J. G. Rhode (1976) *Information and Control in Organizations.* Santa Monica, CA: Goodyear.

Leazes, Francis J., Jr. (1995) "Pay Now or Pay Later": Training and Torts in Public Sector Human Services." *Public Personnel Management* 24, 2 (Summer): 167–180.

Ledvinka, James (1995) "Human Resources Planning," in Jack Rabin, Thomas Vocino, W. Bartley Hildreth, and Gerald Miller, eds., *Handbook of Public Personnel Administration.* New York: Dekker, pp. 217–240.

Lee, Robert D., Jr. (1996) "Federal Employees, Torts, and the Westfall Act of 1988." *Public Administration Review* 56, 4 (July/August): 334–340.

Lee, Robert D., Jr. (1987) *Public Personnel Systems.* Rockville, MD: Aspen.

Lee, Robert D., Jr., and Paul S. Greenlaw (1996) "The Complexities of Human Behavior: Recent Instances of Alleged Quid Pro Quo Sexual Harassment." *Review of Public Personnel Administration* 26, 4 (Fall): 15–28.

Lee, Robert D., Jr., and Paul S. Greenlaw (1997) "Sex and Employment Law: A Partial Catalog." *Review of Public Personnel Administration* 17, 2 (Spring): 57–72.

Lee, Yong (1987) "Civil Liability of State and Local Governments: Myths and Reality." *Public Administration Review* 47, 2 (March/April): 160–170.

Lee, Yong (1992) *Public Personnel Administration and Constitutional Values.* Westport, CT: Quorum Books.

Lepsinger, Richard, and Anntoinette D. Lucia (1997) *The Art and Science of 360-Degree Feedback.* San Francisco: Pfeiffer.

Levine, Charles H. (1978) "Organizational Decline and Cutback Management." *Public Administration Review* 38, 4 (July/August): 316–325.

Levine, Charles H. (1979) "More on Cutback Management: Hard Questions for Hard Times." *Public Administration Review* 39, 2 (March/April): 179–183.

Levine, Charles H., Irene S. Rubin, and George G. Wolohojian (1982) "Managing Organizational Retrenchment." *Administration and Society* 14, 1 (May): 101–136.

Lewis, Carol W., and Anthony T. Logalbo (1980) "Cutback Principles and Practices: A Checklist for Managers." *Public Administration Review*, 40, 2 (March/April): 184–188.

Lewis, Chad T. (1989) "Assessing the Validity of Job Evaluation." *Public Personnel Management* 18, 1 (Spring): 45–63.

Lewis, Chad T., and Cynthia Kay Stevens (1990) "An Analysis of Job Evaluation Committee and Job Holder Gender Effects on Job Evaluation." *Public Personnel Management* 19, 3 (Fall): 271–278.

Lewis, Gregory B. (1988) "Progress Toward Racial and Sexual Equality in the Federal Civil Service?" *Public Administration Review* 48, 3 (May/June): 700–707.

Likert, Rensis (1961) *New Patterns of Management.* New York: McGraw-Hill.

Likert, Rensis (1967) *The Human Organization: Its Management and Values.* New York: McGraw-Hill.

Lindenberg, Karen E., and Laura A. Reese (1995) "Sexual Harassment Policy Implementation Issues: Learning from a Public Higher Education Case Study." *Review of Public Personnel Administration* 15, 1 (Winter): 84–97.

Locke, Edwin A., and Gary P. Latham (1984) *Goal Setting: A Motivational Technique That Works.* Englewood Cliffs, NJ: Prentice Hall.

Locke, Edwin A., K. N. Shaw, L. M. Saari, and Gary P. Latham (1981) "Goal Setting and Task Performance." *Psychological Bulletin* 90: 125–152.

Longenecker, Clinton O., and Dennis A. Gioia (1988) "Neglected at the Top—Executives Talk About Executive Appraisal." *Sloan Management Review* 29, 3: 41–47.

Longenecker, Clinton O., and Nick Nykodym (1996) "Public Sector Performance Appraisal Effectiveness: A Case Study." *Public Personnel Management* 25, 2 (Summer): 151–164.

Longenecker, Clinton, Henry Sims, Jr., and Dennis Gioia (1987) "Behind the Mask: The Politics of Employee Appraisal." *Academy of Management Executive* 1, 3: 183–193.

Lopez, Felix M. (1988) "Threshold Traits Analysis System," in S. Gael, ed., *The Job Analysis Handbook for Business, Industry, and Government.* New York: Wiley.

Lord, Robert G., and J. E. Smith (1983) "Theoretical, Information Processing, and Situational Factors Affecting Attribution Theory Models of Organization Behavior." *Academy of Management Review* 8: 50–60.

Love, Kevin G. (1983) "Empirical Recommendations for the Use of Peer Rankings in the Evaluation of Police Officer Performance." *Public Personnel Management* 12, 1 (Spring): 25–32.

Lovrich, Nicholas (1987) "Merit Pay and Motivation in the Public Workforce: Beyond Concerns of Technique to More Basic Considerations." *Review of Public Personnel Administration* 7, 2 (Spring): 54–71.

Lovrich, Nicholas (1989) "Managing Poor Performers," in James L. Perry, ed., *Handbook of Public Administration.* San Francisco: Jossey-Bass, pp. 412–425.

Lowry, Phillip E. (1988) "The Assessment Center: Pooling Scores or Arithmetic Decision Rule?" *Public Personnel Management* 17 (Spring): 63–71.

Lowry, Phillip E. (1991) "The Assessment Center: Reducing Intrassessor Influence." *Public Personnel Management* 20, 1 (Spring): 19–26.

Lowry, Phillip E. (1992) "The Assessment Center: Effects of Varying Consensus Procedures." *Public Personnel Management* 21, 2 (Summer): 171–183.

Lowry, Phillip E. (1993) "The Assessment Center: An Examination of the Effects of Assessor Characteristics on Assessor Scores." *Public Personnel Management* 22, 3 (Fall): 487–501.

Lowry, Phillip E. (1994) "The Structured Interview: An Alternative to the Assessment Center." *Public Personnel Management* 23, 2 (Summer): 201–215.

Lowry, Phillip E. (1996) "A Survey of the Assessment Center Process in the Public Sector." *Public Personnel Management* 25, 3 (Fall): 307–321.

Lust, J. A., and C. Danehower (1990) "Models of Satisfaction with Benefits." *Journal of Business Psychology* 5: 213–221.

Luthans, Fred, and Alexander D. Stajkovic (1999) "Reinforce for Performance: The Need to Go Beyond Pay and Even Rewards." *Academy of Management Executive* 13, 2 (May): 49–57.

Lynn, Naomi B., and Richard E. Vaden (1979) "Bureaucratic Response to Civil Service Reform." *Public Administration Review* 39, 4 (July/August): 333–343.

Lynn, Naomi, and Richard E. Vaden (1980) "Federal Executives: Initial Reaction to Change." *Administration & Society* 12, 1 (May): 101–120.

McBriarty, Mark A. (1988) "Performance Appraisal: Some Unintended Consequences." *Public Personnel Management* 17, 4 (Winter): 421–434.

McCabe, Douglas M. (1990) "The Federal Sector Mediation and Labor Management Relations Process: The Federal Sector Management Experience." *Public Personnel Management* 19, 1 (Spring): 103–122.

McCelland, David C. (1961) *The Achieving Society.* New York: Free Press.

McCelland, David C. (1975) *Power: The Inner Experience.* New York: Irvington.

McCormick, Ernest J. (1979) *Job Analysis: Methods and Applications.* New York: AMACOM.

McCrae, R. R., and O. P. John (1992) "An Introduction of the Five-Factor Model and Its Applications." *Journal of Personality* 60: 175–215.

McDaniel, Michael A., Deborah L. Whetzel, Frank L. Schmidt, and Steven Mauer (1994) "The Validity of Employment Interviews: A Comprehensive Review and Meta Analysis." *Journal of Applied Psychology* 79: 599–616.

McEvoy, Glenn M. (1990) "Public Sector Manager's Reactions to Appraisals by Subordinates." *Public Personnel Management* 19, 2 (Summer): 201–212.

McGehee, W., and Paul W. Thayer (1961) *Training in Business and Industry.* New York: Wiley.

McGregor, Douglas (1957) "An Uneasy Look at Performance Appraisal." *Harvard Business Review* 35: 39–49.

McGregor, Eugene B., Jr. (1988) "The Public Sector Human Resource Puzzle: Strategic Management of a Strategic Resource" *Public Administration Review* 48, 6 (November/December): 941–950.

McGuire, Jean B., and Joseph R. Liro (1986) "Flexible Work Schedules, Work Attitudes, and Perceptions of Productivity." *Public Personnel Management* 15, 1 (Spring): 65–73.

McGuire, Jean B., and Joseph R. Liro (1987) "Absenteeism and Flexible Work Schedules." *Public Personnel Management* 16, 1 (Spring): 47–59.

McKinney, William R. (1987) "Public Personnel Selection: Issues and Choice Points." *Public Personnel Management* 16, 3 (Fall): 243–257.

McKinney, William R., and John R. Collins, Jr. (1991) "The Impact on Utility, Race, and Gender Using Three Standard Methods of Scoring Selection Examinations." *Public Personnel Management* 20, 2 (Summer): 145–169.

MacLean, Paul (1973) *A Triune Concept of the Brain and Behavior.* Toronto, Canada: University of Toronto Press.

Madigan, Robert M., and Frederick S. Hills (1988) "Job Evaluation and Pay Equity." *Public Personnel Management*, 17, 3 (Fall): 323–330.

Madigan, Robert M., and D. J. Hoover (1986) "Effects of Alternative Job Evaluation Methods on Decisions Involving Pay Equity." *Academy of Management Journal* 29: 84–100.

Madlin, N. (1987) "Computer Based Training Comes of Age." *Personnel* 64, 11: 64–65.

Mahler, Julianne (1997) "Agency Learning: Conditions and Barriers." Paper presented at the American Political Science Association Annual Meeting, Washington, DC (August 28–31).

Maier, Norman R. F. (1958) "Appraisal on the Job: Three Types of Appraisal Interviews." *Personnel* 54, 2 (March/April): 27–40.

Maier, Norman R. F. (1976) *The Apprasial Interview: Three Basic Approaches.* La Jolla, CA: University Associates.

Mani, Bonnie G. (1991) "Difficulties, Assumptions, and Choices in Evaluating Employee Assistance Programs," *Review of Public Personnel Administration* 12, 1 (September–December): 70–80.

Mani, Bonni G. (1995) "Old Wine in New Bottles Tastes Better: A Case Study of TQM Implementation in the IRS." *Public Administration Review* 55, 2 (March/April): 147–158.

Mareschal, Patrice M. (1998) "Providing High Quality Mediation: Insights from the Federal Mediation and Conciliation Service." *Review of Public Personnel Administration* 18, 4 (Fall): 55–67.

Markowich, Michael M. (1993) "Does Money Motivate?" *HRFocus* (August): 1, 6.

Markman, Gideon D. (1997) "Motivation vs Pay." *HRNET@cornell.edu* listserv (May).

Marshall, Neil (1998) "Pay-for-Performance Systems: Experiences in Australia." *Public Productivity & Manangement Review* 21, 4 (June): 403–418.

Martin, David C., and Kathryn M. Bartol (1986) "Training the Raters: A Key to Effective Performance Appraisal." *Public Personnel Management* 15, 2 (Summer): 101–109.

Martino, Joseph (1975) *Technology Forecasting for Decisonmaking.* New York: Elsevier.

Marzotto, Toni (1986) "The Senior Executive Service: The Balance Between Responsiveness and Capacity." Paper presented at the American Political Science Association Annual Meeting, Washington, DC.

Marzotto, Toni (1993) "Wither the Generalist Manager: Reinventing the Senior Executive Service." Paper presented at the American Political Science Association Annual Meeting, Washington, DC.

Maslow, Abraham H. (1943) "A Theory of Human Motivation." *Psychological Review.* 50 (July): 370–396.

Maslow, Abraham H. (1965) *Eupsychian Management.* Homewood, IL: Irwin/Dorsey.

Maslow, A. P. (1976) "The Role of Testing in Training and Development," in R. L. Craig, ed., *Training and Development Handbook.* New York: McGraw Hill, pp. 10–1–10–13.

Masters, Marick F., and Robert S. Atkin (1989) "Bargaining Representation and Union Membership in the Federal Sector: A Free Rider's Paradise." *Public Personnel Management* 18, 3 (Fall): 311–323.

Masters, Marick F., and Robert S. Atkin (1995) "Bargaining, Financial, and Political Bases of Federal Sector Unions: Implications for Reinventing Government." *Review of Public Personnel Administration* 15, 1 (Winter): 5–23.

Mayer, Roger C., James H. Davis, and F. David Schoorman (1995) "An Integrative Model of Organizational Trust." *Academy of Management Review* 20, 3 (July): 709–734.

Meglino, Bruce M., Angelo S. DeNisi, and Elizabeth C. Ravlin (1993) "Effects of Previous Job Exposure and Subsequent Job Status on the Functioning of a Realistic Job Preview." *Personnel Pyschology* 46, 4 (Winter): 803–822.

Meglino, Bruce M., Elizabeth C. Ravlin, and Angelo S. DeNisi (1997) "When Does It Hurt to Tell the Truth? The Effect of Realistic Job Reviews on Employee Recruiting." *Public Personnel Management* 26, 3 (Fall): 413–422.

Meier, Kenneth (1981) "Ode to Patronage." *Public Administration Review* 41, 5 (September/October): 558–563.

Meier, Kenneth J. (1987) *Politics and the Bureaucracy: Policymaking in the Fourth Branch of Government.* 2nd ed. Monterey, CA: Brooks/Cole.

Mello, Jeffrey A. (1995) "Employment Law and Workers with Disabilities: Implications for Public Sector Managers and Human Resources Practices." *Public Personnel Management* 24, 1 (Spring): 75–87.

Merjanian, Ara (1997) "Striving to Make Performance Measurement Work: Texas Implements Systems Approach to Planning, Budgeting." *PA Times* 20, 6 (June): 1, 19–20.

Mesch, Debra J. (1995) "Grievance Arbitration in the Public Sector." *Review of Public Personnel Administration* 15, 4 (Fall): 22–36.

Mesch, Debra J., James L. Perry, and Lois R. Wise (1995) "Bureaucratic and Strategic Human Resource Management: An Empirical Comparison in the Federal Government." *Journal of Public Administration Theory and Research* 5: 385–402.

Meyer, Herbert H. (1991) "A Solution to the Performance Appraisal Feedback Engima." *Academy of Management Executive* 5, 1 (February): 68–76.

Meyer, Herbert H., Emanuel Kay, and John R. P. French, Jr. (1965) "Split-Roles in Performance Appraisal." *Harvard Business Review* 43 (January–February): 123–129.

Miceli, Marcia P., Bonnie L. Roach, and Janet P. Near (1988) "The Motivations of Anonymous Whistle-Blowers: The Case of Federal Employees." *Public Personnel Management* 17, 3 (Fall): 281–296.

Mikkelsen, Aslaug, Torvald ogaard, and Nicholas P. Lovrich (1997) "Impact of an Integrative Performance Appraisal Experience on Perceptions of Management Quality and Working Environment: Findings from a State Enterprise in Norway." *Review of Public Personnel Administration* 17, 3 (Summer): 82–98.

Milakovich, Michael E. (1990) "Total Quality Management for Public Sector Productivity Improvement." *Public Productivity and Management Review* 14, 1 (Fall): 19–32.

Milkovich, George T., and John W. Boudreau (1991) *Human Resources Management.* 6th ed. Homewood, IL: Irwin.

Milkovich, George T., and Alexandra K. Wigdor, eds. with Ranae F. Broderick and Anne S. Mavor (1991) *Pay for Performance: Evaluating Performance Appraisal and Merit Pay.* Washington, DC: National Academy Press.

Miller, Katherine I., and Peter R. Monge (1986) "Participation, Satisfaction, and Productivity: A Meta-Analytic Review." *Academy of Management Journal*, 29, 4: 727–753.

Milward, H. Brinton, and Keith Provan (1993) "The Hollow State: Private Provision of Public Services." in Helen Ingram and Steven Rathgeb Smith, eds., *Public Policy for Democracy.* Washington, DC: Brookings Insitution, pp. 222–240.

Mintzberg, Henry (1994) *The Rise and Fall of Strategic Planning.* New York: Free Press.

Mintzberg, Henry (1973) *The Nature of Managerial Work.* New York: Harper & Row.

Mintzberg, Henry, D. Raisinghami, and A. Theoret (1976) "The Structure of Unstructured Decisions." *Administrative Science Quarterly* 21: 246–275.

Mitchell, Daniel J. B. (1986) "Concession Bargaining in the Public Sector: A Lesser Force." *Public Personnel Management* 15, 1 (Spring): 23–40.

Mitchell, Terence R., and R. C. Liden (1982) "The Effects of the Social Context on Performance Evaluations." *Organizational Behavior and Human Performance* 29: 241–256.

Mitchell, Terence R. and W. G. Scott (1987) "Leadership Failures, the Distrusting Public, and Prospects of the Administrative State." *Public Administration Review* 47, 6 (November/December): 445–452.

Mobley, W. H. (1982) "Supervisor and Employee Race and Sex Effects on Performance Appraisal—A Field Study of Adverse Impact and Generalizability." *Academy of Management Journal* 25, 3: 598–606.

Moe, Terry M. (1984) "The New Economics of Organization." *American Journal of Political Science* 28, 4 (November): 739–777.

Mohrman, Allan, and Edward E. Lawler III (1983) "Motivation and Performance Appraisal Behavior," in Frank Landy, F. Zedeck, and Jeannette Cleveland, eds., *Performance Measurement and Theory.* Hillsdale, NJ: Erlbaum.

Mohrman, Allan M., Jr., Susan M. Resnick-West, and Edward E. Lawler III (1989) *Designing Performance Appraisal Systems: Aligning Appraisals and Organizational Realities.* San Francisco: Jossey-Bass.

Moore, Christopher W. (1986) *The Mediation Process: Pactical Strategies for Resolving Conflict.* San Francisco: Jossey-Bass.

Moore, Mary Virginia, and Yohannan T. Abraham (1992) "Comparable Worth—Is It a Moot Issue?" *Public Personnel Management* 21, 4 (Winter): 455–472.

Moore, Mary Virginia, and Yohannan T. Abraham (1994) "Comparable Worth: Is It a Moot Issue? Part II: The Legal and Juridical Posture." *Public Personnel Management* 23, 2 (Summer): 263–286.

Moore, Perry (1989) "Health Care Cost Containment in Large American Cities." *Public Personnel Management* 18, 1 (Spring): 87–100.

Moore, Perry (1991) "Comparison of State and Local Employee Benefits and Private Employee Benefits." *Public Personnel Management* 20, 4 (Winter): 429–440.

Morrisey, George L. (1976) *Management by Objectives and Results in the Public Sector.* Reading, MA: Addison-Wesley.

Morrison, Elizabeth Wolfe, and Robert J. Bies (1991) "Impression Management in the Feedback-Seeking Process: A Literature Review and Research Agenda." *Academy of Management Review* 16, 3 (July): 522–541.

Moses, J. L. (1987) "Assessment Centers." in R. L. Craig, ed., *Training and Development Handbook.* New York: McGraw-Hill, pp. 248–262.

Mosher, Frederick C. (1982) *Democracy and the Public Service.* 2nd ed. New York: Oxford University Press.

Muczyk, Jan P., and Bernard C. Reimann (1989) "MBO as a Complement to Effective Leadership." *Academy of Management Executive* 3, 2 (May): 131–138.

Murphy, Kevin J. (1987) *Effective Listening: Hearing What People Say and Making It Work for You.* New York: Bantam Books.

Murphy, Kevin R., and Jeanette N. Cleveland (1995) *Performance Appraisal: An Organizational Perspective.* Boston: Allyn and Bacon.

Murray, Brian, and Barry Gerhart (1998) "An Empirical Analysis of Skill-Based Pay Program and Plant Performance Outcomes." *Academy of Management Journal* 41, 1 (February): 68–78.

Nadler, D. A. (1977) *Feedback and OD.* Reading, MA: Addison-Wesley.

Naff, Katherine C. (1991) "Labor-Management Relations and Privatization: A Federal Perspective." *Public Administration Review* 51, 1 (January/February): 23–30.

Naff, Katherine C. (1993) "Perceptions of the Glass Ceiling: The Nature of Subjective Discrimination in the Federal Government." Paper presented at the American Political Science Association Annual Meeting.

Naff, Katherine C., and John Crum (1999) "Working for America: Does Public Service Motivation Make a Difference?" *Review of Public Personnel Administration* 19, 4 (Fall): 5–16.

Naff, Katherine C., and Raymond Pomerleau (1988) "Productivity Gainsharing: A Federal Case Study." *Public Personnel Management* 17, 4: 403–419.

Nathan, Richard (1975) *The Plot That Failed: Nixon and the Administrative Presidency.* New York: Wiley.

Nathan, Richard (1983) *The Administrative Presidency.* New York: Wiley.

National Commission on the Public Service (1989) "Leadership for America: Rebuilding the Public Service—The Report." Washington, DC.

Neikin, Dorothy, and Laurence Tancredi (1989) *Dangerous Diagnostics.* New York: Basic Books.

Nelson, Bob, and Peter Economy (1997) "Can Software Improve Your Performance Appraisals? A Review of Performance Appraisal Software." *IPMA News* (September): 22–23.

Newland, Chet (1987) "Public Executives: Imperium, Sacerdotium, Collegium? Bicentennial Leadership Challenges." *Public Administration Review* 47, 1 (January/February): 45–56.

Newman, Meredith, and Kay Matthews (1999) "Federal Family-Friendly Policies: Barriers to Effective Implementation." *Review of Public Personnel Administration* 19, 3 (Summer): 34–48.

Nice, David C. (1991) "State Regulation of Employee Drug Testing Laboratories." *Review of Public Personnel Administration* 11, 3 (Summer): 66–78.

Nielson, Norma L., and Terry A. Beehr (1994) "Retirement Income for Surviving Spouses." *Public Personnel Management* 23, 3 (Fall): 407–428.

Nigro, Lloyd G. (1981) "Attitudes of Federal Employees Toward Performance Appraisal and Merit Pay: Implications for CSRA Implementation." *Public Administration Review* 41, 1 (January/February): 84–86.

Nigro, Lloyd G. (1982) "CSRA Performance Appraisal and Merit Pay: Growing Uncertainty in the Federal Work Force." *Public Administration Review*, 42, 4 (July/August): 371–375.

Nigro, Lloyd G., and William L. Waugh, Jr. (1998a) "Local Government Responses to Workplace Violence: A Status Report." *Review of Public Personnel Administration* 18, 4 (Fall): 5–17.

Nigro, Lloyd G., and William L. Waugh, Jr. (1998b) "Workplace Violence Policies of U.S. Local Governments." *Public Administration Quarterly* 22, 3 (Fall): 349–364.

Nisbett, Richard, and Lee Ross (1980) *Human Inference Strategies and Shortcomings of Social Judgment.* Englewood Cliffs, NJ: Prentice Hall.

Noe, R. A. (1986) "Trainee's Attributes and Attitudes: Neglected Influences on Training Effectiveness." *Academy of Management Review* 11: 736–749.

Noe, R. A., and Schmitt, N. (1984) "The Influence of Trainee Attitudes on Training Effectiveness: Test of a Model. *Personnel Psychology* 39: 497–523.

Nutt, Paul C., and Robert W. Backoff (1992) *Strategic Management of Public and Third Sector Organizations.* San Francisco: Jossey-Bass.

Odiorne, George S. (1965) *Management by Objectives: A System of Managerial Leadership.* New York: Pitman.

Odiorne, George S. (1971) *Personnel Administration by Objectives.* Homewood, IL: Irwin.

Odiorne, George S. (1987) *The Human Side of Management: Management by Integration and Self-Control.* Lexington, MA: Lexington Books.

O'Hara, Kirk, and Kevin G. Love (1987) "Accurate Selection of Police Officials Within Small Municipalities: *Et tu* Assessment Center?" *Public Personnel Management* 16, 1 (Spring): 9–14.

Olivero, Gerald, K. Denise Bane, and Richard E. Kopelman (1997) "Executive Coaching as a Transfer of Training Tool: Effects on Productivity in a Public Agency." *Public Personnel Management* 26, 4 (Winter): 461–469.

Olshfski, Dorothy F., and Robert B. Cunningham (1986) "Establishing Assessment Center Validity: An Examination of Methodological and Theoretical Issues." *Public Personnel Management* 15, 1 (Spring): 85–98.

Osborne, David, and Ted Gaebler (1992) *Reinventing Government: How the Entrepreneurial Spirit Is Transforming the Public Sector from Schoolhouse to State House, City Hall to Pentagon.* Reading, MA: Addison-Wesley.

Ospina, Sonia (1992) "When Managers Don't Plan: Consequences of Nonstrategic Public Personnel Management." *Review of Public Personnel Administration* 12, 2 (January–April): 52–67.

Osterman, Paul (1995) "Work/Family Program and the Employment Relationship." *Administrative Science Quarterly* 40, 4 (December): 681–700.

Ostroff, Cheri, and Steve W. Kozlowski (1992) "Organizational Socialization as a Learning Process: The Role of Information Acquisition." *Personnel Psychology* 45, 4 (Winter): 849–874.

O'Toole, Daniel E., and John R. Churchill (1982) "Implementing Pay-for-Performance: Initial Experiences." *Review of Public Personnel Administration* 2, 3 (Summer): 13–28.

Ouchi, William G. (1981) *Theory Z.* New York: Addison-Wesley.

Pagano, Michael A. (1984) "The SES Performance Management System and Bonus Awards." *Review of Public Personnel Administration* 4, 2 (Spring): 40–56.

Pajer, Robert (1979) *Employee Performance Evaluation: A Practical Guide to Development and Implementation for State, County, and Municipal Governments.* Washington, DC: Office of Personnel Management, Government Printing Office.

Parasuraman, A., L. L. Berry, and V. A. Zeithaml (1991) "Refinement and Reassessment of the SERVQUAL Scale." *Journal of Retailing* 67: 420–450.

Parasuraman, A., L. L. Berry, and V. A. Zeithaml (1993) "More on Improving Service Quality Measurement." *Journal of Retailing* 69 140–147.

Parasuraman, A., V. A. Zeithaml, and L. L. Berry (1985) "A Conceptual Model of Service Quality and Its Implications for Future Research." *Journal of Marketing* 4, 4: 41–50.

Parasuraman, A., V. A. Zeithaml, and L. L. Berry (1988) "SERVQUAL: A Multiple-Item Scale for Measuring Consumer Perceptions of Service Quality." *Journal of Retailing* 64: 12–37.

Parker, T. C. (1976) Statistical Methods for Measuring Training Results. *Training and Development Handbook* R. L. Craig, ed. New York: McGraw-Hill, pp. 19–1–19–23.

Pascale, Richard T., and Anthony G. Athos (1981) *The Art of Japanese Management.* New York: Simon and Schuster.

Patton, Kevin R., and Dennis M. Daley (1998) "Gainsharing in Zebulon: What Do Workers Want?" *Public Personnel Management* 27, 1 (Spring): 117–131.

Paulsen, Kevin M. (1991) "Lessons Learned from Gainsharing." *HRMagazine* (April): 71–74.

Pearce, Jone L., and James L. Perry (1983) "Federal Merit Pay: A Longitudinal Analysis." *Public Administration Review* 43, 4 (July/August): 315–325.

Pearce, Jone L., W. Stevenson, and James L. Perry (1985) "Managerial Compensation Based on Organizational Performance: A Time Series Analysis of the Impact of Merit Pay." *Academy of Management Journal* 28 (June): 261–278.

Peirce, Ellen, Carol A. Smolinski, and Benson Rosen (1998) "Why Sexual Harassment Complaints Fall on Deaf Ears." *Academy of Management Executive* 12, 3 (August): 41–54.

Perry, James L. (1986) "Merit Pay in the Public Sector: The Case for a Failure of Theory." *Review of Public Personnel Administration* 7, 1 (Fall): 57–69.

Perry, James L. (1993) "Stategic Human Resource Management." *Review of Public Personnel Administration* 13, 4 (Fall): 59–71.

Perry, James L., Canala Hanzlik, and Jone L. Pearce (1982) "Effectiveness of Merit-Pay-Pool Management." *Review of Public Personnel Administration* 2, 3 (Summer): 5–12.

Perry, James L., and Debra J. Mesch (1997) "Strategic Human Resources Management," in Carolyn Ban and Norma Riccucci, eds., *Public Personnel Management: Current Concerns, Future Challenges.* New York: Longman, pp. 21–34.

Perry, James L., and Theodore K. Miller (1991) "The Senior Executive Service: Is It Improving Managerial Performance?" *Public Administration Review* 51, 6 (November/December): 554–563.

Perry, James L., Beth Ann Petrakis, and Theodore K. Miller (1989) "Federal Merit Pay, Round II: An Analysis of the Performance Management and Recognition System." *Public Administration Review* 49, 1 (January/February): 29–37.

Perry, James L., and Hal G. Rainey (1988) "The Public-Private Distinction in Organization Theory: A Critique and Research Strategy." *Academy of Management Review* 13: 182–201.

Perry, James L., and Lois R. Wise (1990) "The Motivational Bases of Public Service." *Public Administration Review* 50, 3 (May/June): 367–373.

Perry, Ronald W., and N. Joseph Cayer (1992) "Evaluating Employee Assistance Programs: Concerns and Strategies for Public Employees." *Public Personnel Management* 21, 3 (Fall): 323–333.

Perry, Ronald W., and N. Joseph Cayer (1997) "Factors Affecting Municipal Satisfaction with Health Care Plans." *Review of Public Personnel Administration* 17, 2 (Spring): 5–19.

Peters, B. Guy, and Donald J. Savoie (1996) "Managing Incoherence: The Coordination and Empowerment Conundrum." *Public Administration Review* 56, 3 (May/June): 281–290.

Peters, Thomas J., and Robert H. Waterman (1982) *In Search of Excellence.* New York: Harper & Row.

Pfeffer, Jeffrey (1998) *The Human Equation: Building Profits by Putting People First.* Cambridge, MA: Harvard Business School Press.

Pfeffer, Jeffrey, and John F. Veiga (1999) "Putting People First for Organizational Success." *Academy of Management Executive* 13, 2 (May): 37–48.

Pfiffner, J. P. (1987) "Political Appointees and Career Executives: The Democracy-Bureaucracy Nexus in the Third Century." *Public Administration Review* 47, 1 (January/February): 57–65.

Phillips, Jean M. (1998) "Effects of Realistic Job Previews on Multiple Organizational Outcomes: A Meta-Analysis." *Academy of Management Journal* 41, 6 (December): 673–690.

Pickett, Les (1998) "Competencies and Managerial Effectiveness: Putting Competencies to Work." *Public Personnel Management* 27, 1 (Spring): 103–115.

Pigors, P. (1987) "Case Method," in R. L. Craig, ed., *Training and Development Handbook.* New York: McGraw-Hill, pp. 414–429.

Pizam, Abraham (1975) "Social Differentiation—A New Pyschological Barrier to Performance Appraisal." *Public Personnel Management* 4: 244–247.

Poister, Theodore H., and Richard H. Harris (1996) "Service Delivery Impacts of TQM: A Preliminary Investigation." *Public Productivity & Management Review* 20, 1: 84–100.

Poister, Theodore H., and Richard H. Harris (1997) "The Impact of TQM on Highway Maintenance: Benefit/Cost Implications." *Public Administration Review* 57, 4 (July/August): 294–302.

Poister, Theodore H., and Gregory Streib (1995) MBO in Municipal Government: Variations on a Traditional Management Tool. *Public Administration Review* 55, 1 (January/February): 48–56.

Pollack, David M., and Leslie J. Pollack (1996) "Using 360-Degree Feedback in Performance Appraisal." *Public Personnel Management* 25, 4 (Winter): 507–528.

Prather, Richard (1974) "Extending the Life of Performance Appraisal Programs." *Personnel Journal* (October): 739–743.

Premack, S. L., and J. P. Wanous (1985) "A Meta-Analysis of Realistic Job Preview Experiments." *Journal of Applied Psychology* 70: 706–719.

Primoff, E. S. (1975) *How to Prepare and Conduct Job Element Examinations.* Washington, DC: Civil Service Commission.

Prince, George (1970) *The Practice of Creativity.* New York: Harper & Row.

Prinz, R. A., and David A. Waldman (1985) "The Merit of Merit Pay." *Personnel Administrator* 30, 1: 84–90.

Pynes, Joan (1993) "What Public Employee Relation Boards and the Courts Are Deciding: Mandatory Subjects of Bargaining." *Review of Public Personnel Administration* 13, 3 (Summer): 58–72.

Pynes, Joan E., and H. John Bernardin (1992) "Mechanical vs. Consensus-Derived Assessment Center Ratings: A Comparison of Job Performance Validities." *Public Personnel Management* 21, 1 (Spring): 17–28.

Quattrone, George A., and Amos Tversky (1988) "Contrasting Rational and Psychological Analyses of Political Choice." *American Political Science Review* 82, 3 (September): 719–736.

Quinn, James Brian (1992a) *The Intelligent Enterprise: A Knowledge and Service Based Paradigm for Industry.* New York: Free Press.

Quinn, James Brian (1992*b*) "The Intelligent Enterprise: A New Paradigm." *Academy of Management Executive* 6, 4 (November): 48–63.

Quinn, James Brian, Philip Anderson, and Sydney Finkelstein (1996) "Leveraging Intellect." *Academy of Management Executive* 10, 3 (August): 7–27.

Rainey, Hal G. (1989) "Public Management: Recent Research on the Political Context and Managerial Roles, Structures, and Behaviors." *Journal of Management* 15: 229–250.

Rainey, Hal G. (1991) *Understanding and Managing Public Organizations.* San Francisco: Jossey-Bass.

Rainey, Hal G., Robert W. Backoff, and Charles H. Levine (1976) "Comparing Public and Private Organizations." *Public Administration Review* 36: 233–246.

Rand, T. M., and Kenneth Wexley (1975) "A Demonstration of the Byrne Similar to Hypothesis in Simulated Employment Interviews." *Psychological Reports* 36: 535–544.

Rea, Louis M., and Richard A. Parker (1992) *Designing and Conducting Survey Research.* San Francisco: Jossey-Bass.

Redford, Emmette (1969) *Democracy in the Administrative State.* New York: Oxford University Press.

Reese, Laura A., and Karen E. Lindenberg (1997) "'Victimhood' and the Implementation of Sexual Harassment Policy." *Review of Public Personnel Administration* 17, 1 (Winter): 37–57.

Reiner, C. A., and Morris H. (1987), in R. L. Craig, ed., "Leadership Development." New York: McGraw-Hill, pp. 519–536.

Renfrow, Patty, Andrew Hede, and David Lamond (1998) "A Comparative Analysis of Senior Executive Services in Australia." *Public Productivity & Management Review* 21, 4 (June): 369–385.

Restak, Richard M. (1979) *The Brain: The Last Frontier.* New York: Warner.

Riccucci, Norma M. (1988) "A Typology for Union Discrimination: A Public Sector Perspective." *Public Personnel Management* 17, 1 (Spring): 41–51.

Riccucci, Norma (1990) "Drug Testing in the Public Sector: A Legal Analysis." *American Review of Public Administration* 20, 2 (June): 95–106.

Riccucci, Norma M. (1991) "Apprenticeship Training in the Public Sector: Its Use and Operation for Meeting Skilled Craft Needs." *Public Personnel Management* 20, 2 (Summer): 181–193.

Richman, Roger (1994) "Balancing Government Necessity and Public Employee Privacy: Reconstructing the Fourth Amendment Through the Special Needs Doctrine." *Administration and Society* 26, 1 (May): 99–124.

Risher, Howard (1997) "Competency-Based Pay: The Next Model for Salary Management." in Howard Risher and Charles Fay, eds., *New Strategies for Public Pay.* San Francisco: Jossey-Bass, pp. 145–158.

Risher, Howard (1999) "Are Public Employees Ready for a 'New Pay' Program?" *Public Personnel Management* 28, 3 (Fall): 323–343.

Risher, Howard, and Brigitte W. Schay (1994) "Grade Banding: The Model for Future Salary Programs?" *Public Personnel Management* 23, 2 (Summer): 187–199.

Roback, Thomas, and Janet C. Vinzant (1994) "The Constitution and the Patronage-Merit Debate: Implications for Personnel Management." *Public Personnel Management* 23, 2 (Fall): 501–513.

Robbins, Stephen P. (1978) *Personnel: The Management of Human Resources.* Englewood Cliffs, NJ: Prentice Hall.

Roberts, Gary E. (1992) "Linkages Between Performance Appraisal System Effectiveness and Rater and Ratee Acceptance." *Review of Public Personnel Administration* 12, 3 (May–August): 19–41.

Roberts, Gary E. (1995) "Developmental Performance Appraisal in Municipal Government: An Antidote for a Deadly Disease?" *Review of Public Personnel Administration* 15, 3 (Summer): 17–43.

Roberts, Gary E., and Tammy Reed (1996) "Performance Appraisal Participation, Goal Setting and Feedback: The Influence of Supervisory Style." *Review of Public Personnel Administration* 26, 4 (Fall): 29–60.

Roberts, Robert N., and Marion T. Dass, Jr. (1991) "The Constitutional Privacy Rights of Public Employees." *International Journal of Public Administration* 14, 3: 315–356.

Robertson, I. T., and Downs, S. (1989) "Work-Sample Tests of Trainability: A Meta-Analysis. *Journal of Applied Psychology* 74: 402–410.

Robinson, Robert K., Billie M. Allen, Geralyn McClure Franklin, and David L. Duhon (1993) "Sexual Harassment in the Workplace: A Review of the Legal Rights and Responsibilities of All Parties." *Public Personnel Management* 22, 1 (Spring): 123–135.

Robinson, Robert K., Ross L. Fink, and Billie Morgan Allen (1996) "The Influence of Organizational Constituent Groups on Rater Attitudes Toward Performance Appraisal Compliance." *Public Personnel Management* 25, 2 (Summer): 141–150.

Rodgers, Robert C. (1986) "An Interesting, Bad Theory of Mediation." *Public Administration Review* 46, 1 (January/February): 67–74.

Rodgers, Robert, and John E. Hunter (1992) "A Foundation of Good Management Practice in Government: Management by Objectives." *Public Administration Review* 52, 1 (January/February): 27–37.

Rohr, J. (1986) *To Run a Constitution: The Legitimacy of the Administrative State.* Lawrence: University Press of Kansas.

Rohr, John A. (1989) *Ethics for Bureaucrats: An Essay on Law and Values.* 2nd ed. New York: Dekker.

Rohr, John A. (1991) "Ethical Issues in French Public Administration: A Comparative Study." *Public Administration Review* 51, 4 (July/August): 283–297.

Romzek, Barbara (1985a) "The Effects of Public Service Recognition, Job Security and Staff Reductions on Organizational Involvement." *Public Administration Review* 45, 2 (March/April): 282–291.

Romzek, Barbara (1985b) "Perceptions of Agency Effectiveness as the Basis for Differences in Organizational Involvement: A Research Note." *Review of Public Personnel Administration* 6, 1 (Fall): 76–85.

Romzek, Barbara (1989) "Personal Consequences of Employee Commitment." *Academy of Management Journal* 32, 3 (September): 649–661.

Romzek, Barbara (1990) "Employee Investment and Commitment: The Ties That Bind." *Public Administration Review* 50, 3 (May/June): 374–382.

Rosen, Bernard (1986) "Crises in the U.S. Civil Service." *Public Administration Review* 46, 3 (May/June): 207–214.

Rosen, Theodore H. (1987) "Identification of Substance Abusers in the Workplace." *Public Personnel Management* 16, 3 (Fall): 197–207.

Rosenbloom, David H. (1971) *Federal Service and the Constitution: The Development of the Public Employment Relationship.* Ithaca, NY: Cornell University Press.

Rosenbloom, David H. (1975) "Public Personnel Administration and the Constitution." *Public Administration Review* 35, 1 (January/February): 52–60.

Rosenbloom, David H. (1981) "The Sources of Continuing Conflict Between the Constitution and Public Personnel Management." *Review of Public Personnel Administration* 2, 1 (Fall): 3–18.

Rosenbloom, David H. (1988) "Constitutional Law and Public Personnel in the 1980s." *Review of Public Personnel Administration* 8, 2 (Spring): 49–65.

Rosenbloom, David H. (1990) "What Every Public Personnel Manager Should Know About the Constitution," in Steven W. Hays and Richard C. Kearney, eds., *Public Personnel Administration: Problems and Prospects.* 2nd ed. Englewood Cliffs, NJ: Prentice Hall: 39–56.

Rosenbloom, David H. (1991) "The Liability of Public Employees for 'Constitutional Torts,'" in Carolyn Ban and Norma Riccucci, eds., *Public Personnel Management: Current Concerns—Future Challenges.* New York: Longman: 129–142.

Rosenbloom, David H. (1992) "Public Administration Liability for Constitutional Torts: The Rehnquest Court and Public Administration." *Administration and Society* 24, 2 (August): 115–139.

Rosenbloom, David H., and James D. Carroll (1995) "Public Personnel Administration and Law," in Jack Rabin, Thomas Vocino, W. Bartley Hildreth, and Gerald Miller, eds., *Handbook of Public Personnel Administration.* New York: Dekker, pp. 71–113.

Rosenbloom, David H., and Rosemary O'Leary (1996) *Public Administration and Law.* 2nd ed. New York: Dekker.

Ross, Cynthia S., and Robert E. England (1987) "State Governments' Sexual Harassment Policy Initiatives." *Public Administration Review* 47, 3 (May/June): 259–262.

Ross, J. D. (1985) "Update on Assessment Center: Implications for Public Sector Selection." *Reiew of Public Personnel Administration* 5, 3 (Summer): 1–8.

Ross, Joyce D. (1983) "Commitment and Loyalty as a Determinant of Performance Ratings." *Review of Public Personnel Administration* 3, 3 (Summer): 105–116.

Rosse, Joseph, and Robert A. Levin (1997) *High-Impact Hiring: A Comprehensive Guide to Performance-Based Hiring.* San Francisco: Jossey-Bass.

Rossi, Peter H., and Howard E. Freeman (1982) *Evaluation: A Systematic Approach.* Beverly Hills, CA: Sage.

Rudner, Lawrence M. (1992) "Pre-Employment Testing and Employee Productivity." *Public Personnel Management* 21, 2 (Summer): 133–150.

Rusbult, Caryl E. (1980) "Commitment and Satisfaction in Romantic Associations: A Test of the Investment Model." *Journal of Experimental Social Psychology* 16: 172–186.

Rusbult, Caryl E. (1983) "A Longitudinal Test of the Investment Model: The Development (and Deterioration) of Satisfaction and Commitment in Heterosexual Involvements." *Journal of Personality and Social Psychology* 45: 101–117.

Rusbult, Caryl E., and Dan Farrell (1983) "A Longitudinal Test of the Investment Model: The Impact of Job Satisfaction, Job Commitment, and Turnover of Variations in Reward, Costs, Alternatives, and Investments." *Journal of Applied Psychology* 68: 429–438.

Rusbult, Caryl E., Dan Farrell, Glen Rogers, and Arch G. Mainous III (1988) "Impact of Exchange Variables on Exit, Voice, Loyalty, and Neglect: An Integrative Model of Responses to Declining Job Satisfaction." *Academy of Management Journal* 31, 3 (September): 559–627.

Ryan, Ann Marie, and Marja Lasek (1991) "Negligent Hiring and Defamation: Area of Liability Relating to Pre-Employment Inquiries." *Personnel Psychology* 44, 2 (Summer): 293–320.

Rynes, Sara L., Robert D. Bretz, Jr., and Barry Gerhart (1991) "The Importance of Recruitment in Job Choices: A Different Way of Looking." *Personnel Psychology* 44, 3 (Autumn): 487–521.

Saal, F. E. (1979) "Mixed Standard Rating Scale: A Consistent System for Numerically Coding Inconsistent Response Combinations." *Journal of Applied Psychology* 64: 422–428.

Saal, F. E., and F. J. Landy (1977) "The Mixed Standard Rating Scale: An Evaluation." *Organizational Behavior and Human Performance* 18: 19–35.

Sackett, P. (1982) "A Critical Look at Some Common Beliefs about Assessment Centers."*Public Personnel Management* 11, 2 (Summer): 140–147.

Sagan, Carl (1977) *The Dragons of Eden: Speculations on the Evolution of Human Intelligence.* New York: Random House.

Sanders, Ronald P. (1997) "Gainsharing in Government: Group-Based Performance Pay for Public Employees." in Howard Risher and Charles Fay, eds., *New Strategies for Public Pay.* San Francisco: Jossey-Bass, pp. 231–252.

Savage, Grant T., John D. Blair, and Ritch L. Sorenson (1989) "Consider Both Relationship and Substance When Negotiating Strategically." *Academy of Management Executive* 3, 1 (February): 37–48.

Sayre, W. (1948) "The Triumph of Techniques over Purpose." *Public Administration Review* 8 (Spring): 134–137.

Schacter, Hindy Lauer (1989) "Frederick Winslow Taylor and the Idea of Worker Participation: A Brief Against Easy Administration Dichotomies." *Administration and Society* 21, 1 (May): 20–30.

Schall, Ellen (1997) "Public-Sector Succession: A Strategic Approach to Sustaining Innovation." *Public Administration Review* 57, 1 (January/February): 4–10.

Schay, Brigitte (1988) "Effects of Performance-Contingent Pay on Employee Attitudes." *Public Personnel Management* 17, 2 (Summer): 237–250.

Schay, Brigitte W. (1997) "Paying for Performance: Lessons Learned in 15 Years of Federal Demonstration Projects," in Howard Risher and Charles Fay, eds., *New Strategies for Public Pay.* San Francisco: Jossey-Bass, pp. 253–271.

Schein, Edgar H. (1985) *Organizational Culture and Leadership.* San Francisco: Josssey-Bass.

Scherkenbach, William W. (1986) *The Deming Route to Quality and Productivity: Roadmaps and Roadblocks.* Milwaukee, WI: American Society for Quality Control.

Schneider, B. (1975) "Organizational Climates: An Essay." *Personnel Psychology* 28: 447–479.

Schneider, B. (1985) "Organizational Behavior." *Annual Review of Psychology* 36: 573–611.

Schneier, Craig Eric, Guthrie, James P., and Olian, J. D. (1988) "A practical approach to conducting and using the training needs assessment." *Public Personnel Management* 17, 2 (Summer): 191–205.

Scholl, Richard W., and Elizabeth Cooper (1991) "The Use of Job Evaluation to Eliminate Gender Based Pay Differentials." *Public Personnel Management* 20, 1 (Spring): 1–18.

Schott, Richard (1986) "The Psychological Development of Adults: Implications for Public Administration." *Public Administration Review* 46, 6 (November–December): 657–667.

Schott, Richard (1991) "Administrative and Organization Behavior: Some Insights from Cognitive Psychology." *Administration and Society* 23, 1 (May): 54–73.

Schott, Richard (1999) "Managers and Mental Health: Mental Illness and the Workplace." *Public Personnel Management*, 28, 2 (Summer): 161–183.

Schwarz, Roger M. (1990–1991) "Participative Decision Making and Union-Management Cooperative Efforts: Attitudes of Managers, Union Officials, and Employees." *Review of Public Personnel Administration* 11, 1–2 (Fall–Spring): 38–54.

Schwarz, Roger M. (1994) *The Skilled Facilitator: Practical Wisdom for Developing Effective Groups.* San Francisco: Jossey-Bass.

Scott, Clyde, and James Suchan (1987) "Public Sector Collective Bargaining Agreements: How Readable Are They?" *Public Personnel Management* 16, 1 (Spring): 15–22.

Scott, K. Dow, Steven E. Markham, and Michael J. Vest (1996) "The Influence of a Merit Pay Guide Chart on Employee Attitudes Toward Pay at a Transit Authority." *Public Personnel Management* 25, 1 (Spring): 103–117.

Senge, Peter (1990) *The Fifth Discipline: Mastering the Five Practices of the Learning Organization.* New York: Doubleday Currency.

Shafritz, Jay (1973) *Position Classification: A Behavioral Analysis for the Public Service.* New York: Praeger.

Shafritz, Jay (1975) *Public Personnel Management: The Heritage of Civil Service Reform.* New York: Praeger.

Shafritz, Jay M., Norma M. Riccucci, David H. Rosenbloom, and Albert C. Hyde (1992) *Personnel Management in Government.* New York: Dekker.

Shareef, Reginald (1994) "Skill-Based Pay in the Public Sector." *Review of Public Personnel Administration* 14, 3 (Summer): 60–74.

Shareef, Reginald (1998) "A Midterm Case Study Assessment of Skill-Based Pay in the Virginia Department of Transportation." *Review of Public Personnel Administration* 18, 1 (Winter): 5–22.

Shaw, Jason D., John E. Delery, G. Douglas Jenkins, Jr., and Nina Gupta (1998) "An Organization-Level Analysis of Voluntary and Involuntary Turnover." *Academy of Mananagement Journal* 41, 5 (October): 511–525.

Shaw, M. E. (1985). Work team development training, Human Resources Management and Development Handbook (W. R. Tracey, ed.). American Management Association, New York, pp. 1113–1124.

Shea, Gordon F. (1992) "Learn How to Treasure Differences: Three Exercises to Help Your Organization Move Beyond Tolerance to Valuing Differences." *HRMagazine* 37, 12 (December): 34–37.

Shore, L. M., and G. C. Thorton (1986) "Effects of Gender on Self-Ratings and Supervisory Ratings." *Academy of Management Journal* 29, 1 (March): 115–129.

Shore, M. (1985). The Action system in learning, Human Resources Management and Development Handbook (W. R. Tracey, ed.). American Management Association, New York, pp. 1425–1433.

Siegel, Gilbert (1996) "Job Analysis in the TQM Environment." *Public Personnel Management* 25, 4 (Winter): 485–494.

Siegal, Sidney R. (1994) "A Comparative Study of Preretirement Programs in the Public Sector." *Public Personnel Management* 23, 4 (Winter): 631–647.

Siegal, Sidney R., and Beth Yvonne Rees (1992) "Preparing the Public Employee for Retirement." *Public Personnel Management* 21, 1 (Spring): 89–100.

Simon, Herbert (1947) *Administrative Behavior.* New York: Macmillan.

Simon, Herbert (1985) "Human Nature in Politics: The Dialogue of Psychology with Political Science." *American Political Science Review* 79, 2 (June): 293–304.

Sims, Henry P., Jr., and Peter Lorenzi (1992) *The New Leadership Paradigm: Social Learning and Cognition in Organizations.* Newbury Park, CA: Sage.

Sims, Ronald R., and Serbrenia J. Sims (1991) "Improving Training in the Public Sector." *Public Personnel Management* 20, 1 (Spring): 71–82.

Singer, Larry (1997) "When Things Go Wrong! A Perspective on Personal Survival in Public Service." Paper presented at the American Society for Public Administration National Conference (July 26–30).

Skinner, B. F. (1971) *Beyond Freedom and Dignity.* New York, NY: Knopf.

Skoien, Diane (1997) "Government Agencies Experience Pass/Fail Assessment." *IPMA News* 63, 4 (April): 7, 10.

Slack, James D. (1990) "Information, Training, and Assistance Needs of Municipal Governments." *Public Administration Review* 50, 4 (July/August): 450–457.

Slaikeu, Karl A. (1996) *When Push Comes to Shove: A Practical Guide to Mediating Disputes.* San Francisco: Jossey-Bass.

Smith, Maureen (1998a) "Employee Privacy Issues: E-Mail and Internet Use in the Workplace." *IPMA News* (August): 12, 15.

Smith, Maureen (1998b) "ADA Accommodations in the Workplace." *IPMA News* 64, 11 (November): 12.

Smith, Maureen (1998c) "Conducting Background Investigations on Current or Prospective Employees." *IPMA News* (September): 19–20.

Smith, Maureen (1998d) "Violence in the Workplace: Are You Protected?" *IPMA News* (October): 12–13.

Smith, Maureen (1998e) "Physical Ability Testing: Who Makes the Grade? *IPMA News* (October): 17–18.

Smith, Maureen (1998f) "Personality Testing for Employee Selection: The Right Choice?" *IPMA News* (October): 19–20.

Smith, P. (1977) "Behaviors, Results, and Organizational Effectiveness: The Problem of Criteria," in Marvin D. Dunnette, ed., *The Handbook of Industrial-Organizational Psychology*. Chicago: Rand McNally.

Smith, P., and C. M. Kendall (1963) "Retranslation of Expectations: An Approach to the Constructions of Unambiguous Anchors for Rating Scales." *Journal of Applied Psychology* 47, 2: 141–155.

Smither, James W., Richard R. Reilly, Roger E. Millsap, Kenneth Pearlman, and Ronald W. Stuffey (1993) "Applicant Reactions to Selection Procedures." *Personnel Pyschology* 46, 1 (Spring): 45–76.

Snell, Scott A., and James W. Dean, Jr. (1992) "Integrated Manufacturing and Human Resource Management: Human Capital Perspective." *Academy of Management Journal* 35, 3 (August): 467–504.

Soden, Dennis L., and Nicholas P. Lovrich (1988) "Motivating the Unmotivated State Employee Through Workplace Participation: Research Note from a Pre- and Post-Intervention Panel Study." *International Journal of Public Administration* 11, 1 (January): 91–115.

Spann, Jeri (1990) "Dealing Effectively with Sexual Harassment: Some Practical Lessons from One City's Experience." *Public Personnel Management* 19, 1 (Spring): 53–69.

Stahl, O. Glenn (1976) *Public Personnel Administration*. New York: Harper & Row.

Starling, Grover (1988) *Strategies for Policy Making*. Chicago, IL: Dorsey Press.

Steadman, S. V., and Clay, M. A. C. (1985) "Needs Assessment," in W. R. Tracey, ed., *Human Resources Management and Development Handbook*. New York: American Management Association, pp. 1338–1352.

Steel, R. P., and N. K. Ovalle (1984) "Self-Appraisal Based on Supervisory Feedback." *Personnel Psychology* 37: 667–685.

Stein, Lana (1987) "Merit Systems and Political Influence: The Case of Local Government." *Public Administration Review* 47, 3 (May/June): 263–271.

Stephenson, Max O., Jr., and Gerald M. Pops (1989) "Conflict Resolution Methods and the Policy Process." *Public Administration Review* 49, 5 (September/October): 463–473.

Stevenson, Jerry G., and Roger Williamson (1995) "Testing for Drugs: Bathrooms or Barbershops?" *Public Personnel Management* 24, 4 (Winter): 467–474.

Stohr-Gillmore, Mary K., Michael W. Stohr-Gillmore, and Nannette Kistler (1990) "Improving Selection Outcomes with the Use of Situational Interviews: Empirical Evidence from a Study of Correction Officers for New Generation Jails." *Review of Public Personnel Administration* 10, 2 (Spring): 1–18.

Strauss, G., and Sayles, L. R. (1980) *Personnel: The Human Problems*. 4th ed. Englewood Cliffs, NJ: Prentice Hall.

Streib, Gregory (1996) "Specialty Health Care Services in Municipal Government." *Review of Public Personnel Administration* 16, 2 (Spring): 57–72.

Strickland, Ruth Ann (1995) "Sexual Harassment: A Legal Perspective for Public Administrators." *Public Personnel Management* 24, 4 (Winter): 493–513.

Strickland, Ruth Ann, and Marsha Lynn Whicker (1989) "Comparing City Policies on Mandatory Drug Testing: A Process Evaluation of a Policy." Paper presented at the Southern Political Science Association.

Stringer, Donna M., Helen Remick, Jan Salisbury, and Angela B. Ginorio (1990) "The Power and Reasons Behind Sexual Harassment: An Employer's Guide to Solutions." *Public Personnel Management* 19, 1 (Spring): 43–52.

Sullivan, John (1996) "What Is Superior to Job Descriptions? Try a Position Expectation Description!" *HRNET@cornell.edu* listserve (October 30).

Suntrup, Edward L. (1989) "Child-Care Delivery Systems in the Government Sector." *Review of Public Personnel Administration* 10, 1 (Fall): 48–59.

Swanson, Cheryl (1993) "Defining a Political Instrumentality Model in a Non-Bargaining Environment: A Casestudy." *Review of Public Personnel Administration* 13, 3 (Summer): 85–93.

Swiss, James E. (1991) *Public Management Systems: Monitoring and Managing Government Performance.* Englewood Cliffs, NJ: Prentice Hall.

Swiss, James E. (1992) "Adapting Total Quality Management (TQM) to Government." *Public Administration Review* (July/August): 356–359.

Talhelm, Daniel R. (1993) "The Community Options Model: A PC Tool for Evaluating Community Choices." Paper presented at the American Society for Public Administration Conference (July).

Taylor, Frederick (1911) *The Principles of Scientific Management.* New York: W. W. Norton.

Taylor, Paul J., and Jon L. Pierce (1999) "Effects of Introducing a Performance Management System on Employees' Subsequent Attitudes and Effort." *Public Personnel Management* 28, 3 (Fall): 423–452.

Taylor, M. Susan, Critina M. Giannantonio, and Judy S. Brown (1989) "Participants' Reactions to Special Assignment Programs: Favorability and Predictors." *Public Personnel Management* 18, 4 (Winter): 430–439.

Teel, K. S. (1986) "Are Merit Raises Really Based on Merit." *Personnel Journal* 65, 3: 88.

Templeton, Jane Farley (1994) *The Focus Group: A Strategic Guide to Organizing, Conducting and Analyzing the Focus Group Interview.* Chicago: Probus.

Terpstra, David E., R. Bryan Kethley, Richard T. Foley, and Wanthanee (Tam) Limpaphayom (2000) "The Nature of Litigation Surrounding Five Screening Devices." *Public Personnel Management* 29, 1 (Spring): 43–54.

Thayer, Frederick (1987) "Performance Appraisal and Merit Pay Systems: The Disasters Multiply." *Review of Public Personnel Administration* 7, 2 (Spring): 36–53.

Thomas, James B., Shawn M. Clark, and Dennis A. Gioia (1993) "Strategic Sensemaking and Organizational Performance: Linkages Among Scanning, Interpretation, Action, and Outcomes." *Academy of Management Journal* 36, 2 (April): 239–270.

Thompkins, Jonathan (1987) "Comparable Worth and Job Evaluation Validity." *Public Administration Review* 47, 3 (May/June): 254–258.

Thompkins, Jonathan (1988) "Sources of Measurement Error and Gender Bias in Job Evaluation." *Review of Public Personnel Administration* 9, 1 (Fall): 1–16.

Thompson, Frank J., Norma M. Riccucci, and Carolyn Ban (1990) "Biological Testing and Personnel Policy: Drugs in the Federal Workplace," in Carolyn Ban and Norma Riccucci, eds., *Public Personnel Management: Current Concerns—Future Challenges.* New York: Longman, pp. 156–171.

Thompson, Frank J., Norma M. Riccucci, and Carolyn Ban (1991) "Drug Testing in the Federal Workplace: An Instrumental and Symbolic Assessment." *Public Administration Review* 51, 6 (November/December): 515–525.

Thompson, James D. (1967) *Organizations in Action.* New York: McGraw-Hill.

Thompson, James R., and Patricia W. Ingraham (1996) "The Reinvention Game." *Public Administration Review* 56, 3 (May/June): 291–298.

Thompson, Kenneth R., Wayne A. Hochwarter, and Nicholas J. Mathys (1997) "Strech Targets: What Makes Them Effective?" *Academy of Management Executive* 11, 3 (August): 48–60.

Tidwell, Gary L. (1984) "Employment at Will: Limitations in the Public Sector." *Public Personnel Management* 13, 3 (Fall): 293–305.

Timmins, William M. (1987) "Smoking versus Nonsmoking at Work: A Survey of Public Agency Policy and Practice." *Public Personnel Management* 16, 3 (Fall): 221–234.

Ting, Yuan (1996) "Workforce Reductions and Termination Benefits in Governments: The Case of Advance Notice." *Public Personnel Management* 25, 2 (Summer): 183–198.

Tjosvold, Dean (1985) "Power and Social Context in Superior-Subordinate Interaction." *Organizational Behavior* 35, 3: 281–293.

Tosi, Henry L., John R. Rizzo, and Stephen J. Carroll (1986) *Managing Organizational Behavior.* Cambridge, MA: Ballinger.

Toulmin, Llewellyn M. (1988) "The Treasure Hunt: Budget Search Behavior by Public Employee Unions." *Public Administration Review* 48, 2 (March/April): 620–630.

Trice, Eleanor (1999) "Cost-Per-Hire: A Worthwhile Calculation? *IPMA News* (March): 17.

Tummala, Hrishna (1987) "Veterans' Preference in the State of Montana: Equal Employment or Affirmative Action?" *Public Personnel Management* 16, 2 (Summer): 159–171.

Tversky, Amos, and Daniel Kahneman (1974) "Judgment Under Uncertainty: Heuristics and Biases." *Science* 185: 1124–1131.

Uniform Guidelines on Employee Selection Procedures." (1978) *Federal Register* 43 (166): 38209–38309.

U.S. Attorney General (1871) *Opinions of the Attorney General:* 516, Washington, DC, August 31, 1871, p. 517.

U.S. Department of Health and Human Services (1988) "Mandatory Guidelines for Federal Workplace Drug Testing Programs." *Federal Register* 53 (April 11): 11970–11989.

U.S. Department of Labor (1977) *Dictionary of Occupational Titles.* 4th ed. Washington, DC: Government Printing Office.

U.S. General Accounting Office (1989) "Drug Testing: Federal Agency Plans for Testing Employees." Washington, DC. GAO/GGD-89-51.

U.S. House Committee on Post Office and Civil Service (1988) "Oversight Hearings on Administration Plans to Drug Test Federal Work Force." Washington, DC: Government Printing Office.

U.S. Merit Systems Protection Board (1988) *Toward Effective Performance Management in the Federal Government.* Washington, DC: Government Printing Office (July).

U.S. Merit Systems Protection Board (1989) *Federal Civil Service Reform: A Survey of Federal Personnel Officials.* Washington, DC: Government Printing Office (November).

U.S. Merit Systems Protection Board (1990b) *Working for America: A Federal Employee Survey.* Washington, DC: Government Printing Office (June).

U. S. Merit Systems Protection Board (1992) *To Meet the Needs of the Nations: Staffing the U.S. Civil Service and the Public Service of Canada.* Washington, DC: Government Printing Office (January).

U.S. Merit Sytems Protection Board (1994a) *Entering Professional Positions in the Federal Government.* Washington, DC: Government Printing Office (March).

U.S. Merit Systems Protection Board (1994b) *Temporary Federal Employment: In Search of Flexibility and Fairness.* Washington, DC: Government Printing Office (September).

U.S. Merit Systems Protection Board (1995) *The Rule of Three in Federal Hiring: Boon or Bane?* Washington, DC: Government Printing Office (December).

U.S. Merit Systems Protection Board (1999a) *Federal Supervisors and Poor Performers.* Washington, DC: Government Printing Office (July).

U.S. Merit Systems Protection Board (1999b) *The Role of Delegated Examining Units: Hiring New Employees in a Decentralized Civil Service.* Washington, DC: Government Printing Office (August).

U.S. Merit Systems Protection Board (2000) Restoring *Merit to Federal Hiring: Why Two Special Hiring Programs Should Be Ended.* Washington, DC: Government Printing Office (January).

U.S. Office of Personnel Management (1989) "Federal Personnel Manual Letter 792-19, Establishing a Drug-Free Federal Workplace." *Federal Register* 54 (April 6): 14024–14033.

U.S. Public Health Service, Alcohol, Drug Abuse, and Mental Health Administration (1986) Q & A Drug Screening. HE20. 8202: EM7V1988.

U.S. Senate Select Committee on Presidential Campaign Activities (1974) *Presidential Campaign Activities of 1972, Book 19.* Washington, DC: Government Printing Office.

U.S. White House (1989) "National Drug Control Strategy." Washington, DC: Government Printing Office.

Ury, William (1991) *Getting Past No: Negotiating with Difficult People.* New York: Bantam Books.

Van Dyne, Linn, and Jeffrey A. LePine (1998) "Helping and Voice Extra-Role Behaviors: Evidence of Construct and Predictive Validity." *Academy of Management Journal* 41, 1 (February): 108–119.

Van Riper, Paul P. (1958) *History of the United States Civil Service.* Evanston, IL: Row, Peterson.

Vega, Arturo, and Michael J. Gilbert (1997) "Longer Days, Shorter Weeks: Compressed Work Weeks in Policing." *Public Personnel Management* 26, 3 (Fall): 391–402.

Vest, Michael J., Fabius P. O'Brien, and Jusanne Meltzer Vest (1990) "Explaining Rights Arbitrator Willingness to Accept Public Sector Interest Arbitration Cases." *Public Personnel Management* 19, 3 (Fall): 331–343.

Vodanovich, Stephen J., and Rosemary H. Lowe (1992) "They Ought to Know Better: The Incidence and Correlates of Inappropriate Application Blank Inquiries." *Public Personnel Management* 21, 3 (Fall): 363–370.

Voltz, W., and D. Costa (1989) "A Public Employee's 'Fair Share' of Union Dues." *Labor Law Journal* 40 (March): 131–137.

Vroom, Victor (1964) *Work and Motivation.* New York: Wiley.

Wagner, John A., III, and Richard Z. Gooding (1987a) "Effects of Societal Trends on Participation Research." *Administrative Sciences Quarterly* 32: 241–262.

Wagner, John A., III, and Richard Z. Gooding (1987b) "Shared Influence and Organizational Behavior: A Meta-Analysis of Situational Variables Expected to Moderate Participation-Outcome Relationships." *Academy of Management Journal* 30, 3: 424–541.

Waldman, David A., Leanne E. Atwater, and David Antonioni (1998) "Has 360 Degree Feedback Gone Amok?" *Academy of Management Executive* 12, 2 (May): 86–96.

Wallington, C. (1987) "Audiovisual Methods," in R. L. Craig, ed., *Training and Development Handbook.* New York: McGraw-Hill, pp. 500–516.

Walsh, James P., and Geraldo Rivera Ungsom (1991) "Organizational Memory." *Academy of Management Review* 16, 1 (January): 57–91.

Walter, Robert J. (1992) "Public Employers' Potential Liability from Negligence in Employment Decisions." *Public Administration Review* 52, 5 (September/October): 491–503.

Walton, Mary (1986) *The Deming Management Method.* New York: Dodd, Mead.

Wamsley, Barbara S. (1997) "Are Current Programs Working? Views from the Trenches," in Howard Risher and Charles Fay, eds., *New Strategies for Public Pay.* San Francisco: Jossey-Bass, pp. 25–39.

Warfield, John N. (1977) *Societal Systems: Planning, Policy, and Complexity.* New York: Wiley.

Warrenfeltz, Rodney B. (1989) "An Achievement Based Approach to Evaluating Engineering Technicians." *Public Personnel Management* 18, 3 (Fall): 243–262.

Weber, Caroline L., and Sara L. Rynes (1991) "Effects of Compensation Strategy on Job Pay Decisions." *Academy of Management Journal* 34, 1 (March): 86–109.

Weeks, J. Devereau (1990) "Public Employee Drug Testing Under Fourth Amendment Limitations After Skinner and Von Raab." Paper presented at the Southeastern Conference on Public Administration.

Wexley, Kenneth N., and Latham, Gary P. (1991) *Developing and Training Human Resources in Organizations.* 2nd ed. Glenview, IL: Scott, Foresman.

Wexley, Kenneth, and W. F. Nemeroff (1974) "Effects of Racial Prejudice, Race of Applicant, and Biographical Similarity on Interview Evaluation of Job Applicants." *Journal of Social and Behavioral Science* 20: 66–78.

Wheeler, Kevin (1999) "The BIG Decision: Buy an Applicant Tracking System or Buy a Service?" *IPMA News* (June): 15–16.

Wherry, R. J., and C. J. Bartlett (1982) "The Control of Bias in Ratings: A Theory of Rating." *Personnel Psychology* 35: 521–555.

White, Leonard (1948) *The Federalists.* New York: Macmillan.

White, Leonard (1951) *The Jeffersonians.* New York: Macmillan.

White, Leonard (1954) *The Jacksonians.* New York: Macmillan.

White, Leonard (1958) *The Republican Era, 1869–1901.* New York: Macmillan.

White, Michael J. (1997) "Qualified and Absolute Immunity." Paper presented at the American Society for Public Administration National Conference (July 26–30).

Whyte, Glen (1989) "Groupthink Reconsidered." *Academy of Management Review* 14, 1 (January): 40–56.

Wiggins, J. S., and A. L. Pincus (1992) "Personality: Structure and Assessment," in M. R. Rosenzweig and L. W. Porter, eds., *Annual Review of Psychology* 43: 473–504.

Wildavsky, Aaron (1988) *The New Politics of the Budgetary Process.* Glenview, IL: Scott, Foresman.

Wilson, Laura A., and Robert F. Durant (1994) "Evaluating TQM: The Case for a Theory-Driven Approach." *Public Administration Review* 54, 2 (March/April): 137–146.

Wilson, Woodrow (1887) "The Study of Administration." *Political Science Quarterly* 2, 1 (June): 197–222.

Wise, Charles R. (1985) "Suits Against Federal Employees for Constitutional Violations: A Search for Reasonableness." *Public Administration Review* 45, 6 (November/December): 845–856.

Wise, Charles R. (1989) "The Liability of Public Administrators," in James L. Perry, ed., *Handbook of Public Administration.* New York: Dekker, pp. 585–601.

Wisensale, Steven K. (1999) "The Family and Medical Leave Act in Court: A Review of Key Appeals Court Cases Five Years After." Paper presented at the 1999 American Political Science Association Meeting.

Wolf, James F., and Frank P. Sherwood (1981) "Coaching: Supporting Public Executives on the Job." *Public Administration Review* 41, 1 (January/February): 73–76.
Wooten, William (1993) "Using Knowledge, Skill, and Ability (KSA) Data to Identify Career Path Opportunities: An Application of Job Analysis to Internal Manpower Planning." *Public Personnel Management* 22, 4 (Winter): 551–563.
Woska, William J. (1988) "Pay for Time Not Worked: A Public-Sector Budget Dilemma." *Public Administration Review* 48, 1 (January/February): 551–556.
Wynia, Bob L. (1974) "Federal Bureaucrats Attitudes Toward a Democratic Ideology." *Public Administration Review* 34, 2 (March/April): 156–162.
Yates, Douglas (1982) *Bureaucatic Democracy: The Search for Democracy and Effectiveness in American Government.* Cambridge, MA: Harvard University Press.
Yeager, Samuel J. (1986) "Use of Assessment Centers by Metropolitan Fire Departments in North America." *Public Personnel Management* 15, 1 (Spring): 51–64.
Yeager, Samuel J., Jack Rabin, and Thomas Vocino (1985) "Feedback and Administrative Behavior in the Public Sector." *Public Administration Review* 45, 5 (September/October): 570–575.
Youndt, Mark A., Scott A. Snell, James W. Dean, Jr., and David P. Lepak (1996) "Human Resource Management, Manufacturing Strategy, and Firm Performance." *Academy of Management Journal* 39, 4 (August): 836–866.
Yukl, Gary (1989) *Leadership in Organizations.* 2nd ed. Englewood, Cliffs, NJ: Prentice Hall.
Zammuto, R. F., M. London, and K. M. Rowland (1982) "Organization and Rater Difference in Performance Appraisals." *Personnel Psychology* 35: 643–658.
Zemke, R. (1979) "Employee Attitude and Opinion Surveys." *Training* (June): 21–33.

Court Cases

Abood v. Detroit Board of Education, 430 U.S. 209 (1977).
AFSCME v. Woodward, 406 F.2d. 137 (1969).
Albermarle Paper Company v. Moody, 442 U.S. 405 (1975).
Beckendorf v. Schwegmann Giant Super Markets, Inc. E. La, Civil Action No. 95-3822 Section K (3), April 21, 1997.
Bishop v. Wood, 426 U.S. 341 (1976).
Board of Commissioners v. Umbehr (1996).
Board of Regents v. Roth, 408 U.S. 564 (1972).
Branti v. Finkel, 445 U.S. 506 (1980).
Brito v. Zia Company, 478 F.2d 1200 (1973).
Carpenter v. Stephen F. Austin State University, 706 F.2d 6708 (1983).
Clay v. City of Chicago, N.D. Ill., No. 96 C 3684, April 8, 1997.
Cleveland Board of Education v. La Fleur, 414 U.S. 632 (1974).
Codd v. Velger, 429 U.S. 624 (1977).
Cole v. Richardson, 405 U.S. 676 (1972).
Commonwealth v. Pullis, Philadephia Cordswainers, Pennsylvania (1806).
Connecticut v. Teal, 457 U.S. 440 (1982).
Elfbrenelt v. Russell, 384 U.S. 11 (1966).
Elrod v. Burns, 427 U.S. 347 (1976).
Griggs v. Duke Power Company, 401 U.S. 424 (1971).
Hafer v. Melo, 116 L. Ed.2d 301 (1991).

Harley v. Schuylkill County, 476 F. Supp. 191 (1979).

Kelley v. Johnson, 425 U.S. 238 (1976).

Lempres v. CBS, Inc., D.D.C. Civil action 95-451 (RMU), Feb. 16, 1996 (1996 U.S. Sist LEXI 2324).

McCarthy v. Philadelpia Civil Service Commission, 424 U.S. 645 (1976).

McClaughlin v. Tilendis, 398 F.2d 287 (1967).

McDonnell Douglas v. Green, 411 U.S. 792 (1973).

Marquez v. Omaha District Sales Office, Ford Division of the Ford Motor Comapany, 440 F.2d 1157 (1971).

National Treasury Employees Union v. Von Raab, 489 U.S. 656 (1989).

Nicoletta v. North Jersey District Water Supply Commission, 77 N.J. 145, 150, 390 A.2d 90, 92 (1978).

O'Connor v. Consolidated Coin Caterers, 1996 Westlaw 142564 (1996).

O'Connor v. Ortega, 480 U.S. 709 (1987).

O'Hare Truck Service v. Northlake 135 L.Ed. 2d 874 (1996).

Patterson v. Alltel Infomation Services, Inc. D.Me., Civil No. 95-188-P-C, March 15, 1996 (1996 U.S. Dist. LEXIS 5253).

Patterson v. American Tobacco Company, 586 F.2d 300 (1978).

Paul v. Davis, 424 U.S. 693 (1976).

Perry v. Sinderman, 408 U.S. 593 (1972).

Pickering v. Board of Education Township High School District 205, 391 U.S. 563 (1968).

Ramirez v. Hofheinz, 619 F.2d 442 (1980).

Rankin v. McPherson, 483 U.S. 378 (1987).

Rowe v. General Motors, 457 F.2d 348 (1972).

Rutan v. Republican Party of Illinois, 497 U.S. 62 (1990).

Skinner v. Railway Labor Executives Association, 489 U.S. 602 (1989).

Thorne v. City of El Segundo, 726 F.2d. 459 (9th Cir 1983), cert. denied, 469 U.S. 979 (1984).

Turner v. State Highway Commission of Missouri, 31 EPD 33, 352 (1982).

United Public Workers v. Mitchell, 330 U.S. 75 (1947).

Wade v. Mississippi Cooperative Extension Service, 528 F.2d 508 (5th Cir. 1976, on remand, 424 F. Supp. 1242 (5th Cir. 1976).

Wards Grove Packing Co. v. Atonio, 490 U.S. 642 (1989).

Wisconsin v. Constantineau, 400 U.S. 433 (1971).

Zell v. United States, 472 F. Supp. 356 (1979).

Index